# Serving the People of God

# Serving the People of God

## The Collected Shorter Writings of J. I. Packer
## Volume 2

**James I. Packer**

paternoster press

# Contents

# Foreword

When Martin Luther wrote the Preface to the first collected edition of his many and various writings, he went to town explaining in detail that theology, which should always be based on the Scriptures, should be done according to the pattern modelled in Psalm 119. There, Luther declared, we see that three forms of activity and experience make the theologian. The first is prayer for light and understanding. The second is reflective thought (*meditatio*), meaning sustained study of the substance, thrust, and flow of the biblical text. The third is standing firm under pressure of various kinds (external opposition, inward conflict, and whatever else Satan can muster): pressures, that is, to abandon, suppress, recant, or otherwise decide not to live by, the truth God has shown from his Word. Luther expounded his point as one who knew what he was talking about, and his affirmation that sustained prayer, thought, and fidelity to truth whatever the cost, become the path along which theological wisdom is found is surely one of the profoundest utterances that the Christian world has yet heard.

In introducing this mass of fugitive pieces I would only say that behind each of them lies a conscious attempt over more than forty years to hew to Luther's line, in hope that by adhering to his theological wisdom I might arrive at substantive wisdom in and through the grace of our Lord Jesus Christ. How far I have attained my goal is something that readers must judge for themselves. In retrospect, writing this material does not seem to have been time wasted, and it is my prayer that no one who explores it will feel that their time has been wasted either.

I thank Jim Lyster, Isobel Stevenson, Tony Graham and the rest of the staff at Paternoster for all their hard work in putting this collection together.

# The Church

# Chapter 1

# The Nature of the Church

The church of God, 'that wonderful and sacred mystery,'[1] is a subject that stands at the very heart of the Bible. For the church is the object of the redemption which the Bible proclaims. It was to save the church that the Son of God became man and died;[2] God purchased his church at the cost of Christ's blood.[3] It is through the church that God makes known his redeeming wisdom to the hosts of heaven.[4] It is within the church that the individual Christian finds the ministries of grace, the means of growth, and his primary sphere for service.[5] We cannot properly understand the purpose of God, nor the method of grace, nor the kingdom of Christ, nor the work of the Holy Spirit, nor the meaning of world history without studying the doctrine of the church.

But what is the church? The fact that we all first meet the church as an organized society must not mislead us into thinking that it is essentially, or even primarily, that. There is a sense in which the outward form of the church disguises its true nature rather than reveals it. Essentially, the church is not a human organization as such, but a divinely created fellowship of sinners who trust a common Saviour, and are one with each other because they are all one with him in a union realized by the Holy Spirit. Thus the church's real life, like that of its individual members, is for the present 'hid in Christ with God,'[6] and will not be manifested to the world until he appears. Meanwhile, what we need, if we are to understand the church's nature, is insight into the person and work of Christ and of the Spirit and into the meaning of the life of faith.

---

THE NATURE OF THE CHURCH was originally published in *Basic Christian Doctrine*, ed. Carl F. H. Henry (Orlando: Harcourt, Brace, 1962), pp. 241–247. Reprinted by permission.

[1] Aquinas.
[2] Eph. 5:25.
[3] Acts 20:28.
[4] Eph. 3:10.
[5] Eph. 4:11–16.
[6] Col. 3:3.

## The Covenant People of God

The church is not simply a New Testament phenomenon. An ecclesiol -
ogy which started with the New Testament would be out of the way at
the first step. The New Testament church is the historical continuation
of Old Testament Israel. The New Testament word for 'church,' *ekklesia*
(in secular Greek a public gathering) is regularly used in the Greek Old
Testament for the 'congregation' of Israel. Paul pictured the church in
history, from its beginning to his own day, as a single olive tree, from
which some natural (Israelite) branches had been broken off through
unbelief, to be replaced by some wild (Gentile) branches. [7] Elsewhere, he
tells Gentile believers that in Christ they have become 'Abraham's seed,'
'the Israel of God.'[8]

The basis of the church's life in both testaments is the covenant which
God made with Abraham. The fundamental idea of biblical ecclesiology
is of the church as the covenant people of God.

What is a covenant? It is a defined relationship of promise and
commitment which binds the parties concerned to perform whatever
duties toward each other their relationship may involve. The two main
biblical analogies for God's covenant with sinners are the royal covenant
between overlord and vassal and the marriage covenant between hus -
band and wife, the former speaking of God's sovereignty and lordship,
the latter of his love and saviourhood. By his covenant, God demands
acceptance of his rule and promises enjoyment of his blessing. Both
thoughts are contained in the covenant 'slogan,' 'I will be your God,
and ye shall be my people';[9] both are implied whenever a believer says
'my [our] God.'

God expounded his covenant to Abraham in Genesis 17, a chapter of
crucial importance for the doctrine of the church. Four points should be
noticed here. First, the covenant relationship was announced as a *corporate*
one, extending to Abraham's seed 'throughout their generations.' [10] Thus,
the covenant created a permanent community. Second, the relationship
was one of *pledged beneficence* on God's part: he undertook to give
Abraham's seed the land of Canaan. [11] This, as he had already told
Abraham, would involve redeeming them from captivity in Egypt. [12]
Third, the end of the relationship was *fellowship* between God and his
people: that they should 'walk before' him, knowing him as they were

---

[7] Rom. 11:16–24.
[8] Gal. 3:29; cf. Rom. 4:11–18; Gal. 6:16.
[9] Cf. Exod. 29:45; Lev. 26:12; Jer. 31:33; 2 Cor. 6:16; Rev. 21:3 etc.
[10] Gen. 17:7.
[11] Gen. 17:8, a type of heaven; cf. Heb. 11:8–16.
[12] Gen. 15:13–21; cf. Exod. 2:24.

known by him.[13] Fourth, the covenant was confirmed by the institution of a "token,"[14] the *initiatory rite* of circumcision.

Later, through Moses, God gave his people a *law* for their lives and authorized forms of *worship* (feasts, exhibiting his fellowship with them, and sacrifices, pointing to the bloodshedding for sin which alone could provide a basis for this fellowship). Also, he spoke to them repeatedly, through his prophets, of their glorious *hope* which was to be realized when the Messiah came.

Thus, emerged the basic biblical notion of the church as the covenant people of God, the redeemed family, marked out as his by the covenant sign which they had received, worshipping and serving him according to his revealed will, living in fellowship with him and with each other, walking by faith in his promises, and looking for the coming glory of the Messianic kingdom.


## New Testament Fulfillment

When Christ came, this Old Testament conception was not destroyed, but fulfilled. Christ, the Mediator of the covenant, was himself the link between the Mosaic and Christian dispensations of it.[15] The New Testament depicts him as the true Israel, the servant of God in Whom the nation's God-guided history is recapitulated and brought to completion,[16] and also as the seed of Abraham in whom all nations of the earth find blessing.[17] Through his atoning death, which did away with the typical sacrificial services forever, believing Jews and Gentiles become in him the people of God on earth. Baptism, the New Testament initiatory sign corresponding to circumcision, represents primarily union with Christ in his death and resurrection, which is the sole way of entry into the church.[18]

Thus, the New Testament church has Abraham as its father,[19] Jerusalem as its mother[20] and place of worship,[21] and the Old Testament as its Bible.[22] Echoing Exodus 19:5f. and Hosea 2:23, Peter describes the

---

[13] Gen. 17:1.
[14] Gen. 17:11.
[15] i.e., the 'old' and the 'new' covenants of Heb. 8–10, chapters which build upon Jer. 31:31ff.
[16] Cf. Matt. 2:15; etc.
[17] Gal. 3:8f., 14–29.
[18] Rom. 6:3ff.; Gal. 3:27ff.; Col. 2:11ff.
[19] Rom. 4:11, 16.
[20] Gal. 4:26.
[21] Heb. 12:22.
[22] Rom. 15:4.

Christian church in thorough-going Old Testament fashion as 'a chosen
generation, a royal priesthood, an holy nation, a peculiar people; . . .
Which in time past were not a people, but are now the people of God.'[23]


## A New Creation in Christ

The New Testament idea of the church is reached by superimposing upon
the notion of the covenant people of God the further thought that the
church is the company of those who share in the redemptive renewal of
a sin-spoiled creation, which began when Christ rose from the dead.[24] As
the individual believer is a new creation in Christ,[25] raised with him out
of death into life,[26] possessed of and led by the life-giving Holy Spirit,[27]
so also is the church as a whole. Its life springs from its union with Christ,
crucified and risen. Paul, in Ephesians, pictures the church successively as
Christ's *building*, now growing unto 'an holy temple in the Lord';[28] his
*body*, now growing toward a state of full edification;[29] and his *bride*, now
being sanctified and cleansed in readiness for 'the marriage supper of the
Lamb.'[30]

Some modern writers in the 'catholic' tradition treat Paul's body
metaphor as having a special 'ontological' significance, and indicating that
the church is 'really' (in a sense in which it is not 'really' anything else) an
extension of the manhood and incarnate life of Christ. But, according to
Paul, the church's union with Christ is symbolically exhibited in baptism;
and what baptism symbolizes is not incorporation into Christ's manhood
simply, but sharing with him in his death to sin, with all its saving fruits,
and in the power and life of his resurrection. When Paul says that the Spirit
*baptizes* men into one body, he means that the Spirit makes us members of
the body by bringing us into that union with Christ which baptism
signifies.[31] Scripture would lead us to call the church an extension of the
resurrection rather than of the incarnation! In any case, Paul uses the body
metaphor only to illustrate the authority of the Head, and his ministry to
his members, and the various ministries that they must fulfil to each other;
and we have no warrant for extrapolating it in other theological directions.

---

[23]  1 Pet. 2:9f.
[24]  Cf. 1 Cor. 15:20; Col. 1:18.
[25]  2 Cor. 5:17.
[26]  Eph. 2:1ff.
[27]  Rom. 8:9–14.
[28]  Eph. 2:21.
[29]  Found, as well as in Ephesians 4, in Rom. 12, 1 Cor. 12 and Col. 1.
[30]  Eph. 5:25ff., cf. Rev. 19:7ff.
[31]  1 Cor. 12:13.

## Ministry in the Church

The New Testament conceives of all ministry in the church as Christ's ministry to and through the church. As the church is a priestly people, all its members having direct access to God through Christ's mediation, so it is a ministering people, all its members holding in trust from Christ gifts of ministry (i.e., service) for the edifying of the one body.[32] Within the context of this universal ministry, Christ calls some specifically to minister the gospel,[33] giving them strength and skill for their task[34] and blessing their labours.[35] As spokesmen and representatives of Christ, teaching and applying his Word, church officers exercise his authority; yet they need to remember that, as individuals, they belong to the church as its servants, not the church to them as their empire. The church is Christ's kingdom, not theirs.[36] This is a basic point which Luther accused the papacy of forgetting.

## Universal and Local

Paul speaks not merely of the whole body but also of local groups in an area, and even of a Christian household, as ' *the* church.' No local group is ever called 'a church.' For Paul does not regard the church universal as an aggregate of local churches (let alone denominations!); his thought is rather that whenever a group of believers, even Christ's statutory two or three,[37] meet in his name, they *are* the church in the place where they meet. Each particular gathering, however small, is the local manifestation of the church universal embodying and displaying the spiritual realities of the church's supernatural life. So Paul can apply the body metaphor, with only slight alteration, both to the local church (one body in Christ)[38] and to the universal church (one body *under* Christ).[39]

## Visible and Invisible

The Reformers drew a necessary distinction between the church visible and invisible; that is, between the one church of Christ on earth as God

---

[32]  1 Cor. 12:4–28; Rom. 12:6–8; cf. 1 Cor. 16:15; 2 Cor. 9:1.
[33]  Eph. 4:11; cf. Rom. 1:1,5,9; 15:16.
[34]  1 Cor. 3:10; 15:10.
[35]  1 Cor. 3:6f.
[36]  Cf. 2 Cor. 4:5.
[37]  Matt. 18:20.
[38]  Rom. 12; 1 Cor. 12.
[39]  Eph. 4.

sees it and as man sees it; in other words, as it is and as it seems to be. Man sees the church as an organized society, with a fixed structure and roll of members. But (the Reformers argued) this society can never be simply identified with the one holy catholic church of which the Bible speaks. The identity between the two is at best partial, indirect, and constantly varying in degree. The point is important. The church as God sees it, the company of believers in communion with Christ and in him with each other, is necessarily invisible to men, since Christ and the Holy Spirit and faith, the realities which make the church, are themselves invisible. The church becomes visible as its members meet together in Christ's name to worship and hear God's Word. But the church visible is a mixed body. Some who belong, though orthodox, are not true believers – not, that is, true members of the church as God knows it – and need to be converted.[40] The Reformers' distinction thus safeguards the vital truth that visible church membership saves no man apart from faith in Christ.

Another matter on which this distinction throws light is the question of church unity. If a visible organization, as such, were or could be the one church of God, then any organizational separation would be a breach of unity, and the only way to reunite a divided Christendom would be to work for a single international super-church. Also, on this hypothesis, it would be open to argue that some institutional feature is of the essence of the church and is therefore a *sine qua non* of reunion. (Rome, for instance, actually defines the church as the society of the faithful *under the Pope's headship;* some Anglicans make episcopacy in the apostolic succes - sion similarly essential.) But, in fact, the church invisible, the true church, is one already. Its unity is given to it in Christ.[41] The proper ecumenical task is not to create church unity by denominational coalescence, but to recognize the unity that already exists and to give it worthy expression on the local level.

In the purposes of God, the church, we have seen, is glorious; yet on earth it remains a little flock in a largely hostile environment. Often, its state and prospects seem to us precarious. But we need not fear. Christ himself, the King who reigns on Zion's hill, is its Saviour, its Head, its Builder, its Keeper. He has given his promise: 'the gates of hell shall not prevail against it.'[42] And he is not accustomed to break his word.

---

[40] Cf. Matt. 13:24ff.,47ff.; 2 Cor. 13:5; 1 Cor. 15:34.
[41] Eph. 4:3.
[42] Matt. 16:18.

# Chapter 2

# Body Life

'The body is a unit, though it is made up of many parts; and though all its parts are many, they form one body. So it is with Christ . . . Now you are the body of Christ, and each one of you is a part of it' (1 Cor. 12:12,27).

These words are part of an illustration of which Paul was fond. Indeed, it was his standard illustration for making clear the nature of the inner life of the church. There is, we know, one church universal which is invisible in its own nature. It is the company of those who have living faith in Christ and so are united to each other because they are united to him. But that church becomes visible wherever the people of God, either many or few, meet together to do the things the church does: worship, pray, maintain the ministry of the Word, spread the gospel, fellowship, cele - brate the sacraments and share the things of God. So Paul, writing to the local church at Corinth, says, 'You are the body of Christ.' Just you!

He would say the same thing to every congregation he was privileged to address. Each local congregation is a microcosm (a small-scale presentation) of the church universal. Therefore, when folks look at this or any other congregation, they should see the life of the world church concentrated in that one place.

What sort of life should it be? Body life, the life in which all the limbs (the Greek word for 'members' literally means limb) are contributing to the welfare of the whole body. Our bodies give us trouble when any part is not working properly. When the parts work properly, the body's life is a wonderful thing. In the same way, Paul wants us to understand that the life of a church is a wonderful thing as in the power of God's Spirit each limb, unit, bit, piece, joint and muscle does its best and contributes to the health of the whole. As he says in Ephesians 4:16, 'The whole body joined and held together by every supporting ligament, grows and builds itself up in love, as each part does its work.'

Today, 'church growth' commonly refers to an increase in the membership rolls or attendance. But the New Testament perspective is that God is interested in quality even more than he is interested in

BODY LIFE was originally published in *Tenth*, (Philadelphia: Tenth Presbyterian Church), July, 1981, pp. 2–11.

quantity. He calls for the evangelizing of the world, but most of all he is concerned that the functioning of the church, the company of the faithful, should always and everywhere bring glory to him as this supernatural life of fellowship with Christ is displayed, lived out, deepened and ripened.

## A Lively Church

First Corinthians 12–14 is a passage of Scripture which makes painful reading for thoughtful evangelical believers. Why? Is it because Corin - thian public worship as described in chapter 14 was such a chaotic uproar?

Is it because of the apparent unseemliness of services in which many folk were talking at once, some in ecstatic gibberish, and in which some women were screeching to be heard above the general noise? Because, in other words, it was a scene of confusion? That is how it seems to have been, as some of Paul's statements in chapter 14 show. But it is not for this reason that I speak of these chapters as painful. These chapters make painful reading because, whatever evils they confront us with, they do at least show us a local church in which the Holy Spirit was working in power. So reading the passage makes one painfully aware of the impov - erishment, inertia, dryness and deadness of so many churches at the present time.

If our only reaction to these chapters is to preen ourselves and feel glad because our churches are free from Corinthian disorders, we are fools indeed and ought to think again. I fear that many of our churches today are orderly simply because they are asleep. And in many cases I fear it is the sleep of death. It is no great thing, is it, to have perfect order in a cemetery?

These Corinthian disorders were due to an uncontrolled overflow of Holy Spirit life. There was real carnality and immaturity in these Corin - thians. It was deplorable enough, and Paul censures it strongly. But this must not blind us to the fact that they were nevertheless enjoying the ministry of the Holy Spirit in a way which most today are not. Remember how, at the start of the letter, Paul wrote, 'I always thank God for you because of his grace given you in Christ Jesus. For in him you have been enriched in every way – in all your speaking and in all your knowl - edge. . . . You do not lack any spiritual gift' (1 Cor. 1:4,5,7). This was not just empty politeness. Paul meant what he said. He always did, and this statement is no exception. The Corinthians really had been enriched by Jesus in the manner described. So, when they met for fellowship they brought with them gifts and contributions in abundance. Whereas con - gregations today too often gather in a spirit of unexpecting apathy, scarcely aware that they come to church to receive, let alone to give, these Corinthians met with eagerness, excitement and expectation, anxious to share with their fellow believers the 'manifestation of the Spirit' that was theirs (12:7). Paul says, 'When you come together, everyone has a hymn, or a word of instruction, a revelation, a tongue, or an interpretation' (14:6).

Public worship at Corinth was thus the very opposite of a drab routine. Every service was an event, for every worshiper came ready and anxious to share something God had given him. Paul gave regulations, not for creating this state of affairs, but for handling it in a way that was orderly and edifying once it had arisen. The state of affairs was itself the spontaneous creation of the Holy Spirit in that church. And when the Corinthians met for worship, the presence and power of God in their midst was an experienced reality.

This is the basic dimension of spiritual revival. Within the Corinthian fellowship there was a sense of the presence of God that struck awe into people's hearts, just as had happened at Jerusalem in the early days. The knowledge of God, the sense of God's presence among these people, was too much for casual, irresponsible contact. That is how it always is in revival times, and that is how it was at Corinth. The awareness of God that was there gave every word that was spoken in God's name heart-searching power.

On this Paul utters what is perhaps the most remarkable throw-away line in the whole New Testament. 'If an unbeliever or someone who does not understand comes in while everyone is prophesying (I think this means "preaching the gospel"), he will be convinced by all that he is a sinner . . . and the secrets of his heart will be laid bare. So he will fall down and worship God, exclaiming, "God is really among you!" ' (14:24,25). Paul affirms this as a certainty! His confidence is breath-taking.

Could that seriously be said to any church known to you at this present time? Say it in our churches, and the only reaction will be, 'How marvellous if that would happen! It is not happening here.' Yet in revival times this has happened over and over again. This word comes out of revival experience. It obviously had happened at Corinth more than once that a casual visitor, coming by accident into a church service and hearing what was said in God's name, had his or her heart searched and broken and was transformed and went out a renewed man or woman.

The Corinthian disorders were grievous, that we grant. But the Corinthian church was being carried along by a great surge of divine life. Disorder, as such, is demonic. I do not question that. Disorder is not in the least to be desired. But it remains a question whether Holy Ghost life, with all its exuberance and risk of disorder, is not preferable to spiritual deadness, neat and tidy thought that deadness might be.

Three centuries ago, in his discourse on spiritual gifts, John Owen, the Puritan, reviewed the Puritan revival of the first sixty years of the seventeenth century and frankly acknowledged the misuse of spiritual endowments that had disfigured the era.

By some, I confess, they have been abused; some have presumed on them; some have been puffed up with them; some have used them disorderly in the churches, and to their hurt; some have boasted . . . all which miscarriages also befell the primitive churches. [But] I had rather have the order, rule, spirit and practice of those churches which were planted by the apostles, with all their troubles and disadvantages, than the carnal peace of others in their open degeneracy from all these things.

Frankly, I would rather have it too. I hope you feel the same. Give me life with all its disorder rather than death with its tidy inertia.

## Sharing Our Common Life

Let us spend a little time exploring what the New Testament says about fellowship or, if you want a two-syllable word instead of a three-syllable one, 'sharing,' which is what fellowship really is. What does the thought of fellowship mean to you when you hear the word in the ordinary course of Christian conversation? Does it suggest to you a cup of coffee in the church parlour? Gossip on the steps outside after the service? A spell at a Christian family camp? Touring Scotland or the Holy Land with a coachful of church people? We often say we have had fellowship when all we mean is that we have taken part in some Christian social enterprise. We ought not to talk like that. The fact that we share social activities with other Christians does not of itself imply that we are having fellowship with them, not at all.

Do not mishear me. I am not denying that there is a place in the life of God's people for activities of this kind. My only point is that to equate these activities with fellowship is an abuse of Christian language, and a dangerous one. It fools us into thinking that we are thriving on fellowship when all the time our souls may be starving for lack of it. It is not a good sign when a person sees no difference between sucking sweets and eating a square meal. Equally it is not a good sign when Christians see no difference between social activities in Christian company and what the New Testament calls fellowship in Christ.

'Fellowship' is one of the great words of the New Testament. It denotes something that is vital for our spiritual health and central to the church's true life. We notice, as we read the New Testament, that fellowship features in the first description of the young church: 'They devoted themselves to the apostles' teaching and to the fellowship' (Acts 2:42).

What is meant here? Gossip? Cups of tea? Tours? No, what is being referred to is something of quite a different order and on quite a different level. The New English Bible has an illuminating paraphrase of these verses. Here are the key phrases: 'They met constantly to hear the apostles teach, and *to share the common life* [that is the paraphrase for fellowship], and to break bread, and to pray. A sense of awe was everywhere. . . . All whose faith had drawn them together held everything in common. . . . With one mind they kept up their daily attendance at the temple, and, breaking bread in private houses, shared their meals with unaffected joy, as they praised God' (vv. 42–47). That is fellowship as the New Testament understands it, and there is clearly a world of difference between that and mere social activities.

I believe that one of the reasons why great sections of the modern church are so often sluggish and feeble, compared with our counterparts of one or two centuries ago, is that the secret of fellowship has been lost. Christ rebuked the Laodiceans for complacently supposing that they had all they needed when they were actually in a state of spiritual bankruptcy. I believe he would rebuke us for talking so glibly about the happy fellowship we have with each other when lack of fellowship really is one of our glaring shortcomings. A body in which the blood does not circulate properly is always below par, and fellowship corresponds to the circulation of the blood in the body of Christ. We gain strength through fellowship and lose strength without it. We grow in fellowship. We go back if we live in isolation from one another. How then should we analyse fellowship and focus it before our minds?

The Greek word for fellowship comes from a root meaning 'common' or 'shared.' So fellowship means common participation in something either by giving what you have to the other person or receiving what he or she has. Give and take is the essence of fellowship, and give and take must be the way of fellowship in the common life of the body of Christ.

Christian fellowship is *two-dimensional*, and it is first vertical before it can be horizontal. That is, we must know the reality of fellowship with the Father and with his Son Jesus Christ before we can know the reality of fellowship with each other in our common relationship to God. You get this spelled out very clearly in the first chapter of 1 John. He writes, 'Our fellowship is with the Father and with his Son, Jesus Christ' (v.3). But he also says, 'We proclaim to you what we have seen and heard, so that you also may have fellowship with us' (v.3) – fellowship with us, that is, in our fellowship with God. That is clear enough, is it not? Fellowship with the Father and the Son makes the Christian. Fellowship with the Father and the Son is the experience of one who is truly a limb in the body of Christ. The person who is not in fellowship with the Father and the Son is no Christian at all, and so cannot share with Christians the realities of their fellowship. This vertical dimension is presupposed when we think of the horizontal dimension of fellowship.

The fellowship of sharing with one another what we have received from the Lord is *a spiritual necessity*. For God has not made us self-sufficient. We are not made so we can keep going on our own. This is often illustrated from the coals of a coal fire. Put the coals together and the fire burns. Separate them out, one from each other, and each goes out quite quickly. So it is in the body of Christ. We are made not for isolated and self-sufficient living but for togetherness in dependence on each other.

The writer to the Hebrews, seeking to stir up the flagging faith and zeal of those harassed Jewish Christians, urges them (among other things) to have more fellowship: 'Let us not give up meeting together, as some are in the habit of doing, but let us encourage one another all the more as you see the Day approaching' (Heb. 10:25). The church will always flourish where there is strong fellowship. The church will always be stagnant, moribund and ineffective where there is no fellowship. There may be orthodoxy, but this is more than orthodoxy. It is the sharing life which the people of God are called to live.

Christian fellowship is also the *family activity* of God's sons. In a good family there is plenty of sharing among the siblings. In the family of God that is also the way it is meant to be. Like fellowship with the Father and the Son, it is two-way traffic: you give and you take, as we said. When it is fellowship with the Father and the Son, you receive the gift of a relationship with God and you give yourself to the Father and the Son in grateful response. That is your reasonable service. In the horizontal dimension of fellowship, sharing with our brother Christians, we give as God has given to us, and we receive.

So Christian fellowship is *seeking to share with others* what God has made known to you, while letting them share with you what they know of him, as a means of finding strength, refreshment and instruction for one's own soul. Gratefully one receives what others share. Equally, one labours to give. And in the giving, no less than in the taking, one finds renewal and strength.

You see this in Paul. A very remarkable scripture, I think, is Romans 1:11,12. Paul is writing to the Romans, people that he has never met before: 'I long to see you so that I may impart to you some spiritual gift to make you strong . . .' Then, lest he give the impression that he thinks the fellowship between him and them is one-way traffic only – all give and no take, all giving and no receiving – he hastens to add as a kind of explanatory modification of what he has just said, 'that is, that you and I may be *mutually encouraged* by each other's faith.'

Preachers know this experience. Special joy comes from opening the Word of God to folk who are obviously hungry and obviously apprecia - tive. The knowledge that folk have received what the preacher has sought to give does his heart good. Those who preach must then, however, be open to receive whatever ministry comes back to them from those to whom they have spoken. Proud aloofness here would be killing.

In Romans 1 Paul is envisioning not only the joy of knowing that the Romans will receive the things he is sharing. He also wants to know the joy of receiving from them what the Lord has given them. God forbid that we should be so self-sufficient in our pride and vain-glory that we should be unwilling to receive and ready only to give, so that for us fellowship becomes a sort of ego trip. This attitude of 'I'm the one who gives, but I don't need to take' has ruined the ministry of more pastors than I can number. Paul was not too proud to look forward to receiving, and so being strengthened in fellowship with the people to whom he ministered. So I say to my brothers in the ministry, as I say to everyone who rejoices to share the things of God: seek from the Lord the humility that is willing to take and to be ministered to, as well as to minister.

## A Threefold Definition

Christian fellowship, then, is an expression of both love and humility. It springs from a desire to bring benefit to others coupled with a sense of personal weakness and need. It has a double motive: the wish to help and the wish to be helped, the wish to edify and the wish to be edified. It is thus a corporate seeking by Christian people to know God better through sharing with each other what individually they have learned already. We seek to do others good, and we seek that others will do us good.

We can therefore say three things about fellowship. First, it is *a means of grace*. Through fellowship and in fellowship one's own soul is refreshed and fed by the effort to communicate one's knowledge of divine things, to come and pray for others, and to receive from God through them.

Second, fellowship is *a test of life*. Fellowship means opening one's heart to one's fellow Christians. The person who is free to eschew pretense and concealment about himself when talking to his fellow believers is the one who is being open and honest in his daily dealings with God. He is the one who is walking in the light, as John puts it in the first chapter of his first letter ('If we walk in the light, as he is in the light, we have fellowship with one another,' 1 John 1:7). If we are not walking in the light we do not have fellowship with one another. If we are not letting the light of God shine full on our whole life, we shall never have free fellowship with others because we shall be unwilling to open up to them. After all, why would we be willing to tell them the shameful secrets of our hearts when we are not prepared to open up to God and let him deal with these things? Those who will not walk in the light with God will never walk in light with their brethren.

Third, fellowship is *a gift of God*. The New English Bible translates Paul's blessing in 2 Corinthians 13:14 like this: 'May the grace of the Lord Jesus Christ, and the love of God, and *the fellowship of the Holy Spirit* be with you all.' The kind of fellowship of which I am speaking, which has as its motive love to our brothers in Christ as an expression of our love to the Lord, and which involves real openness with each other and real reliance on each other – that kind of fellowship comes only as God's gift in and through the Holy Spirit. It is only where the Holy Spirit has been given, where we are spiritually alive to God and anxious to grow in grace ourselves and help others do the same, that such fellowship will be a possibility. It is only as the Spirit enables us that we shall actually be able to practice it.

When does fellowship become a reality? Whenever two or more Christians desiring to help each other to know God better do, in fact, share with each other such knowledge of God and experience of God as they individually possess. It happens when they take responsibility for each other in that sharing situation, when they advise, pray for, encourage and seek in every way to uphold their brother or sister in his or her life and testimony.

It can happen in many circumstances. It can happen in preaching. It can happen as we pray together. It can happen in group Bible study. It can happen in talk between friends over a meal. It can happen in talk between husband and wife at home in the evening. But what happens in every case will be the same thing: the Lord's presence and power will be realized, and we will realize afresh through the words, attitudes, actions and love of a fellow Christian the truth of that promise from the Lord Jesus Christ to be present where 'two or three come together in [his] name' (Matt. 18:20). That promise applies no less to informal acts of fellowship than to public worship. It finds fulfilment when Christians meet together to share informally just as it does at the stated hours of worship on Sunday.

## Fellowship and Reformed Theology

You ask me, 'Is this a Reformed emphasis? Did Calvin give this teaching about fellowship? Did the Puritans talk about it? Did Spurgeon discuss it?' For some folk, what was said one, two, three or four hundred years ago must be decisive, and what was not stressed then cannot be important now. But I want to break away from that frame of reference and say three things.

First, even if this was not an emphasis in our favourite Reformed authors, it *should be an emphasis* in our Reformed churches today. For, what we are talking about is the form and fruit of spontaneous Holy Ghost life, wherever it exists. In fact, wherever new life from God has come to the churches, this sort of fellowship has begun to appear spontaneously, without anyone's needing to search the Puritans, Spurgeon, or whomever, to find precedents for practicing it.

But, of course, it did become a reality among the Puritans. Yes, it did! Often they met together to talk about divine things, and to pray. Sharing and praying together at home was for them a basic activity of Christian family life. And they urged from time to time that every believer should seek from God the priceless gift of one 'bosom friend' – that was their phrase. Every Christian, they said, needs 'one bosom friend,' someone to whom you can say just anything about yourself and ask for help and support in any matter, someone who will care for you, pray for you, someone to whom (expressing this in modern language, which the Puritans did not use, although this was their thought) you will be accountable, someone who will watch over you in the Lord. Over and above ordinary pastoral care from the clergy, so they insisted, this kind of peer relationship is something that every Christian needs.

And what about the Wesleyan revivals? Wesley was converted in a fellowship meeting, a Moravian Pietist Society meeting in Aldersgate Street. Wesley, Whitefield and other leaders of the eighteenth-century evangelical awakening founded fellowship groups, societies as they were called then, in order to 'maintain the glow' which God had brought into the heart of their converts. They insisted that one cannot keep Christians on an even keel, alive and bubbling over with the life of God on a day-to-day basis, unless they belong to such societies.

Again, revivals began in East Africa in the 1930s and immediately there were revival fellowships. They just happened. The folk who had come alive to God met together spontaneously to share, pray, sing and encour-age each other in the Lord. They did it because they found themselves wanting to do it. They do it still, and the revival still goes on.

It seems that every time there has been spiritual quickening anywhere the pattern of Malachi 3:16 has been fulfilled: 'Those who feared [knew and loved] the LORD talked with each other.' They got together for this purpose. I think that the small-group movement of our time, if rightly guided by true ideals of church life, holds tremendous potential for renewal in the churches. The fellowship pattern is there, ready made; what it needs is the touch of God. The full potential of these small-group structures is yet to be realized.

Second, *Reformed leaders have known this principle* of fellowship and have urged the importance of groups. Take George Whitefield. He was a great evangelist and in himself the unity figure of the world-wide English-speaking evangelical movement in the eighteenth century. He led for thirty-five years. He preached 18,000 sermons at least, averaging ten a week, and gave many more informal discourses. By common consent, his ministry had more impact on the eighteenth century than that of anyone else. Wesley and Jonathan Edwards were the first to admit it. Well, here is Whitefield:

> If we look into church history we shall find that as the power of God prevails, Christian societies and fellowship meetings prevail proportionately.
>
> My brethren, let us plainly and freely tell one another what God has done for our souls. To this end you would do well as others have done, to form yourselves into little companies of four or five each and meet once a week to tell each other what is in your hearts, that you may then also pray for and

comfort each other as need shall require. None but those who have experienced it can tell you the unspeakable advantage of such a union and
communion of souls. And none that I think truly loves his own soul, and his
brethren as himself, will be shy of opening his heart in order to have the advice,
reproof admonition and prayers of his brethren. A sincere person will esteem
that one of the greatest blessing.

We see in Whitefield the third and, I think, final stage of the evolution
of the evangelical ideal of the ministry. Sixteenth-century (Reformation)
emphasis: the pastor must be a teacher of the Bible and a preacher of the
gospel. Seventeenth-century (Puritan) emphasis: in addition to that, the
pastor must be shepherd, counsellor, one who can deal one-to-one with
each of the sheep in the flock for which he is caring. Eighteenth-century
emphasis (found in Whitefield): in addition to being a preacher and
counsellor, the minister must be a centre, source and facilitator of
fellowship. One of the tests of his work is that wherever he brings the
word of life, he gathers those who are alive to God and shows them how
to fellowship together in groups, as Whitefield was doing in the quotation
just given.

   Third, in fellowship of this sort, *Reformed theology can restrain excesses*
which, in fact, have often crept into some of these groups. I spoke of
accountability, but I would now add that it must be an accountability under
God. Reformed theology will never let you forget that God alone is Lord
of the conscience. One error that is widespread in certain circles is the
insistence that every Christian must be in a relation of absolute obedience
to some other Christian. Here the idea of accountability has been taken too
far. It has become a domination of the authority figure over the one under
authority, which is real tyranny, for the authority figure now stands as lord
of the conscience in God's place, just as medieval priests used to do. God
alone is Lord of the conscience, and fellowship relations of the kind of which
I am speaking must be practiced under the ultimate and acknowledged
authority of the Lord, who from his Word shows his children what is right
and what is wrong for their lives. In fellowship relations, as in all else, the
appeal to Scripture is needful and decisive.

## Spiritual Gifts

Fellowship is carried on through the reality of spiritual gifts. In these days
much has been taught about spiritual gifts. I will content myself with brief
remarks on the theology and practical approach to the doctrine and use
of gifts.

   What is a spiritual gift? It is in essence a God-given capacity to express
or minister Christ so that those to whom service is rendered will see Christ
and grow in Christ to his glory. It may be a gift of speech, behaviour,

conduct, service in any form. It may be the practical gift of relieving needs, Samaritan-style, just as it may be the teacher's gift of explaining things from the Word. But whatever it is, it is a God-given ability to make Christ known. When gifts are exercised in the power of the Spirit by whom they are bestowed, the reality of the situation is this: Christ himself, on his throne but through his Spirit in us, is ministering as he ministered to people in the days of his flesh. We become his mouth, his hands, his feet. We should seek each day thus to be his hands, mouth and feet, to fulfil his ministry to others by exercising the spiritual gifts we have been given.

Usually others see our gifts better than we see them ourselves. Usually others can tell us more exactly what we can and cannot do for the Lord than we are able to discern by introspection. Realizing then that the finding and use of gifts is fellowship business, we should ask others to watch us and tell us what our gifts are, and so be guided by them.

Our charismatic friends seem to me to be wrong in their idea that the sign gifts which authenticated the apostles are maintained by God in every age, this age included. I think this is a total mistake. But my charismatic brethren, it seems to me, are absolutely right to stress, as they do, the importance of every-member ministry in the body of Christ. I ask you, what is your ministry? What is your gift or gifts? What are the things you can do to express and communicate Christ? If you have never sought the answer to that question, begin to seek that answer now in the fellowship of the Christians who know you best, and go on from there.

Let me close by warning that there are many hindrances to body life. We need to search our hearts as to whether these are not impeding the reality of body life in our churches.

Among the clergy, clericalism can impede body life. Clericalism is a conspiracy. It is the state of affairs in which the minister says, 'You leave the spiritual ministry to me; that's my job.' And the congregation says, 'Yes, that's absolutely right, and so we will.' That can be said the other way. The congregation may say to the minister, 'We hired you to do the spiritual ministry. Get on with it! That's the job you're paid to do.' And the minister says what a minister should never consent to say, namely, 'I accept that, and so I will.' For us who serve God as clergy and pastors it is necessary to challenge that conspiracy and decline to be a party to it, to insist on the principle of every-member ministry.

We should seek the state of affairs reflected by a letterhead from a southern church, which I received a few years ago. On the letterhead was: 1) the name of the church; 2) 'ministers: the congregation'; and 3) 'assistant to the ministers': the name of the pastor! That is how it should be in every church.

In another church I saw on the vestry door a little plaque saying: 'Head Coach.' That was right also!

Another hindrance to body life is formalism, the supposition that if you are doing things correctly (as Presbyterians in particular are so anxious to do) then all is well. That formal correctness will be an empty shell of church life, a barren sham, if the realities of body life are not there backing it up.

Self-sufficiency on the part of any in the congregation, standoffishness which is unwilling to open up to brother Christians, complacency with the church as it is – these things too will hinder body life. Be warned!

To conclude, then, I say: for your own sake, for the sake of our churches, for the glory of our Lord Jesus Christ, for the blessing of the world through churches that are really alive – seek body life in its fullness in your congregation. Practice body life in its fullness. Do not rest until every-member ministry is a reality. Love one another; pray for one another; end those wretched divisions and the cliquishness and all the other things which quench the Spirit and prevent fellowship from being what it ought to be. Seek true fellowship, and do not rest until it becomes a reality for you through the power of the Spirit of God. Then your church will really be alive, a beacon for Christ in the place where God has set it, and it will grow in the full scriptural sense of that word.

# Chapter 3

# Divisions in the Church

My subject is divisions in the church, and I shall creep up on it cautiously. It is a subject on which I do not want to be divisive.

I am speaking to a diverse group of people. We are diverse denomina - tionally to start with. Some of us are Anglicans. Others are Presbyterians. We have representatives from the United Church of Canada, the Christian Reformed Church, Baptists, Lutherans, independent community churches, and probably others.

Directionally, too, we are diverse. Some of us are in process of discovering Reformed piety. What really turns us on about this confer - ence is the testimony it gives to godliness according to the Reformed faith, and church issues have not so far bothered us much. Others of us, I am sure, are Reformed pietists who know all about this element but who are now discovering the glory of God's purpose for his church. Some of us come from congregations that have split, or may split; some of us face deep-rooted denominational complacency and wonder how long we can or should endure it.

How am I to talk to so diverse an audience about divisions in the church? I am going to start where I know all of us do start, whatever other differences there may be. I start at the point at which we are united, the point on which the previous addresses of this conference have united us, if we were not united on it before: namely, our belief in the one church of God in Christ, which is our conference theme.

## Our Common Ground

As Reformed people we are committed to what has sometimes been called the 'spiritual idea' of the church, that is to say, a view of the church not primarily as an institution (like a club) nor a body created by the automatic operation of the sacraments, but as the community of those

DIVISIONS IN THE CHURCH was originally published in *The Church: God's New Society*, (Philadelphia: Tenth Presbyterian Church, 1985), pp. 34–44. Reprinted by permission.

who have faith in Jesus Christ. It is the relationship to Christ that makes the church. The church is one because everyone who is in the church is one with Christ. The church may be pictured like the wheel of a bicycle. Christ is the hub. You and I are spokes. Because we are linked with Christ we belong to the church and have something to give by way of stability and usefulness to the rim of the wheel, that is, the church's outward witness, worship and life. United to the one Saviour we are united to each other in the one universal Christian church

This church is the family of God. It is also the body of Christ. The New Testament speaks of 'members,' not of the church, but of Christ; 'membership' is part of the notion of the church as Christ's body. 'Members' means 'limbs,' not people who sit in pews and pay their dues but people vitally united to Christ – limbs, organs and units in his body, which is the visible church worldwide.

The church is also the fellowship of the Holy Spirit. Believers share in the life of the Spirit, giving and taking in the fellowship which the Spirit sustains. 'Give and take' is the constant formula of Christian fellowship. Surely we are agreed on all this.

We are agreed, too, that the church is central in God's plan. We know that

> Christ loved the church and gave himself up for her to make her holy, cleansing her by the washing with water through the word, and to present her to himself as a radiant church, without stain or wrinkle or any other blemish (Eph. 5:25–27).

We are being caught up into this glorious destiny appointed by the Saviour. This is the centre of God's plan for history: the redemption and perfection of the church.

Finally, we know that local churches, congregations such as those from which you and I come, are outcroppings of this one universal church composed of all believers. Each local church is a bit of the church universal becoming visible in a particular place. It is a microcosm, a small-scale presentation of the larger church. I am sure we are all agreed on that. Here, then, is our starting point for thinking about divisions in the church as it presents itself before the eyes of men.

## Shameful Divisions

The church, we have said, is the family of God. Tell me, now, how ought families – siblings, specifically brothers and sisters – to behave? Well, you are not going to deny that siblings ought to act like and look like parts of a family. If brothers and sisters never meet together, never speak to each other, appear to be entirely indifferent to each other – that is an unnatural and scandalous state. That would be true of any human family. I put it to you without fear of contradiction: the same is true of the family of God.

I ask another question. How does a body function? Let me answer by reading you something Paul says in 1 Corinthians 12, picking up halfway through verse 24:

> God has combined the members of the body and has given greater honour to the parts that lacked it, so that there should be no division in the body, but that its parts should have equal concern for each other. It one part suffers, every part suffers with it; if one part is honoured, every part rejoices with it (vv.24–26).

How *does* a body function? Paul says that it functions as a support system. If one part of your body is in pain – your toe, finger, tooth – you feel completely out of sorts. The whole body resonates with pain. If a part of your body is substandard in its functioning, other parts – nerves, muscles and so on – overdevelop in order to make up. That is part of the meaning of the picture. The body of Christ is a great, worldwide support system.

Or is it? It should be.

I ask another question. How does a fellowship function? Fellowship, we said, means give and take, share and share alike. I give you what God has given me; you give me what God has given you. That is the pattern which the church ought to exhibit everywhere. None of us is to live to himself, any more than any of us can die to himself. We are to live in the give and take of the one fellowship of the Holy Spirit.

I am arguing that divisions in the church which prevent the family from acting like one family and the body from functioning like one body and the one fellowship from operating with free give and take are unnatural; unnatural to the point of being shameful. Brothers and sisters, such things ought not to be. Listen to Paul, writing in the second half of Ephesians.

> As a prisoner for the Lord, then, I urge you to live a life worthy of the calling you have received. Be completely humble and gentle; be patient, bearing with one another in love. Make every effort to keep the unity of the Spirit through the bond of peace (Eph. 4:1–3).

The unity of the Spirit is a fact already, according to these verses. We are not to create it, as if it did not exist; the Spirit who invited us to Christ has created it; we are to maintain it and express it. That is the first and basic thing it means to walk worthy of the calling to which we have been called. If we are not doing that our behaviour is scandalous.

This is why Paul was so distressed to discover that at Corinth, in that bright and lively but immature and carnal church, there were people separating into parties according to which was the favourite preacher for each group: 'I belong to Paul,' 'I belong to Apollos,' 'I belong to Cephas.' And evidently there were a few people who in face of this, tried to keep their end up as simple Christians saying 'I belong to Christ; I don't know about you, but Christ is the one to whom I give loyalty.' Well, it distressed Paul that there should be divisions in that congregation. That was not walking 'worthy' of the calling to which Christians are called.

When we study division in the churches we have to say that although we cannot deny the unity that the Lord has created, we can fail to express it, and the theme of this study is Christian failure.

Let me state that point another way. If we are going to study division in the church, we had better recognize that we are studying something pathological. We are studying a form of spiritual ill-health in Christ's body. Our study is comparable to a doctor studying blindness in the eye or paralysis in the limbs. Division in the church means that 'something is wrong.' The body is out of sorts.

Why does this illness of division exist? The question is not hard to answer. It exists because of Satan and sin. Satan keeps pace with God in attempting to spoil what God is doing. God is busy uniting all sorts and conditions of people out of every nation and tongue, and Satan is trying to stop this from happening. He wants to divide the family, split the body, spoil the fellowship.

And sin? Sin in our imperfectly sanctified nature is what you might call an instinct for division. The first thing that sin did when it came into the world was to estrange Adam and Eve from each other. Then it caused Cain to kill Abel. Sin has always produced divisions and, alas, the sinful impulse, whenever let loose, is still a divisive impulse. So we can see clearly enough why the people of God fail to practice unity as they should and Christ appears to be divided.

## Inescapable Divisions

Sometimes, of course, division, though not desirable, is inescapable. It is a necessary evil, the best thing that the situation admits of. Still it is always a sad thing when the situation arises which makes it the best thing to do.

How are we to evaluate the divisions that have actually appeared in the professed body of Christ? Here I wish to offer what I suppose academics would call a descriptive typology of the different kinds of division that come into church life. I think it important that we should try to list them, because different sorts of divisions have to be approached and judged in different ways. Not all types of division are equally good, equally bad, equally necessary or equally excusable.

First, there are *divisions about beliefs and doctrine*. To start with, in the New Testament you have divisions whereby *the authentic church differentiates itself from what is really the non-church*, where previously the two were confused. This sort of division, which identifies the body rather than divides it, can clear the air in a helpful way.

This is one of the things John wanted his readers to understand when he wrote his first letter. There had been a split in the fellowship, because some folks claimed to have received new understanding and eventually left the fellowship to pursue it. John writes to those who stayed behind to assure them that in staying with the apostolic preaching they were showing they were true believers and that the others were not Christians at all. It was a necessary sorting out. John says,

> They went out from us, but they did not really belong to us. For if they had belonged to us, they would have remained with us; but their going showed that none of them belonged to us (1 John 2:18,19).

The particular matter on which the heretics claimed to have received new light was the person and atoning death of Jesus Christ. The history books describe their view by the technical term 'gnostic.' They believed that there had never been any true incarnation, that Jesus had only appeared to be man but was not so really and that he had not really died on the cross. He saves people, they maintained, by his teaching but not by any atonement made for them. John assures his readers that what the apostles taught about the incarnation and atonement is truth and what the heretics taught were lies. They did not believe the true gospel. Therefore, the sorting out had been salutary.

The heretics had taken the initiative in making the separation. But the separation, says John, had to be made. Thus, when you get to his second letter you see him exhorting Christians who are up against this doctrine to take the initiative themselves in separating from it.

> Many deceivers, who do not acknowledge Jesus Christ as coming in the flesh, have gone out into the world. Any such person is the deceiver and the antichrist. . . . If anyone comes to you and does not bring this teaching, do not take him into your house or welcome him. Anyone who welcomes him shares in his wicked work (2 John 7–11).

This is a salutary sorting out but, strictly speaking, it is not division within the church. I deal with it first only so that we may not be confused by supposing that perhaps it is.

Second, there are occasions *when the faithful church withdraws from the scandalous church*. The historical sixteenth-century Reformation was one such case.

In Galatians 1:8, Paul declares a curse on those who bring a message other than the good word of justification by faith, with faith through Jesus Christ only. He says, 'But even if we or an angel from heaven should preach a gospel other than the one we preached to you, let him be eternally condemned!' As the letter goes on to show, he was fighting the view that justification is by Christ plus works. Justification by faith alone was being obscured by that view. Again, in Colossians 2:18, 19 he writes,

> Do not let anyone who delights in false humility and the worship of angels disqualify you for the prize. Such a person goes into great detail about what he has seen, and his unspiritual mind puffs him up with idle notions. He has lost connection with the Head from whom the whole body, supported and held together by its ligaments and sinews, grows as God causes it to grow.

It is ruinous to add anything to Christ as mediator. Salvation is through Christ alone. Any church that is taken in by any form of 'Christ-plus' teaching is scandalous and in deep spiritual trouble.

That is what happened in the medieval church. It taught that salvation is by Christ plus works, and claimed that the church had been graced with the gift of infallibility so that none of its teachings could be challenged. When the Reformers opposed those errors, they found resistance at every point. So they had to withdraw to save the gospel. Protestantism was thus born. It is sad that it had to happen. But it did have to happen, or the gospel could never have been preserved for us. That is one kind of division that has sometimes been necessary.

Third, there are divisions that happen *when a forthright church* (or forthright group of Christians) *withdraws from a fuzzy church*, where faithful believers have tried but failed to maintain a clear witness to God's grace according to the Scriptures. It may be a matter of withdrawing from a particular denomination. It may be just withdrawing from a local congregation.

Why does this happen? It happens for the same reason the Reformers withdrew from the Roman communion – to keep the channel of truth clear so that the life of God may flow along it. Folk who withdraw in this way have seen that God's pattern is as Paul describes it in the first half of Ephesians. We are to:

> no longer be infants, tossed back and forth by the waves, and blown here and there by every wind of teaching and by the cunning and craftiness of men in their deceitful scheming. Instead, speaking the truth in love, we will in all things grow up into him who is the Head, that is, Christ (Eph. 4:14,15).

That can happen only if gospel truth is constantly set forth and thus taken into people's hearts and minds. The forthright church withdraws from the fuzzy church in situations where it seems that this cannot happen any more. It is a sad thing when this happens, but it has to happen if growth is going to be maintained.

In this situation the pastoral purpose is kept at the forefront. Truth is for people. Thus, those who under pressure become firebrands for truth and forget the pastoral purpose for which God has given it cannot but dishonour God by their separating.

I expect that I address people who have left congregations for exactly this reason. You tried to maintain a clear testimony to the gospel, but there came a point at which it could not be done. You proved the situation, tested out its possibilities. But you could see that there was no hope. So you withdrew and united with another congregation. Maybe you belong to a group who withdrew. I hope you did it in love, sadness, quietness and pastoral concern. But if it was for the sake of keeping the gospel clear and the channel of life free from obstructions, well then, it had to be done, however regrettable it was.

Fourth, there are *divisions over church order*. You do not find this in the New Testament, but you do find it in our Protestant denominations. Incompatible views about how the church should order its life have broken surface, and therefore particular groups of congregations have had to go their own separate ways. Basically, there have been three unavoidable causes of denominational separation of this kind

1. Some believe in covenant baptism for the children of believers, and some do not. These two practices do not marry, and this has necessitated division. Baptist and Baptistic churches go one way. Presbyterian and related churches go another.

2. Some believe in episcopacy and liturgy, and some do not. Not all Christians believe that diocesan episcopacy can be a fruitful pastoral institution. Not all Christians believe that a thought-out, carefully wrought liturgical form for the worship of God is always best. Those who have not been able to accept these views have regrettably had to leave the Anglican communion.

3. Some believe that congregations should be linked to each other in synods, that is, central deliberative bodies which have legislative power, and some do not. This has been the Presbyterian way and the way of all national (state) churches, but it is not the independent way. Those who believe that the New Testament favours congregational independence rather than presbyterianism have had to separate at this point.

In all these matters of divergence, a case can be made from Scripture on both sides. We know this, for it is actually done, over and over again. None of us, therefore, whatever his or her own personal convictions, should feel entitled to say with absolute confidence that the Bible excludes the other way. We are in the realm, not of certainties of faith, but of matters of more or less probable opinion. The most we can say is that 'I *think* the Bible excludes the other way; I *think* my practice is the one Scripture directs.' That degree of humility ought to make us sensitive to maintain fellowship in the fundamentals with those who in matters of church order have felt obliged to go a different way from us, as we have gone in a different way from them.

In that connection it is worth reading some words out of Mark's Gospel which, I think, speak directly to the case of Protestant believers who agree on the doctrines of God's grace but are ecclesiastically divided.

> 'Teacher,' said John, 'we saw a man driving out demons in your name and we told him to stop, because he was not one of us.'

> 'Do not stop him,' Jesus said 'No one who does a miracle in my name can in the next moment say anything bad about me, for whoever is not against us is for us' (Mark 9:38, 39).

On this basis, in spite of our separate denominational groups, we ought to maintain fellowship every way we can. Conferences like ours, and joint local activities, are among the means of doing this.

Fifth, there are *divisions for non-theological reasons*, divisions, for example, over people's race, class, age or style. There are ethnic churches. The Mennonite Church is an ethnic church. The Christian Reformed Church and the Reformed Church in America are ethnic churches. The Swedish Covenant Church is an ethnic church. There are Black and Hispanic and West Indian churches. It would be foolish to say that these distinctions ought not to be sufficient warrant for churches like these to be formed. What is important is that we share the same faith and attest to it.

Not all white Reformed Christians would be at home in Black congregations which, nonetheless, maintain the same faith as themselves; and so on across the board. What we must do here is take care that our programs testify to our oneness with Christians of different ethnic backgrounds, colours and social classes.

It is a different story, however, when divisions are over such non-theological factors as *the personalities of leaders*, like that division described in 1 Corinthians 1. That sort of division we must reject categorically, because, Paul says, it is wrong. Oh, to be sure, we have our favourite preachers, but that is no reason for dividing the local congregation. You must have been in the faith long enough to have learned that God blesses different people through different preachers. But do not divide the body over that! It would be Spirit-quenching, very much the devil's work and very dishonouring to the Saviour, to be part of a division over preachers.

## Dealing With Division

That is enough of an analysis. Let me turn now to strategies that have been proposed for dealing with areas of tension, where outward division either threatens or has already taken place. On these I simply offer comments – no more.

Strategy number one: *separation*. It has been maintained that the best thing for evangelicals to do when in mixed and imperfectly focused denominations is to withdraw and get together, thus (it is said) realizing what Paul longed to see at Philippi.

> Whatever happens, conduct yourselves in a manner worthy of the gospel of Christ. Then, whether I come and see you or only hear about you in my absence, I will know that you stand firm in one spirit, contending as one man for the faith of the gospel (Phil. 1:27).

The thing has happened, of course, in our time. That is the story of the Presbyterian Church in America. I would not suggest for a moment that it was wrong for evangelical Presbyterians to reorganize themselves along these lines. It was not schism, that is, causeless separation. Maybe it cleared the air in a fruitful way.

However, as we contemplate this type of action we must remember that it does not automatically guarantee blessing to those who thus separate. I think of a small Presbyterian body which withdrew from a much larger Presbyterian body about fifty years ago but which has never grown. It is faithful to the Scriptures. Yet to all intents and purposes it is very stuck in the mud. Let us remember too that in a small, separated body you always have the problem of Diotrephes, the man who loved to have pre-eminence. The smaller the pond, the bigger the problem presented by the man who wants to be a big fish in it. The smaller the pond, the narrower the vision of the Christian calling in this world is likely to be.

So there are cons as well as pros as one contemplates separating. Separation is a last resort, and no one should ever think of it as a standard solution. It brings all kinds of dangers with it.

Strategy number two: *church union*. This is presented as a step toward regaining the visible oneness of Christ's church that denominational separation obscures. It has been greatly pushed by the ecumenical movement for the last sixty years.

I offer these principles. First, remember that church union assumes that the basic dimensions of Christian unity are already there: oneness of belief, love and commitment to the work of Christian mission. In John 17:20–23 the Saviour prays that all his people may be one in him in the same way that he and the Father are one with each other – and that means oneness of mind, love and common purpose, as well as of divine essence. Where these dimensions of Christian unity are not found, talk about church union is so inappropriate as to be painful. You cannot have a successful marriage where the man and woman do not agree about anything important. Yet that is what the church union program has so often been trying to encompass.

Second, separated churches ought to unite where this will further the church's work. Assuming they are one in faith and purpose, well, if resources can be better deployed through being pooled, none of us should be so stuck in the mud as to refuse to come together. But only where there is common faith and love one for the other and common under- standing of the church's calling can the question of union be sensibly raised.

The last principle governing the strategy of church union is that efforts like these will waste an enormous amount of Christians' time to no purpose where there is no genuine unity in faith matters. There comes a time in some union talks when Christians ought to protest that they really have more important things to do. So be careful about union schemes, good though it is to diminish the enormous number of denominations in Christendom.

Strategy number three: *co-operation*, such as is illustrated by a conference of this kind. Here members of different congregations and denominations come together to testify to their true unity in faith, love and commitment to the Lord's work. I am all for maximizing this sort of co-operation as a way of exhibiting and deepening our real, Christ-created, Spirit-given unity; I hope you are too.

Strategy number four: *maturation*, that is, seeking to lead others to true maturity in Christ. Immaturity is one great cause of division. The church at Corinth was divided into warring groups because, says Paul, they were childish. The gospel had not gotten deep enough into their system to make them appreciate what the practice of unity requires. They had to grow at that point.

We hear different notions of what constitutes carnal Christianity. Note, however, that the carnality of which Paul is speaking in 1 Corinthians 3:1 is failing to understand that we have to practice unity as part of our calling in the body of Christ. Even Reformed people can be thus carnal and immature. What is going to help us at this point? Only maturation – seeking better to understand the gospel of God's grace, the reality of the oneness in Christ that God has given us, the forbearance and patience that are involved in expressing that unity in fellowship with our brethren, and humility (so that we do not push our own opinions, when we know really that they are not more than opinions, on other people). This is a temper that we always need in our church life.

# Chapter 4

# The Doctrine and Expression
# of Christian Unity

Our aim in this essay is to focus the biblical notion of the unity of the Church, and draw from it some lines of approach to current questions about the uniting of churches.

The theme is hackneyed, no doubt. Our era has seen a flood of writing on it already. For fifty years the world Church has concentrated on problems of unity in a quite unprecedented way. This has been due to several converging factors. First, this has been due to a steady build-up of external pressures against the Church's mission. Our world continues to shrink, and to absorb in every continent the cultural patterns of the 'secular cities' of the West. The Communist bloc has put up the shutters against Christianity, and the old Eastern faiths, revitalized by nationalism, have grown strong, while by every outward standard of reckoning the Chris - tian tide has ceased to flow in Afro-Asia and is ebbing in the West. In an age which knows the power of centralized administration and big technological battalions, as seen in the industrial empires of the West and the to talitarian regimes of the East, the churches, thrown on to the defensive and conscious of their weakness, have come to see today as in a special sense 'a time for unity' (to quote the title of the Bishop of Bristol's recent treatment of this theme). United, it is felt, we shall stand, whereas divided we cannot but fall.

One sign of our times is that all over the world members of the older Protestant church families in particular are hopefully looking to union schemes to renew the Church's life. This is disturbing, for neither Scripture nor experience encourages such hopes. The New Testament links revival with the outpouring of God's Spirit to empower the Word, but suggests no connection between this and uniting separated churches; and the witness of history is that, where movements of revival have neither presupposed nor produced such unions, no union to date – the Church

---

THE DOCTRINE AND EXPRESSION OF CHRISTIAN UNITY was originally published in *Churchman*, One Body in Christ, LXXX, 1966. Reprinted by permission.

of Scotland, the English Methodist Church, the Church of South India, or any other – has led to any kind of spiritual awakening. This unpalatable fact should be squarely faced. Whatever fringe benefits union schemes may have brought, they have not so far resulted in any discernible deepening of spiritual life, nor any notable evangelistic advance. How - ever, hope springs eternal in the churchman's breast – is not ecclesiastical optimism a standard counterfeit for Christian hope? – and many are sincerely convinced that our stagnant churches will find in union their elixir of life. Hence thoughts of union bulk large in many minds.

Then, second, modern theology has rediscovered the Church. The consequent redirection of interest has been quite dramatic. The nine - teenth century was for Protestant Europe and America an era of religious individualism, while Roman thought about the Church was wholly institutional, juridical, and authoritarian.

But all that has changed. From study of the biblical themes of God's covenant, God's people, and Christ's body has sprung a new vision of the Church as the redeemed community, a single organism, 'visible' by its very nature, and central in God's plan. Realization that the kingdom of God is essentially neither socialism, as liberal Protestants thought, nor ecclesiasticism, as Roman Catholics had assumed, but is the realm of God's saving, subduing, and renewing action, dynamic in character and cosmic in range, has opened a new chapter of thought about the Church's mission and the conditions of its earthly life. Hence has come a new theological interest in unity, as part of God's will for the Church on earth.

What this unity involves, however, is not yet agreed. Easy agreement was never, indeed, on the cards. Participants in the debate have viewed the new insights from conflicting basic standpoints, and have been constantly tempted to assume – as we would all start by doing – that the highroad to unity is for everyone else to become like themselves. Discussion continues, and though the ground is now mostly familiar, old positions have constantly to be re-thought and re-stated. This is what, within its limits, the present essay seeks to do.

We would first call attention to two contrasts between New Testament teaching and our usual way of thinking about the Church.

First: we regularly treat the Church as a topic on its own, a distinct theme for conferences, lectures, and books, to be discussed only in relation to problems of schism and settlement. This in itself is no more improper than is the isolating of any other biblical theme for study; yet we need to remember that the New Testament does something different. Instead of isolating the doctrine of the Church, it integrates it into the doctrine of grace. Its interest in ecclesiology is not institutional, but evangelical. The subject of all New Testament theology, the thing that all the New Testament books are consciously *about*, is the work of God in Christ. New Testament teaching is kergymatic, in the sense of being, first to last, exposition and application of the Gospel of redeeming love. The doctrine of the Church belongs as part of this exposition.

This reflects ultimately the God-centredness of the Bible. If, as is popular these days, we view the Bible from the standpoint of its narrative, as a *drama*, we have to acknowledge the Triune God as author, producer, and chief performer. Or if, in the older manner, we see the Bible as a *message*, 'God's Word written,' we have to recognize God himself as its source, subject, and actual speaker. From either standpoint, it would be as absurd to say that the Bible is about the Church as to say that it is about the Middle East. The Bible is about *God* – the Creator redeeming. And when it shows us the Church, the substance of what it is showing us is God's work of redemption – particularly, what older divines called the *applying* of redemption.

To study the Christian life – calling, justification, sanctification con - flict, preservation, glorification – is to study the applying of redemption to individuals; to study the Church – its nature, notes, life, ministry, sacraments – is to study *the same subject* in its corporate aspect. The doctrine of the Church, as we said, is part of the doctrine of grace. Had Paul been asked the theme of his 'Church epistles' Colossians and Ephesians – or, for that matter, Romans and Galatians which, as modern expositors recognize, have as good a claim to be called 'Church epistles' as have the other two – he would certainly have said: the grace of God in Christ.

Whether the common claim that 'the Church is part of the Gospel' is true or false depends how the word 'Church' is being used. If it is taken in a 'Catholic' sense, to denote a sacramental institute of salvation with a built-in hierarchical structure – a view only attainable in any case by appeal to extra-biblical authority – then the statement is false. It is true, however, when 'Church' is defined as the family community of those redeemed, called, and united to God – when, in other words, the Church is *defined in terms of the Gospel*. Our point is that this is how it should be defined, and that its nature and life should be analysed in entire correlation to the work of God in grace as the New Testament sets it forth.

Second: we regularly treat the Church's unity as problematical and uncertain by reason of the plethora of divisions not merely between denominational groups, but within them as well. (The theological differ - ences between evangelicals and others in the older Protestant bodies, for instance, seem actually to go deeper than any of the differences between these bodies as such.) Here again, however, the New Testament is different. Though the first churches also lacked effective uniformity of doctrine, worship, and government, and though 'organic union' in the modern sense was neither known to them nor sought by them, the apostolic writers never saw the Church's unity as a problem. Rather, they proclaimed it as a fact. This shows again how theocentric, evangelical, and, in the sense explained, non-institutional, their thought about the Church was.

Our way is to start from the Church as we see it: hence what strikes us is the fact of division, and we wonder in what sense, if any, the Church can be one. This perplexity is reflected in William Temple's half-jocular remark: 'I believe in the Holy Catholic Church and sincerely regret that it does not at present exist!' At one time it seemed that the ecumenical movement would never rise above this point of view. What it reveals, however, is the imperfect sanctification of our minds, for this is not the apostolic approach. The New Testament way is to start from the cross of Christ, whereby God reconciled Jew and Gentile, bond and free, Greek and Barbarian, male and female, not only to himself, but also to each other. In the New Testament, therefore, unity is integral to the fact of the Church, and the problem is not how the divided Church can be one, but how the Church can be divided.

> 'He (Christ) is our peace', writes Paul, 'who made both one. . . having abolished in his flesh the enmity . . . that he might create inmself of the twain one new man, so making peace; and might reconcile them both in one body unto God through the cross . . .' (Eph. 2:14ff.).

Jesus himself had said: 'Other sheep I have, which are not of this fold; them also I must bring, and they shall hear my voice; and they shall become one flock, one shepherd' (John 10:16) – a thought which John underlined by observing that Jesus was to die 'not for the nation only, but that he might also gather together into one all the children of God that are scattered abroad' (11:52). Here is a unity given to the Church by the very acts of redemption and calling. So Paul tells the Galatian Christians 'ye are all one man in Christ Jesus' (Gal. 3:28).

This unity is given and established by an act of God; Christians neither made it nor, in the ultimate sense, can they break it, any more than they can fall out of their Saviour's hand (John. 10:29f.). Christ is not divided (1 Cor. 1:18), and those whom he has baptized through the Spirit into one body (1 Cor. 12:13, cf. Rom. 12:5, Eph. 4:4) cannot be severed from that body. 'If the foot shall say, Because I am not the hand, I am not of the body; is it therefore not of the body?' (1 Cor. 12:15). Like it or not 'all of us, united with Christ, form one body, serving individually as limbs and organs to one another' (Rom. 12:5, NEB). The unity of this 'one body in Christ' can be ignored and denied, but it cannot thereby be destroyed. Invariably, therefore, the New Testament views the empirical facts of Christian division in the light of the antecedent fact of Christian unity; not vice versa!

What is the nature of the Church's given and indestructible unity? This question is not answered merely by naming factors which are thought to effect unity, or to manifest its existence and safeguard its continuance. Explanations of the Church's unity are often given in terms of common subjection to the Papacy, or the historic episcopate, or 'catholic tradition', or the doctrines of the Protestant confessions, or the authority of the Scriptures. But all such explanations miss the heart of the matter. The items listed could not, in their very nature, be more than outward means and signs of unity. The Church's unity has to be explained in terms of its union with God.

The Church is one because Christians share a common relation to the three Persons of the one Godhead – a relation that is common, not merely in the sense of being similar in every case, but in the further sense of being a single, communal relation whereby God, Father, Son, and Holy Spirit, holds all Christians, every moment, in saving union with himself. God's relation to the whole Church is numerically one, just as a father's relation to his whole family is numerically one, embracing both the group ('my children') and each individual within it ('my child'). This unitary action of God causing sinners to stand in his grace is what makes and keeps the Church one, as a glance at the New Testament account of the Church will show.

This account has two focal points, the covenant and the new creation. The covenant idea indicates the Church's continuity with Old Testament Israel, as the inheritor under the 'new' covenant of what Israel looked forward to under the 'old'. The thought of new creation, by contrast, underlines the discontinuity between the Church's resurrection-life 'in the heavenlies' and the Adamic realm of death from which Christ delivered her. The covenant idea speaks of *pledged fellowship* between God and his Church, in faithfulness and love, on the basis of remission of sins.

Complementary to this, the new creation concept speaks of *vital union* between God and his Church through his vitalizing action in raising her from death to a new life of righteousness. With the former notion may be grouped the New Testament's 'community' images of the Church, as God's nation, family, city, flock, kingdom, and priesthood, and Christ's bride; with the latter belong its 'organic' images of the Church as a vine, temple, body, and man, in Christ. Both these streams of thought (which, of course, come together in both sacraments) testify to the Church's unity.

Moreover, both testify to two further facts in connection with this unity – first, that the one Church owes its existence to the sovereign initiative of the one God, second, that the one Church has all its life through the effective mediation of the one Christ. Regarding the first fact, it is enough to observe that the biblical analogue of God's covenant is not a negotiable contract between equals, but covenants of monarchy and marriage, in both of which a unilaterally defined relationship is offered at the discretion of the offerer; while the biblical analogue of new creation is the old creation, which, in the nature of the case, was God's work entirely. Regarding the second fact, we need only note that Christ is set forth, on the one hand, as both heir of God's covenant in its original form (Gal. 3:15ff.) and mediator of it in its final form (Heb. 8:6) and, on the other hand, as both 'the beginning' of the new creation through his own resurrection (Col. 1:18; see C. F. D. Moule *ad loc.* and also the One in whom 'new creation' becomes a reality for us through faith in him (2 Cor. 5:17; cf. John. 3:3–15; Col. 2:10–12). Here, then, is the grace of God in Christ which creates and sustains in being the one Church. When Paul proclaims the Church's unity 'one body, one Spirit . . . one hope . . . one Lord, one faith, one baptism, one God and Father of all . . .' (Eph. 4:4f.) – it is of this grace that he is bearing witness.

A further point must be made here. Paul speaks of 'one faith' through which, as he tells us elsewhere, men receive God's grace and actually come to belong to the one Church. What is this 'one faith'? Paul's answer certainly would have been: faith in Jesus Christ according to my Gospel – in other words, trust in the person of the Saviour on the basis of certain truths about his work and its effects. So the idea of the Church is of a community which knows God's grace through believing in Jesus Christ, and which knows Jesus Christ through believing specific doctrines about him.

Here is the basis for insisting, as it is necessary (though unfashionable) to do, that the Church is, by its very nature, a confessional body. The common playing-down of faith in doctrines, as if faith in Christ did not require it, is shallow thoughtlessness – indeed, if pressed, it is utter nonsense. Christ is not an unknown 'x,' but a specific historical personage, now glorified. The notion of faith in him lacks content till we know those facts about him which are relevent to our condition, and it is precisely these facts which have historically been called doctrines. In a recent battle of the Joneses,[1] Professor Douglas Jones attacked Dr. D. M. Lloyd-Jones for saying that Christian unity exists only where the central doctrines of Paul's Gospel are believed. This is not so, argued Professor Jones, for belief in doctrines is not the same thing as faith in Christ. But this fell short of the point at issue. That you can have belief in doctrines without faith in Christ was not in dispute.

Dr. Lloyd-Jones' thrust was rather that you cannot have faith in Christ without faith in the doctrines of the Gospel. No doubt it is beyond our power to determine how much false doctrine, or how little true doctrine, concerning Jesus is compatible with 'justifying faith' in any particular case. No doubt we must be cautious in judging the spiritual state of heretics, knowing that the lapses induced by intellectual besetting sins can be no less astounding than the depths of evil into which the regenerate can backslide. Yet in principle Dr. Lloyd-Jones' position is unchallengeable. Integral to the Pauline concept of the one church is the notion of a Pauline commitment, confessed in worship, witness, and life, to Jesus Christ as set forth in the Pauline Gospel.

★ ★ ★

---

[1] See D. R. Jones, *Instrument of Peace* (London 1965), pp. 68–73, commenting on D. M. Lloyd-Jones, *The Basis of Christian Unity* (London, 1962).

The idea of the Church as a single worldwide community of believers, not divided by their separateness in space and time, one because God is one, and Christ is one, and grace is one, was used by the New Testament teachers to interpret and guide the corporate life of 'the churches' – that group of small and obscure communities who confessed Jesus Christ as Lord.

The New Testament dignifies each such community as 'the church' in its own place, viewing it (as scholars since Hort and Harnack all agree) as a local 'outcrop' – P. T. Forsyth's word – of the one Church universal; the Church cosmic in microcosm. We cite some of Forsyth's statements on this point, for no one ever expressed it better than he: [2]

> The total Church was not made up by adding the local churches together, but the local Church was made a Church by representing there and then the total Church.

> The Church in the town, or in the house of So-and-so, means the total Church as emerging there, looking out there, taking effect there.

> The one Church is to the many as England to her counties.

> It is not strictly speaking correct to speak of the Corinthian Church, but of the Church of Corinth, as it comes to the surface there. And the Church in a private house was as much the Church as the whole Christianity of Corinth. So in the one locality you might have a multitude of Churches with an equal place in the whole Church everywhere.

In fact, the New Testament knows only these two applications of the word 'Church' – to the one universal Church as such, and to individual congregations, the twos and threes who meeting in Christ's name, locally manifest the one Church's life.

Is it right, then, to call a group of congregations a 'church,' and speak of (say) the Church of England, or the Methodist Church? In principle, one can justify this usage, inasmuch as the banding together of local congregations into a team for mutual aid and more effective evangelism – which is, from one standpoint, every denomination's formal rationale – is itself a characteristic manifestation of the life of the Church universal, no less than is the meeting of a single congregation. But when different families of churches live side by side, in a state of local overlap, yet do not practice regular communion with each other, nor exercise active care for each other, and when each congregation is forced by this situation to announce itself, not as Christ's church (i.e., the universal Church out - cropping) in a particular place, but as the local representative of the

---

[2] *The Church and the Sacraments* (London, 1947 ed.), pp. 65ff.

Congregational, or Methodist, or Anglican, or Baptist denomination, the position is actually scandalous, for it hides from view the true unity of the one Church of God.

In such a situation all parties are in the same boat, even if the oldest retains its original geographical title and calls itself (say) not 'the Anglican Church' but 'the Church of England.' The logic of the situation turns the church families involved into denominations and indeed sects *de facto*, whatever they may call themselves. Whatever value Protestant denomi - nationalism may have conserved, and whatever potency for good it may have had, it is in itself a deformed growth, although to seek to eliminate it by regional reunions, so as to manifest the given unity of God's Church, is a positive duty.

When the Reformers and their successors sought to show how New Testament teaching would correct the institutionalist mode of thought which underlay the identification of the Church of Christ with the Church of Rome, they found need to draw an explicit distinction between the Church as *visible* and as *invisible*. This distinction, which goes back to Luther and Zwingli, was a basic element in all Anglican ecclesi - ology till the end of the Caroline period. In recent years it has been so misunderstood that one hesitates to use it; nevertheless, as long as the mental habits which the Reformers were up against survive (as they still do, and not merely in the Church of Rome), one seems to have no choice. As long as the claim is made that the Church of Christ is essentially a visible community, to be identified with some existing organization or group of organizations, so long will it be necessary to protest that Christ's Church is essentially invisible, and that its identity with existing ecclesi - astical bodies cannot in the nature of the case be more than indirect and incomplete.

The persistent mistake about this distinction is to regard it as a distinction between two churches, the thrust of which is to suggest that what appears to be the Church all over the world is not really such, since the 'real' Church is somewhere out of sight. On the basis of this mistake, it is assumed that those who hold the 'real' Church to be invisible will be indifferent to the organized life of actual local churches, feeling that it does not directly concern them, since these do not constitute the 'real' Church at all. Hence ecumenical theologians as a body – with exceptions, notably among the Lutherans – are hostile to the distinction, which they see as a lapse into Platonic dualism tending to inhibit interest in visible union.

But this is a complete misunderstanding of what, historically, this distinction meant. It was drawn, not between two churches, but between two aspects of the one Church – that which it wears to the eyes of men, who see only the appearance, and that which it has to the eye of God, who looks on the heart and knows things as they are, and whose estimate of spiritual realities, unlike ours, is unerring. This distinction does not deny that the one Church, by its very nature, has a visible aspect; it is not, therefore, refuted by the true observation of H. Burn-Murdoch that, of the 110 occurences of *ekklesia* in the New Testament, all save one (Heb. 12:23) denote a community living in this world a visible, identifiable life of continuance in the apostolic fellowship. [3] The purpose of the distinction was, and is, simply to clarify three points about the one Church, as follows.

The first point concerns its *nature*. The Church is essentially a fellow-ship of believers, the totality of those whom Christ has united to himself through the Holy Spirit. What constitutes the Church is not any of its historical outward features – papacy, hierarchy, succession, or any insti - tutional means of grace – but the actual grace-given reality of faith in the Christ of the Gospel. Faith is primary, because Christ, and the Holy Spirit, and the forgiveness of sins, are primary. But since these primary realities are not in any sense visible to human eyes, the Church which they bring into being cannot be visible either. As Luther insisted, the Holy Catholic Church of the Creeds is an object, not of sight, but of faith. The distinction was thus, in the first place, a protest against all views of the Church which stop short at its formal and external aspects, however correctly these may be conceived.

The second point concerns the *identification* of the Church. Where the Gospel is, faith is, and where faith is, there the Church is, whatever institutions may be lacking; but no group or organization can be acknow - ledged as the Church while it lacks the Gospel. The Church becomes visible and identifiable, not by flaunting some historical pedigree of ministerial succession, but by professing and proclaiming the apostolic Gospel by word and by sacrament.

On this basis the Reformers held, first, that their separation from Rome was no sin since Rome had effectively unchurched herself by corrupting the Gospel; second, their separation was no breach of the Church's unity, since neither papal government and order, nor any other particular form, was essential to that unity; third, that by recovering their own church-character through their renewed confession of the Gospel the Reformed churches had actually recovered unity, and were now waiting for Rome itself to join their new-found fellowship. The distinc - tion was thus, in the second place, the basis for a defence of the Reformation as a renewal rather than a disruption of the Church.

The third point concerns *membership* of the Church. In the visible Church, as in Old Testament Israel and New Testament churches too, persons may be present whom God sees to have no place there, since their profession of faith, though perhaps orthodox, is 'notional' and hypocriti - cal, and their hearts remain hardened against the practice of repentance. Such may, like Simon Magus, have received the sacraments, but not as yet the grace of the sacraments; they still need to be converted, and unless

---

[3] *Church, Continuity, and Unity* (Cambridge, 1945), p. 29.

they are converted churchmanship and sacraments will not save them. The distinction was thus, in the third place, a call to churchmen to seek that living faith in the living Christ which the Reformers delineated so vividly, and which alone makes salvation sure.

Much, no doubt, has changed since the Reformers' day. For one thing, Roman theology, albeit with oscillating motion, comes closer to the Gospel nowadays than it was prepared to do in the sixteenth century, and this requires some reassessment of earlier attitudes. But as long as Rome – not to mention the Orthodox churches – continues to identify the Church with an ecclesiastical institution, and while Protestant thought on the subject, preoccupied with problems of liturgy and order, remains as institutionalized as it is at present, the visible-invisible distinction will still be needed to make plain the Church's true nature.

What obligations have Christians, and local churches, with regard to the Church's unity? Not to create it, as if it did not already exist, but to acknowledge and express it in every way possible. 'The unity of the Spirit,' says Paul (Eph. 4:3). What does this involve? One thing that it involves is the removing of obstacles to the expression of the unity that exists. It is noticeable that the obstacles to which the New Testament constantly points are not institutional, but personal – lack of love, and care, and forbearance; pride and party spirit; unwillingness to maintain liberty for the other man's conscience in secondary matters, even though you judge him to be wrong (Rom. 14; 1 Cor. 8).

Biblical ecumenism starts with loving your neighbour in your own home church, and twentieth-century ecumenism will prove a hollow sham if it does not start here too. But current interest is focused – dangerously, perhaps – on relations between congregations and denomi - nations in a divided Christendom. Here the prime obstacles to manifesting unity take the form, not so much of lovelessness and jealousy, as of disagreement about the faith to be confessed, and barriers at the Lord's table. What lead does Scripture give in these matters? We close by suggesting three principles which, if our foregoing exposition has been right, would seem to be biblical imperatives for a sound ecumenical policy today.

### (1) We must stop regarding all separations, past and present, as acts of schism

The word 'schism,' which in the New Testament means a needless division in the local church, occasioned, not by disputes about revealed truth, but by arrogance and lack of love (1 Cor. 1:10, 11:18f., 12:24f.), was in the patristic period applied exclusively to separation, for whatever cause, from the Catholic Church – an act which the Fathers, not distinguishing between the church visible and invisible, equated with separation from Christ and saving grace. Rome maintains this view, though allowing that schism through invincible ignorance may not prove to be damning. Recently, under Anglican guidance stemming from men like T. A. Lacey and O. C. Quick, world Protestantism has embraced the notion that the Church is in a state of 'internal schism' and the ecumenical movement has been called an association of 'penitent schismatics.' But this is surely unhelpful and misleading. It suggests that all our separations, as such, are morally blameworthy and unjustifiable. But this is not so.

To separate for truth's sake, at the summons of a biblically enlightened conscience, is not sin. When, without failure of love or respect, men dissociate themselves from their previous church connections in order to be free to obey God, this is not, and never was, schism. It may be their duty – as the Reformers thought it their duty to break with Rome over the Gospel, and as the Baptist and Independent dissenters of 1662 thought it their duty to stand apart from the re-established Church of England and gather churches according to what they held to be the biblical model.

For such separations the word 'schism' is a pejorative misnomer, which should be dropped from ecumenical discussion. It can only engender a false sense of guilt about divisions which are rooted in cleavage of principle, and encourage an ungodly attitude of 'union at any price.' Union between separated churches in the same area is certainly to be sought – after all, as Forsyth said, 'union is unity taking effect' [4] – but it may not be bought at the cost of truth, or the compromise of conviction.

### (2) We must practice intercommunion with Christians and congregations of sound faith

In 1 Cor. 10:16f., Paul speaks of the Lord's Supper, the communion of the body and blood of Christ, as a means whereby the union of Christians with Christ, and in Christ with each other, is both expressed and deepened. The 'one loaf' both evidences and contributes to our oneness in the one body. Fellowship at the Lord's Table is thus a means of maintaining 'the unity of the Spirit.' Here is the theological argument for an open communion table, from which no adherent of an orthodox Christian body is barred; and it is an unanswerable argument, for to decline to express at the Lord's Table the union which we have with our fellow-believers would actually be a breach of unity. We may regret that the Church of England is so grudging and slow to move at official level in the matter of eucharistic fellowship with non-episcopal lovers of Jesus Christ, but evangelicals can give a lead here, both in welcoming Free Churchmen to our communion services and in communicating with them at theirs, and this we should actively do.

---

[4] Op. cit., p. 67.

### *(3) We must insist that evangelical doctrine is the only proper basis for closer church relations*

It is commonly said that Anglican unity is 'cultic' rather than 'confes -
sional,' and that the Anglican Communion is not a 'confessional' body.
It is assumed that this is to its credit; but the truth is the reverse. Basic to
the biblical ideas of the Church, as we saw, is the thought of acknow -
ledging and maintaining the 'one faith.' Every church, therefore, should
be a 'confessional' body. Our historic formularies show that this was our
Reformers' ideal for the Church of England. Unhappily, in recent years
the Church has appeared to be more concerned about episcopal order
than about evangelical faith, and in interchurch negotiations it has been
the former rather than the latter which she has stressed as the necessary
basis of unity. It is good, no doubt, that she should be in full communion
with the Old Catholics, who have the historic episcopate, even though
their faith is as yet far from evangelical; but it is deplorable that we should
not yet have entered into comparable relations with, for instance, the
Church of Scotland. It is hard to say which feature of the 1963 Anglican-
Methodist conversations report was the more regrettable, its calculated
laxity in handling the authority of Scripture or its assiduity in writing the
whole substance of episcopal ordination for Methodist clergy into the
Service of Reconciliation.

The times, of which these things are signs, call us to right the balance
by recovering the historic Anglican awareness that the true and sufficient
basis of the unity which closer church relations are to manifest lies not in
the realm of ministerial order, but of catholic – that is, evangelical – faith.

# Chapter 5

# The Gospel and the Lord's Supper

My business in this article is to set some parameters and directions for
thought and practice in the administration, or celebration (I accept both
words), of the Lord's Supper. The first thing I want to do is look at the
present state of the eucharistic discussions that affect Anglicans, so creating
the situation of which we are part and within which we have to glorify
God by using the Lord's Supper aright.

Two aspects of the present discussions call for comment. The first is
the repositioning of Rome and the second is the reformulating of the
Gospel. Let us take the repositioning of Rome first.

## The Repositioning of Rome

In two ways the Roman Catholic Church has changed, not its stand, but
its stance, that is its way of standing for the things for which it does stand.
The first change is a new insistence that the lay folk must learn to pray
the mass. Previously the idea had been that it is the priest who celebrates
the mass and, though it is important for the lay folk to be there, it is not
important for them to know what is going on, so they may pursue their
own devotions or read the Bible or do whatever they want to do.

This change has issued now in the production of a new mass in the
vernacular. This liturgy is very similar to the revised forms which the
various provinces of the Anglican Communion have been using these last
twenty years, even to the point of having four different eucharistic prayers.
So Rome has a new mass, but it doesn't have a new doctrine of the mass
and that is the important fact to hold on to.

The second change is a new attitude to ecumenical discussion.
ARCIC, the official Anglican/Roman Catholic conversation, has pro -
duced a series of statements on matters that have historically divided the

THE GOSPEL AND THE LORD'S SUPPER was originally published in
*Mission and Ministry*, the quarterly publication of Trinity Episcopal School for
Ministry, Vol. 8, Number 1, Summer, 1990, pp. 18–24. Reprinted by
permission.

Roman Catholic communion from Anglicanism. The Eucharist was the first of the subjects to be tackled.

The ARCIC statement was offered as a consensus statement. Roman Catholic authorities have examined it and have decided that it isn't fully a Catholic statement. Anglican Evangelicals have examined it and decided that it isn't fully an evangelical statement. Just as you cannot square the circle, so you cannot state the Catholic doctrine of the mass in terms that will satisfy Evangelical Anglicans, and you cannot state the historical Anglican doctrine of the Lord's Supper in a way that will satisfy Roman Catholics. It wasn't to be expected.

On the other hand, the exercise was a clarifying exploration of just how far the two positions could converge and where still they are not able to come together. We are where we were in terms of substantive doctrine, though a significant change has taken place in terms of our attitude to each other, friendliness having replaced hostility and coolness.

## Reformulating the Gospel

Another significant change in the Church that bears on our thinking about the Lord's Supper is the widespread reformulation of the Gospel. Here my searchlight is trained on Protestantism.

I formulate the Gospel this way: it is information issuing in invitation; it is proclamation issuing in persuasion. It is an admonitory message embracing five themes. First, God: the God whom Paul proclaimed to the Athenians in Acts 17, the God of Christian theism.

Second, humankind: made in God's image but now totally unable to respond to God or do anything right by reason of sin in their moral and spiritual system. Third, the person and work of Christ: God incarnate, who by dying wrought atonement and who now lives to impart the blessing that flows from his work of atonement.

Fourth, repentance, that is, turning from sin to God, from self-will to Jesus Christ. And fifthly, new community: a new family, a new pattern of human togetherness which results from the unity of the Lord's people in the Lord, henceforth to function under the one Father as a family and a fellowship.

Now, there are three alternative versions of the Gospel competing for our attention with the formulation I have just summarized.

## Barth's Gospel

There is, first, the Gospel according to Karl Barth, which proclaims that the whole human race was in Christ when he died. That was humankind reprobated and rejected. And the whole human race was in Christ when he was raised from the dead. That – hear me well – is all humankind elected and accepted.

So the good news is that everyone, without exception, has already been redeemed and restored to God and the only problem is that the world is full of people who don't know that they are, so that Gospel preaching is merely a matter of telling people that this has happened. Responsive faith is then simply a matter of acknowledging Christ and his salvation as realities that already include you.

Barth's gospel doesn't issue in the kind of evangelism that Evangelicals have been doing for centuries and, please God, will go on doing until the Lord comes back. It is an imparting of information without any invitation, or rather the invitation is simply a matter of persuading people to believe the information, as distinct from summoning them to turn and trust and begin a new life.

## Hick's Gospel

Then there is the Gospel according to John Hick. Hick is a Presbyterian, not an Anglican, but his voice is heard in many Anglican circles. Hick affirms the gospel of pluralism, which is that God manifests himself savingly in all the world's religions on equal terms.

There is nothing unique, therefore, about Jesus Christ and his work of atonement, and it is not necessary to evangelize the world. Humankind doesn't need Christ. All that humankind needs is some religion or other, and the world is full of people who already have some religion or other. Why bother them?

This is Hick's pluralism. In an age in which Christian leaders are tempted to feel swamped by the magnitude of the evangelistic task and the reality of cultural apostasy from Christian moorings, many find this kind of thinking very alluring. It gets us off the hook; if it is true, we need no longer feel swamped or see ourselves as failures. But we have to ask ourselves whether it is true, and I write as one who doesn't think it is.

## The Mainstream Gospel

Then there is a third alternative version of the Gospel which is much less focused and which I will call the Gospel of the Anglican mainstream. I might name it 'Christianity and water,' borrowing the phrase from C. S. Lewis.

It represents a shift from what historically has been called Augustini - anism, the belief in the lostness, helplessness, and hopelessness of fallen human nature without grace, to what historically has been called semi-Pelagianism, the doctrine that despite the Fall human nature remains basically good, although we have become weak and lack the moral resources to carry out the good purposes of our hearts, so that we are constantly betrayed into bad behaviour.

On this view of man the Gospel of the Anglican mainstream says: though everyone is fundamentally good, what we all need and what Christ gives us is help and enrichment to fulfil our human potential and to become the people that in our hearts we are seeking to be. This doctrine, which the new Anglican liturgies of our day so clearly reflect, relativizes the absolutes of biblical teaching – in Romans 8, for example – about lost humankind at enmity with God and about the sovereignty of the saving grace of God. I don't believe that those absolutes may be relativized.

We ought to be prepared to say that the Lord's Supper is not about the Gospel according to Barth, nor about the Gospel according to Hick, nor about this scaled down Anglican mainstream Gospel. The Lord's Supper is about the Gospel of the marvellous sovereign grace of God, saving sinners who are fundamentally and radically bad until grace finds them and makes them new.

Our present melee requires no change in our convictions, but a frank recognition that we face some new postures and new noises from those around us. Gently but firmly we have to contradict these novelties in order to stand firm where Anglican Evangelicals have always stood, and where the Bible, I believe, directs us to stand.

## What are we to do?

So in this situation, in which Roman doctrine has not changed and the Gospel is challenged from several sides, what are we to do? With regard to the Lord's Supper, there are two things we are called to do. First, the liturgy of the Lord's Supper, today as always, must express the Gospel, and it is our task to see that in our parishes, it does. Second, sharing in the Lord's Supper must edify the faithful, and it is our task to ensure that in our parishes that also happens.

The liturgy of the Lord's Supper must express the Gospel. For the Lord's Supper is, as the 28th *Article of Religion* says, 'a Sacrament of our redemption by Christ's death.' It is the Word of the Gospel made visible.

Here Thomas Cranmer's genius has given us a lead. Cranmer, as the reformer of worship in the Church of England, faced the question: how does one put the Gospel into liturgical form? He wanted congregational worship; he wanted simple worship; he wanted edifying worship; he wanted evangelical worship, not only in his Bible services, Morning and Evening Prayer, but also in his sacramental services, Baptism and the Lord's Supper. How was he to get it? He found an answer so simple and so cogent that it ought to be categorized as a stroke of genius.

You secure evangelical worship, Cranmer saw, by designing your services with a sequence of three themes. Theme one is the detecting and confessing of *sin*. Theme two is the announcing of *grace*, in the form of God's promise to pardon and restore the penitent through Christ.

Then theme three is the exercising of *faith*, first in believing God's promise and trusting him for that promised pardon and then in grateful acts of praise, testimony, intercession, and receiving and obeying instruction.

## The Sequence in Practice

See this first in Cranmer's Bible services. In Morning and Evening Prayer we begin with penitence for sin: 'We have erred and strayed from thy ways like lost sheep.' That is the first theme.

The second theme is the good news of grace: '[God] pardons and absolves all them that truly repent and unfeignedly believe his Holy Gospel.' Cranmer called it an absolution, but essentially it is an evangelical proclamation.

The third theme follows: it is the exercising of faith in that pardoning grace, first by saying the Lord's Prayer, with special stress on 'forgive us our trespasses,' then by praise (the Psalms), then in intercession and (ideally!) in responding to the sermon. It is all the trustful devotion of sinners who by faith know themselves loved and saved.

In a more complex way, Cranmer built this sin–grace–faith sequence into his second Communion service, that of 1552, which in all essentials became the Holy Communion service of England's 1662 *Prayer Book*. He built this service out of three cycles of the sequence. They operate like three turns of a screw. A screw holds more firmly with every turn.

Each of Cranmer's three turns of the screw makes its own contribution to fixing the Gospel in our hearts, so that his Communion service really is the Good News, first made audible and then made visible in the sacramental action, confirming what has been heard. The second cycle adds to the first a sharpened application, and the third adds to the second a sacramental confirmation. It is built up like this.

## The Sequence in Holy Communion

What we call the antecommunion is the first cycle. In it, there is first an acknowledgement of sin in the Collect for Purity ('cleanse our hearts by the inspiration of thy Holy Spirit') and the hearing of the Law (with the response, 'Lord, have mercy upon us').

Second, the grace that restores sinners is proclaimed in the New Testament readings, the Epistle and the Gospel. The third element in the personal sequence is the responsive exercise of faith and this is fourfold:

saying the Creed, which is confession ('I believe . . .'); learning of God through listening to the sermon; giving to God in the collection; and joining in prayer for the well-being of the Church on earth.

That is Cranmer's antecommunion. It is the first cycle of the sin, grace, faith sequence. It is still recognizable in our revised liturgies, though it is not quite as clear there as it was in Cranmer's form.


## The Second Cycle

Then comes the second journey through the sequence, at the beginning of the communion itself. It starts with the very poignant acknow-ledgement of sin in the confession ('Have mercy upon us . . . Forgive us all that is past'). Next comes the equally poignant proclamation of pardoning and restoring grace, first in the prayer of absolution and then in the declaration of the promises of God to sinners ('hear what comfortable words our Saviour Christ saith unto all that truly turn to him').

There follows a very dramatic responsive exercise of faith. We give thanks for the grace that pardons our sins, great and grievous though they are, by swinging into the *Sursum corda*: 'Let us give thanks unto our Lord God.' 'It is meet and right so to do.' 'It is very meet, right, and our bounden duty, that we should at all times, and in all places, give thanks . . .'

It is a dramatic change of mood, it is sudden, it is emphatic, it is glorious. What are we giving thanks for? We are giving thanks for the pardon of sin. This is faith expressing itself in grateful praise for the reality of that forgiveness.


## The Third Cycle

Having moved through the second cycle of the sin, grace, faith sequence in an applicatory and dramatic way, thus raising the tension of the service very strikingly, Cranmer's liturgy now confirms the Gospel to us by a third journey through the cycle. This time we focus on the sacramental action whereby the Lord, who gave us this action as his visible Word to us, confirms all that we have learned thus far about God's pardoning grace.

So Cranmer, having finished the great outburst of praise in the *Sursum corda*, goes back to the beginning of the sequence with the 'prayer of humble access.' He put this prayer before the long eucharistic prayer – not after it, as we are used to in our revised forms – because it is the first part of the third sin, grace, faith sequence. In the prayer we remind ourselves and the Lord that we come to him as sinners not 'worthy to gather up the crumbs under [his] table.'

Then comes the second part of the sequence, beginning with the great eucharistic prayer which expounds the Cross. It begins with an utterance of gratitude and praise for 'the full, perfect, and sufficient sacrifice, oblation, and satisfaction for the sins of the whole world' which Christ offered on Calvary and then goes on to celebrate the institution of the Lord's Supper as 'a perpetual memory [or memorial] of that his precious death until his coming again.' That leads straight into the giving of the bread and the wine to each worshiper. Thus the good word of grace is individualized now to each person who comes to the table and receives the Lord's gifts ('Feed on him in thy heart by faith . . . drink this in remembrance . . . and be thankful.')

The service closes with the third stage in the sequence, responsive faith in fresh thanks, self-giving, and adoration of God in the words of the *Gloria*, which Cranmer with the simplicity of his liturgical genius saved to be the climactic utterance of triumphal praise before we are dismissed with the blessing. It is sad that all the modern revisions put it up at the front and so disrupt completely the three-fold sequence in the first part of the communion service.

The brilliant simplicity of Cranmer's evangelical liturgy is something which all the modern Anglican revisions of the communion service disregard. In an inarticulate but real way, Anglican worshippers all the world over have felt the power of Cranmer's liturgy, for they all at first received it in something like its original form. The new eucharistic liturgies are differently structured and don't have the power which the old one had, and was felt to have. Liturgically, it seems to me, we've traded a precious birthright for a fair mess of liturgical pottage.

What we need more than anything else at the Lord's Table is a fresh grasp of the glorious truth that we sinners are offered mercy through faith in the Christ who forgives and restores, out of which faith comes all the praise that we offer and all the service that we render. Cranmer's liturgy ministered this fresh grasp magnificently. Whatever form of liturgy we now use, we need to ensure, so far as we can, that it does the same: for this everlasting gospel of salvation for sinners is what in Scripture the Lord's Supper is all about.

## Edifying the Faithful

And now a word on how sharing the Lord's Supper must edify the faithful. There needs to be understanding, and so there must be teaching and learning.

I don't think we do enough teaching on the meaning of the Lord's Supper and the way to enter into eucharistic worship. One very simple way of getting into this is to study together the *Articles of Religion* which deal with the Lord's Supper (Numbers 25 through 31). They are very full and thorough, and congregational exploration of them would be found illuminating by many.

I would urge secondly that as there must be understanding through teaching and learning, so there must be involvement. I don't think we can ever say too much about the importance of an active exercise of mind and heart at the communion service. I am sure it demands more of our minds and hearts than is demanded of us when we come to a Bible service, Morning or Evening Prayer.

Holy Communion demands of us private preparation of heart before the Lord before we come to the table. We need to prepare ourselves for fellowship with Jesus Christ the Lord, who meets us in this ceremony. We should think of him both as the host at the communion table and as enthroned on the true Mount Zion referred to in Hebrews 12, the city of the living God where the glorified saints and the angels are.

The Lord from his throne catches us up by his Spirit and brings us into fellowship with himself there in his glory. He certainly comes down to meet us here, but he then catches us up into fellowship with him and the great host of others who are eternally worshipping him there.

We are also to learn the divinely intended discipline of drawing assurance from the sacrament. We should be saying in our hearts, 'as sure as I see and touch and taste this bread and this wine, so sure is it that Jesus Christ is not a fancy but a fact, that he is for real, and that he offers me himself to be my Saviour, my Bread of Life, and my Guide to glory. He has left me this rite, this gesture, this token, this ritual action as a guarantee of this grace; He instituted it, and it is a sign of life-giving union with him, and I'm taking part in it, and thus I know that I am his and he is mine forever.' That is the assurance that we should be drawing from our sharing in the Lord's Supper every time we come to the table.

## Togetherness with Christ

And then we must realize something of our togetherness in Christ with the rest of the congregation. A strange perverse idea has got into Anglican hearts that the Lord's Supper is a flight of the alone to the Alone: it is my communion I come to make, not our communion in which I come to share. You can't imagine a more radical denial of the Gospel than that.

The communion table must bring to us a deeper realization of our fellowship together. If I go into a church for a communion service where not too many folk are present, to me it is a matter of conscience to sit beside someone. This togetherness is part of what is involved in sharing in eucharistic worship in a way that edifies.

And finally, lest you think that I am one of these sourpusses who is always nostalgic about the past and negative about the present, let me say something positive about the present. One good thing which the

Charismatic movement has brought back into our worship is a tremen -
dous emphasis on the importance of adoration. There are other ways of
adoring, no doubt, than to raise your hands and arms in the air and sing
folk-type music: diversity here is to be cheerfully accepted.

But the stress on adoration itself is something to pick up and run with,
and this we should do unanimously. In the Evangelical worship at the
Lord's Table in my youth there was nothing like enough heartfelt
adoration. There is more today because of the Charismatic influence.
There needs to be more still, in my judgement, even in Charismatic circles
themselves. At the Holy Table, above all, let there be praise!

# Chapter 6

# The Real Meaning of the Real Presence

At the end of Cranmer's treatise *The True and Catholick Doctrine of the Sacrament*, he describes his understanding of Christ's presence in the Holy Communion this way: 'If by real presence you mean the presence of Christ *in re* [Latin for "in the thing", the thing in this case being the bread and the wine] we reject it.'

But, he says, 'If by real presence you mean the presence of Christ with his people at the eucharistic celebration, we affirm it.' He plays with the phrase 'real presence,' negating it in one sense and affirming it in the other.

## Personally and Objectively Present

This is the teaching Anglican Evangelicals have continued to uphold. Let me quote from an open letter to the Bishops at the last Lambeth Conference, a letter signed by dozens of Anglican Evangelical theologians:

> We ourselves strongly affirm that at every eucharist Jesus Christ is Himself personally and objectively present, ready to make Himself known through the breaking of bread and to give Himself to us so that we may feed on Him in our hearts by faith.

We rejected the Roman Catholic idea that the bread and wine were physically changed into the body and blood of Christ. We accepted what Hugh Latimer said at his last trial:

> That which before was bread now has the dignity to exhibit Christ's body and yet the bread is still bread and the wine is still wine. For the change is not in the nature, but in the dignity. This has been called transignification, as distinct from transubstantiation.

---

THE REAL MEANING OF THE REAL PRESENCE first appeared in *Mission and Ministry*, the quarterly publication of Trinity Episcopal School for Ministry, Vol. 8, Number 1, Summer, 1990. pp. 10–11. Reprinted by permission.

The letter then stated our position in quotations from the Reformation authorities.

> We also believe that Christ's body and blood are 'very and indeed taken and received by the faithful in the Lord's Supper' [from the Catechism]. We believe that 'the means whereby the body of Christ is received and eaten in the Supper is faith' [from *Article 28*]. We believe further that those 'lacking a lively faith in no wise are partakers of Christ' [from *Article 29*].

> Therefore [we concluded, quoting Richard Hooker], the real presence of Christ's most blessed body and blood 'is not to be sought for in the sacraments [meaning the bread and wine as such] but in the worthy receiver of the sacrament.'

## The Only Clear-Headed Way

I think that Hooker, and before him Cranmer, were right and that this is the only clear-headed way to bring out what the Scriptures teach about the way that Christ blesses us through the sacramental means of grace, whereby he does bless us. Christ is really present with us according to his promise whenever two or three meet together in his name to do something that he told us to get together and do.

The Lord's Supper, of course, stands at the head of those activities. As in the rest of them, so in the Supper: the presence is not in the elements, the bread and wine, but in the fellowship and in the heart.

# Revival in the Church

# Chapter 7

# What is Revival?

The way to find out what a group of people are really like is to see what they habitually talk about. And the most revealing commentary on the state of British evangelicalism over the past forty years is a list of the topics which have occupied evangelical minds during that time. Thus, in the twenties the great talking-point was evolution and the truth of the Bible, for evangelicals had their backs to the wall. In the thirties, the talking-points were guidance and prophecy, for evangelicals felt adrift, and unsure as to where they were going. In the forties and early fifties, evangelicals recovered vigour, and the chief subject of discussion was ways and means of evangelism. Now, at the start of the sixties, it seems that evangelicals are recovering vision; the impotence of our churches and our evangelism in face of the entrenched ungodliness of today is becoming a burden to us, and the recurring theme of our talk is coming more and more to be revival. One thanks God for this; it means that evangelicalism is putting down roots again, and seeking, after a century in the wilderness, to re-enter the world of spiritual realities in which our forefathers lived. May God look in mercy on our blindness, and lead us further in this direction.

The really odd thing in all this is not that the topic of revival is concerning evangelicals now, but that it has for so long failed to concern them, so much so that some find this renewed interest in it disconcerting and distasteful. The strange truth is that for the past hundred years, although the churches, and evangelicalism within the churches, have been continuously losing ground, Christian people have not been longing for revival. Interest in the subject, where it has existed at all, has been guarded and a little patronizing: the news of what God did in Wales in 1904–5, and in Manchuria in 1906–8, does not seem to have stirred English evangelical hearts as did the news of the much smaller awakening in the Hebrides in 1949. On the whole, the faithful have been preoccupied throughout this period with other things.

This comparative unconcern about revival marks a break with the earlier evangelical outlook. For a century after the days of Whitefield and

WHAT IS REVIVAL? was originally published in *The Best of Crusade* (London: Victory Press, 1963), pp. 89–93. Reprinted by permission.

Jonathan Edwards, the immediate reaction of evangelicals when the fires of life burned low in the churches was to appoint times for self-humbling and confession of sin and special prayer that God would visit them again. They regarded revivals as the chief means by which the gospel advanced; they believed, and often declared in print, that without revivals churches could not stay alive. But after about 1860 evangelicals ceased to think in these terms. We may well ask, why? The deepest reason seems to be that their minds were possessed by two thoughts which, taken together, made any desire for revival seem positively improper. The one was an optimistic belief that the mounting number of organized evangelical activities – missions, campaigns, conventions, Christian Unions and inter-denominational doings of all sorts – would suffice of themselves to meet the situation. The other was a pessimistic notion, born of J. N. Darby's esoteric dispensationalism, that the great final apostasy had begun and there was, therefore, no possibility of any real recovery of the churches' fortunes. The first thought implied that revival was not really needed; the second, that it was in any case out of the question.

It is worth pointing out that, even if Darbyite suspicions were justified (and non-Darbyites have their doubts), they could not justify Christians in ceasing to pray for revival. Christ taught his disciples to pray, 'Hallowed be Thy name.' God's 'name' means God himself as he has made himself known. That which dishonours and profanes God's name is lukewarmness and deadness in the churches, the gospel belied by the lives of its adherents, and paganism triumphant in the world. That which hallows God's name is the reversal of these conditions – strong faith and victorious holiness in the churches, and the winning of lost souls to the Saviour (see Ezek. 36:20–23). To pray 'Hallowed be Thy name' with understanding in days of spiritual decline therefore involves praying for revival. If, then, it is right to think that the Lord will return at a time of great apostasy, does it not follow that when he comes he should find the faithful on their knees praying for revival? And does it not follow too that whenever the churches find themselves weak and ineffective, whenever their defeats reveal that the judgement of God is upon them for their past unfaithfulness, the saints should begin to pray for revival? Such circumstances should bring to their lips Habakkuk's prayer: 'O Lord, revive thy work in the midst of the years . . . in wrath remember mercy' (Hab. 3:2). And the worse things are, the more earnestly should the cry for revival go up, as it did in Israel of old. (See the great Bible prayers for revival in the Old Testament: Ps. 44, 74, 79, 80, 85:4–7; Is. 63:15–64:12; Lam. 5). In these days of growing apostasy and secularism, we should be inexcusable if we were prepared to be content with anything less than revival, and did not make the cry for revival our own: 'Wilt thou not revive us again; that thy people may rejoice in thee?' (Ps. 85:6).

But what exactly *is* revival?

There are two factors in our situation which obstruct right thinking about this question. The first is a matter of language; the second is a mistake in theology.

The first obstructing factor is a *restricted usage*. In the eighteenth century, the word 'revival' took its place in the evangelical vocabulary as a description of the kind of spiritual movements which were taking place on both sides of the Atlantic. But since then the word has come to be used in two narrower senses. Some (especially in America) give the name 'revival' to what we would call an evangelistic campaign, and designate its leader as a 'revivalist.' Others speak of 'personal revival' and 'continu - ous revival,' meaning the restoration of individual backsliders and cold-hearted Christians to a state of spiritual health, and the maintaining of that state once it is recovered. The very existence of these narrower usages encourages the idea that successful evangelism and the quickening of believers is all that revival really amounts to. But this is not so. Both these things happen in revivals; but both happen also apart from revivals. Neither can be equated with revival, for revival includes both, and much more. It would make for clarity, therefore, if we could drop these narrower usages entirely.

The second obstructing factor I call *the antiquarian fallacy*. It consists of building up a mental blueprint of revival from the history of revivals, or of one particular revival, in the past, and treating this as a norm to which all revivals in the future must correspond. In fact, what we have to look into is not the outward forms that revival has taken in history, but the inward pattern of God's reviving work as presented in the Bible.

The biblical evidence falls into three main categories. First there are prayers for revival (the main passages under this head were mentioned earlier). Second, there are prophetic pictures of revival, given in Old Testament terms with immediate reference to Old Testament situations, but disclosing the permanent principles of God's action whenever he restores a church in decline (see especially Is. 35:3–10; 40–46; Jer. 31; Ezek. 34; 36:16–38; Joel 2:12–32; Zech. 1–8). Third, there are narratives of revival (under Asa, 2 Chron. 15; Hezekiah, 2 Chron. 29–31; Josiah, 2 Chron. 34, 35; Ezra, Ezra. 9, 10; Nehemiah., Neh. 8–10; and – foremost in importance – the revival that began with Pentecost, Acts 2–12).

The main points in the biblical presentation of revival are these:

1. Revival is *God renewing the Church*. Revival is a work of restoring life (that is what the word 'revive' means), and it is the people of God who are the subjects of it. It is a social, corporate thing. Every Bible prayer for revival implores God to quicken, not *me* but *us*. Every Bible prophecy of revival depicts God visiting and enlivening, not one or two individual Israelites, but Israel, the whole people. Every record of revival, in biblical and later Christian history, tells of an entire community being affected. Revival reaches Christians individually, no doubt, but it is not an individualistic affair; God revives, not just the Christian, but the Church,

and then the new life overflows from the Church for the conversion of outsiders and the renovation of society.

2. Revival is *God turning away his anger from the Church*. For God's people to be impotent against their enemies is a sign that God is judging them for their sins. The cry for revival springs from the sense of judgement (Ps. 79:4–9; 80:12–14; 85:4–7; Hab. 3:2); the coming of revival is God's comforting of his people and restoring them after judgement.

Revival is God *manifesting himself to his people*; visiting them (Ps. 80:14; Jer. 29:10–14), coming to dwell with them (Zech. 2:10ff.), pouring out His Spirit on them (Joel 2:28; Acts 2:17ff.), quickening their consciences, showing them their sins and exalting Christ in their eyes in his saving glory. In times of revival, there is a deep awareness of God's presence and an inescapable sense of being under his eye; spiritual things become overwhelmingly real and the truth of God becomes overwhelmingly powerful, both to wound and to heal. Conviction of sin becomes intolerable; repentance goes very deep; faith springs up strong and assured; spiritual understanding grows quick and keen, and converts mature in an amazingly short time; joy overflows (Ps. 85:6; 2 Chron. 30:26; Neh. 8:12, 17; Acts 2:46f.; 8:8), and loving generosity abounds (Acts 4:32); Christians become fearless in witness and tireless in labour for their Saviour's glory. The manifesting of God's gracious presence in revival awakens them out of sleep and energises them to serve their Lord in a quiet unprecedented way. Indeed, they recognize their new experience as a real foretaste of the life of heaven, where God will disclose himself to them so fully that they will never be able to rest day or night from singing his praises and doing his will.

3. Revival, lastly, is *God making known the sovereignty of his grace*. Revival is entirely a work of grace, for it comes to churches that deserve only judgement; and God brings it about in such a way as to show that his grace is entirely sovereign in it, and human plans and schemes have had nothing to do with it. We can organize conventions and campaigns, but the only organizer of revival is God the Holy Ghost. Revival, when it comes, comes suddenly, unexpectedly, as at Pentecost, breaking out often in obscure places through the ministry of obscure people; God sends revival in a way that shows that he is its only source, and all the praise and glory of it must be given to him alone.

God is sovereign in revival, and men cannot extort it from him by any endeavour or technique. What, then, should those who long for revival do?

Two things. First, preach and teach God's truth; second, pray. Preach and teach because it is *his* truth, and the blessing of revival cannot reach further than the gospel has gone. Pray, because God has told us that we need not expect to receive unless we ask, and, in the words of Jonathan Edwards, the classic theologian of revival, 'When God has something very great to accomplish for his Church, it is his will that there should precede it, the extraordinary prayers of his people; as is manifest by Ezek. 36:37 [see the context]. And it is revealed that, when God is about to accomplish great things for his Church, he will begin by remarkably pouring out the spirit of grace and supplication (Zech. 12:10)' ( *Thoughts on the Revival in New England*, chap. 5:3). God help us, then, to seek his face till he come and rain righteousness upon us; and to him shall be all the glory and the praise.

# Chapter 8

# Renewal and Revival

I am in the middle of writing a book on revival in the church, and have just finished a chapter examining revival as a corporate experience of five things together, following a spell of widespread coldness and deadness. The following analysis has emerged:

*God comes down*, in the sense that he gives a deepened awareness of his inescapable presence as the Holy One, mighty and majestic, dwelling among his people. Revival experience begins with being forced to realize, like Isaiah in the temple, the intimacy of the supernatural and the closeness of the living God.

*God's Word comes home*, in the sense that the Bible, its message and its Christ re-establish the formative and corrective control over faith and life that is theirs by right. In revival the divine authority of the Bible is realized afresh, and Christians find that this collection of Hebrew and Christian literary remains is still the means whereby God speaks to them and feeds their souls.

*God's purity comes through*, as God uses his Word to quicken consciences; the perverseness, ugliness and guiltiness of sin are seen and felt with new clarity, and the depth of one's own sinfulness is realized as never before, so that the forgiveness of sins becomes the most precious truth in the creed.

*God's people come alive*. Joyful assurance of salvation, conscious communion with a living Saviour, a spirit of prayer and praise, a readiness to share with other believers, and a love that reaches out to all in need, are the characteristic marks of revived Christians. Inhibitions dissolve, and a new forthrightness in utterance and initiative in action take their place.

*Outsiders come in*, drawn by the moral and spiritual magnetism of what goes on in the church. Whence came this analysis? First, from accounts of revival in Scripture – the early chapters of Acts, plus the narratives of awakenings under Asa, Hezekiah, Josiah and Ezra (2 Chr. 15, 29–31, 34, 35; Ezra 9–10; Neh. 8–10). Second, from the theology of revival in Scripture, in such prophets as Isaiah, Ezekiel and Zechariah, and such

RENEWAL AND REVIVAL was originally published in *Renewal*, Number 62, April, 1976. Reprinted by permission.

Psalms as 44, 67, 80 and 85. Third, from the annals of similar stirrings in the Protestant Evangelical awakenings of the eighteenth century under men like Jonathan Edwards in America and George Whitefield, Daniel Rowlands and John Wesley in Britain; revivals round the globe in the 1850s and again in the 1900s; and later movements like the East African revival, which began in the 1930s and still goes on. The family likeness of these movements, both to each other and to biblical prototypes, is remarkable, and makes a fascinating study.

What is the thrust of this analysis? It is that Scripture shows, and history confirms, that revival is a distinctive and recurring work of God whereby he has again and again revitalized flagging churches and through the consequent evangelistic outflow vastly extended the kingdom of Christ. Revival, therefore, is the highest hope for the church on earth until the Lord comes to take us home. This thesis, I hasten to say, is not new; Edwards spelt it out more than two centuries ago, the first two generations of evangelical missionary pioneers held it almost to a man, and I am merely restating it for our time.

It is, I think, a fact that it is only Protestant Evangelicals who use the word 'revival' as a theological term, and as a label for the hope which they cherish for the period preceding the Lord's return. It is true that some Evangelicals over the past century-and-a-half have pessimistically abandoned this hope on the grounds of a somewhat esoteric interpretation of prophecy, but these can hardly be regarded as typical.

For Evangelicals generally, 'revival' is a glowing and evocative word of precise meaning, marked by hallowed associations from the past and precious hopes for the future. This reflects the impact of books like Edwards' *Thoughts on the Revival of Religion in New England* (1742) and Charles Finney's famous *Lectures on Revivals of Religion* (1835), the most influential 'revivalist' handbook of all time, plus the familiar use of labels like 'the Evangelical revival' and 'the Welsh revival' for such breathtaking episodes as those of the mid-eighteenth century and 1904, plus two hundred years of prayer (not wholly unanswered, either) that God would grant new impetus in the church for the spread of the gospel.

Perhaps other sections of the church feel that 'revival' is a word so directly identified with historic evangelical interests that it will not serve to express their own hopes for the church. At all events, they prefer to speak of 'renewal' rather than 'revival'. Ecumenicals seek 'one church *renewed* for mission,' and charismatics proclaim charismatic *renewal* as both their hope and their present experience.

It was Thomas Hobbes who reminded the world that words are the counters of wise folk, the coinage of fools. The wise person knows that two people can use different words and mean the same thing, just as they can use the same word and mean different things. Nonetheless when different words are used the presumption is that something different is meant. Is that so here?

As one who is convinced that revival as defined is the modern church's deepest need, and that to seek anything less for God's people now is to fiddle while Rome burns (Rome here covering Protestantism and Or - thodoxy too!), I ask the question with some anxiety. How close do ecumenical and charismatic renewal come, both in idea and in experience, to evangelical revival?

It seems clear that the ecumenical notion of renewal (taking that first) has only a limited overlap with the evangelical concept of revival. The ecumenical notion is broader, for it includes a new reforming energy, Bible-directed and self-critical, in the realms of technical theology, liturgy and the church's human structures. The historic notion of revival has only ever touched these matters incidentally; it has tended to focus all attention on the quickening of individuals in their relationship to God, their fellowship with each other, and their outreach ministry, sometimes even in avowed antithesis to these other concerns. (Which of course was a mistake – the concerns of reformation are not opposed to those of revival, but should be classed among them.) Yet the historic evangelical notion of revival goes deeper, for it highlights the crucial truth that there is no significant quickening at any point at all save through a personal visitation of the living God, apart from which Christians, whatever they do, will never 'cut ice' for God in this fallen world.

It is tragic that exponents of ecumenical renewal seem blind to this truth. For where God's quickening visitation is not sought nor found, everything suffers – theological renewal is just a word-game, union of churches and renewing of structures just a power play, and liturgical change just a new formalism in place of the old. Indeed, it seems true to say that for lack of God's quickening visitation all the seemingly creative movements of our time which ecumenical spokesmen have hailed as signs of renewal are currently withering away.

The biblical and theological renewal, so called, which was sparked off over half a century ago through Karl Barth, is fragmenting and sinking deeper and deeper into subjectivism. The liturgical movement, having sponsored a vernacular mass in Roman Catholicism and the 'you-who' style of worship in Protestantism, seems to have shot its bolt, while the church union movement, which achieved its objective in South and North India and for the small Christian community of Sri Lanka, has for the present run out of steam everywhere else.

Without suggesting for a moment that any of these movements, or any other items in the present-day ecumenical programme, are worthless or wrong-headed in themselves, I cannot avoid the conclusion that they have neither quickened the church spiritually in any fundamental way, nor contributed much to the evangelizing of the world in our time; nor, while they are pursued without regard for the need of revival, are they likely to be more fruitful in the future than they have been thus far. This is a verdict which I would rather not have to pass, but it seems inescapable.

What, now, of the idea and experience of charismatic renewal? How does this appear from the standpoint of an evangelical theology of revival? Several things need to be said.

First, the charismatic movement is young, multiform in practice, not theologically unanimous (Protestant and Roman Catholic charismatic theology are by no means identical, and spokesmen have acknowledged the movement as a spirituality seeking a theology), and moreover still rapidly developing from within. So one can only generalize about it with great caution.

I am writing as one who has read its literature, shared its worship (Protestant forms), admired its adherents, criticized its theology (Protes - tant and Catholic versions), and defended its spirituality; I think I am as well qualified as the next person to attempt generalizations, but others will have to judge this when they see what my generalizations are. (In any case, whatever I say, I have no hope of pleasing everybody!)

Second, the familiar accusation that some charismatics are immature, unstable, escapist, obsessive, credulous, unrealistic, angular, opinionated and divisive must be admitted to be true. But this proves nothing, because there are non-charismatic Christians of whom the same things are equally true. These qualities are human weaknesses brought to the movement rather than engendered by it. Whether standards of discipline and care within the movement are such that these weaknesses get recognized and Christians suffering from them are helped to move beyond them seems to be a question which would have to be answered differently in different circles, just as it would in the non-charismatic world.

Third, though I have not seen any full-scale theology of revival put out from a charismatic source (perhaps my reading is deficient), it seems clear that much that is central to the movement coincides strikingly with the historic evangelical concept. A few years ago it was hard to be sure that 'charismatic renewal' was more than a new pietistic individualism, like the old Oxford Group, based on a common experience of 'baptism in the Holy Spirit' and expressing itself by forming groups where this experience could be spread. Now, however, it really takes invincible ignorance to remain unaware that those whose goal is 'charismatic renewal' aim at a quickening of the whole church by seven means:

1. Rediscovery of the living God and his Christ, and the supernatural dimensions of Christian living (this, fundamentally, is what 'baptism in the Holy Spirit' and glossolalia are held to secure and safeguard).

2. Returning to the Bible as the inspired Word of God, to nourish one's soul on it.

3. Habits of private and public devotion designed to bring the whole person, body and soul, into total expectant dependence on the Holy Spirit.

4. A leisurely, participatory style of public praise and prayer.

5. A use of spiritual gifts for ministry in the Body by every member of Christ.

6. Thorough exploration of the possibilities of ministry through a communal life-style.

7. An active commitment by this and other means to reach out to the needy in service and evangelism.

The parallels between this and the evangelical idea of revival are plain.

Fourth, it is doubtful whether the devotional distinctives of 'charis - matic renewal' are as distinctive as is sometimes thought. Does the glossolalic's exercise of heart in praise and intercession really differ from that of the non-glossolalic? Do the convictions as to what God is saying which some cast into the form of 'prophecy' really differ qualitatively from those of other Christians who communicate them without casting them into that form? Does the difference between the slow, improvisa - tory, Bruckner-and-Wagner-like charismatic worship style and the brisker Bach-and-Mozart-like style of non-charismatic worship argue a different awareness of God?

Is it only charismatics who experience that strong witness to adoption, the Father-love, and the hope of glory which seems always to be at the heart of what is called (unfortunately, because unscripturally, as I think) 'baptism in the Holy Spirit'?

It is not obvious to me that the answer to any of these questions is yes, and I am much struck by parallels between experiences of praying privately in tongues and of contemplative prayer as taught by Catholic masters.

Fifth, the way to test whether 'charismatic experiences', or any other form of professedly Christian experience, are a genuine manifestation of the Holy Spirit is to apply to them the New Testament's own doctrinal and ethical tests. The doctrinal test is whether the experience leads to the honouring and magnifying of the Christ of the gospel (cf. John 16:14; 1 Cor. 12:3; 1 John 4:1–6); the ethical test is whether it leads to Christ-likeness of character (cf. Gal. 5:22; 1 Cor. 13, in the context of 12–14), with boldness (*parrhesia*) in witness to the Lord Jesus (cf. Acts 4:31) and joy in all things (cf. Rom. 14:17; John 15:11, 16:12–22). I am sure I have observed a great deal of charismatic experience, as I have of non-charismatic, which passes these tests with flying colours. And where such experience is found, there renewal is real.

Sixth, though I joyfully recognize much that bears the signature of the Spirit in the charismatic movement, as I also do outside it, I do not think that in Britain, at any rate, either its adherents or any other Christian grouping is currently experiencing revival, or anything like it. The galvanizing sense of God, and the humility, integrity, depth and power which this brings are simply not there: by which I mean, not here. This remains a day of small things, and we are still pygmy Christians.

It is my conviction that those who seek evangelical revival and those who aim at charismatic renewal should recognize the essential identity of their purposes; that they should accept each other's spirituality as being genuinely from God – flawed by human weakness, no doubt, but yet authentically God's way for those who follow it – and so should forsake Spirit-quenching attitudes of mutual suspicion and devotional imperial - ism; and that we should set ourselves to seek an outpouring of the Holy Spirit together. I am glad to have had the opportunity of writing to commend this conviction in the pages of *Renewal.*

# Chapter 9

# Steps to the Renewal of the Christian People

## The Task and the Method

In the following presentation I address myself to a two-fold task: first, to formulate a clear view of what the renewal of the church really is, and then to say what needs to happen in order to get us there, starting from where we are. And in tackling that twofold task I have a twofold goal: to speak both to your minds and to your hearts. For I shall try, not just to state God's truth, but also to apply it by way of challenging your concern and your action. So, as I hope that this will not be less than a responsible theological discourse, I also hope that it will be more than that. I intend, you see, not just to lecture but also to preach.

Who am I, you may ask, to set myself this agenda? Let me tell you. I am an expatriate Englishman, an Episcopal pastor by calling and a Reformed theologian by trade, who in 1945, soon after his conversion, was given a copy of Charles G. Finney's *Lectures on Revivals of Religion* (1835), and who since that time has carried a personal burden of concern for the renewing of God's people through a fresh outpouring of the Holy Spirit. On this subject I have spoken repeatedly, written occasionally, and thought constantly throughout those years. Now I seek to enlist you for the pursuit of the same interest, and I am grateful for the opportunity to do so.

There is, however, one thing that I need to say at the very outset about the manner of pursuing an interest of this kind. Renewal in all its aspects is not a theme for dilettante debate, but for humble, penitent, prayerful, faith-full exploration before the Lord, with a willingness to change and be changed, and if necessary to be the first to be changed, if that is what the truth proves to require. To absorb ideas about renewal ordinarily costs

STEPS TO THE RENEWAL OF THE CHRISTIAN PEOPLE was originally published in *Summons to Faith and Renewal*, ed. Peter Williamson and Kevin Perrotta (Ann Arbor: Servant Press, 1983), pp. 107–127. Reprinted by permission.

nothing, but to enter into renewal could cost us everything we have, and we shall be very guilty if, having come to understand renewal, we then decline it. We need to be clear about that. John Calvin once declared that it would be better for a preacher to break his neck while mounting the pulpit if he did not himself intend to be the first to follow God.[1] In the same way, it would be better for us not to touch the study of renewal at all if we are not ourselves ready to be the first to be renewed. I speak as to wise people; please judge what I say.

By what method, now, shall we approach our subject? Here the gates of two 'by-path meadows,' to use Bunyan's phrase, stand invitingly open. First, it is tempting to come at the renewal theme *sociologically*. That would mean defining 'the Christian people' in external and institutional terms as an organized association with specific goals; equating renewal with the achieving of those goals; and then occupying ourselves in pragmatic reflection on what structural and attitudinal changes would have to be engineered in order to realize these goals in a statistically measurable way. The idea that the church's health problems can be solved by such manipulation is not unfamiliar, at least to members of major Protestant denominations in North America; analysts both inside and outside de - nominational headquarters do a great deal of thinking at this level. Nor do I dismiss such analysis as useless; on the contrary, it does much to make us aware of lacks and needs in the church's life. But I urge most emphatically that the renewal of the church is in essence a spiritual and supernatural matter, a work of the Holy Spirit enriching our fellowship with the Father and the Son, and it takes more than clever social engineering to bring this about.

Again, it is tempting to come at our theme *historically*. That would mean identifying past movements of renewal and revival, from the Old Testament records of Israel's return to Yahweh under Asa, Hezekiah, Josiah, Ezra, and others, and the New Testament story in Acts of revival in Palestine after Pentecost; through to the Cistercian and Dominican and Franciscan movements; the ministry of Savonarola; the Western Refor - mation; the early Jesuits; English Puritanism and Lutheran Pietism; the Evangelical Awakenings in old England and New England in the eight - eenth century; the repeated stirrings of the Spirit in Wales and Scotland between the seventeenth and nineteenth centuries; the first hundred years of the Protestant missionary movement; the frontier revivals in America; the world-wide quickenings among Protestants in the 1850s and again in the 1900s; the East African revival, now fifty years old and still continuing; the awakenings in Lewis, off the west coast of Scotland, in the 1950s, in Western Canada in the 1960s, and in Indonesia and the Californian 'Jesus movement' in the 1970s; the impact of the world-wide charismatic

---

[1] Quoted from T. H. L. Parker, *The Oracles of God: An Introduction to the Preaching of John Calvin* (London: Lutterworth Press, 1947), p. 60.

movement over the past twenty years; and so on. It would then mean analysing, comparing, reconstructing, and characterizing these move - ments in the way that historians do, and seeking to produce out of this exercise generalized typologies of renewal for future reference.

Now I do not wish to minimize the very great value of this kind of study. The psalmists charge us to keep God's mighty works in remem - brance, and we should be glad that in our day so much printed material on past renewal movements is available to us. [2] But if all we did was study renewal historically, we should in the first place be looking at it in a merely external and this-worldly way, as the phenomenon of changed outlooks and activities in certain persons' lives, and in the second place we could hardly avoid lapsing into what I call the antiquarian fallacy about renewal, the assumption, that is, that any future renewal will become recognizable by conforming to some pattern set in the past.

That there are such patterns is not in doubt; they merit careful exami - nation, and in that connection I commend in particular Richard Lovelace's pioneer theological phenomenology of renewal, *Dynamics of Spiritual Life* (1979). But we should limit God improperly, and actually quench the Spirit, if we assumed that future movements of renewal will correspond in outward form to some past movement, and that we can rely on this correspondence as a means of identifying them. Renewal is precisely God doing a new thing, and though as we shall see every work of renewal has basic qualities, or

---

[2] Note especially the pioneer studies by J. Edwin Orr of post-Methodist awakenings: *The Second Evangelical Awakening in Britain* (London: Marshall, Morgan & Scott, 1949); *The Second Evangelical Awakening in America* (Grand Rapids, Mich.: Zondervan, 1952); *The Fervent Prayer: The World Wide Impact of the Great Awakening of 1858* (Chicago: Moody Press, 1974) (all three dealing with the movement of 1957–60); *The Eager Feet: Evangelical Awakenings, 1790–1830* (Chicago: Moody Press, 1975); *The Flaming Tongue: Evangelical Awakenings, 1900–1910* (Chicago: Moody Press, 2nd ed., 1975); *The Light of the Nations: Evangelical Renewal and Advance in the Nineteenth Century* (Exeter: Paternoster Press and Grand Rapids: Eerdmans, 1965); *Campus Aflame: Evangelical Awakenings in College Communities* (Glendale, CA.: Regal Books, 1971); *Evangelical Awakenings in Southern Asia* (Minneapolis, Minn.: Bethany Fellowship, 1975); *Evangelical Awakenings in Africa* (Minneapolis: Bethany Fellowship, 1975); *Evangelical Awak- enings in the South Seas* (Minneapolis: Bethany Fellowship, 1976). Note also J. T. Carson, *God's River in Spate* (Presbyterian Church of Ireland, 1958; on the Irish revival of 1859); J. Goforth, *By My Spirit* (Grand Rapids, Mich: Zondervan, 1967; on the Chinese revivals of 1908); E. Eifion Evans, *When He is Come* (Bridgend, Wales: Evangelical Press of Wales; 2nd ed., 1967; on the Welsh revival of 1859); and *The Welsh Revival of 1904* (Bridgend, Wales: Evangelical Press of Wales, 1969). See too the critical analysis by Ian Murray, *Revival and Revivalism: the Making and Marring of American Evangelicalism, 1750–1858* (Edinburgh: Banner of Truth, 1994).

dimensions, in common with every other, we must recognize that the contours of the cultures within which the church has from time to time lost its vitality, and also the contours of that loss in itself, have varied; which means that it is not safe for us to assume that the outward forms and phenomena of revival in this or any future age will always prove to have exact historical precedents. At this point sad mistakes in judgement have been made in the past, and I suspect are being made by some in the present. Let us strive not to be of their number.

What I have said makes it apparent, I hope, that our basic need in studying renewal is for categories and criteria that are neither sociological nor historical but theological, which for me at least means biblically-based. With scripture as our guide, therefore, we shall now discuss, first, the *theology* of renewal (that is, the overall account that should be given of renewal as a work of God); second, the *elements* in renewal (that is, specific things that occur when this work of God is in progress); third, the *quest* for renewal (that is, the steps in seeking renewal which we and the segments of the body of Christ to which we belong could take, starting now).

## The Theology of Renewal

For some decades the word 'renewal' has been used loosely in the world church, with applications as wide as they are unfocused. The general sense that renewal is needed because the church is not all that it should be is welcome, but the vague way in which the word is thrown around is unhelpful, to say the least. Contemporary voices celebrate liturgical renewal, theological renewal, lay renewal, ecumenical renewal, charis - matic renewal, and renewal in other departments too; indeed, it seems that any new outburst of activity in the church, any cloud of dust raised by the stamping of excited feet, will be hailed as renewal by somebody.

Certainly, there is no renewal without activity, and when renewal is a reality every area of the church's life should benefit. But the implicit equating of renewal with enthusiasm and activity is inadequate in two ways. First, it gives an idea of renewal which is far too *inclusive*: horizon-tally, so to speak, it embraces too much. For in biblical thought and experience, renewal is linked with divine visitation, purging judgement, and restoration through repentance, and no amount of hustle and bustle qualifies as renewal where these notes are absent. Second, this equation gives an idea of renewal which is far too *superficial*: vertically, so to speak, it does not include enough. It views renewal in terms of externals only, and takes no account of the inward exercise of heart in encounter with God in which true renewal as scripture depicts it always begins. But hustle and bustle do not constitute renewal apart from this inward dimension.

How then should we define renewal? The word is one of a group – spiritual, renewal, revival, awakening, visitation, reformation – which tend to be used together and need to be defined together. Five of these six are correlated by Richard Lovelace in a way which both corresponds to usage and clarifies the realities involved. I quote him.

> *Spiritual* (as in *spiritual life, spiritual gifts*) . . . means *deriving from the Holy Spirit*, which is its normal significance in scripture. *Renewal, revival*, and *awakening* trace back to biblical metaphors for the infusion of spiritual life in Christian experience by the Holy Spirit (see Rom. 6:4, 8:2–11; Eph. 1:17–23, 3:14–19, 5:14). Usually they are used synonymously for broad-scale movements of the Holy Spirit's work in renewing spiritual vitality in the church and in fostering its expansion in mission and evangelism. *Reformation* refers to the purifying of doctrine and structures in the church, but implies also a component of spiritual revitalization. Renewal is sometimes used to encompass revival and reformation, and also to include *aggiornamento*, the updating of the church leading to a new engagement with the surrounding world.[3]

To Lovelace's definitions I add that *visitation*, the sixth word in the group, signifies the initial divine approach to spiritually moribund communities out of which their renewal comes.

Lovelace's two definitions of *renewal* alert us to the fact that this is one of those 'concertina-words' which in use keep alternating between a narrower and a broader significance. The term carries its narrowest meaning (concertina closed) when it is used of the personal quickening of an individual. Used so, it signifies that his spiritual life – that is, his God-given fellowship with the Father and the Son through the Spirit, the saving relationship which finds expression in his praise and prayer, his devotion and character, his work and his witness – has been decisively deepened through God's visiting his soul. ('His,' by the way, in that last sentence includes 'hers'; I am not suggesting that only males experience personal renewal!)

At the other end of the scale, *renewal* has its broadest meaning (concertina open) when it is applied to the church, for here, in idea at any rate, it signifies revitalizing at every level, starting with believers' inner lives (what Puritans called their 'heart work') and extending to all the characteristic public activities in which the body of Christ is called to engage.

Following the thrust of the definite article in my assigned title when it speaks of 'renewal of *The* Christian people,' I focus in this paper on the latter, broader application of the word. You cannot, of course, have corporate renewal of any part of the body of Christ on earth without personal renewal of those who make it up, although the quickening of individuals can and does constantly occur without it being part of any larger local movement; but here I shall speak of personal renewal only in

---

[3] Richard F. Lovelace, *Dynamics of Spiritual Life* (Downers Grove: InterVarsity Press, 1979), pp. 21f.

the context of corporate renewal, the quickening of 'the Christian people' in this place or that.

In terms of biblical theology, now, we can characterize God's work of renewal in the following three ways. First, renewal is an *eschatological* reality, in the sense that it is a general experiential deepening of that life in the Spirit which is the foretaste and first instalment of heaven itself. Assurance of both the shameful guiltiness and the total pardon of our sins; joy, humble but exalted, in the awareness of God's love for us; knowledge of the closeness of the Father and the Son in both communion and affection; a never-ending passion to praise God; an abiding urge to love, serve, and honour the Father, the Son, the Spirit, and the saints, and inward freedom to express that urge creatively and spontaneously – these things will be the essence of the life of heaven, and they are already the leading marks of spiritually renewed individuals and communities in this world. To describe situations of renewal, as Protestants using the word *revival* are prone to do, as heaven on earth is not devotional hyperbole; intrinsically and ontologically, that is exactly what the renewal of the Christian people is.

Second, renewal is a *Christological* reality, in two ways. First, it is *subjectively* Christocentric, in the sense that awareness of the gracious, beneficent personal presence of the glorified Lord Jesus – 'Jesus, my Shepherd, Husband, Friend, my Prophet, Priest and King, my Lord, my life, my way, my end,' as Newton's marvellous hymn puts it; Jesus, who guards, guides, keeps, and feeds me, and finally receives me to be with him forever in glory is the very heart of the renewed Christian's sense of reality. The vision of Christ's glory, the realization that every one of God's good gifts comes to us through him and the passion to love and adore him come to pervade the minds and hearts of persons in renewal to a degree that is a major anticipation of heaven, as was said in the last paragraph. The lady who explained to me her identification with a certain renewal movement by saying, 'I just want the Lord Jesus to run my life,' could not have been better directed: she was after the right thing, and she was looking for it in the right place.

It is precisely in renewal that love to Jesus and fellowship with him become most clear-sighted and deep. The most obvious evidence of this is the hymnology of renewal movements. Charles Wesley was the supreme poet of love to Jesus in a revival context: think of his 'Jesus, lover of my soul,' and the final stanzas of 'Thou hidden source of calm repose' –

> Jesus, my all in all thou art,
> My rest in toil, my ease in pain,
> The medicine of my broken heart,
> In war my peace, in loss my gain,
> My smile beneath the tyrant's frown,
> In shame my glory and my crown;

In want my plentiful supply,
In weakness my almighty power,
In bonds my perfect liberty,
My light in Satan's darkest hour,
In grief my joy unspeakable,
My life in death, my heaven in hell.

Or think of this, from the supreme preacher of love to Christ in a renewal context, Bernard of Clairvaux:

Jesus, the very thought of thee
With sweetness fills my breast;
But sweeter far thy face to see,
And in thy presence rest.

O hope of every contrite heart,
O joy of all the meek,
To those who fall how kind thou art!
How good to those who seek!

But what to those who find? Ah! this
Nor tongue nor pen can show:
The love of Jesus, what it is,
None but his loved ones know.

Jesus, our only joy be thou,
As thou our prize wilt be;
Jesus, be thou our glory now
And through eternity.

One mark of spiritual authenticity in the renewal songs of our time – Christian camp fire songs, as they have sometimes been called – is that in them the theme of Christ's love to us and ours to him surfaces once more, and strongly.

Second, renewal is *objectively* Christocentric, in the sense that through it believers are drawn deeper into their baptismal life of dying with Christ in repentance and self-denial and rising with him into the new righteousness of combating sin and living in obedience to God. Authentic revivals have deep ethical effects; they produce authentic sanctity – really, though not always uniformly, tidily, or calmly – along with authentic ministry one to another; and both these features of authentic Christianity should be viewed as the supernatural life of Christ himself living and serving in and through his members by means of the operation of the Spirit. Also, the intensified communion with Christ should be seen as based upon the dynamic reality of this our union with him – or, better, this his union with us.

The third point in the biblical concept of renewal is that it is a *pneumatological* reality, in the sense that it is through the action of the Holy Spirit doing his New Covenant work of glorifying the glorified Christ before the eyes of the understanding of his disciples, as was described above, that renewal actually takes place. Here, incidentally, is a sure test of whether particular stirrings of excitement about interior experience of God are instances of Holy Spirit renewal or not: as Jonathan Edwards argued against critics of the Great Awakening, it is not the devil who exalts Christ, but the Holy Spirit, so that if the experiences in question deepen Christ-centred devotion, that proves their source. And if they do not, that proves their source too. For Satan's strategy is always to distract us from Christ, and getting us to concentrate on exotic experiences – visions, voices, thrills, drug trips, and all the mumbo-jumbo of false mysticism and nonrational meditation – is as good a way for him to do it as any other.

In addition to characterizing renewal in this way, biblical theology answers for us the question, what place has renewal in God's overall purposes? 'Restore us again, O God of our salvation,' prays the psalmist, 'and put away thy indignation toward us! Wilt thou be angry with us for ever? Wilt thou prolong thy anger to all generations? Wilt thou not revive us again, that thy people may rejoice in thee?' (Ps. 85:4–6). Those verses, which can be matched from many passages in the psalms and the prophets, beg for a quickening visitation to the community ('restore, or revive, us again') which will have a twofold experiential significance.

First, this reviving will be experienced as *the ending of God's wrath*, the termination of the impotence, frustration, and barrenness which have been the tokens of divine displeasure for unfaithfulness.

Second, this reviving will be experienced as *the exulting of God's people*: joy will replace the distress which knowledge of God's displeasure has made the faithful feel. Then, third, as appears most clearly from the Acts narrative, such reviving is also experienced as *the extending of God's kingdom*. God's visitation to renew his own household regularly has an evangelistic and cultural overflow, often of great power, leading to the fulfilment in churchly terms of what Zechariah foresaw in terms of the post-exilic restoration: 'Ten men from the nations of every tongue shall take hold of the robe of the Jew, saying "Let us go with you, for we have heard that God is with you" ' (Zech. 8:23). Again and again, for the glory of God in and through his church, this pattern of events has needed to recur, and has in fact recurred, both in and since the biblical period.

In *Dynamics of Spiritual Life*, Dr. Lovelace argues that the apparent antithesis between the two models of cyclical and continuous renewal which the Old and New Testaments respectively seem to throw up is not absolute since the same spiritual forces operate in both types of situations. [4]

---

[4] Op. cit., esp. chapter 2.

I agree, and to clarify the point I offer a distinction between *renewing* or *reviving* as an act of God – that is, the initial visitation which sparks off a new movement – and *revival* or *renewal* itself – that is, the state of revivedness in which God's people continue until for whatever cause the power of the original visitation is withdrawn. Thus one may say that Pentecost was a day of renewing; that renewal conditions surrounded all the protagonists of the church history recorded in Acts, as the New Testament letters also show by the quality of the devotional experience to which they testify; but that six of the seven churches of the Apocalypse had quenched the Spirit, so that the quality of their inward responsiveness to Jesus Christ was now noticeably reduced, and repentance on their part and a fresh visitation from their Lord were urgently needed.

How this might bear on the present life of our own churches, and on our own roles and responsibilities within them, is something at which we must look with some care. But first we should spend a moment reviewing the *elements* in revival, which I announced as the second part of our discussion.

## The Elements in Renewal

The phenomena of renewal movements merit much more study by church historians, theologians, and exponents of Christian spirituality than they have yet received. At surface level, they vary widely, as do the movements within which they appear, and we should not be surprised at that. For, in the first place, spiritual movements are partly shaped by pre-existing needs, which in their turn reflect all sorts of nonrecurring cultural and economic factors, as well as many aspects of the morbid pathology of sin and spiritual decline; and, in the second place, the spiritual experiences of Christians are determined in part by temperament, by atmosphere, and by pressure groups, all of which are variables; and, in the third place, God the Lord appears to delight in variety and never quite repeats himself.

At the level of deeper analysis, deeper, that is, than verbal and cultural variants and pre-set interpretative grids, there are constant factors recognizable in all biblical and post-biblical revivals and renewals of faith and life, whatever their historical, racial, and cultural settings. They number five, as follows: awareness of God's presence; responsiveness to God's word; sensitiveness to sin; liveliness in community; fruitfulness in testimony. Let me illustrate them briefly.

### (1) *Awareness of God's presence*

The first and fundamental feature in renewal is the sense that God has drawn awesomely near in his holiness, mercy, and might. This is felt as the fulfilling of the prayer of Isaiah 64:1f.: 'O that thou wouldst rend the heavens and come down, that the mountains might quake at thy presence . . . to make thy name known to thine adversaries, and that the nations may tremble at thy presence.' God 'comes,' 'visits' his people, and makes his majesty known.

The effect is regularly as it was for Isaiah himself, when he 'saw the Lord sitting on a throne' in the temple and heard the angels' song – 'Holy, holy, holy' – and was forced to say, 'Woe is me, for I am ruined! Because I am a man of unclean lips, and I live among a people of unclean lips' (Is. 6:1–5). It is with this searching, scorching manifestation of God's presence that renewal begins, and by its continuance that renewal is sustained. Says Arthur Wallis: 'The spirit of revival is the consciousness of God.'[5] Wrote Duncan Campbell, out of his experience of revival in Lewis from 1949 to 1953: 'I have no hesitation in saying that this awareness of God is the crying need of the church today.'[6] This, and nothing less than this, is what the outpouring of the Spirit in renewal means in experiential terms.

## (2) Responsiveness to God's word

The sense of God's presence imparts new authority to his truth. The message of Scripture which previously was making only a superficial impact, if that, now searches its hearers and readers to the depth of their being. The statement that 'the word of God is living and active, sharper than any two-edged sword, piercing to the division of soul and spirit, of joints and marrow, and discerning the thoughts and intents of the heart' (Heb. 4:12) is verified over and over again. Paul thanked God that when the Thessalonians heard from the missionaries 'the word of God . . . you accepted it not as the word of men but as what it really is, the word of God' (1 Thess. 2:13). They did this because 'our gospel did not come to you in word, but also in power and in the Holy Spirit and with full conviction' (1:5). It is always so in renewal times. God's message – the gospel call to repentance, faith, and holiness, to praise and prayer, witness and worship – authenticates itself unambiguously to men's consciences, and there is no room for half-measures in response. That leads to our next point.

## (3) Sensitiveness to sin

Deep awareness of what things are sinful and how sinful we ourselves are – *conviction* of sin, to use the old phrase – is the third phenomenon of

---

[5] Arthur Wallis, *In the Day of Thy Power* (London: Christian Literature Crusade, 1960), p. 20.
[6] Duncan Campbell, *The Lewis Awakening 1949–1953* (Edinburgh: Faith Mission, 1954), p. 29.

renewal that calls for notice. No upsurge of religious interest or excite - ment merits the name of renewal if there is no deep sense of sin at its heart. God's coming, and the consequent impact of his word, makes Christians much more sensitive to sin than they previously were: con - sciences become tender and a profound humbling takes place. The gospel of forgiveness through Christ's cross comes to be loved as never before as folk see their need of it so much more clearly.

Conviction of sin was very much part of the early Christian story, and the opening chapters of Acts give us three examples of it. In Acts 2:37–41 we see conviction *accepted*. Peter's congregation was 'pierced to the heart' (2:37) with a sense of their guilt for compassing Jesus' death. The Greek word for 'pierced' means literally to inflict a violent blow; it is a painfully vivid image for what was an acutely painful experience. Shattered, the congregation cried out, 'Brethren, what shall we do?' Peter showed them the way of faith, repentance, and discipleship, and three thousand of them took it. Thus, conviction was the means of their blessing.

In Acts 7:54–60 we see conviction *resisted*. Stephen has accused his Jewish judges of resisting the Spirit, murdering the Christ, and showing contempt for the law (7:51–53). They are 'cut to the quick' (7:54) – the Greek word literally means 'sawn apart'; it expresses the inner turmoil arising from the conjunction of inescapable guilt and uncontrollable anger.

Too proud to admit they had been wrong, they ground their teeth, yelled at Stephen, stopped their ears, mobbed him, ran him out of town, and stoned him to death. The trauma of felt guilt had driven them into hysteria. Conviction in this case was the means of their hardening.

Then in Acts 5:1–10 we see conviction *killing* – literally. Peter tells Ananias that he has lied to the Holy Spirit and so to God, and Ananias dies. A divine judgement, certainly; but what account of it should we give in human terms? The most natural view is that in that revitalized community, where sensitiveness to the presence of God and hence to the foulness of sin was exceedingly strong, the realization of what he had done so overwhelmed Ananias that his frame could not stand it, and he died of shock; and Sapphira the same. They literally could not live with their sin. Thus, conviction became the means of their judgement.

What do we learn from this? That under revival conditions consciences are so quickened that conviction of sin becomes strong and terrible, inducing agonies of mind that are beyond imagining till they happen. But conviction of sin is a means, not an end; the Spirit of God convinces of sin in order to induce repentance, and one of the more striking features of renewal movements is the depth of repentance into which both saints and sinners are led. Repentance, as we know, is basically not moaning and remorse, but turning and change: 'about turn, quick march' is a good formula to express its meaning. In 2 Corinthians 7:10, Paul says, 'The sorrow that is according to the will of God produces a repentance without regret, leading to salvation,' and in the next verse he applauds the robustness of the Corinthians' repentance in the matter about which he had rebuked them. 'What earnestness . . . this godly sorrow has produced in you: what vindication of yourselves, what indignation, what fear, what longing, what zeal, what avenging of wrong!' Vivid conviction produces vigorous repentance.

In times of renewal the impulse constantly recurs, often in defiance of cultural conditioning, to signalize and seal one's repentance by public confession of what one is renouncing: as was done at Ephesus, apparently spontaneously, when 'many . . . of those who had believed kept coming, confessing and disclosing their practices' (Acts 19:18), and some occult practitioners went so far as publicly to burn their very valuable books of spells – a costly and humbling gesture, no doubt, but equally certainly a liberating one for those who made it.

One or more of three motives prompts public confession. It is partly for *purgation*: individuals feel that the only way to get evil things off their conscience and out of their lives is by renouncing them publicly. Sins are also confessed for *healing* (Jas. 5:16): pocketing pride and admitting one's faults and failings to others is part of God's therapy. And, finally, sins are confessed for *doxology*: 'Come and hear, all who fear God, and I will tell of what he has done for my soul' (Ps. 66:16). This kind of confession is likely to appear spontaneously wherever there is genuine renewal.

### (4) Liveliness in community

Love and generosity, unity and joy, assurance and boldness, a spirit of praise and prayer, and a passion to reach out to win others are recurring marks of renewed communities. So is divine power in their preachers, a power which has nothing to do with natural eloquence. John Howe, the Puritan, once Cromwell's chaplain, spoke of this in a passage in a sermon on Ezekiel 39:29 ('I have poured out my Spirit upon the house of Israel, saith the Lord God'). Preaching in 1678 and looking back on the great days of the Puritan revival under the Commonwealth, he told his congregation:

'When the Spirit shall be poured forth plentifully . . . I believe you will hear much other kind of sermons . . . than you are wont to do now-a-days. . . . It is plain, too sadly plain, that there is a great retraction of the Spirit of God even from us. We [preachers] know not how to speak living sense [= *sensus*, a feeling, felt reality] unto souls, how to get within you; our words die in our mouths, or drop and die between you and us. We even faint when we speak; long experienced unsuccessfulness makes us despond. We speak not as persons that hope to prevail, that expect to make you more serious, heavenly, mindful of God, and to walk more like Christians. . . . When such an effusion of the Spirit shall be as is here signified . . . ministers . . . shall know how to speak to better purpose, with more compassion and sense, with more seriousness, with more authority and allurement, than we now find we can.'[7]

Also in renewal times God acts quickly: his work accelerates. When Paul left Thessalonica after between two and three weeks' ministry there, he left behind him a virile church whose quality can be gauged from 1 Thessalo - nians 1–3. God had moved fast. No wonder Paul asks them to pray that 'the word of the Lord may speed on [literally, run] and triumph, as it did among you' (2 Thess. 3:1). Truth spreads, and people are born again and grow in Christ, with amazing rapidity under renewal conditions.

### (5) Fruitfulness in testimony

Revival of the church always has an evangelistic and ethical overspill into the world: Christians proclaim by word and deed the power of the new life, souls are won, and a community conscience informed by Christian values emerges.

Such in outline is the constant pattern by which genuine movements of renewal identify themselves. Christians in renewal are accordingly found living in God's presence (*coram Deo*), attending to his word, feeling acute concern about sin and righteousness, rejoicing in the assurance of Christ's love and their own salvation, spontaneously constant in worship, and tirelessly active in witness and service, fuelling these activities by praise and prayer. The question that presses, therefore, is not whether renewal is approved as a theological idea or claimed as a shibboleth of fashion (to say 'we are in renewal' is almost mandatory in some circles nowadays). The question that presses is whether renewal is actually displayed in the lives of Christian individuals and communities: whether this quality of Christian life is there or not. Which brings us to our final section.

## The Quest for Renewal

This is where analysis finally merges into application and lecturing becomes preaching. I have three points to develop: First, our guilt in not being renewed, and God's call to us to repent of it; second, our inability to renew ourselves, and God's call to us to seek renewal from him; third, our obligation to remove obstacles to our being renewed, and God's call to us to act now in this matter. What this amounts to is a summons to us all to be more honest with God, more simple and thoroughgoing in our response to his grace, more open and straightfor - ward both with him and with others, than we may have been hitherto. Let me try to spell this out as I understand it.

---

[7] John Howe, *Works* (London: F. Westley and A. H. Davis, 1832), p. 575.

Theme one: our guilt in not being renewed, and God's call to us to repent of it. For this I need only refer you once more to the letters of our Lord to the seven churches of the Revelation. With only one of them, the Philadelphian congregation, was the Saviour pleased; the Ephesian church was condemned for having left its first love (2:4f.), the church at Sardis for being dead (3:1), and the church at Laodicea for being self-satisfied and self-deceived. 'I know your works,' says Jesus to the Laodiceans; 'you are neither cold nor hot. Would that you were cold or hot! So, because you are lukewarm, and neither cold nor hot, I will spew you out of my mouth. For you say, I am rich, I have prospered, and I need nothing; not knowing that you are wretched, pitiable, poor, blind, and naked . . . Those whom I love I rebuke and chasten; so be zealous and repent' (3:15–17, 19). It is hard to doubt that this is the mind of Jesus with regard to many churches in North America and Britain today.

Biblical theology knows no middle condition, for churches or for Christians, between spiritual advance under God's blessing and spiritual decline under his displeasure. The root of spiritual decline is always human unfaithfulness in some form, and its fruit is always chastening judgement from God, whose gracious plan and supernatural enabling are hereby slighted and dishonoured. Marks of decline include high tolerance of half-heartedness, moral failure, and compromise; low expectations of holiness in oneself and others; willingness to remain Christian pygmies; apathy about the advancement of God's cause and his glory; and contentment, even complacency, with things as they are.

Charles Finney once said, 'Christians are more to blame for not being revived than sinners are for not being converted.'[8] Was he right? It is, at the very least, a question worth thinking about as we reflect on the relevance to ourselves of Jesus' words to the Laodiceans. And perhaps in doing this we shall need to make our own the words of the Anglican litany: 'From hardness of heart, and contempt of thy word and commandment, good Lord, deliver us.'

So we move to theme two: our inability to renew ourselves, and our need to seek this blessing from God by prayer. The point here is that whereas self-reliance, expressing self-sufficiency, is natural (we might almost say, instinctive) to us in our fallenness, it is beyond us to compass spiritual renewal by any form of activity that we organize. The principle is that underlying Isaiah 22:8–14, where Judah's feverish bustle of defen - sive activity in face of trouble was ruling out anything in the nature of a genuine return to God and a genuine dependence on him for the deliverance which only he could give. To look to human ingenuity, however, for that which only God in his grace can give is arrogant, inept, and in the outcome barren.

---

[8]   Charles G. Finney, *Revivals of Religion* (London: Oliphants, 1928), p. 20.

That is how it is in the matter of renewal. When Christians, by the Laodicean character of their lives and their ecclesiastical systems, have quenched the fire of God's Spirit, and so brought about a withdrawal of God's presence and glory, it is beyond their power to kindle the fire again, much as they might wish to do so; only God himself, by his own quickening visitation, can renew, and for this we have to wait on him in patient, persistent, penitent prayer until he is pleased to act. Charles Finney, who for a decade after his conversion was used by God in a continuous revival ministry, came to think, evidently generalizing from that experience, that self-examination and earnest prayer on a congrega - tion's part would always secure a divine visitation and fresh outpouring of the Spirit immediately. But the experience of many who have sought to implement this formula, and indeed the different and disappointing experience of Finney himself in later years, shows that this is not so.

In no situation can revival be infallibly predicted or precipitated; there are no natural laws of renewal for man the manager to discover and exploit. That, however, is no cause for discouragement, for the other side of the coin is that the possibility of renewal can never be precluded either; no one can set limits to the graciousness of God who has promised that we shall find him when we seek him with all our hearts. To seek God and his renewing grace, recognizing that he can renew us though we cannot renew ourselves, is in this instance the only constructive thing that is open to us to do. 'Ask, and it will be given you; seek, and you will find,' says our Lord (Matt. 7:7). The Psalter provides several pattern prayers for this purpose, notably Psalms 44, 67, 74, 79, and 85. Waiting on God in constant acknowledgement of need, pleading that he should move in mercy, is the way forward here.

Finally, we move to theme three: our obligation to remove hin - drances to renewal, and God's call to us to begin doing this now. A moment ago I said that we cannot precipitate a visitation from God. That is true; God is sovereign in these matters and takes action to answer prayer at his own speed and in his own good time. Yet there is something we can do at this present moment to bring spiritual quick - ening nearer, and that is to break with things that are in their own nature Spirit-quenching.

For instance: surely *clericalism* as a leadership style is Spirit-quenching. Clericalism, which on my analysis involves more persons than the ordained, is a sort of conspiracy between leaders and those led: the one party (it does not matter which) says, 'all spiritual ministry should be left to the leader,' and the other party says, 'yes, that's right.' Some leaders embrace clericalism because it gives them power; others, running scared, embrace it because they fear lest folk ministering alongside them should overshadow them, or because they feel incapable of handling an every-member-ministry situation. But every-member ministry in the body of Christ is the New Testament pattern, and anything which obstructs or restricts it is an obstacle to a renewing visitation from God. What does this suggest that leaders, and others, ought to do now?

Again: surely *formalism* as a worship style is Spirit-quenching. But many churches seem to view worship in a way that can only be called formalistic, for their interest is limited to performing set routines with suitable correctness, and there is no apparent desire on anyone's part actually to meet God. What does this suggest that leaders, and others, ought to do now?

Yet once more: surely personal attitudes of *complacency* about things as they are is Spirit-quenching. Think of your own church or fellowship: to what extent do you see in it the reality of worship? faith? repentance? knowledge? holiness? Do its members resolutely, energetically, passion - ately love the Lord? Do they love each other? How do they pray? How do they give? How much support do they get from each other in times of personal need? How much sharing of their faith do they do, or try to do? Ought you to be content with things as they are? Think also of yourself, and of what these folk see in you. Ought either they or you to be content with what you are? It must be expected that those led will become like their leaders; that is the natural thing to happen; but if it happens so in your church or fellowship, will that be good enough? What does this line of thought suggest that leaders, and others, ought to do now?

The first step, perhaps, to the renewal of the Christian people is that leaders should begin to repent of their too-ready acceptance of too-low levels of attainment both in themselves and in those whom they lead, and should learn to pray from their hearts the simple-sounding but totally demanding prayer in Edwin Orr's chorus: ' *Send a revival – start the work in me.*' The second step, perhaps, is for leaders to challenge their followers as to whether they are not too much like the Laodiceans of Revelation, and whether Jesus' searing words to these latter – 'you are lukewarm . . . you say, I need nothing; not knowing that you are wretched, pitiable, poor, blind, and naked . . . be zealous, and repent. Behold, I stand at the door and knock . . .' – do not apply directly to themselves, here and now. The third step, perhaps, is for us all, leaders and led together, to become more serious, expectant, and honest with each other as we look to God in our use of the means of grace – sermon and sacrament, worship and witness, praise and prayer, meditation and petition – and as we seek to make our own the psalmist's plea: 'Search me, O God, and know my heart! Try me and know my thoughts! And see if there be any wicked way in me, and lead me in the way everlasting!' (Ps. 139:23–24). Then the fourth step, perhaps, will be to trust the Holy Spirit to lead us on from there.

Does this prospect strike awe into you? I am sure that it does, and it has the same effect on me. But that is no justification for drawing back from it, when our need of it is so plain.

'O Lord, I have heard the report of thee, and thy work, O Lord, do I fear. In the midst of the years renew it; in the midst of the years make it known; in wrath remember mercy' (Hab. 3:2).

Let all the people say: amen.

# Chapter 10

# The Holy Spirit and the Local Congregation

Our theme is the work of the Holy Spirit in connection with the local church, and for a biblical lead on this we naturally turn to 1 Corinthians 12–14, the classical passage on the subject. It is a passage which cannot but make painful reading for thoughtful evangelical Christians today.

Now why do I say that? Because Corinthian public worship, as there described, was such a chaotic uproar? Because of the apparent unseem - liness of services in which, as it seems, many talked at once, some in ecstatic gibberish, and women screeched to be heard above the general noise (cf. 14:26–35)? Because of the amount of rivalry and self-display that there was in connection with leading the prayers, and singing, and preaching? Do I mean that it is painful to contemplate a situation in which such disorders, liturgical and moral and spiritual, had become a matter of course? No, I do not mean that. What I mean is that these chapters make painful reading because, whatever evils they confront us with, they do in fact show us a local church in which the Holy Spirit was working in power. Reading this passage makes one painfully aware of the degree of impoverishment and inertia which prevails in our churches at the present time. If our only reaction to reading these chapters is to preen ourselves and feel glad because our churches are free from Corinthian disorders, we are fools indeed. I fear that many of our churches today are orderly simply because they are asleep; and with some, one fears it is the sleep of death. After all, it is no great thing, is it, to have order in a cemetery?

The Corinthian disorders were due to an uncontrolled overflow of Holy Ghost life. The real and deplorable carnality and immaturity of the Corinthian Christians, which Paul censures so strongly elsewhere in this

THE HOLY SPIRIT AND THE LOCAL CONGREGATION was originally published in *Churchman*, LXXIX. 2, June, 1964. Reprinted by permission. Biblical quotations in this article are from the KJV. No attempt has been made to disguise the fact that it was originally an address to a conference of Anglican clergy.

epistle, must not blind us to the fact that they were enjoying the ministry of the Holy Spirit in a way in which we today are not.

At the start of the epistle, Paul had written (1:4):

> I thank my God always on your behalf, for the grace of God which is given you by Jesus Christ; that in everything you are enriched by him, in all utterance, and in all knowledge; even as the testimony of Christ was confirmed in you: so that you come behind in no gift . . .

This was not empty politeness. Paul had not got his tongue in his cheek; he meant what he said.

The Corinthians really had been 'enriched' by Christ in the manner described. Consequently, when they met for the fellowship of worship they brought with them gifts and contributions in abundance. Whereas congregations today too often gather in a spirit of aimless and unexpectant apathy, scarcely aware that they come to church to receive, let alone to give, the Corinthians met with eagerness and excitement, anxious to share with their fellow-believers the 'manifestation of the Spirit' (12:7) that was theirs.

'When you come together', wrote Paul (14:26), 'every one of you hath a psalm, hath a doctrine (some instruction, NEB), hath a tongue, hath a revelation, hath an interpretation.' Public worship at Corinth was the reverse of a drab routine; every service was an event, for every worshipper came ready and anxious to contribute something that God had given him.

In the words quoted, Paul is not (*pace* our Brethren friends) prescribing an order for worship, making a rule that Christian worship always and everywhere should take the form of an American tea, or potluck support, where every guest brings something for the common pool; he is just describing the actual state of affairs in one particular church, and giving directions, not for creating it, but for handling it now that it had arisen. The state of affairs itself, however, was the spontaneous creation of the Holy Spirit.

Furthermore, when the Corinthians met for worship the presence and power of God in their midst was an experienced reality. There was a sense of God among them that struck awe into men's souls, as at Jerusalem in the early days (cf. Acts 5:11–13), and gave every word that was spoken in God's name heart-searching force. Hence Paul – who, remember, knew the church, having watched over the first eighteen months of its life, and could therefore speak of it at first-hand – could write to them almost casually words that would sound staggering, indeed fatuous, if spoken to a congregation today. 'If therefore the whole church be come together into one place,' Paul declared 'and all . . . prophesy' (that is, announce the message of God in intelligible speech – whether by direct inspiration or biblical exposition we need not here determine), and there come in one that believeth not, or one unlearned, he is convinced of all, he is judged of all: and thus are the secrets of his heart made manifest; and so falling down on his face he will worship God, and report that God is in you (among you, RV) of a truth (14:23–25).

Can you imagine that being seriously said to any local congregation of your acquaintance today? Yet Paul could say it to the Corinthians in a matter-of-fact manner, without the least sense of unreality, as if it were unquestionably true. How was this possible?

It could only have been possible if in fact the statement was one whose truth both Paul and the Corinthians had repeatedly proved in experience. This alone can explain why Paul made it, and why he expected the Corinthians to accept it, as he clearly does. Evidently, then, it had happened more than once at Corinth, and no doubt elsewhere in Paul's experience, that a casual visitor, coming in by accident to a church service, had heard all that was spoken as a message from God to his heart, and had gone out a changed man. Nor should we be surprised at this; for the same thing has happened many times since Paul's day under revival conditions, when the sense of God's presence among his people has been strong.

Granted that the Corinthian disorders were grievous, yet the Corin - thian church was being carried along by a great surge of divine life. Disorder, as such, is demonic, and not to be desired, but it remains a question whether Holy Ghost life, with all its exuberance and risk of disorder, is not preferable to spiritual deadness, neat and tidy though that deadness may be.

It is true that there is no problem of disease or malfunctioning where death reigns, but is lifelessness therefore the ideal? Three centuries ago, in his *Discourse of Spiritual Gifts*, John Owen reviewed the Puritan revival (for revival it truly was) and frankly acknowledged the extravagance and misuse of spiritual endowments that had disfigured it.

By some, I confess, they [that is, 'the eminent abilities of a number of private Christians'] have been abused; some have presumed on them; . . . some have been puffed up with them; some have used them disorderly in churches, and to their hurt; some have boasted . . . all which miscarriages also befell the primitive churches.

And then he went on to say:

And I had rather have the order, rule, spirit, and practice of those churches which were planted by the apostles, with all their troubles and disadvantages, than the carnal peace of others in their open degeneracy from all these things.[1]

---

[1] *Works*, ed. W. H. Goold (London: Banner of Truth, 1967), IV. 518.

Frankly, and before God I say it, so had I, and I hope my readers feel the same. But it cannot be denied that if one thinks as Owen does, 1 Corinthians 12–14 makes, as we said, painful reading.

We ought to stop here for a moment and ask ourselves why it is that we know so little of the power of the Spirit in our churches today. Both Testaments tell us that to enjoy a rich outpouring of the Holy Spirit is a characteristic privilege of the New Testament church. For a church to lack the Spirit's powerful working in its corporate life is therefore by biblical standards unnatural, just as heresy is; and this unnatural state of affairs can only be accounted for in terms of human failure.

The New Testament has a phrase for the failure in question: we may, it says, *quench* the Spirit by resisting or undervaluing his work, and by declining to yield to his influence.[2] The image is of putting out a fire by pouring water on it. It is noteworthy that in 1 Thessalonians 5:19 the words 'quench not the Spirit' are flanked, on the one hand, by exhorta - tions to follow the good, and to rejoice, pray, and give thanks at all times, and, on the other hand, by warnings against disregard for 'prophesyings' (the messages of God, however and by whomsoever declared), failure to discriminate, and evil involvement. It is natural to suppose that these things were connected in Paul's mind, and that he wished his readers to gather that heedlessness of these exhortations and warnings at any point was likely to quench the Spirit, not only in the Christian's personal life but also in the common life of the church.

It is noteworthy too that while one may effectively put out a fire by dousing it, one cannot start it burning again simply by stopping pouring water; it has to be lighted afresh. Similarly, when the Spirit has been quenched it is beyond man's power to undo the damage he has done: he can only cry to God in penitence to revive his work.

It seems undeniable that evangelicals today inherit a situation in which the Holy Spirit has been quenched. Why and how this has happened since the last widespread movement of the Spirit over the country, in 1859, is far too broad and complex a question to try to answer here, though the general devaluing of the Bible and its gospel since that time has plainly had a great deal to do with it. But we need to ask ourselves whether we who down the years have stuck to the 'old paths' of evangelical faith in connection with the Bible and the gospel may not ourselves be guilty of contributing to our present barrenness in other ways, by our own Spirit-quenching attitudes and inhibitions on the practical level, which impede and stifle the Spirit's work in our congregations. Here are some specific questions which it seems to me that we who are clergy need to put to ourselves:

Are we not quenching the Spirit by *clericalism*? By that I do not mean the priestly pretensions of the heirs of the Oxford Movement, but rather the subtler clericalism which proceeds on the assumption that apart from

---

[2]  cf. Acts 7:51; Heb. 10:29.

the Sunday school, all spiritual ministry is the clergyman's preserve, and which therefore declines to encourage lay initiative in this department.

How much responsibility do we give our laity in connection with evangelism? visiting? prayer meetings? home meetings? How often do we ask our lay readers to preach? How much help do we give them to develop their preaching gifts? Do we train our laity as conscientiously as we try to train our non-stipendiary associates and our assistant curates? Do we treat our lay readers as colleagues in the ministry? How often do we have them in to a staff meeting? It is irony indeed when the foremost critics of prelacy in the diocese appear as last-ditch defenders of it in the parish! We need to examine ourselves.

Again, are we not quenching the Spirit by *formalism*? By that I do not mean the blatant formalism of some ritualists, but the subtler formalism which assumes that Prayer Book services as set, simply and straightfor - wardly read, must under all circumstances constitute spiritual worship, and so ignores the possibility that some may not understand them and neglects to teach their meaning and to train Christians in the Prayer Book way of worship.

How hearty and intelligent is the worship of our own congregation? How much Prayer Book teaching have they had from us during the past three years? How much do we propose to give them during the coming twelve months? How much thought do we and they regularly give together to the problems of ordering worship – the problem, for instance, of making the two sacraments genuinely congregational acts? There may be more of the evil of formalism in the use of prescribed forms into which people do not enter than in the use of prohibited ones into which they do! Here, too, we need to examine ourselves.

Again, do we not quench the Spirit by *conventionality*? By this I do not mean the unprincipled and superficial conventionality that follows all the latest fashions in churchmanship and theology, just to keep 'with it,' whatever 'it' may be, but the subtler conventionality which, however much times change, remains wedded to the way things were said and done about a hundred years ago and refuses to face the possibility that these ways may need amending today if we are to make contact with people at the point where they now are.

And do we not quench the Spirit by *complacency*? – not the blatant complacency of those who refuse to allow that anything in the church is really wrong, but the subtler complacency of simply accepting as normal a situation in which nothing is happening and contentedly jogging along in it year after year.

Once more, we need to examine ourselves – for these attitudes in the clergy will certainly quench the Spirit, as they will frustrate the congre - gation, in any local church, and will effectively keep us from seeking the revival which we desperately need. But I must not pursue this line of thought further at present.

★ ★ ★

The New Testament witness to the Holy Spirit is summed up for us in the creedal phrase, 'the Lord and giver of life.' He is 'the Lord,' a divine Person, free and sovereign, who as Vicar of Christ on earth (for there is no better phrase than that to describe him) exercises Christ's authority and continues his ministry of teaching and guiding his people.

The lordship of the Spirit resolves into the lordship of the Christ whose Spirit he is. And he is 'the giver of life,' who brings us to the new birth, who changes us from glory to glory, who brings forth in the regenerate the fruit of Christ-like character, who strengthens and equips for service, and who will one day, at the Saviour's word, raise the dead. I propose now to speak of his work as Lord and Life-Giver in connection with the local church, first as *creating* it, second as *animating* it, third in its *order*, fourth in its *growth*.

### (i) *The work of the Holy Spirit in creating the local church*

The work whereby the Spirit creates the local congregation is identical with the work whereby he creates the church universal, of which each local church is a visible manifestation. What work is that? It is the work of causing sinful men to hear and respond to the divine summons to repentance and faith in Christ, and of uniting them savingly to the crucified and risen Lord.

In 1 Corinthians 12, Paul speaks first of the Spirit as the One who leads men to faith ('no man can say that Jesus is the Lord' – the primitive baptismal confession – 'but by the Holy Ghost,' verse 3), and later on of the Spirit as grafting all who believe into Christ ('by one Spirit are we all baptized into one body,' verse 13). No doubt it is right to find in the latter passage an implicit reference to Christ as the baptizer, and to understand the words as in effect an exposition of the promise, 'he shall baptize you with the Holy Ghost' (Matt. 3:11).

Yet the Spirit is not a passive element, to be manipulated, like the water in water-baptism; he must be thought of as the agent, rather than the instrument, of the Saviour's action. In this verse, Paul uses the imagery of both sacraments ('by one Spirit are we all *baptized* . . . and have all been made to *drink* into one Spirit') to denote the single reality to which both point; which is, precisely, saving union with Christ.

This union is a creative act on God's part. 'If any one is in Christ, he is a new creation.'[3] It is mysterious in character, for it is a fresh putting forth of the power that raised Jesus from the dead. The risen Jesus is at present out of our sight, and neither his life nor that which Christians enjoy in union with him is open to human inspection. 'Your life is *hid* with Christ in God.'[4] But this vitalizing union with Christ is none the less real for being mysterious, as appears from its transforming effects.

---

[3] 2 Cor. 5:17, RSV.

[4] Col. 3:3.

From man's standpoint, it is nothing less than a new birth, a regenerating act of God whereby, as Christ explained to Nicodemus, one is born
afresh of the Spirit in the course of coming to faith in Jesus as one's divine
Saviour.[5] Its effect is to make it natural – one might almost say, instinctive
– for the future to believe God's truth, to eschew sin, to love God and
his children, and to fulfil his commands.[6] Those born again are indwelt
by the Spirit, as branches in the vine which is Christ, and the fruit of the
Spirit grows in them. Analysed christologically (as always by Paul), this
new birth consists of union with Christ in his death and resurrection,
leading to fellowship with him henceforth in his risen life.[7] Some speak
of the church as the extension of the incarnation, but the basic biblical
objection to that is surely that it locates our union with Christ at the
wrong point.

Biblically, if the church is the extension of anything, it is the
extension of the resurrection. Union with Christ in his death – co-
crucifixion[8] and co-burial,[9] as Paul puts it – means, first, that our guilt
is gone ('he that hath *died* is justified from sin,'[10] – as the NEB puts it, 'a
dead man is no longer answerable for his sin'); second, that our former
life under the rule of sin is gone, and a new life of fellowship with Christ
and righteousness, discontinuous with the old life, has begun. ('Reckon
ye also yourselves to be *dead indeed unto sin* . . . sin shall not have
dominion over you.'[11]) For resurrection with Christ means effective
deliverance from slavery to sin to live in the Spirit, being conformed to
Christ ever more thoroughly in mind and heart, attitude and outlook.
By his Spirit, Christ himself is not merely with us, to direct us, but in
us, to make us observe his directions; so Paul writes: 'I am crucified
with Christ: nevertheless I live; yet not I, but *Christ liveth in me.*'[12] This
is what union with Christ means; and it is the Spirit who is the agent
of it all.

Union with Christ implies union with all others who are Christ's. In
Christ, my fellow-believer is my brother, for we both belong to the same
family. More than that, he is in a real sense part of me. Because we are
both vitally linked to our common Saviour, we have a vital link with each
other – we are, in Paul's phrase, 'members one of another';[13] as the NEB
puts it, 'all of us are the parts of one body.'

---

[5] John. 3:3–15.
[6] cf. 1 John. 2:29, 3:9, 4:7, 5:1.
[7] cf. Rom. 6:1–13; Col. 2:12–3:4.
[8] Gal. 2:20, 6:14; Rom. 6:6.
[9] Rom. 6:3; Col. 2:12.
[10] Rom. 6:7, RV.
[11] Rom. 6:11, 14.
[12] Gal. 2:20.
[13] Eph. 4:25.

On this foundation rests the New Testament teaching about God's covenant people, the church. Writing to the Ephesians, Paul portrays this double union – with Christ, and in Christ with each other – by no less than four 'organic' metaphors for the church: the body of Christ, the bride of Christ, the new man in Christ, the temple.

Three of these images point directly to the church's subjection to Christ: He is the body's head, the bride's husband, and the corner-stone of the temple (head of the arch, fixing the rest in place).[14] Three of the images point to the church's destiny in Christ: the body, the new man, and the temple *grow* towards a predestined perfection.[15] And three of the images point to the new relationship of mutual involvement and dependence which binds the regenerate together in Christ.

In the body, all are members of one another; in the new person, racial distinctions (and sexual and social distinctions too[16]) are transcended;[17] in the temple, the stones are 'fitly framed together' for firm integration.[18] From these passages we learn that in and under Christ, Christians are called to 'fit in' with each other, to feel for one another, and to stand together in love, loyalty, and care.

Now all this applies directly at the local level, for the local church is no more – and no less – than an outcrop, a microcosm, of the church universal. Paul applies the body-image to local church life in 1 Corinthians 12 and Romans 12, just as he does to the life of the universal church in Ephesians. 'Ye are the body of Christ,' he tells the Corinthians.[19]

The local church, then, must not be thought of as a club, a mere human organization, but as a divine creation, a sample of the church universal, called to glorify Christ by being an exemplary instance of the work that he is doing in different places all over the world. It is better not to speak at all of church 'members,' for in the New Testament 'members' are not subscribers to a society, but parts of a body, and it is not the church that has 'members,' but Christ.

The right to belong to the local church rests on the claim to belong to Christ, and on that alone. If we go, as we should, with modern ecumenical theology in emphasizing the supernatural status of the local church, as the body of Christ visibly exhibited, then we should let this emphasis lead us – as, unhappily, it does not always lead ecumenical theology – to a renewed insistence that everyone who links himself to the outward fellowship *must be born again*; for only the regenerate are members of Christ.

---

[14]  cf. Eph. 1:22f., 5:23ff., 2:20ff.
[15]  cf. Eph. 4:12–16, 2:21.
[16]  Gal. 3:28.
[17]  Gal. 2:15f.
[18]  Gal. 2:21.
[19]  1 Cor. 12:27.

### (ii) The work of the Holy Spirit animating the local church

As an outcrop and sample of the church universal, created in Christ by the Holy Spirit of God, the local church has its own proper life to live – a life lived on very different principles and for very different ends from the life of the world around. The church's life, we are told, must be one of *love*, a life of gratitude to God, in which we seek to imitate our Saviour by love towards all people, and particularly those who are both his brothers and sisters and ours. 'The members,' wrote Paul 'should have the same care one for another.'[20] Specifically, this life of love is to be a life of *fellowship*, whereby we share (for that is what 'fellowship' really means) the good things that God has given us individually.

No one is self-sufficient; we all need each other and what God has given each other; we must learn, therefore, to express our love in the give-and-take of Christian fellowship. And this loving fellowship must take the form of *ministry* (*diakonia* in Greek), literally in English 'service.' 'By love *serve* one another.'[21] In this basic sense, the church's ministry is a vocation to which every Christian is called.

It is for this life of ministry, in which every part of the body is called to make its own contribution,[22] that God gives *gifts*. Gifts and ministry are in this sense correlative; God gives each his or her gift, not primarily for themselves, but for others, to be used for their good in the fellowship of the body's life.[23] The body-image provides on each occasion the context in which Paul's teaching about spiritual gifts is set out.[24] We may summarize this teaching in the form of answers to four questions.

(1) *What are gifts?* Their names give clues to their nature. Ephesians 4:8 calls them Christ's *domata* (presents). In 1 Corinthians 12 (five times) and 1 Peter 4:10 they are referred to as *charismata*, gifts springing from divine *charis* (grace). In 1 Corinthians 12:1 they are termed *pneumatika*, literally 'spirituals' – that is, powers from the Spirit.[25] 1 Corinthians 12:6 calls them *energeiai*, 'operations'; the verse after terms them 'the *manifestation* of the Spirit,' implying that by their use the divine life of God's people is exhibited both to themselves and others.

What, essentially, are they? Is there a common formula covering such varied abilities and activities as those listed in (say) 1 Corinthians 12:28–30? Yes, there is; it is this: a spiritual gift is *an ability to express and communicate in some way one's knowledge of Christ and his grace*. It is not a mere natural endowment, though usually it is given through the sancti - fying of a natural endowment. Spiritual gifts have a spiritual content: they

---

[20]   1 Cor. 12:25.

[21]   Gal. 5:13.

[22]   Eph. 4:16.

[23]   cf. 1 Cor. 12:7.

[24]   cf. Rom. 12:4ff.; 1 Cor. 12:4ff.; Eph. 4:8ff.

[25]   cf. 'distributions of the Holy Ghost,' Heb. 2:4, RV, margin.

display the riches of Christ, by manifestation of something received from him. All forms of service which do this involve an exercise of spiritual gifts, for profit[26] and edifying.[27]

(2) *What kinds of gifts are there?* Very many; there is no reason to treat even 1 Corinthians 12:28–30 as an exhaustive list, and it is doubtful whether in principle such a list could be compiled. Paul compares the variety of gifts in the body of Christ to the variety of functions in the human body, where ear, eye, hand, foot, and many inelegant organs, all have a part to play in the healthy functioning of the whole.[28] Gifts vary in value, according to whether they give more or less help to others; thus, speaking the word of God in intelligible terms is better than speaking it in a tongue. 'Covet earnestly the best gifts.'[29]

What are the best gifts? Clearly, ministries of the word: wisdom, knowledge, prophecy, power to teach and apply truth, the gifts that qualify men to be apostles, preachers, evangelists, and pastors. In 1 Corin - thians 12:28ff., these gifts are mentioned first; in Eph. 4:11, they alone are in view. But the list in 1 Corinthians 12 mentions other gifts, fitting us for other forms of service: extraordinary gifts like healing and miracles, more ordinary ones like 'governments' (skill in administration!) and 'helps' (the Greek word suggests the idea of 'taking over').

These gifts, though unspectacular, are as much needed in the church's life as preaching abilities, and so are many more forms of service not listed here at all. In Romans 12:6ff., Paul's charge to his readers to use their gifts starts, as one might expect, with the ministry of the word, but it soon broadens (verses 8ff.), without any sense of a change of subject, into a general plea for the exercise of Christian graces towards others – showing mercy, kindness, consideration, hospitality, and so on. For in fact to show these qualities in serving others is to enjoy the privilege of exercising one's spiritual gift no less really than a clergyman does when he preaches. No doubt 'gifts' and 'graces' are distinct in idea, but in practice much of our employment of the former is simply an exercising of the latter, informally or spontaneously, in giving such help as we can, according to human needs.

(3) *Which persons have gifts?* Every single Christian, says Paul.[30] All can serve others in some way, and all are called to do so; and such service, whatever its form, falls under the definition of an exercise of gifts. This is a doctrine of the ministry of all believers. Peter teaches the same: 'As every man hath received the gift, even so minister the same one to another, as good stewards of the manifold grace of God.'[31]

---

[26]  1 Cor. 12:7.
[27]  cf. Eph. 4:12,16.
[28]  1 Cor. 12:15–25.
[29]  1 Cor. 12:31; cf. 14:12–19.
[30]  Rom. 12:6; 1 Cor. 12:7; Eph. 4:7, 16.
[31]  1 Pet. 4:10.

(4) *What purpose have gifts?* Edification, as we saw; which means, literally, a 'building up' of Christians, leading them forward towards their ultimate perfection. The reason why Paul views speaking in tongues as a comparatively insignificant gift is because, at most, it only edifies the speaker, whereas comprehensible utterance of God's word edifies the whole church.[32] The public exercise of gifts must always be regulated 'unto edifying.'[33]

### (iii) The work of the Spirit in the local church's order

Order (*taxis*) means arrangement; disorder means lack of arrangement. Order is required in local church life;[34] but of what sort, and to what end? The purpose of order, as Paul explains it,[35] is to allow gifts to be exercised to edification. Church order is meant not to stifle gifts, but to secure a situation in which all gifts may be used to the best advantage. We need to ask ourselves: does our existing church order – by which I mean, not primarily our Prayer Book uniformity, but the overall pattern of congregational life – have this effect in our local churches?

Our Brethren friends would shake their heads at this point, for their constant complaint is that the Church of England has a 'one-man ministry,' which represses gifts among the unordained by removing all room for their exercise. I venture to say that if this is really true, it is a damning indictment, and we need not look any further to find out what it is that is quenching the Spirit in these days, but I am also bold to say that it ought never to be possible to accuse an Anglican parish church of having a 'one-man ministry.' And I do not mean by that that all churches should have one or more assistant curates! I mean, simply, that the structure of their congregational life should be such as to call forth and utilize all the gifts of all the congregation.

Thus, others beside the clergy have God-given gifts of wisdom, knowledge, speech, prayer; what note are we taking of these gifts in our own congregations, and what arrangements do we make for their respon - sible and edifying exercise? Others beside the clergy have gifts of pastoral care; what responsibilities in this field do we delegate to persons so gifted within our own flocks?

The Church of Scotland has its lay eldership; many evangelical Free Churches have a pastoral diaconate; Methodism in the days of its greatest spiritual effectiveness had its class leaders; what have we? What provision is made in our churches to meet the need which has been met at different times and in different places by the evangelical society, the class meeting,

---

[32]  1 Cor. 12:4.

[33]  1 Cor 14:26.

[34]  1 Cor. 14:40.

[35]  cf. 1 Cor. 14:26.

the group Bible study, the cottage meeting, the revival fellowship meeting, and similar institutions – the need, that is, for a decentralized fellowship of prayer, study, testimony, and evangelism, in groups so small as to admit of no 'passengers,' but encouraging each member to make a full contribution of all that he or she has to give?

Is it not a happy sign that in several churches recently there has been a retreat from the pattern of more and more weeknight meetings 'up at the church,' and a serious attempt to rediscover the – surely healthier – pattern of more small meetings in people's homes? This, at least, is clear: that where spiritual gifts are neglected and inhibited, the local church fails to fulfil its calling to be the body of Christ in action in the place where it is set, and effectively quenches the Spirit by ingratitude for what he has given; and therefore we need constantly to seek his guidance in develop - ing a pattern of congregational life in which all gifts may be used to the full. The right pattern will vary from church to church, and from one year to another in the same church, and only the Spirit, who gives the gifts, can show us the way to order each church's life here and now so that his gifts will find full employment.

### (iv) The work of the Holy Spirit in the local church's growth

As the human body grows and keeps fit through exercise, so the local church will advance towards maturity through the faithful exercise of spiritual gifts within its fellowship; and as it grows inwardly stronger, so its outreach will become more effective. But in applying this truth we have to start from where we are.

We have to ask: how can we foster gifts in Christian people? And the answer is: through feeding them with the word of grace till their heartfelt cry is, 'What can I do for my Lord? how much can I do for the one who did so much for me?' When men and women, clergy with their laity and laity with their clergy, are constantly taking this question back to God in prayer, then spiritual gifts become apparent as the Spirit's way of indicating his answer to the question in each case. But how far the clergy and laity of the Church of England – even, as it seems, evangelical clergy and laity of the Church of England – are from such a state of heart! We need grace to be discontented with things as they are, grace to refuse comfort till God has changed them, grace to lay hold of God and not let him go till by his mercy the power and gifts of the Spirit are shed abroad abundantly again. Then God's work will be revived, and our long-stunted churches will at last grow. May that day come soon!

# Chapter 11

# Piety on Fire

*Despite the longevity and vibrancy of the charismatic movement, when CHRISTI -ANITY TODAY surveyed readers about the questions most on their minds, Is the charismatic renewal from God? made the top-ten list. Responses to the movement have been diverse. Some Christian leaders have called it 'demonic,' while others have belittled it as mere emotionalism. At the other extreme are those who view it as the sole answer to the apathy and institutionalism that often plague the church.*

*We asked J. I. Packer, author of* Keep in Step with the Spirit *(Revell), to give us a brief but careful look at this movement that provokes such strong reactions. This essay is just one of the ten collected in* Tough Questions Christians Ask *(Christianity Today/Victor Books).*

To ask whether or not the charismatic movement is from God is like asking whether today's motor vehicles are efficient. In each case the true answer doubtless is: In some respects yes, in others no. But both questions are too broad and unfocused for that answer to get us very far. If all we want to know is whether God ordinarily blesses where the charismatic renewal movement takes root, a simple yes will suffice, for that is in truth the fact. But if our goal is to assess how mature and God-honouring charismatic patterns of godliness are as compared with other forms, past and present, some discussion is needed.

There are two extremes of opinion. Some Christians pan the renewal as Ralph Nader used to pan American cars (remember *Unsafe at Any Speed?*). These critics dismiss charismatic distinctives as either self-induced or demonically inspired, and they tell us that embracing these distinctives is always spiritually stultifying and retrograde. Others applaud the renewal in what might be called Star Wars terms, seeing it as God's final triumphant move for preserving the church and spreading the gospel in today's anti-Christian world. Mediating assessments fan out between these two extremes. Where does biblical wisdom lead us to position ourselves on this spectrum? That is what we must try to see.

PIETY ON FIRE was originally published in *Christianity Today*, vol. 33, May 12, 1989, pp. 18–23. Reprinted by permission.

## A Growing Phenomenon

First, let us make sure we know what we are talking about. The charismatic movement, also called the renewal movement and the char- ismatic renewal, is a worldwide phenomenon some thirty years old. Some refer to it as the second Pentecostal wave, in distinction from the first wave that produced the Pentecostal denominations at the start of this century. It emerged in California, as did its predecessor, and has touched most Christian bodies, including the Roman Catholic community. Pen- tecostals are relatively unaffected, but that is natural since, from their standpoint, charismatic renewal is just the rest of the church catching up with what they themselves have known for two generations.

The movement has spread far and fast. An educated guess is that something like twenty-five million Christians outside the Pentecostal churches have adopted a recognizably charismatic approach to Christian and church life.

What is that approach? It is a matter of embracing some, if not all, of the following items:

1. A hermeneutical claim that all elements of New Testament min- istry and experience may with propriety be hoped for, sought, and expected today, none of them having permanently ceased when the apostolic age ended.

2. An empirical claim that among the elements of New Testament ministry and experience now enjoyed within the renewal are (a) experi- ential post-conversion Spirit-baptism, as seen in Acts 2:1–4; 8:14–17; 10:44–46 with 11:15–17; 19:1–6; (b) tongues, understood as glossolalia (uttering language-like sounds) rather than xenolalia (speaking languages one never learned) and as given primarily for private devotional use; (c) interpretation of tongues, when spoken in public; (d) prophecy, under- stood as receiving and relaying messages directly from God; (e) miraculous healing through prayer; (f) deliverance from demonic influences through exorcism; and (g) words of knowledge, understood as supernatural disclosing of information about individuals to those who seek to minister to their needs.

3. A high valuation of one's own glossolalia as a personal prayer language, and deliberate, frequent use of it.

4. Emphasis on the church as the body of Christ, upheld and led on to maturity by the Holy Spirit through the mutual love and supernaturally empowered service of its members.

5. A concern to identify and harness each Christian's spiritual gift or gifts for body ministry.

6. Insistence that worship is central in the church's common life, and that the heart and climax of true worship is united praise as distinct from preaching and the Eucharist (which have been the historic focal centres of Protestant and Roman Catholic worship respectively).

7. The cultivation of a relaxed, leisurely, intimate, informal style of corporate worship, aimed at evoking feelings of awe and joy before the Lord and at expressing love and loyalty to him for his saving grace.

8. The use for this purpose of simple, repetitive choruses and 'renewal songs,' often consisting of biblical texts set to music in a modern folk idiom for performance with guitar accompaniment. Guitars may be reinforced by melody instruments and also by tambourines, bongos, and jazz drums, as in a dance band's rhythm section.

9. The congregational practice of 'singing in the Spirit' – that is, sustaining ad lib, and moving within, the full-close chord with which a hymn or song ends, vocalizing extemporarily and sometimes glossolalically in the process.

10. Encouragement of physical expression of the spirit of praise and prayer by raising hands, swinging the body, dancing, prostrating oneself, and other such gestures. Bodily movements of this kind are held to deepen worship by intensifying the mood being expressed, and thus to glorify God.

11. Expectation of prophecy in worship gatherings, either as an immediate on-the-spot message from God or as the remembered fruit of a vision or a dream, and the provision of opportunity to utter it to the congregation.

12. The typical perception of people both outside and inside the community of faith less as guilty sinners than as moral, spiritual, and emotional cripples, scarred, soured, and desperately needing deliverance from bondages in their inner lives; and the structuring of counselling and prayer ministries to meet their need, thus viewed.

13. The practice of prayer with laying on of hands, for all who desire it, as a regular conclusion to worship gatherings. Those who are sick, disabled, and troubled in mind are particularly urged to receive this ministry, and to expect benefit through it.

14. A counselling technique of leading pained, grieved, inhibited, and embittered souls to visualize Christ and involve him therapeutically in the reliving of their traumatic hurts, as a means to inner healing.

15. A confident assumption that it is not ordinarily God's will that any of his children should continue in pain, or in any mental and emotional state other than joy, and a consequent downplaying of the older Christian stress on the spiritual benefit of humbly accepted suffering.

16. An insistent claim that miraculous-looking 'signs and wonders' (especially 'healings') have evidential value that will convince modern Westerners of the truth and power of the gospel, and that 'signs and wonders' should therefore be sought from God by prayer in each congregation.

17. A firm belief that some, if not all, disturbed people with addictive enslavements (bondages) are under the influence of demons who must be detected and exorcised.

18. A commitment to aggressive evangelism, aimed at inducing the self-willed to repent and open their lives to Jesus Christ and his Holy Spirit.

19. Emphasis on the benefit of communal and community living; of prayerfully sharing all one's concerns with 'the body,' normally in small groups, and of accepting discipline and guidance from other Christians in authoritative mentor relationships.

20. Insistence that established patterns of personal and church life must always be open to change so that Holy Spirit life may find freer expression, and expectation that all Christians, fellowships, and congregations will need to make such change over and over again.

21. Expectant openness to divine guidance by prophecy, vision, and dreams.

22. Confidence that a shared charismatic experience and lifestyle unifies Protestants and Roman Catholics at a deeper level than that at which doctrine divides them.

23. A devotional temper of exuberant euphoria, expressing a sense of loving intimacy with the Father and the Son that has in it little self-assessment and self-criticism, but is affectionate and adoring in a happily childlike way.


## From all Angles

How should we bring this kaleidoscopic phenomenon into focus? Evaluation needs to be made from a number of angles.

Sociologically, the charismatic movement is a restrained, white, mid-dle-class reinvention of original working-class, black-style, 'holy roller' Pentecostalism, from which it has borrowed much of its theology. Its relative uninhibitedness frequently approaches, but rarely transgresses, the bounds of educated good taste.

Spiritually, it is a recognizable mutation of the Bible-based conver-sionist piety fostered in seventeenth-century Puritanism, in New Eng-land's Great Awakening, and in nineteenth-century Protestant missionary movement – the type of piety that is nowadays labelled 'evangelical.' Original Pentecostalism was an adaptation of this piety in its Wesleyan form, but Calvinistic charismatics are currently found in some strength.

Doctrinally, the renewal is in the mainstream of historic evangelical orthodoxy on the Trinity, the incarnation, the objectivity of Christ's atonement and the historicity of his resurrection, the need of regeneration by the Holy Spirit, personal fellowship with the Father and the Son as central to the life of faith, and the divine truth of the Bible. There is nothing eccentric about its basic teaching.

Culturally, the charismatic movement appears as a child of our time in its anti-traditionalism, its anti-intellectualism, its romantic emotionalism, desire for thrills and emotional highs, its narcissistic preoccupation with physical health and ease of mind, preference for folk-type music with poetically uncouth lyrics, and its cultivated informality. In all these respects, the renewal reflects the late twentieth-century Western world back at itself.

Theologically, charismaticism is a mixed bag, as witnesses this perceptive vignette by Richard Lovelace:

> The charismatic renewal continues to express the mystical spirituality of the Puritan and awakening eras, but often without the rational and theological checks against error and credulity maintained by evangelicals. As a consequence, charismatics have some of the problems of the radical spiritualists in the anabaptist and Puritan left wing. Gifts of the Spirit are more prominent than the call to sanctification. The charismatic garden has a luxuriant overgrowth of theological weeds, including the health-and-wealth gospel, the most virulent form of the American heresy that Christianity guarantees worldly success. A fuzzy and unstructured ecumenism lives side by side with rampant sectarianism.[1]

Granted, the renewal has an enviable track record of enlivening the spiritually dead and energizing the spiritually paralysed, but whether it commands the resources to lead them on to full-orbed Christian maturity is another matter. When the liturgical and pastoral innovations that initially channel the new life become routines as stylized as those they replaced, and the limitations listed by Lovelace are accepted as normal, is not some writing beginning to appear on the wall? And the question, How may the renewal be renewed? does not seem to have been faced as yet, let alone answered.

## Not from God?

But even if the charismatic movement has no more to give to the church than it has given already, it is surely strange that it should ever be dismissed as not 'from God' – that is, as manifesting throughout something other than God's grace, so that every element of it should be explained as merely human or actually demonic. Yet that verdict has on occasion been voiced. How should we respond?

Our first comment must be that such thinking is largely emotional and irrational. The human mind has an unhappy tendency to jump from specifics we dislike to blanket condemnations of the larger reality of which the specifics are part. Someone misbehaves once, so we tag him as a no-good forever. We think a store cheated us over one purchase, so we

---

[1] 'Evangelical Spirituality: A Church Historian's Perspective,' *Journal of the Evangelical Theological Society* 31, no. 1 [March 1988], p. 33.

resolve never to shop there again. Our car gives trouble, so we henceforth refuse all cars of that make. So, too, if charismatic phenomena offend our sense of social, liturgical, or theological propriety, and charismatic indi - viduals embarrass us and make us feel threatened, we are very apt to respond by abusing the whole movement and denying that there is anything of God in it at all. But how silly! And how nasty! This is a reaction of wounded pride and wilful prejudice, and as such is bad thinking in every way.

Our second comment must be that by biblical standards the negative verdict is impossible. This can be seen from an argument classically set out by Jonathan Edwards in the aftermath of the much-criticized Great Awakening, of which he became the prime defender. In *The Distinguishing Marks of a Work of the Spirit of God*, Edwards reasons as follows: Any movement that (1) exalts Jesus Christ as Son of God and Saviour, leading people to honour him as such; (2) opposes Satan's kingdom by weaning people from sin and worldliness; (3) teaches people to revere and trust the Bible as the Word of God; (4) makes people feel the urgency of eternal issues and the depth of their own lostness without Christ; and (5) stirs up in people new love of Christ and of others, must be a divine work at its heart, whatever disfigurements may appear on its surface, since these are effects that Satan and fallen humankind have no wish to induce, and in fact try to avoid. But the Great Awakening had these distinguishing marks; therefore, it was a work of God.

That the charismatic renewal has had the same fivefold effect is beyond dispute; therefore, it too must be adjudged a work of God. No doubt human folly breaks surface in it, as happens in all movements involving human excitement; no doubt Satan, whose nature and purpose is always to spoil any good God produces, keeps pace with God in it, engineering lunatic fanaticism within its ranks as he did in the Great Awakening. But to diagnose human and satanic disfigurements of this contemporary work of God is altogether different from seeing it as intrinsically the fruit of psychological freakiness or satanic malice.

Our third comment must be that aspects of the renewal raise real theological problems that should not be ignored or glossed over, even if the movement as a whole is given a relatively clean bill of health. We need to reflect on some of these:

1. Charismatics sometimes claim that their distinctive doctrines are proved true by the blessing that God gives through the teaching of them and the ministry based on them. This, however, is a mistake. Because God is gracious, those who seek him with their whole hearts find his blessing even if their thoughts about that blessing are, and remain, askew. The deadening effect of views that keep people from seeking blessings that are there for them (for instance, medieval teaching on faith, which by telling folk to trust themselves to the church stopped them from seeking assured forgiveness from Christ's own hand) is

obvious; but that is not the problem here. If charismatics err, they err only by expecting to receive from God, whose face they seek, more than he has actually promised. Whether the expectations of charismatics are biblically realistic and whether they really receive what they expect are open questions, but the certainty that God meets and blesses all who seek him in honest and hearty prayer is beyond all question. Scripture is explicit on that.[2] Striking answers to humble prayers do not, however, guarantee that one's understanding of God's promises is correct, or that God means these striking answers to become the rule rather than remain the exception.

2. Sharing charismatic experience is often declared, as we noted earlier, to unify Protestants and Roman Catholics at a deeper level than that at which their doctrine divides them. This, if so, gives charismaticism great ecumenical significance, but for some the mere making of such a claim destroys the credibility of the renewal as a work of God. I am, myself, a Protestant who finds the official papacy and its trappings grotesque, and official Roman Catholic teaching on the church's infallible authority, on the Mass, and on Mary grossly and grievously mistaken, and therefore I sympathize with those for whom this charismatic claim demonstrates that at its heart the renewal is unspiritual and blind. But I do not accept the critics' assumption that if the love and reverence for Scripture that charismatic experience evokes was truly from God it would lead Romanists to question these doctrines and the system that maintains them in the way that Protestants do.

Everyone observes that Protestant charismatics are concerned for the church not as a confessing and theologizing institution, but as a worship - ping and serving fellowship. And we also observe that the renewal among Protestants is a pietistic phenomenon, interdenominational because un - denominational, concerned, first, with the spiritual life that flows from a living relationship to each person of the godhead in saving grace, and, second, with fruitful fellowship and outreach on the part of those who have thus come to life.

Unsurprisingly, the same is true of Roman Catholics. They had their reasons for being Roman before they met the renewal, and part of the Catholic package is that the institutional church has the last and decisive word in biblical interpretation, so that using Scripture to challenge church teaching is off limits. So one should not treat the failure of renewed Roman Catholics to mount such a challenge as evidence that their experience, and the movement that midwifed it, are somehow spiritually phony.

The truth is that charismatic ecumenism, if we are to call it that (and many do), is a limited and truncated thing, just because charismatics put

---

[2] See 2 Chron. 7:14; 15:2, 12–15; Ps. 9:10; 24:3–6; 27:7–14; 70:4; 119:2, 58; Prov. 8:17; Jer. 29:13, Matt. 6:33; 7:7–11.

all their energy into transdenominational concerns and leave questions of official church teaching and structures on one side. I personally believe that developing a shared spirituality is far and away the most constructive and necessary form of ecumenical action that can be taken in the world church today. But that does not mean that charismatic renewal constitutes a full-orbed ecumenism just because it majors in spirituality. Someday in the future, divergences of belief between and within churches will have to be discussed again; they are the present issues that cannot be shelved indefinitely. In the meantime, however, the fact that the professedly Bible-based renewal shelves church questions should not be held to destroy its claim to be a genuine work of God, embodying and projecting for popular consumption a significant form of ecumenical piety. That claim must be decided on other grounds.

3. The charismatic insistence that what are sometimes called 'sign-gifts' (tongues and interpretation, healing gifts, prophecy, words of wisdom and knowledge) are still given, with its corollary that those who do not seek them miss something important, raises problems. Paul speaks of 'signs, wonders and miracles' as 'things that mark an apostle.' [3] Hebrews 2:34 speaks of them as confirming the apostles' testimony, and the Book of Acts knows them only in connection with the apostles' personal ministry. The common assumption that God withdrew the 'sign-gifts' after the apostolic age cannot, perhaps, be proved, but it cannot be disproved, either.

It is gratuitous to take for granted that every form of God's working in New Testament times is meant to be reproduced today: Who among us nowadays raises the dead? And comparisons of contemporary charis-matic phenomena with their alleged New Testament prototypes is inconclusive. New Testament tongues were used in public, and there is no single unambiguous statement that they were ever used any other way. But charismatics value their tongues as a private prayer language. Can they, then, be an identical manifestation?

Again, it cannot be made plausible that New Testament interpretation of tongues and prophecy corresponded exactly to the phenomena that go by those names today, nor is it at all likely that the 'word' ('message,' NIV) of wisdom and knowledge in 1 Corinthians 12:8 corresponded to the (apparently) sanctified telepathy that goes by those names today. And the immediate, organic, large-scale, and uniformly successful healings as-cribed to Christ and the apostles in the New Testament are certainly not matched by the frequently abortive efforts of present-day healing minis-tries. The claim that the apostolic 'sign-gifts' continue is thus more than can be proved, and the verdict that charismatic manifestations are from God can only be reached by first acknowledging that they have no exact New Testament precedent and then judging them on the basis of their

---

[3] 2 Cor. 12:12.

effect on people's moral and spiritual lives. Charismatics need to recognize this.[4]

4. Charismatics view Spirit baptism as a necessary post-conversion experience, which God always models on the apostles' experience re-corded in Acts 2:1–4 and identifies to its latter-day recipients by the gift of glossolalia. This thesis, borrowed from mainstream Pentecostalism, also raises problems.

What is at issue is not whether the Holy Spirit initiates and sustains states of mind in believers in which the love of the Father and the Son, the power of the Spirit himself, and the reality of spiritual evil are vividly grasped. Not only Pentecostal-charismatic accounts of Spirit baptism, but all mainstream Christian accounts of 'infused' communion with God are given in these terms, and believers of all traditions follow the lead of the Psalms in asking God to grant and deepen this kind of experience. Nor is the issue whether the Spirit ever bestows mountain-peak moments of assurance, or ever induces glossolalia by his loving pressure upon us; we know, or should know, that on occasion he does both, and sometimes (not always) simultaneously.

What is in question is precisely this: whether Luke's narrative of Pentecost is teaching us that Christians who lack one such momentary experience, marked by tongues, are second-rate and not fully filled with the Holy Spirit whatever else they may have experienced and done; or, putting it differently, whether Acts 2:1–4 is a revealed experiential norm for us all, as official Pentecostalism affirms. Against the claim that it is, I bring the following arguments.

(a) This is nowhere stated or implied in Acts, nor anywhere else in Scripture.

(b) The claim is inconsistently made by those who make it. If the apostles spoke known languages at their Pentecost, why is not the same expected of us at ours? On what basis is glossolalia, which is not the speaking of known languages, accepted as a substitute? And why is not hearing a tornado sound and seeing fiery tongues, as the apostles did, required as part of the prescribed experience? If Acts 2:1–4 is to be taken strictly as the norm of Spirit baptism, no one today experiences Spirit baptism at all. If, however, the post-conversion experience of God's integrating and empowering love through Christ is to be called Spirit baptism, as being somewhat like the apostles' experience on Pentecost morning, then Acts 2:1–4 is not strictly a norm – only a case of partial similarity: But if that is so, it would be better not to label this particular Christian experience 'Spirit baptism' at all. Used thus unbiblically, the label can only confuse.

---

[4] I have been here applying the principle insisted on by Edwards in his *Thoughts on the Revival of Religion in New England (1742)*; see *Edwards on Revival* (Edinburgh: Banner of Truth, 1994). I have discussed 'sign-gifts' more fully in *Keep in Step with the Spirit* (Old Tappan, N.J.: F. H. Revell, 1984), pp. 200–34.

(c) The reason why the apostles' experience of the new covenant ministry of the Spirit began at Pentecost, after they came to faith, was not personal but dispensational. It had nothing to do with the quality or specific acts of their previous discipleship, but with the dawning of a new era of human enjoyment of God's grace here on earth. Nowhere in the world was the Spirit's new covenant ministry operative till nine o'clock on Pentecost morning. The apostles' two-stage experience was thus unique to themselves and is not a norm for us. The New Testament norm is stated in Peter's Pentecost sermon: All who believe and repent receive the Holy Spirit in the fullness of his enhanced ministry right at the outset. [5] In line with this, Paul refers to Spirit baptism as one aspect of our initiation into Christ at conversion[6] and insists that all who are Christ's have the Spirit from the start.[7]

(d) Acts 4:8, 31; 6:3, 5; 7:55; 9:17; 11:24 and 13:9, 52 all speak of persons being filled with, or full of, the Spirit, with no reference to tongues as accompanying that fullness. But if some were Spirit-filled without glossolalia then, some may also be now.

(e) Luke records four cases of 'pentecostal' manifestations – one involving Jesus' disciples,[8] one involving Samaritans,[9] one involving Gentile 'God-fearers,'[10] and one involving Ephesian followers of John the Baptist.[11] The design of Acts makes it natural to think that he does this to exhibit God's acceptance on equal footing in the church of four different groups whose togetherness in Christ might otherwise have been doubted. Nothing suggests that his purpose is to establish norms of complete Christian experience for all; the impression left, rather, is that these manifestations were exceptional signs from God, not matched in the experience of other believers. Certainly, the burden of proof rests on anyone who would argue the contrary.

While believing, then, that through the Spirit many Christians experience intense moments of joyful assurance, and glossolalia becomes for some an authentic mode of praise and prayer, I reject the opinion that Acts 2:1–4 exhibits an experience that every Christian needs, and that God calls every Christian to seek, promising that those who seek will find. By the same token I reject the view that those who cannot testify to this experience necessarily live on a lower plane than those who can.

---

[5]  Acts 2:38.
[6]  1 Cor. 12:13.
[7]  Rom. 8:9.
[8]  Acts 2:1–4.
[9]  Acts 8:14–17.
[10]  Acts 10:11–17.
[11]  Acts 19:1–7.

## Test Everything

Now we must draw the threads together.

The charismatic renewal has brought millions of Christians, including many clergy, to a deeper, more exuberant faith in Christ than they had before. It has quickened thousands of congregations, invigorating their worship, making love and fellowship blossom among them, increasing their expectancy and enterprise, and giving a stimulus to their evangelism. Charismatic insistence on openness to God has transformed countless lives that previously were not open to him. Is this from God? The question answers itself.

The pride and folly of triumphalism and the schismatic temper threaten the movement constantly, however, and need to be watched against unceasingly. Some things in the renewal are magnificent, but others are not right yet, and the liveliest Christian movements are naturally the objects of Satan's most diligent attention.

Some attitudes to the renewal, however, among Christians not in-volved in it, are not right either, and Satan loves to lure Christians into opposing the work of God. So the word to Christians both inside and outside the charismatic movement would seem to be: 'Do not put out the Spirit's fire . . . Test everything. Hold on to the good. Avoid every kind of evil . . . The grace of our Lord Jesus Christ be with you.' [12] Let all the people say, Amen!

---

[12]  1 Thess. 5:19–22, 28.

# Chapter 12

# Theological Reflections on the Charismatic Movement

## I

My subject is a complex and still developing phenomenon which over the past generation has significantly touched the entire world church, Roman Catholic, Orthodox, Anglican and non-Episcopal Protestant, at all levels of life and personnel and across a wide theological spectrum. [1] Sometimes it is called Neo-Pentecostalism because, like the older Pentecostalism which 'spread like wildfire over the whole world' [2] at the start of this century, it affirms Spirit-baptism as a distinct post-conversion, post-water-baptism experience, universally needed and universally available to those who seek it.

---

THEOLOGICAL REFLECTIONS ON THE CHARISMATIC MOVEMENT was originally published in *Churchman*, XCIV 1980, 1 and 2, 7–25. Reprinted by permission.

[1] Best surveys: Walter J. Hollenweger, *The Pentecostals* (London: SCM, and Minneapolis: Augsburg, 1972), a magisterial profile of old and new Pentecostalism together, marred only by an obtuse anti-fundamentalism; Richard Quebedeaux, *The New Charismatics* (New York: Doubleday, 1976), a well-informed descriptive report; Edward D. O'Connor, *The Pentecostal Movement in the Catholic Church* (Notre Dame: Ave Maria Press, 1971); Kevin and Dorothy Ranaghan, *Catholic Pentecostals* (New York: Paulist Press, and London: Fountain Trust, 1969); Michael P. Hamilton (ed.), *The Charismatic Movement* (Grand Rapids: Eerdmans, 1975), a balanced set of analytical studies, pro and con, with a gramophone record of glossolalia thrown in. Most useful bibliographies: on Pentecostal churches past and present, Hollenweger, op. cit., pp. 523–57; on Pentecostal origins and history in N. America, Vinson Synan, *The Holiness-Pentecostal Movement in the United States* (Grand Rapids: Eerdmans, 1971), pp. 225–39; on the charismatic movement among Protestants, Quebedeaux, op. cit., pp. 223–42; on the Catholic charismatic renewal, Edward D. O'Connor, in Edward D. O'Connor (ed.), *Perspectives on Charismatic Renewal* (Notre Dame: University of Notre Dame Press, 1978), pp. 145–84.

[2] Hollenweger, op. cit., p. 63.

The movement has grown, however, independently of the Pentecostal denominations, whose suspicions of its non-separatist inclusiveness have been – and in some quarters remain – deep, and its own preferred name for itself today is 'charismatic renewal.'[3] For it sees itself as a revitalizing re-entry into a long-lost world of gifts and ministries of the Holy Spirit, a re-entry which immeasurably deepens individual spiritual lives, and through which all Christendom may in due course find quickening. Charismatic folk everywhere stand on tiptoe, as it were, in excited expectation of great things in store for the church as the movement increasingly takes hold.

Already its spokesmen claim for it major ecumenical significance. 'This movement is the most unifying in Christendom today,' writes Michael Harper; 'only in this movement are all streams uniting, and all ministries being accepted and practised.'[4] The claim is true: apart from Sri Lanka and North India, all the main union schemes of the sixties (Anglican-Methodist in England, Anglican-United Church in Canada, the multi - lateral Nigerian and New Zealand plans, and the huge Consultation on Church Union [COCU] in the USA) effectively collapsed, and it is a common complaint that ecumenical energy of the conventional sort is waning; but trans-denominational charismatic fellowship, with its inter - national leadership and attendant linking organizations,[5] goes from

---

[3] 'At first, Neo-Pentecostals called their emerging movement a "Charismatic revival" – heralding the restoration of the charismata to the life of the contemporary church. Soon, however, the term "revival" was generally replaced with 'renewal' to 1) dissociate the movement from revivalistic fundamentalism and 2) link it with the larger goal of not only reintroducing spiritual gifts to the historic denominations, but also of relating the charismata to spiritual and institutional Christian renewal more inclusively and comprehensively.' (Quebedeaux, op. cit., p. 116).

[4] M. Harper, *None can Guess* (London: Hodder & Stoughton, and Plainfield: Logos, 1971), pp. 149, 153. Harper provides an interesting profile of the movement, as he sees it from inside, in *Three Sisters* (Wheaton: Tyndale House, 1979).

[5] Leaders and organizations are surveyed in Quebedeaux, op. cit., chaps. 3 and 4. Internationally prominent are Dennis Bennett (Anglican), under whom charismatic life first blossomed in California in 1960; Graham Pulkingham (Anglican), Harald Bredeson (Reformed Church), Howard Ervin (Baptist), Larry Christenson (Lutheran), all linked with the Californian movement from the start; Michael Harper (Anglican: 'editor and theoretician,' as Quebedeaux calls him), who founded the Fountain Trust in 1964 and the journal *Renewal* in 1966; David du Plessis ('Mr. Pentecost'), senior statesman among the Pentecostal churches; Ralph Wilkerson (Assemblies of God), founder, pastor and director of Melodyland Christian Centre, a combined church, seminary and conference headquarters opposite Disneyland in the Los Angeles conurbation; Leon Joseph Cardinal

strength to strength. Ecumenically, its technique is distinctive; it seeks first and foremost to realise oneness in Christ experientially, in celebration and ministry, confident that theological convergence will follow.

> This open stance [writes Richard Quebedeaux] 'whereby the Holy Spirit is seen to lead people to theological truth *following* (rather than prerequisite to) a common experience, is clearly ascendant throughout Neo-Pentecostalism; it is one reason why [in it] evangelicals, liberals and Roman Catholics have been joined together (spiritually, at least) for the first time.'[6]

Though in each 'mainline' denomination charismatics are a relatively small minority, the movement's cumulative impact is considerable, and is likely to be greater rather than less as the future unfolds.

Writing in 1953, before the current charismatic renewal began, Lesslie Newbigin typecast the Protestant and Catholic views of the church as 'the congregation of the faithful' and 'the body of Christ' respectively, and went on to describe the Christianity of the Pentecostal churches as an authentic third stream of Christian awareness, embodying a view of the church as 'the community of the Holy Spirit.' This, he said, is now needed to fertilize and irrigate the other two views. He put his point as a question:

> May it not be that the great churches of the Catholic and Protestant traditions will have to be humble enough to receive [a new understanding of the Holy Spirit] in fellowship with their brethren in the various groups of the Pente-costal type with whom at present they have scarcely any fellowship at all?[7]

Newbigin's question still looms, and with an extended application, as we survey the pervasive phenomenon of charismatic renewal a quarter of a century later.

-----

[5] *(continued)* Suenens, Roman Catholic Archbishop of Malines-Brussels; Arnold Bittlinger (Lutheran), a pastor of the United Church of the Palatinate, West Germany; among many others.

Backing organizations include the world-wide and very wealthy Full Gospel Business Men's Fellowship International (FGBMFI), a laymen's organization founded in 1953 by the American Pentecostal millionaire dairyman Demos Shakarian for world evangelization with Spirit baptism and healing. Among successful 'house journals' for the movement have been *Trinity*, *Renewal*, *Full Gospel Business Men's Voice* and *Logos Journal*.

Widely-selling charismatic authors include Bennett, Harper, Christenson, Merlin Carothers, David Wilkerson, John L. Sherrill, and David Watson. Leading publishers of charismatic material include Hodder & Stoughton (London) and Logos International (Plainsfield, New Jersey).

[6] Op. cit., p. 111.

[7] L. Newbigin, *The Household of God* (London: SCM Press, 1954), 110.

## II

What are the distinctive contentions of this transdenominational, cross-traditional movement?

The first thing to say is that, in relation to the creeds and confessions of their own churches, charismatics usually have nothing distinctive to say at all. They appear as theological primitives, recalling their churches not only to apostolic Christian experience but also to the 'old paths' of supernaturalist belief. They are 'sound' (though perhaps superficial) on the Trinity,[8] the incarnation, the objective significance of the atonement and the divine authority of the Bible,[9] and they see Christianity conven-tionally in terms of the three traditional R's – Ruin, Redemption and Regeneration. But theological reflection does not turn them on; they know that this is not what their movement is really about. Their biblical exposition is simple to the point of naiveté, and few of them seem to know or care that in their own ranks different theologies of charismatic experience are promoted.

In their own denominations, their concern is not so much to rethink inherited traditions, doctrinal and devotional, as to reanimate them: so Roman Catholics pray the Mass, invoke the Virgin (whom they view as a pioneer charismatic), and run through the rosary with renewed ardour, while Anglicans rejoice to find that Cranmer's liturgy is now marvellously alive for them. ('Every word of it glows,' a middle-aged woman said to me.) Generally speaking, and ignoring the centrifugal lunatic fringe which every lively movement in this fallen world produces sooner or later, charismatics are loyal denominationalists who, taking as their starting-point what their church professes, devote their thoughts, prayers and efforts to revitalizing its practice. And it is in connection with the

---

[8] Quebedeaux reports that 'there are now even a few Unitarian-Universalist Charismatics' (op. cit., p. 127). This would seem to illustrate the assertion that the renewal experience does not ordinarily affect one's commitment to the doctrines of one's church: though it also prompts questions about the nature of the experience, at least in this particular case. Hollenweger (op. cit., pp. 31f., 71, 311f.) tells of the 'Jesus only' Pentecostal churches which apparently hold a modalist doctrine of the Trinity, but this fruit of naive Bible-searching has no counterpart in the charismatic movement. For the history of Pentecostal unitarianism, see Synan, op. cit., pp. 153–63.

[9] Charismatic experience regularly intensifies the sense of the divine authority of Scripture (which is what a believer in the Reformed doctrine of the Spirit's inner witness to Scripture [*testimonium internum Spiritus Sancti*] would expect where a genuine experience of the Spirit has taken place). Quebedeaux cites Jean Stone (lay leader in California, 1960–66), as saying in 1962: 'The Lord appears to be making a lot of Episcopalian Fundamentalists in these end time days!' (op. cit., p. 149; cf. Hollenweger, op. cit., p. 5).

revitalizing of practice through the renewing of experience that the charismatic distinctives are voiced.

They are five in number, and though each of the five is affirmed with a wide variety of emphasis, sophistication and flexibility, and fitted into various theological schemes according to who is speaking, they stand together as in broad terms the ideological masthead of charismatic renewal all the world over. They are as follows:

### 1) A decisive enriching of personal Christian experience

It is claimed that usually, if not invariably, a momentous divine work takes place in each Christian's experience some time after they have begun actively to respond to God. This work differs in idea from both conversion as understood by evangelical Protestants, and baptismal incorporation into Christ as traditionally understood by Catholic sacramentalists, Roman, Orthodox and Anglican. Usually (so the claim runs) this blessing needs to be sought from God specifically, and perhaps at length (though this belief characterizes the old Pentecostalism rather than the new, which more often stresses the immediate availability of the Spirit's fullness). The name usually given to it, commonly though not invariably on the basis that the New Testament phraseology echoed does in fact refer to this second work of grace, is baptism in, or with, or by, the Holy Spirit. [10]

Spirit-baptism is ordinarily expounded as a vast intensifying of the Christian's consciousness of four things: 1) the sovereign love to him of the God who through redemption and adoption has become his heavenly Father, and his own consequent privilege as an heir of glory, and in a real sense already a possessor and inhabitant of heaven; 2) the closeness and

---

[10]  Historically, the first evangelicals to speak of baptism(s) of the Spirit for the increase of love, zeal and power for life and service were Wesley's designated successor, John Fletcher of Madeley (*Works*, New York, 1851, II: 356, 632–69, IV: 230–32), and his wife Mary (see G. H. Williams and Edith Waldvogel in Hamilton (ed.), *The Charismatic Movement*, p. 81). Fletcher, with Wesley, saw the Christian life as a two-stage process in which full inward sanctity (Christian perfection, perfect love, cleansing of the heart, entire sanctification) is given experientially some time after conversion, and he envisaged Spirit-baptisms following sanctification as needed and as sought. Early North American Pentecostalism, which grew out of the Methodist holiness tradition, posited one Spirit-baptism only but then split over whether it was a third experience following the 'second blessing' of sanctification, or a second, the 'finished work' of sanctification having been wrought, at least in principle, at conversion. The latter view ('Baptist' as distinct from 'Wesleyan') is now that of the Assemblies of God, the largest Pentecostal denomination, and of a statistical majority of North American Pentecostals (cf. Hollenweger, op. cit., pp. 24ff., 29, 47; Synan, op. cit., pp. 147–53), and all latter-day charismatics appear to assume it.

adequacy of Jesus Christ the Lord as his living, loving Saviour, Master and Friend; 3) the indwelling, enabling and supportive power of the Holy Spirit in all dimensions and depths of his personal life; 4) the reality of the demonic (personal evil), and of spiritual conflict with 'the world-rulers of this darkness' (Eph. 6:12) as a basic element in Christian life and service.

This account is strikingly parallel to the experience of the Spirit's sealing described by the seventeenth-century Puritan Thomas Good - win,[11] to the experience of 'perfect love,' or 'entire sanctification' ('scrip - tural holiness' and 'Christian perfection') taught by John Wesley in the eighteenth century and by Wesleyan conservatives from that day to this;[12] to the experience of 'baptism in the Holy Spirit' as an enduring of the Christian with power for service, which such nineteenth-century Ameri - can teachers as Charles G. Finney, Asa Mahan, A. B. Simpson, D. L. Moody and R. A. Torrey described;[13] and to the so-called 'Keswick experience' of being 'filled with the Holy Spirit' through consecration and faith for victory over all known sin, as described in the late nineteenth and early twentieth century by such Americans as W. E. Boardman and Hannah Whitall Smith and such Englishmen as the Anglican Evan Hopkins and the Baptist F. B. Meyer.[14]

---

[11] T. Goodwin, *Works*, ed. J. C. Miller (London, 1861), 1:227–52 (sermons on Eph. 1:13).

[12] Wesley set out his view in 'A Plain Account of Christian Perfection' (various revisions, 1739–77; *Works*, ed. T. Jackson, London, 1872, pp. 366–488); it is well summarized in F. D. Bruner, *A Theology of the Holy Spirit* (Grand Rapids: Eerdmans, 1970, and London: Hodder & Stoughton, 1971), pp. 323–32. 'A gradual work of grace constantly precedes the instantaneous work of both justification and sanctification . . . As after a gradual conviction of the guilt and power of sin you was (sic) justified in a moment, so after a gradually increasing conviction of inbred sin you will be sanctified in a moment.' (*The letters of the Rev. John Wesley*, ed. John Telford, Letter of 21 June 1784; London: Epworth Press, 1931, VII: 221f.).

[13] In his *Memoirs* (New York, 1876), pp. 17f., Finney tells how he wept and 'bellowed out the unutterable gushings' of his soul when he received a baptism of the Spirit in 1821; Mahan describes his experience extensively in Part II of *Out of Darkness into Light* (London, 1875); in 1871 Moody 'dropped to the floor and lay bathing his soul in the divine' while his room 'seemed ablaze with God' (W. R. Moody, *The Life of Dwight L. Moody*, New York, 1900, pp. 146f.); A. B. Simpson expounded the baptism as 'power to receive the life of Christ' in *The Holy Spirit, or Power from on High* (Harrisburg, 1896). Torrey's exposition is in *The Person and Work of the Holy Spirit* (London: Nisbet, 1910), pp. 213–37. Bruner summarizes his views, op. cit., pp. 335–37.

[14] W. E. Boardman, *The Higher Christian Life* (Boston, 1859); Hannah Whitall Smith, *The Christian's Secret of a Happy Life* (New York, 1870); Evan H. Hopkins, *The Law of Liberty in the Spiritual Life* (London, 1884); on Boardman and Mrs.

It has much in common, too, with spiritual intimacies recorded by exponents of the Christian mystical tradition, Catholic and Protestant, as well as by such reticent and ordinarily unmystical people as the Anglican Bishop Moorhouse of Melbourne and Manchester, who in a testimony written for posthumous publication spoke of the night when, in the year before his ordination, after anxious prayer for closer communion with God, he

> awoke filled with the most marvellous happiness, in such a state of exultation that I felt as though a barrier had fallen, as though a door had suddenly been opened, and a flood of golden light poured in upon me, transfiguring me completely. I have never felt anything in the least like it . . .[15]

What these similarities may mean we shall consider later; for the moment, we simply note that they are there.

### 2) Speaking in tongues

Glossolalia (uttering sounds unintelligible to oneself)[16] is claimed to be the usual accompaniment and sign of baptism in the Holy Spirit.[17] It is seen

---

[14] *(continued)* Smith. cf. B. B. Warfield, 'The "Higher life" Movement,' in *Perfectionism* (Grand Rapids: Baker, 1958), pp. 216–311: on 'Keswick,' cf. Steven Barabas, *So Great Salvation* (London: Marshall, Morgan & Scott and Grand Rapids: Eerdmans, 1953); on F. B. Meyer. cf. Bruner, op. cit., pp. 340f.

[15] E. C. Rickards, *Bishop Moorhouse of Melbourne and Manchester* (London: John Murray, 1920), pp. 15f. The account continues: 'At the time I did not think of it as Christ, but as God the Father: but now I see that he manifested himself through Christ.' In a description of the same experience written in a letter when he was 83, Moorhouse said: 'To prevent myself from crying aloud in my joy, I was obliged to wrap myself in my bedclothes. And for days this divine rapture lasted . . . it made me love everyone intensely . . . it was heaven . . . I had been in heaven' (pp. 245f.).

[16] For clarity, glossolalia (uttering sounds unintelligible to anyone) should be distinguished from xenolalia or xenoglossia (speaking a language one has not learned and does not know oneself to be speaking). Isolated cases of xenolalia in charismatic circles, in the older Pentecostalism and earlier (cf. Bennett and Williams in *The Charismatic Movement* pp. 27ff., 69ff.; R. W. Harris, *Spoken by the Spirit* (Springfield: Gospel Publishing House, 1973); Don Basham, *The Miracle of Tongues* (Old Tappan: Revell, 1973)) seem solidly attested; I believe myself to have verified one such. But most Pentecostal and charismatic tongue-speaking has been glossolalia, lacking any discernible language structure (see Quebedeaux, op. cit., pp. 199–203, and the academic literature there cited).

[17] Following the first Pentecostals, and the defined doctrine of such major Pentecostal bodies as the Assemblies of God, most Protestant and some Catholic

as a God–given capacity for prayer and praise; valuable because, as experience shows, it enables worshippers to sustain and indeed heighten moods of adoration, penitence, petition and intercession in a way they could not do otherwise. The gift is regarded as mainly, though not entirely, for private devotional use.

Subjectively, it is a matter of letting one's vocal chords run free as one lifts one's heart to God, and, as with learning to swim, confidence in entrusting oneself to the medium (the water in the one case, babbling utterance in the other) has much to do with one's measure of success and enjoyment. Glossolalia is not, as is often thought (and as the NEB mistranslations in 1 Corinthians 14 suggest [18]), an ecstatic thing: 'Christian speaking in tongues is done as objectively as any other speaking, while the person is in full possession and control of his wits and volition, and in no strange state of mind whatever' [19] and, once the novelty has worn off, 'at times the glossolalia feels a singular *lack* of emotion while speaking

---

[17] *(continued)* charismatics claim that glossolalia is the invariable sign of Spirit-baptism. Their point is plainly nullified, however, if linked, as it sometimes is, to direct instruction on how to start speaking in tongues. Other Catholic charis-matics deny the claim: 'Some people begin speaking in tongues at the moment of the baptism. Others do not begin until hours, days, or even weeks later, and some never do' (O'Connor, *The Pentecostal Movement in the Catholic Church*, p. 134). Josephine Massyngberde Ford censures 'The Team Manual' for the Life of the Spirit Seminars, by a fellow Roman Catholic, for making the quest for tongues integral to seeking Spirit-baptism:

> 'It would seem that tongues are of very special importance to those who prepared this manual and that their stress on this gift, together with various techniques which they employ to induce tongues, and the importance of the authority figure . . . presents an enormous risk of hypnosis followed by regression of the ego and personality transference. My own advice would be to abstain from this emphasis, these techniques, and from praying over people for tongues, and to leave the gift entirely to the Holy Spirit. I believe that there is a genuine gift of tongues bestowed by God without human intervention.' (*The Charismatic Movement*, pp. 122f.).

[18] Eleven times in 1 Cor. 14 (verses 2, 4, 5, 6, 9, 13, 18, 19, 23, 26, 27), and in 12:28, 13:8, NEB renders glossa(i) as tongues of ecstasy or ecstatic speech. O'Connor's observation is on target: 'The New Testament nowhere describes prayer in tongues as "ecstatic utterance." That term has been coined by modern scholars in their efforts to conjecture what the gift must have been like. The experience of the Pentecostal movement suggests that their guess-work has been ill-advised' (op. cit., p. 126).

[19] Bennett, in *The Charismatic Movement*, p. 32. Bennett is warding off the idea that Christian glossolalia is schizophrenic, hypnotic or demonic in origin.

in tongues.'[20] Usually, though not invariably, glossolalia persists in the experience of those who have once begun it, as a mode of prayer which seems real and right for them, into which they can slip at will; and though they allow it to be a lesser gift, according to Paul's estimate in 1 Corin - thians 14:1–19,[21] yet they prize it because of the devotional help it brings them. Whether one's first entry into it was spontaneous and involuntary, or by learning a vocal technique for it (both happen), does not affect its devotional value once one can manage it.

### 3) Spiritual gifts

Understanding gifts as capacities to express and communicate the knowl - edge and power of Christ for the edifying of the church (which certainly seems to be Paul's concept of a *charisma*),[22] charismatics usually claim that all the 'sign-gifts' (so-called) of the New Testament period – not only tongues, but also gifts of interpretation, miracles, healing powers, and the receiving of direct communications from God through visions, dreams and inward impressions for relaying as prophecy – are now once more being given, after centuries of almost total abeyance. That the more ordinary gifts of teaching, rule, management, giving and supporting [23] have been constantly bestowed down the Christian centuries, and are being given still, is not denied. Nonetheless, the renewal of 'sign-gifts' is seen as, so to speak, icing on the church's cake, showing that at this point unbelief and apathy – the result of mistakenly assuming that these gifts were permanently withdrawn when the apostolic age closed – have now given place to eager and expectant faith which God honours according to the dominical formula 'according to your faith be it done to you.' [24]

Persons baptized in the Holy Spirit, it is urged, ordinarily receive several gifts, and no Christian is entirely giftless. Therefore, every

---

[20]  Richard Baer, quoted by Ford, in *The Charismatic Movement*, p. 115.

[21]  That Paul in this passage discourages tongues in Christian gatherings so as to make way for intelligible speech is well shown by C. W. Parnell, *Understanding Tongues-Speaking* (Johannesburg: S. African Baptist Press, 1972), pp. 74–81. On 'I want you all to speak in tongues' (v.5), O'Connor rightly says: 'This text cannot be used as an argument that everyone ought to speak in tongues, since Paul has expressly declared . . . that the Holy Spirit does not give this or any other of the charisms to all men but only to some (1 Cor. 12:4, 10, 11, 30). Rather, this is a concessive clause . . . the sense of the passage is, "The gift of tongues is always good, but prophecy is better" ' (op. cit., p. 125).

[22]  Cf. Arnold Bittlinger, *Gifts and Graces: a Commentary on 1 Cor. 12–14* (London: Hodder & Stoughton, 1967); *Gifts and Ministries* (Grand Rapids: Eerdmans, 1973).

[23]  Cf. Rom. 12:4ff.; 1 Cor. 12:28–30.

[24]  Matt. 9:29.

member ministry, achieved by discerning and harnessing each Christian's gifts, should become standard practice throughout the body of
Christ on earth, and congregational behaviour-patterns must be sufficiently decentralized, flexible and leisurely to permit and not inhibit
this. All gifts are for building up the body and must be regulated in
exercise for the furthering of that purpose, according to Paul's 'body-
model' of diverse functions expressing mutual care. [25] In the first days of
the charismatic renewal, there was some reason to fear that interest was
limited to forming clusters of quickened individuals apart from the
churches in the manner of the now-deceased Oxford Group; but
charismatic leaders and their followers have during the past decade made
it abundantly clear that the revitalizing of the church as such is central
in their prayers and purposes, and unity in the Spirit, not division, is
their goal. If there are cantankerous and disruptive charismatics, it is
enough to say that this is despite the teaching they are given, not because
of it, and to point out that in any case the charismatic community has
no monopoly of this particular character type.

### 4) *Worship in the Spirit*

Worshipping God should be a personal realizing of fellowship with the
Father and the Son through the Spirit, and thereby a realizing of spiritual
community with the rest of God's assembled family. As Jesus Christ must
be central in all worship as the Mediator and Redeemer, who with the
Father and the Spirit is loved and adored, so worshippers must constantly
seek to grasp and explore their God-given identity in the family where
they are all God's children and Jesus Christ is their elder brother. So when
the congregation meets, the liturgical structure of worship must be loose
enough to allow for spontaneous contributions, and sufficiently relaxed,
informal and slow-moving to let all bask in the sense of togetherness with
God and each other.

   Different charismatic communities work for this in different ways, but
the goal is common; and in general it is true that both in its pace and in
its way of highlighting points by repetition, slightly varied but not much,
charismatic worship is to, say, historic Anglican and Roman Catholic
liturgical forms as Bruckner is to Haydn or the later Wagner to Mozart.
Perhaps it would not be wholly misleading to call charismatic worship
romantic, concentrating on the expression of responsive attitudes and

---

[25]  See 1 Cor. 12:4–26.

   This emphasis, always characteristic of the Brethren movement and recently
prominent in the ecumenical theology of the laity, was not a main feature of the
old Pentecostalism. The late Alan Stibbs (d. 1971) is gratefully remembered by
many as an Anglican pioneer of it. Cf. J. I. Packer, 'The Holy Spirit and the Local
Congregation,' in *The Churchman*, June 1964, pp. 98–108.

feelings, whereas the older liturgical style is classical, exalting God and uplifting worshippers by its majestic excellence of form. [26] At all events, charismatic worship aims above all to achieve genuine openness to God at the deepest level of our personal being, so that each worshipper will move beyond the mere churning over of notions to find God himself, and to celebrate and enjoy the realities of life in him. For this, so charismatics insist, time is needed and time must be taken. And it is, I think, not peculiar to me to find that a two- or three-hour session of worship in the charismatic style, so far from leaving one exhausted, can be deeply cleansing and invigorating at the motivational and emotional level.

### 5) God's strategy of renewal

Charismatics as a body are sure that, however much or little there may have been of charismatic manifestations and ministry between the first and twentieth centuries, charismatic renewal is certainly central at present in God's purpose of revitalizing his church. Those who identify with the movement thus feel themselves not merely free but obliged to think and talk big, sometimes in ways that strike other Christians as naive, concerning the significance of this particular way of knowing God of which they find themselves trustees. The form of this conviction, that charismatic renewal is the key to the church's health today, varies from spokesperson to spokesperson, but on the conviction itself there is substantial agreement.

Such are the characteristic charismatic certainties. Genetically, they all find their origin in the Pentecostal wave that broke over world Protes-tantism in the first years of this century. [27] Doctrinally, apart from the claim that Spirit-baptism is instantly available (which older Pentecostals did not say), and the fashionable emphasis on 'body-life' as mutual ministry, most charismatics have simply taken over, at least in broad outline, the older Pentecostal theology, which was a relatively traditional evangelical pie-tism of Wesleyan descent, laying its own stress on Spirit-baptism as a post-conversion necessity, on tongues and (a matter I have not stressed)

---

[26] So in hymnology: the repetitive, slow-moving, sometimes incoherent style of charismatic hymns and choruses contrasts strikingly with the more theologically and poetically accomplished words, and brisker tunes, of earlier days.

[27] Original Pentecostalism sought to be an 'ecumenical revival movement' rather than a denomination (Hollenweger, op. cit., pp. 505f.) but was forced to create its own denominational structures because the older churches rejected it as false fire, fanatical and to many minds Satanic. G. Campbell Morgan called it 'the last vomit of Satan' (cited in Synan, op. cit., p. 144); German evangelicals condemned it as diabolical (Hollenweger, op. cit., pp. 223ff.).

on healing.[28] In their spirituality, the charismatics' goal of realizing the life of God in the Christian soul emotionally, existentially and evidentially, as well as cerebrally, also corresponds to that of the older Pentecostalism.

Sociologically and psychologically, interesting questions arise about the observable correlations between inward and outward stress (pains, pressures, personal crises) on the one hand, and the embracing of charismatic spirituality on the other.[29] Pastorally, there is much to be said about the strengths, weaknesses and vulnerabilities of the charismatic way in practice. These are proper fields of enquiry, which are increasingly being explored today. But theological reflection is our present business, and to this we now proceed.

## III

First, we must note that the charismatic movement is theologically diverse. Says Quebedeaux, rightly, as we have begun to see:

> Protestants and Catholics, conservatives and liberals, do not automatically discard their own theological and ecclesiastical differences when they come together in the movement. Nor do the movement's leaders themselves agree on the precise definition of the Baptism of the Holy Spirit. Protestant Neo-Pentecostals, for instance, often view the Baptism of the Holy Spirit as

---

[28] Hollenweger, op. cit., pp. 291ff., expounds Pentecostal doctrine with formal accuracy if not full sympathy. The 'Fourfold Gospel' of the Presbyterian A. B. Simpson, founder of the Christian and Missionary Alliance, seems to have been one source of it; the characteristic Pentecostal message was and is the 'Fourfold Gospel' (Christ as Saviour through personal conversion, Sanctifier through baptism in the Spirit, Healer through specific faith for healing, and Coming King through pre-millennial return) with the second item enlarged to include tongues as evidence of the baptism (see note 16 above). Simpson denied that glossolalia was the invariable or sure evidence of the baptism, but in 1907 defined an attitude to tongues ('seek not – forbid not') that was friendlier and more tolerant than that of other evangelicals in his day (see Synan, op. cit., p. 145).

[29] Cf. Quebedeaux: 'Pentecostalism was a legitimate way to dismantle inhibition and to enjoy emotional release, which for a long time was limited in modern society. In some ways, it may be anti-cultural (or counter-cultural?), but it may also function as a safety valve, and may thus in the long run prevent emotions from running into socially nihilistic channels. It might be interesting to speculate why in the 1900–60 period the lower socio-economic levels of society needed this kind of release; and why in the 1960s and 1970s the middle class needs it. The need could, perhaps, be linked to the declining relative position of the middle class in a period of economic redistribution and the reduction of status differences (i.e., a limited experience of relative deprivation)' (op. cit., pp. 230f.).

a 'second work of grace' after conversion . . . Roman Catholics . . . look at the Baptism of the Holy Spirit as an interior experience (usually with outward manifestations) of the Spirit's filling and transforming power in the life of a believer who has received the Holy Spirit through the sacrament of water baptism. The exact nature of the *charismata* (such as tongue speaking and divine healing) and their operation as outlined in 1 Cor. 12–14 are also debated.[30]

Broadly speaking, the position is this. Most Protestants theologize charismatic experience in terms of *restoration*, claiming that in response to faith God is reproducing today all that he did at Pentecost and later in Samaria, Caesarea and Ephesus,[31] and also in Corinth[32] – or, at least, all that he did in giving gifts at Corinth.[33] Roman Catholics usually theologize charismatic experience in terms of *realization* of what was latent before, namely the indwelling of God's Spirit to further man's recovery of God and of wholeness in him by whatever means help each individual.

Protestants tend to read all the details of New Testament charismatic experience as paradigms and, in effect, promises of what God *will* do for all who ask, while Catholics read them rather as demonstrating what God *can* do as spiritual need requires. The two notions are not, of course, exclusive: the restoration is attributed partly, at least, to a realization of the indwelling Spirit's power, and the realization is seen as resulting in a restoration of lost dimensions of Christian experience.

The two approaches, however, lead to different attitudes towards charismatic phenomena and lack of them. For most Protestants, and some Catholics, it becomes virtually mandatory to insist that all New Testament manifestations of the Spirit are available and intended for all churches everywhere; and Christians and churches which fail to seek, and therefore to find them are thereby shown to be at least in this respect second-rate. Roman Catholics, however, need not say more than that

---

[30] R. Quebedeaux, *The Young Evangelicals* (New York: Harper & Row, 1974), 43; cf. *The New Charismatics*, pp. 153f.

[31] Acts 2, 8, 10, 19.

[32] 1 Cor. 12–14.

[33] German Pentecostals mostly dissociate themselves from the two-stage understanding of baptism in the Spirit. The charismatic Lutheran Arnold Bittlinger writes: 'We Christians do not look for a special act of the reception of the Spirit in "sealing" or "the baptism of the Spirit," but we know that the Holy Spirit dwells in every Christian and desires to be visible in every Christian' (Hollenweger, op. cit., p. 247. cf. p. 15). A similar viewpoint is expressed in Thomas Smail, *Reflected Glory* (London: Hodder & Stoughton, and Grand Rapids: Eerdmans, 1976), and in the joint 'charismatic' – 'non-charismatic' Anglican evangelical statement *Gospel and Spirit*, sec. 2 (London: Fountain Trust/Church of England Evangelical Council, 1977; also in *Churchman*, April 1977).

current charismatic phenomena are analogous to those mentioned in
the New Testament, and that God now gives them in freedom when
and as he sees that they will be beneficial.

Let me say at once that this latter position seems to me sounder, partly
because current charismatic phenomena do not fully correspond to those
of 1 Corinthians 12–14, and partly because the assumption that what God
did in first-century Jerusalem and Corinth he will want to reproduce
everywhere in every age is more than I can defend. But the only point I
am making at present is that there is more than one charismatic theology,
and our reflections must take account of that fact.

How, theologically, should we evaluate the charismatic movement?
It claims to be a manifestation of spiritual renewal, but some, convinced
that the 'sign-gifts' were for the apostolic age only[34] and/or discerning no
biblical basis for the norm of two-stage entry into full Christian experi -
ence,[35] have been inclined to dismiss it as eccentric, neurotic or even
demonic. Scripture, however, yields principles for judging whether
professedly Christian movements are God-inspired or not; principles
about God's work, will and ways which the apostles are seen applying in
letters like Galatians, Colossians, 2 Peter and 1 John to various supposedly
super-spiritual versions of the faith. Two basic tests emerge: one credal,
one moral.

The credal test may be formulated from two passages, 1 John 4:2–3
and 1 Corinthians 12:3. The first passage says that any spirit – that is,
evidently, anyone claiming to be Spirit-inspired – who fails to confess the
incarnation is not of God. The thrust of this fully appears only as we recall
that for John the incarnation of God's Son led on to his sacrificial death

---

[34]  Chrysostom (late fourth century) wrote:

> In the beginning, charismata were given even to the unworthy, because the
> ancient period needed this help to foster the faith; but now they are not given
> even to the worthy because faith is strong and firm enough not to need this
> support (J. P. Migne, ed., *Patrologia Graeca*, 51:81).

This, the common position at all times, was restated by B. B. Warfield, *Counterfeit
Miracles* (New York: Scribners, 1918), *Miracles Yesterday and Today* (Grand
Rapids: Eerdmans, 1953), who argued that since the charismata 'were part of the
credentials of the Apostles as the authoritative agents of God in founding the
church . . . they necessarily passed away' with the Apostolic age (*Miracles Yesterday
and Today*, p. 6). Later presentations of this view (e.g. Walter J. Chantry, *Signs of
the Apostles: Observations on Pentecostalism Old and New*, rev. edn. Edinburgh:
Banner of Truth, 1973) lean heavily on Warfield.

[35]  Cf., e.g., F. D. Bruner, *A Theology of the Holy Spirit* (Grand Rapids: Eerdmans,
1970 and London: Hodder and Stoughton, 1971); J. D. G. Dunn, *Baptism in the
Holy Spirit* (London: SCM Press, 1970); J. R. W. Stott, *Baptism and Fullness* rev.
edn. (London: IVP and Downers Grove: Inter-Varsity Press, 1976).

for our sins,[36] and denial of the former entailed denial of the latter too. The second passage affirms that the Spirit of God leads no one to say 'cursed (*anathema*) be Jesus,' but leads men rather to call him Lord ( *kyrios*), which otherwise they could never sincerely do.[37] This accords with the pervasive New Testament witness that the Holy Spirit in his character as the Spirit of Christ fulfils what we may call a floodlight ministry of enabling sinful men to discern Christ's glory, and to trust and love him accordingly. So the credal test, for charismatics as for all other professed Christians, is the degree of honour paid by confession, attitude and action to the Son whom God the Father has made Lord.

The moral test is given by statements such as those of John, that he who truly knows and loves God will show it by keeping his command - ments, avoiding all sin and loving his brethren in Christ.[38] When we apply these tests to the charismatic movement it becomes plain that God is in it. For, whatever threats and perhaps instances of occult and counterfeit spirituality we may think we detect round its periphery (and what movement of revival has ever lacked these things round its periphery?), its main effect everywhere is to promote robust Trinitarian faith, personal fellowship with the divine Saviour and Lord whom we meet in the New Testament, repentance, obedience, and love to fellow-Christians, ex - pressed in ministry of all sorts towards them; plus a zeal for evangelistic outreach which puts the staider sort of churchmen to shame.

This suggests our next question. What particular features of the charismatic movement call for unambiguous approval when biblically assessed? A dozen suggest themselves at once.

1) Its stress on personal fellowship with, and devotion to, the living Christ.

2) Its stress on the need to be filled with the Spirit, and to be living a life which one way or another displays the Spirit's power.

3) Its recognition of, and provision for, the necessary emotional dimension – necessary because we are human beings – in apprehending and responding to the love of God in Christ.

4) Its stress on the need to cultivate an open, ardent, constant, whole-hearted habit of prayer (which, as we saw, is where glossolalia comes in).

5) Its stress on the need to cherish and express Christian joy in both speech and song.

6) Its insistence that each Christian be thoroughly involved in the church's worship; not necessarily by speaking in the assembly (though that kind of participation, when orderly and well done, must surely be approved), but primarily by opening one's heart to God in worship and

---

[36] John 1:1–2:2, 3:16, 4:8–10.

[37] See 1 Cor. 2:14.

[38] Cf. 1 John 2:4, 3:9ff., 17–24, 4:7–13, 20f., 5:1–3.

seeking to realize for oneself the divine realities about which the church sings, prays and learns from Scripture.

7) Its concern that all Christians be actively involved in ministry; finding and using their gifts, whatever these prove to be, for others' welfare.

8) Its missionary zeal and concern to share Christ.

9) Its awareness of the potential of groups. Hummel, with his eyes on the USA, writes of

> the hundreds of interdenominational fellowship meetings in homes through-out the country. They convene weekly for worship and praise, Bible study, mutual encouragement and exercise of gifts as the Holy Spirit manifests them. These groups supplement the regular services of churches in which the members are usually active.[39]

The same is true in England and elsewhere. In a remarkable way the charismatic movement has discovered, or rediscovered, the value of small groups for prayer and ministry.

10) Its stress on the need for church structures to be flexible enough to allow all gifts within a congregation to be fully used.

11) Its experiments in community living; in particular, the estab-lishing of extended families composed of nuclear families who unite to fulfil ministries of shelter and support which no nuclear family on its own could manage.

12) Its cultivation of childlike openness, spontaneity, warmth, and expectancy in relationships with both God and men.

Now a balancing question. What charismatic characteristics might impede that corporate maturity in Christ at which New Testament teaching aims? Ten defects of charismatic qualities – defects sometimes observed, at least on the movement's fringes, and always threatening – call for mention here.

1) *Elitism*. In any movement in which significant-seeming things go on, the sense of being a spiritual aristocracy, the feeling that 'we are the people who really count,' always threatens at gut-level, and verbal disclaimers of this syndrome do not always suffice to keep it at bay. Here elitist tendencies are reinforced by the restorationist theology which sees charismatic experience as the New Testament norm for all time and is inevitably judgmental towards non-charismatic Christianity. When you have gone out on a limb, as many have, in order to seek and find something which you now think everyone should be seeking, though many are not, it is hard not to feel superior.

---

[39] Charles E. Hummel, *Fire in the Fireplace: Contemporary Charismatic Renewal* (Downers Grove: Inter-Varsity Press, 1978), p. 47; cf. the description of charismatic prayer groups among Roman Catholics in USA in O'Connor, *The Pentecostal Movement in the Catholic Church*, pp. 111–21.

2) *Sectarianism*. The absorbing intensity of charismatic fellowship, countrywide and worldwide, can produce a damaging insularity whereby charismatics limit themselves to reading charismatic books, hearing char - ismatic speakers, fellowshipping with other charismatics and backing charismatic causes; and this is the thin end of the sectarian wedge in practice, however firm one's profession of aiming at catholic unity.

3) *Emotionalism*. Only a fine line divides healthy emotion from unhealthy emotionalism, and any appealing to or playing on emotion crosses that line every time. Though the white-collar charismatic move - ment of today is (for cultural rather than theological reasons, it seems) generally calmer than original blue-collar Pentecostalism ever was, its preoccupation with expressing feelings of joy and love makes it vulnerable here. Its warmth and liveliness attract highly emotional and disturbed people to its ranks, and many others find in its ritual emotionalism some relief from strains and pressures in other areas of their lives (marriage, work, finance, etc.). But such sharing in group emotion is a self indulgent escapist 'trip' which must debilitate in the long run. Generally, the movement seems to teeter on the edge of emotional self-indulgence in a decidedly dangerous way.

4) *Anti-intellectualism*. Charismatic preoccupation with experience observably inhibits the long, hard theological and ethical reflection for which the New Testament letters so plainly call. The result often is naiveté and imbalance in handling the biblical revelation; some themes – gifts and ministry in the body of Christ, for instance – being run to death while others, such as eschatology, get neglected. Looking for a prophecy (supposedly, a direct word from God) when difficult issues arise, rather than embracing the hard grind of prayerful study and analysis, is a tendency that sometimes obtrudes; so at other times does a doctrinaire insistence that for Spirit-filled, Bible-reading Christians all problems of faith and conduct will prove to be simple. The charismatic movement has been called 'an experience seeking a theology'; 'lacking' and 'needing' would fit, but whether 'seeking' is warranted is open to doubt, sometimes anyhow.

5) *Illuminism*. Sincere but deluded claims to direct divine revelation have been made in the church since the days of the Colossian heretic(s) and the Gnosticizers whose defection called forth 1 John, and since Satan keeps pace with God they will no doubt recur till the Lord returns. At this point the charismatic movement, with its stress on the Spirit's personal leading, and the revival of revelations via prophecy, is clearly vulnerable. The person with unhealthy ambitions to be a religious leader, dominating a group by giving them the sense that he is closer to God than they are, can easily climb on the charismatic band-wagon and find there good-hearted, emotionally dependent folk waiting to be impressed by him; so, too, the opinionated eccentric can easily invoke the Spirit's direction when he refuses to let his pastor stop him disrupting the congregation

with his odd ideas. Living as it does on the edge of illuminism, the movement cannot but have problems here.

6) '*Charismania*.' This is O'Connor's word for the habit of mind which measures spiritual health, growth and maturity by the number and impressiveness of people's gifts, and spiritual power by public charismatic manifestations.[40] The habit is bad, for the principle of judgment is false; and where it operates, real growth and maturity are likely to be retarded.

7) '*Super-supernaturalism*.' This is my word for that way of affirming the supernatural which exaggerates its discontinuity with the natural. Reacting against 'flat-tire' versions of Christianity which play down the supernatural and do not expect to see God at work, the super-supernatu - ralist constantly expects miracles of all sorts – striking demonstrations of God's presence and power – and he is happiest when he thinks he sees God acting contrary to the nature of things, so confounding common sense[41] For God to proceed slowly and by natural means is to him a disappointment, almost a betrayal. But his undervaluing of the natural, regular and ordinary shows him to be romantically immature, and weak in his grasp of the realities of creation and providence as basic to God's work of grace. Charismatic thinking tends to treat glossolalia, in which mind and tongue are deliberately and systematically dissociated, as the paradigm case of spiritual activity, and to expect all God's work in and around his children to involve similar discontinuity with the ordinary regularities of the created world. This makes for super-supernaturalism almost inevitably.

8) *Eudaemonism*. I use this word for the belief that God means us to spend our time in this fallen world feeling well, and in a state of euphoria based on that fact. Charismatics might deprecate so stark a statement, but the regular and expected projection of euphoria from their platforms and pulpits, plus their standard theology of healing, show that the assumption is there, reflecting and intensifying the 'now-I-am-happy-all-the-day-and-you-can-be-so-too' ethos of so much evangelical evangelism since D. L. Moody.

---

[40]  O'Connor, *The Pentecostal Movement* . . ., pp. 225ff.

[41]  'Thus, there are people who want their entire lives to be guided by heavenly messages and revelations, and hence neglect the planning and deliberation that are within their power. Some people want all sicknesses to be healed miraculously, and refuse to see a doctor or take medicine. On similar grounds, others would like to see theological study and sermon preparation replaced by a kerygma [= pulpit utterance] of purely charismatic inspiration and the institutional offices in the Church . . . replaced by a purely charismatic leadership.' (O'Connor, *The Pentecostal Movement* . . ., p. 227) All this expresses very clearly and typically the super-supernaturalist cast of mind.

Charismatics, picking up the healing emphasis of original restorationist Pentecostalism – an emphasis already strong in 'holiness' circles in North America before Pentecostalism arrived – regularly assume that physical disorder and discomfort is not ordinarily God's beneficent will for his children.[42] On this basis, with paradigmatic appeal to the healings of Jesus and the apostles, plus the claim, founded on Isaiah 53:3–6 and 10 as interpreted in Matthew 8:16f. and 1 Peter 2:24, that there is healing in the atonement,[43] plus reference to Paul's phrase '*charismata* of healings' ('gifts of healings,' AV; 'healers,' RSV) in 1 Corinthians 12:28, they make supernatural divine healing (which includes, according to testimony, lengthening of legs, straightening of spines and, in South America, filling of teeth) a matter of constant expectation,[44] and look for healing gifts in their leaders almost as a matter of course. But the texts quoted will not bear the weight put upon them,[45] and New Testament references to

---

[42] 'The longing for the supernatural and for the healing of sickness by prayer is a constant feature of nineteenth-century works of edification.' (Hollenweger, op. cit., p. 353). See A. B. Simpson, *The Gospel of Healing* (1877), A. J. Gordon, *The Ministry of Healing* (1882), etc. and cf. Hollenweger, pp. 115–20, 353–76. Otto Stockmayer (Switzerland) and Andrew Murray (South Africa) were among leaders who held out hope of regular conquest of illness by prayer.

[43] 'Deliverance from sickness is provided in the atonement and is the privilege of all believers' (Declaration of Faith of the Assemblies of God, 12); ' "Divine healing" is provided for all in the atonement' (Declaration of Faith of the Church of God (Cleveland), 11): cited from Hollenweger, pp. 515, 517. That total healing for the body with total sinless perfection are 'in the atonement,' in the sense that entire personal renewal in Christ's image flows from the cross (cf. Rom. 8:23; Phil. 3:20f.) is true, but it is a potentially disastrous mistake to expect on earth what will only be given in heaven.

[44] Cf., for instance, Francis MacNutt, *Healing* (Notre Dame: Ave Maria Press, 1974), pp. 13f. 'I would no longer have to tell people whose sicknesses were disintegrating their personalities that their illness was a God-sent cross, but I would hold up the hope that God wanted them well even when medical science could not help.' Assessing claims to supernatural bodily healing through prayer is hard, for the evidence is regularly incomplete and disputed. Sample sceptical evaluations highlighting this difficulty are B. B. Warfield, *Counterfeit Miracles*, and W. Nolen, *Healing: A Doctor in Search of a Miracle* (New York: Random House, 1974), a study of the healing ministry of Kathryn Kuhlman, who in 1962 had ventured to publish a book called *I Believe in Miracles*. My argument does not depend on, nor does it justify, assessments as negative as these, though it is hard to see on what grounds one could safely be more positive.

[45] Cf. John F. MacArthur, *The Charismatics: A Doctrinal Perspective* (Grand Rapids: Zondervan, 1978), pp. 55ff.; W. Hendriksen, *Exposition of the Gospel According to Matthew* (Grand Rapids: Baker, 1973 and Edinburgh: Banner of Truth, 1977), pp. 400f.

sickness among Christian leaders that was not supernaturally healed [46] make it plain that good health at all times is not God's will for all believers.

Also, the charismatic supposition loses sight of the good that can come in the form of wisdom, patience and acceptance of reality without bitterness when Christians are exposed to the discipline of pain and of remaining unhealed. [47] Moreover, the charismatic supposition creates appalling possibilities of distress when a person who seeks healing fails to find it, and then perhaps is told that the reason lies not in God's unwillingness or inability to heal, but in his or her own lack of faith. [48] Without doubting that God can and sometimes does heal supernaturally today, and that healings of various kinds do in fact cluster round some people's ministries, I judge this expression of the eudaemonist streak in charismatic thought to be a major mistake, and one which makes against Christian maturity in a quite radical way.

9) *Demon-obsession*. In recovering a sense of the supernaturalness of God, charismatics have grown vividly aware of the reality of supernatural personal evil, and there is no doubt that their development of 'deliverance' ministry and the impulse they have given to the renewal of exorcism [49] have been salutary for many. But if all life is seen as a battle with demons in such a way that Satan and his hosts get blamed for bad health, bad thoughts and bad behaviour without reference to physical, psychological and relational factors in the situation, a very unhealthy demonic counter - part of super-supernaturalism is being developed. There is no doubt that this sometimes happens, and that it is a major obstacle to moral and spiritual maturity when it does.

10) *Conformism*. Group pressure is tyrannical at the best of times, and never more so than when the group in question believes itself to be super-spiritual, and finds the evidence of its members' spirituality in their power to perform along approved lines. Inevitably, peer pressure to perform (hands raised, hands outstretched, glossolalia, prophecy) is strong in charismatic circles; inevitably, too, the moment one starts living to the group and its expectations rather than to the Lord, one is enmeshed in a

---

[46] Epaphroditus, Phil. 2:27; Timothy, 1 Tim. 5:23; Trophimus, 2 Tim. 4:20; Paul himself, the agent of widespread supernatural healings of others (cf. Acts 28:8f., etc.) according to the natural exposition of 2 Cor. 12:7ff., where 'thorn' points to physical pain and 'flesh' to created, flesh-and-blood humanity.

[47] See on this the superb book by the quadriplegic Joni Eareckson-Tada and Steve Estes, *A Step Further* (Grand Rapids: Zondervan, 1978, and Glasgow: Pickering & Inglis, 1979).

[48] 'Healing does not fail because of the will of God, but because of the unbelief of his children.' (Pentecostal evangelist Richard Vinyard, 1958; Hollenweger, op. cit., p. 358) See Hummel, op. cit., pp. 219f.

[49] Cf. John Richards, *But Deliver us from Evil* (London: Darton, Longman & Todd, 1976).

new legalistic bondage, whereby from yet another angle Christian maturity is threatened.

Yet, having said all this, it is well to remind ourselves that those who live in glass houses should not throw stones. No type of Christian spirituality is free from dangers, weaknesses and threats to maturity arising from its very strengths, and it is not as if Christian maturity (which includes all-round liveliness of response to God, as well as sobriety of judgement) were overwhelmingly visible in non-charismatic circles today. In matters of this kind it is the easiest thing in the world to dilate on specks in my brother's eye and to ignore logs in my own; so we had better move quietly on.

Next, we ask: How far are the distinctives of 'charismatic experience' confined to professed charismatics? This seems an important question, for I suspect that something of an optical illusion tends to operate here, creating a quite mistaken sense that 'charismatic' spirituality is totally different from anything found outside 'charismatic' circles. Earlier I noted the similarity between testimonies to charismatic Spirit-baptism and other accounts of 'second blessings' given by other Christians of other times, and the list of parallels can be extended. One man voices the ardour of his praise or the agony of his prayer in glossolalia, another in his native tongue; but is the exercise of heart essentially different?

Dr. Baer affirms a 'fundamental functional similarity between speaking in tongues and two other widespread and generally accepted religious practices, namely, Quaker silent worship and the liturgical worship of the Catholic and Episcopal churches,' in all three of which the analytical reason rests to allow deeper dimensions of the person to be touched by God.[50] Is this idea obviously wrong? Or take the Spirit-wrought awareness of how the God of the Bible sees us, and how his word in Scripture applies to our life-situations: if one man objectifies it by calling it prophecy and announcing it in oracle-form, while another expresses it as his personal certainty of what God is saying to him and to others, does that argue any essential difference in the inward work of God in the heart in the two cases?

Is it only charismatics who ever seek or find bodily healing through prayer, or who ever practise successful exorcism by prayer in Jesus' name? Is it only charismatics who minister in love to each other, however little others may have been instructed in the developed doctrine of spiritual gifts? I suggest that, in reality, charismatic and non-charismatic spiritualities differ more in vocabulary, self-image, groups associated with, and books and journals read, than in the actual ingredients of their communion with the Father and the Son through the Spirit. Charismatic experience is less distinctive than is sometimes made out.

---

[50] Cited from Josephine Massyngberde Ford in *The Charismatic Movement*, pp. 115f.

## IV

We move now to the main question, to which we have thus far been clearing the way. In what terms should we theologize – that is, explain in terms of God – the characteristic charismatic experience? What should we take the Holy Spirit to be doing in the lives of charismatics at the point where they profess a spiritual experience transcending that of other Christians? This is in fact the major question which the movement raises, and by concluding from its central convictions and ethical fruits that God is in it, and by finding closer correspondence between 'charismatic' and 'non-charismatic' spirituality than is sometimes noticed, I have made it more difficult than it would be otherwise. For the fact we must now face is that the theology most commonly professed within the movement concerning its own claimed distinctives is deeply unbiblical.

Granted, the movement disclaims any specifically theological purpose, and claims to be a renewal of experience, not doctrine, and so is impatient of intellectual niceties. But 'experience' is a slippery word, and 'experi -ences' (i.e., specific states of thought and feeling) coming to imperfectly sanctified sinners cannot but have dross mixed with their gold, and no 'experience' just by happening can authenticate itself as sent by God to further his work of grace. The mere fact that a Christian has an experience does not make it a Christian experience. The sign that an experience is a gift of God's grace is that when tested by Scripture it proves to have at its heart an intensified awareness of some revealed truth concerning God and our relationship to him as creatures, sinners, beneficiaries, believers, adopted sons, pledged servants or whatever. But if experiences are pointed to as evidencing and confirming beliefs which appear biblically to be mistaken, we then have only two options: either to reject the experiences as delusive and possibly demonic in origin, or to re-theologize them in a way which shows that what they actually evidence and confirm is something different from what was first alleged. This is the choice we now have to make with regard to at least the main stream of charismatic testimony.

Some, noting the mistakes which charismatic experience is said to verify, have taken the first course and written off the movement as delusive and dangerous. Nor can one altogether blame them when one thinks of the euphoric conceit with which the mistaken assertions are sometimes (not always) made, the naive mishandling of Scripture that often goes with them, and – most distressing of all – the seeming unconcern of charismatic spokesmen about questions of truth, with their inability to see what difficulties of principle they raise by their bland assumption that once conservative and liberal Protestants and conservative and liberal Roman Catholics share together in the Spirit all their doctrinal differences may safely be left to look after themselves. I confess myself to be one among the many whom these features bother.

Nonetheless, I think I see God's touch in charismatic experience; and therefore I venture upon the second course, that of re-theologizing. The reader must judge how I get on.

First we glance at the traditional Pentecostal account of charismatic experience, for which most charismatics outside Germany have settled more or less. This, the *restorationist* view as I called it, makes the essence of the disciples' experience on Pentecost day, as described in Acts 2, and of the Corinthian experience as described in 1 Corinthians 12–14, into norms, ideals and goals for Christians now.

The view centres on a conception of Spirit-baptism as 'an experience distinct from and usually subsequent to conversion in which a person receives the totality of the Spirit into his life and is thereby fully empowered for witness and service.'[51] Until Spirit-baptism takes place, the Christian lacks essential resources which God has in store for him; therefore he is charged to seek this experience till he finds it.[52] When it comes thus to upgrade him, glossolalia occurs as the outward sign of what has happened.[53]

Since only hereby does he receive 'the totality of the Spirit' (however that odd phrase be construed), his experience as thus theologized may properly be viewed as completing his initiation into Christ, just as in Anglo-Catholic theory receiving the Spirit in confirmation has been seen as completing the initiation which water-baptism began.[54] (Baptismal imagery is, of course, intrinsically initiatory.) Recent thorough examinations of this view by J. D. G. Dunn, F. D. Bruner, J. R. W. Stott and A. A. Hoekema[55] make it needless for us to weigh it in detail here. Suffice it to say, first, that it compels an evaluation of non-charismatic Christianity – i.e., Christianity which neither knows nor seeks post-conversion Spirit-baptism – as low-road, second-class and lacking something vital; and, second, that it cannot be established from

---

[51] A. A. Hoekema, *Holy Spirit Baptism* (Grand Rapids: Eerdmans, and Exeter: Paternoster, 1972) p. 10.

[52] Cf. the Statement of Fundamental Truths of the Assemblies of God (USA), 7: 'All believers are entitled to, and should ardently expect, and earnestly seek, the Baptism in the Holy Ghost and fire, according to the command of our Lord Jesus Christ. This was the normal experience of all in the early Christian Church . . .'.

[53] This is the usual Pentecostal view, though the British-based Elim Foursquare Gospel Alliance, the Swiss Pfingstmission and some German Pentecostal bodies dissent (Bruner, *A Theology of the Holy Spirit*, p. 77, note 30). Some charismatics who value tongues also dissent, e.g. Larry Christenson (cf. Hoekema, op. cit., p. 31) and O'Connor (cf. note 18 above).

[54] For this idea see Bruner, op. cit., pp. 185ff.; J. D. G. Dunn, *Baptism in the Holy Spirit*, G. W. H. Lampe, *The Seal of the Spirit* (London: Longmans, Green, 1951).

[55] In works already cited.

Scripture, for it has no coherent answer to biblical counter-questions like these:

*1) Can it be convincingly denied that 1 Corinthians 12:13 ('We were all baptized by one Spirit into one body – whether Jews or Greeks, slave or free – and we were all given the one Spirit to drink,'* NIV) *refers to one aspect of what we may call the 'conversion-initiation complex' with which the Christian life starts, so that according to Paul every Christian as such is Spirit-baptized? Surely not.*

The only alternative to this conclusion would be to hold, as the late R. A. Torrey influentially did, [56] that Paul here speaks of a 'second blessing' which he knew that he and all the Corinthians had received, though some Christians today have not. But 1) this hardly squares with Paul's earlier description of the Corinthians as, despite all their gifts, unspiritual babes in Christ, unable as yet to take solid food (3:1 and 2) it forces one *either* to deny that Christians who lack the 'second blessing' belong to the one body of Christ or to disregard the natural meaning of 'into one body' and render it as 'for the sake of' or 'with a view to benefiting,' which the Greek can hardly stand; and 3) if the latter line is taken, it constitutes a vote of censure on Paul for a needlessly and almost mischievously misleading use of words. [57]

Some, accepting this conclusion, have urged that this initiatory baptism by the Spirit in 1 Corinthians 12:13 is distinct from Christ's subsequent baptism *with* or *in* the Spirit, referred to in Mark 1:8 = Matthew 3:11 = Luke 3:16; John 1:33; Acts 1:5, 11:16. But in all seven passages the same preposition *(en) is* used, making the Spirit the 'element' in which Christ baptizes, so that the distinction is linguistically baseless. [58]

*2) Can it be convincingly denied that the narratives of Acts, from Pentecost on, assume that faith-repentance (Luke alternates these words when specifying response to the gospel) and the gift of the Spirit in the fullness of his new covenant ministry come together? I do not think so.*

Peter's words at the close of the first Christian evangelistic sermon, 'Repent, and be baptized every one of you in the name of Jesus Christ for the forgiveness of your sins; and you shall receive the gift of the Holy Spirit' (Acts 2:38), are unambiguously clear on this point. So, as Luke narrates it, is the abnormal character of the 'two-stage' Samaritan

---

[56] Cf. *The Person and Work of the Holy Spirit*. pp. 177f.; the baptism is potential for all, actual only for some. Bruner notes Torrey's role as 'a kind of John the Baptist figure for later international Pentecostalism' (op. cit., p. 45).

[57] Cf. Dunn, op. cit., pp. 127ff.

[58] Cf. Hoekema, op. cit., pp. 21f.

experience (8:14–17)[59] – the only such abnormality, be it said, in the whole book, for the Ephesian disciples who had not received the Spirit (cf. 19:2–6) were not Christians when Paul met them, any more than Cornelius was before hearing Peter (cf. 11:13). The case of Cornelius, who received the Pentecostal gift while faithfully drinking in Peter's gospel, confirms the conjunction between faith-repentance and be – stowal of the Spirit which Peter affirmed in Acts 2:38, and further shows (as Peter's words in 2:38 did not) that it is the outgoing of the heart to God, rather than the water-baptism which from the human side expresses it, that occasions God's gift.[60]

*3) Can it be convincingly denied that, as Luke presents the matter, the sole reason why Jesus' first disciples had a 'two stage' experience, believing first and being Spirit-baptized after, was dispensational, inasmuch as nine o'clock on Pentecost morning was the moment when the Spirit's new covenant ministry among men*

---

[59] Bruner, op. cit., pp. 177f., urges from Luke's 'not yet' (οὐδέ ω) in v.16 that for a believer 'to be baptized and not to have received the Spirit was an abnormality, in fact . . . an impossible contradiction in Christian realities . . . The meaning is this: The Spirit is to come with baptism, but this coming had "not yet" occurred. The relation of baptism to the Spirit . . . is the relation of cohesion,' baptism guaranteeing that the Spirit must and would also be given, the only question being when. This may be over-arguing, but at least οὐδέ πω implies expectation. The guess (it cannot be more) that God withheld the manifestation of the Spirit (in Luke's language, 'the Holy Spirit' simply) till his apostles might be its channel so as to stop the Samaritan-Jewish schism being carried into the church seems rational and reverent. The gift showed that Samaritans and Jews were being equally blessed through Christ; the mode of its giving showed that all Christians, Samaritan and Jewish equally, must recognize the divinely established leadership and authority of Christ's Jewish apostles. Heb. 2:4 mentions charismata as authenticating the apostles' witness, and all such manifestations which the New Testament notices were connected with their personal ministry; though that, pace Warfield and Hoekema, is no proof that there never were any that were not so connected, or that there are none now.

[60] Bruner, op. cit., pp. 196f., rightly quoted Acts 2:39, 3:16, 26, 5:31, 11:18, 13:48, 15:8f., 16:14, 18:27 to show that in Acts faith and repentance are no less God's gift than is the Spirit. Dunn, op. cit., pp. 101f., maintains, against a good deal of German and British exegesis, that to understand Luke we must 'acknowledge both that Spirit-baptism and water-baptism are distinct entities and that the focus and nerve centre of Christian initiation is the gift of the Spirit. At this point certainly Luke was no "early Catholic," and the attention which theologians have devoted to water-baptism on the assumption (implicit or explicit) that it is the most important element of conversion-initiation and that the salvation-gifts of God (including the Spirit) are somehow dependent on it, is to be regretted.'

*began; so that their 'two-stage' experience must be judged unique, and not a norm for us at all? Surely this, too, is certain.*

The common Pentecostal-charismatic handling of Acts 2, like that of the holiness teachers (Torrey, etc.) from whom it came, misses this point; yet it is really inescapable. Luke's theology of the Pentecostal even as fulfilling Jesus' promise and Joel's prediction (1:4f., 2:17f.), and the thrust of Acts as a whole, combine to put it beyond doubt. It is evident that Luke wrote his second volume to tell how the age of the Spirit dawned following Jesus' ascension, and how in the Spirit's power the gospel ran from Jerusalem to the capital of the Empire. He recorded particular experiences – Pentecost itself; the conversions of the Ethiopian eunuch, Paul, Cornelius, Lydia and the gaoler; Ananias' and Sapphira's heart failure when their duplicity was exposed; the humbling of simoniacal Simon and the blinding of Elymas; the visions of Stephen, Cornelius, Peter and Paul – as so many milestones on the gospel's road to Rome, not as models or paradigms of how God always acts. I guess Luke would have been both startled and distressed had he foreseen how some of his latter-day readers would misconstrue him in these matters. For in so far as his story is paradigmatic, it is 'an object lesson in the nature of the church and its mission'[61] rather than in the stages of universal Christian experience. [62]

*4) Can it be convincingly denied that when Paul wrote, 'Do all speak in tongues?' (1 Cor. 12:30) he expected the answer 'No'? Again, surely not.*

---

[61] Bruner, op. cit., p. 161.

[62] Against the Pentecostal-charismatic thesis that the reception of the Spirit by the apostles at Pentecost after prayer, with glossolalia, as a second stage of their Christian experience, is presented in Acts as a revealed norm for all subsequent believers, it must be said: 1) This is nowhere stated or implied in Acts itself. 2) It is inconsistent: if speaking in tongues is part of the universal pattern, why not hearing a roaring wind? 3) In the other recorded instances of the Spirit and tongues being bestowed together (Samaritans probably, cf. 8:18; Cornelius, group and the Ephesians definitely, 10:46, 19:6) these gifts came through apostles to folk not seeking, praying or 'tarrying' for them (cf. Luke 24:49, AV). 4). In all four cases the manifestation of the Spirit came to whole groups, not just to seeking individuals within those groups to the exclusion of non-seekers. 5) Acts 4:8, 31, 6:3, 5, 7:55, 9:17, 11:24, 13:9, 52, speaks of persons being filled with, or full of, the Spirit with no reference, explicit or implicit, to tongues. But if being Spirit-filled without glossolalia was the lot of some then, it may be God's will for some now. 6) From the way he tells his story, Luke seems to have understood his four cases of 'Pentecostal' manifestations as God's testimony to his acceptance on equal footing in the new society of four classes of folk whose co-equality here might otherwise have been doubted – Jews, Samaritans, Gentiles and disciples of John. Whether any more such manifestations took place in the apostolic age we do not know, but it would be gratuitous to

Older Pentecostals distinguished between glossolalia as a universal, one-off, involuntary manifestation attesting Spirit-baptism and as a con‐tinuing, non-ecstatic, controllable gift which not all have.[63] Most charis‐matics agree with most Pentecostals that glossolalia is the universal sign of Spirit-baptism, and seem to go beyond them both in their valuation of it as a devotional aid and in their expectation that all Spirit-baptized Christians will practise it regularly.[64] But in this their restorationism, unlike that of the Pentecostal churches, takes them beyond Paul; which gives point to the next question.

*5) Can charismatic glossolalia, which is frequently a learned skill and technique, which lacks language-structure, and which its own practitioners regard as mainly for private use, be convincingly equated with the tongues of 1 Corinthians 12–14, which were for public use, which were a 'sign' to unbelievers 'a negative sign towards their judgement,' as Stendahl explains it*[65]*), and which Paul (I quote Stendahl again) 'thought about as a language,' conveying meaning and therefore capable of being interpreted?*[66] *Can the identity of these two glossolalic phenomena be convincingly affirmed? Surely not. The negative resemblance of unfruitful*

---

[62] *(continued)* assume without evidence that they did in any situations where the lesson of co-equality in Christ was already understood.

Clearly much that cannot be read out of Acts has to be read into it to make the Pentecostal case.

[63] This is the point of the otherwise enigmatic sentence in the Statement of Fundamental Truths of the Assemblies of God, 8: 'The Evidence of the Baptism in the Holy Ghost . . . The speaking in tongues in this instance is the same in essence as the gift of tongues (1 Cor. 12:4–10, 28), but different in purpose and use.'

[64] Cf. the quotations in Hoekema, op. cit., pp. 31, 47. Kevin and Dorothy Ranaghan write: 'We are convinced that as far as the charismatic movement is concerned everyone touched by it is meant to pray in tongues.' 'Once a person has yielded to the gift of tongues and given his body-person over so radically to the operation of the Spirit, the power and dynamic begin to flow tangibly and visibly through his life' (*Catholic Pentecostals*, New York: Paulist Press, and London: Fountain Trust, 1969, pp. 222, 221). This is extreme, and some Catholic charismatics explicitly dissent (cf. note 17); nonetheless, it is a statement to which most charistmatics, it seems, would assent, as consonant with their own experi‐ence. Glossolalia is certainly the movement's badge in the eyes of the Christian public everywhere, and it is clear that charismatics as a body are happy to have it so. Cf. John L. Sherrill, *They Speak with Other Tongues* (London: Hodder & Stoughton, 1964; Westwood, N.J.: Spire Books, 1965).

[65] In *The Charismatic Movement*, p. 53.

[66] Op. cit., p. 60, note 12.

*understanding (1 Cor. 14:14) may be thought to be there*[67] *but the extent of the correspondence overall is quite uncertain.*

On the nature, worth, provenance and cessation of New Testament tongues much is obscure and must remain so: Various interpretations on key points are viable, and perhaps the worst error in handling the relevant passages is to claim or insinuate that perfect clarity or certainty marks one's own view. The texts (Acts 2:4–11, 10:46, 11:17, 19:6; 1 Cor. 12–14) are too problematical for that.

Some exegetes, with Charles Hodge, regard both the Pentecostal and the Corinthian tongues as a gift of languages (xenolalia, xenoglossia). [68] Others, with Abraham Kuyper, regard both as the uttering of unintelli - gible sounds (which Kuyper guesses may be the language we shall all speak in heaven), so that the Pentecostal miracle ('we hear them telling in our own tongues the mighty works of God!' Acts 2:11) was one of miraculous hearing rather than miraculous speaking (unless Kuyper's guess is right, in which case it was both). [69] Most, with Calvin, think the Pentecostal tongues were languages and the Corinthian tongues were not; but there is no unanimity. Each case is arguable, and Hoekema is right when he says, 'It seems difficult, if not impossible, to make a final judgement on this matter.'[70]

Then, too, opinions vary as to how far Paul's *thelo* in 1 Corinthians 14:5 expresses positive desire rather than concessive willingness, cour - teously phrased, for the Corinthians to speak in tongues, and why he thankfully records that he speaks in tongues more than all of them

---

[67] Or it may not. *Akarpos* (unfruitful) in verse 14 may mean either 'helping nobody' (Goodspeed; so in Eph. 5:11; Tit. 3:14; 2 Pet. 1:8; Jude 12) or 'blank.' The former meaning is consistent with the speaker understanding the tongue he utters, which Charles Hodge (*An Exposition of the First Epistle to the Corinthians* , London: Banner of Truth, 1958, p. 288) held to be implicit in the passage. But today's charismatics confessedly do not understand their tongues.

[68] Hodge, op. cit., pp. 248–52, 276–302. Robert G. Gromacki, *The Modern Tongues Movement* (Philadelphia: Presbyterian and Reformed, 1967), p. 113, takes this view.

[69] Kuyper, *The Work of the Holy Spirit* (Grand Rapids: Eerdmans, 1946). pp. 133–8. Of a piece with Kuyper's suggestion is the view, often met, that Paul saw Christian glossolalia as 'tongues of angels' (1 Cor. 13:1), angelic as distinct from human language. But while this, like so much else that is proposed in the discussion of 1 Cor. 12–14, is not absolutely impossible, Paul's words in 13:1 are sufficiently explained as a rhetorical hyperbole meaning simply 'no matter how wonderful a performance my glossolalia may be.'

[70] Hoekema, *What about Tongue-Speaking?* (Grand Rapids: Eerdmans, and Exe-ter: Paternoster, 1966), p. 83; cf. p. 128: 'The baffling question remains: how can Pentecostals . . . be sure that what goes on in tongue-speaking circles today is the same thing that went on in New Testament days?'

(14:18): whether because he wanted to testify that tongues enriched his ministry or his devotions, or simply because he wanted leverage for making his point about necessary restraint in the next verse. Again, different viewpoints are defensible.

Views vary too as to what Paul meant by 'the perfect' (*to teleion*) at whose coming tongues will cease (13:10): whether it is maturity in love, [71] or the complete New Testament canon and the fully-equipped state of the church that has it, [72] or (the majority view) the life of heaven upon which Christians will enter when the Lord comes. The second view entails that the gift of tongues was withdrawn before the first century closed; the first and third leave that question open, just as the question whether 'sign-gifts' were ever given apart from the apostles' personal ministry must finally be left open.

But one thing is clear: prima facie, Paul is discussing public use of tongues throughout 1 Corinthians 13 and 14, and it is neither necessary nor natural to refer any of his statements to glossolalia as a private exercise. Charismatics often explain 14:4 ('he who speaks in a tongue edifies himself') and 18 ('I speak in tongues more than you all') in terms of private glossolalic prayer, but exegetically this is a guess which is not only unable to be proved, but not in fact very plausible. It involves a gratuitous modelling of first-century experience on the charismatics' own ('Paul and the Corinthians must have been like us'); furthermore, it is hard to believe that in verse 4 Paul can mean that glossolalists who do not know what they are saying will yet edify themselves, when in verse 5 he denies that the listening church can be edified unless it knows what they are saying. [73] But if in verse 4 Paul has in view tongue-speakers who understand their tongues, today's charismatics cannot regard his words as giving them any encouragement, for they confessedly do not understand their own glos - solalia. And the supposition that these verses relate to private glossolalia cannot in any case be supported from Paul's flow of thought, to which private glossolalia is irrelevant. This supposition can be read into the text, as so much else can in these chapters, but not read out of it.

---

[71] Cf. Nils Johannson, '1 Cor. XIII and 1 Cor. XIV,' *New Testament Studies*, vol. 10, no. 3, April 1964, p. 389.

[72] Cf. Gromacki, op. cit., pp. 125–9.

[73] Cf. Hodge on verse 4: 'The speaker with tongues did not edify the church, because he was not understood; he did edify himself, because he understood himself . . . the understanding was not in abeyance.' On verse 18 he says: 'That Paul should give thanks to God that he was more abundantly endowed with the gift of tongues, if that gift consisted in the ability to speak in languages which he himself did not understand, and the use of which, on that assumption, could according to his principle benefit neither himself nor others, is not to be believed.' Hodge's axiom that edification presupposes understanding is hard, biblically, to get round; accepting it, however, entails the conclusion that glossolalia as practised today cannot edify, which is a most unfashionable view.

As for the tongues spoken for two generations in Pentecostal churches[74] and nowadays by millions of charismatics also, linguists, sociologists, doctors, psychologists and pastors have studied them first-hand with some thoroughness.[75] The study has its hazards, for the phenomenon is widespread among all sorts of people, and the risk of generalizing from untypical cases is high. Also, it is clear that some students find glossolalic piety unsettling, indeed unnerving, so that strong defensive

---

[74] Interestingly, Nils Bloch-Hoell in his authoritative survey, *The Pentecostal Movement* (London: George Allen & Unwin, 1964, p. 146) noted that 'glossolalia is definitely decreasing within the Pentecostal Movement.' Whether this was what the charismatic Derek Prince had in mind when he said in 1964: 'They have programmed the Holy Spirit out of most Pentecostal churches, do you know that?' (*Baptism in the Holy Spirit*, London: Fountain Trust, 1965, p. 27) can only be surmised. Virginia H. Hine, in an enquiry into tongues-speaking that embraced the USA, Mexico, Colombia and Haiti, found that second-generation Pentecostals generally used tongues less than did their fathers, and that 'the most frequent glossolalics were those who had been least socialized to accept the practice' – in other words, those for whom it had most charm of novelty and boldness of breaking with their past ('Pentecostal Glossolalia: Towards a Functional Interpretation,' *Journal for the Scientific Study of Religion*, 8 (1969), pp. 221f. I am told by British charismatic leaders that glossolalia has been less stressed in their circles during the past decade than it was before, but I cannot test that generalization.

[75] See, among recent books, William J. Samarin, *Tongues of Men and Angels* (New York: Macmillan, 1972, an authoritative, broad-based socio-linguistic study); John P. Kildahl, *The Psychology of Speaking in Tongues* (New York: Harper & Row, and London: Hodder & Stoughton, 1972, a careful and fair-minded report on a ten-year investigation), plus his chapter, 'Psychological Observations,' in *The Charismatic Movement*; Morton T. Kelsey, *Tongue Speaking* (New York: Doubleday, 1964 and London: Epworth Press, 1965, a welcoming assessment bringing Jungian personality theory to bear). See also Virginia H. Hine, art. cit. More negative assessments, reflecting older models, are those of Julius Laffal, *Pathological and Normal Language* (New York: Atherton Press, 1965; glossolalia voices, while yet concealing, a 'conflicted wish') and Wayne Oates, Frank E. Stagg, Glenn Hinson and Wayne E. Oates in *Glossolalia* (Nashville: Abingdon, 1967; glossolalia is a regressive symptom of a deprived personality). Among older authorities, George B. Cutten, *Speaking in Tongues* (Northford Cosin: Elliotts, 1927) sees glossolalia as a syndrome found among non-verbalizers of low mental ability and social privilege, and Emile Lombard, *De la Glossolalie chez les Premiers Chrétiens et des Phénomènes Similaires* (Lausanne: Bridel, 1910), depicts it as a kind of entranced automatic speech. A well-digested pastoral treatment is C. W. Parnell, *Understanding Tongues-Speaking* (Johannesburg: South African Baptist Press, 1972). See also Hoekema's two books already cited.

prejudices arise to cloud their judgement. [76] However, there seems to be, if not unanimity, at least a growing agreement among present-day investigators on the following points.

i) Whatever glossolalists may believe to the contrary, glossolalia is not language in the ordinary sense, though it is both self-expression and communication; and whatever Freudian theorists may have suspected or feared, it is not a product of the kind of disassociation of mind and bodily function which argues stress, repression or mental sickness. It is, rather, a willed and welcomed vocal event in which, in a context of attention to religious realities, the tongue operates within one's mood but apart from one's mind in a way comparable to the fantasy-languages of children [77] and the scat-singing of the late Louis Armstrong. [78] It is not the prerogative

---

[76] 'Quite clearly, available evidence requires that any explanation of glossolalia as pathological must be discarded. Even among those who accept this position, however, there often remains a sort of non-specific suspicion of emotional immaturity, of sub-clinical anxiety, or of some sort of personal inadequacy. This is particularly true of church leaders in whose denominations the ranks of Spirit-filled Christians are swelling.' (Hine, art. cit., p. 217).

[77] Cf. Samarin, op. cit., pp. 142f. and Dennis Bennett in *The Charismatic Movement*, pp. 25f. Bennett identifies childish pseudo-languages with the glosso-lalic gift, and on this basis claims that 'it is not unusual to find a person who has been speaking in tongues ever since childhood but who did not know the significance of what he or she was doing.' How this squares with Bennett's conviction that glossolalia is a Spirit-given consequence of conversion is not clear, but it shows most helpfully what sort of thing Bennett takes glossolalia in himself and in those to whom he ministers to be.

[78] 'There is no mystery about glossolalia. Tape-recorded samples are easy to obtain and to analyze. They always turn out to be the same thing: strings of syllables, made up of sounds taken from among all those that the speaker knows, put together more or less haphazardly but which nevertheless emerge as word-like and sentence-like units because of realistic, language-like rhythm and melody . . . Nothing "comes over [the speaker's] vocal chords." Speech . . . starts in the brain . . . when someone speaks in tongues, he is only using instructions [to the vocal organs] that have lain dormant since childhood. 'Finding' them and then being willing to follow them are the difficult things. So the only causes that need to be found are those that explain why a person should want to use these rules again and how he becomes willing to do so.' (Samarin, op. cit., pp. 227f.) Samarin parallels glossolalia with the 'nonsense vocalizations' of Armstrong, Ella Fitzgerald and others; he might have added to his list Adelaide Hall in Duke Ellington's 1927 Creole Love Call and Billy Banks in Yellow Dog Blues (1932), once a candidate for the title of the hottest track ever. It is unfortunate that Samarin miscalls scat-singing, be-bop (pp. 145f.); be-bop was a name for 'progressive' instrumental jazz, and was coined in 1946.

of one psychological type rather than another, nor is it the product of any particular set of external circumstances or pressures.

ii) Though sometimes starting spontaneously in a person's life, with or without attendant emotional excitement, glossolalia is regularly both taught (loosen jaw and tongue, speak nonsense-syllables, utter as praise to God the first sounds that come, etc.) and learned, and is in fact easy to do if one wants to.

iii) Contrary to the sombre ideas of earlier investigators, who saw it as a neurotic, psychotic, hysterical or hypnotic symptom, psycho-pathological or compensatory, a product of emotional starvation, repression or frustra - tion, glossolalia argues no unbalance, mental disturbance or prior physical trauma.[79] It can and does occur in folk so affected, for whom it is often, in effect, a support mechanism;[80] but many if not most glossolalics are persons of at least average psychological health, who have found that glossolalia is for them a kind of exalted fun before the Lord.

iv) Glossolalia is sought and used as part of a quest for closer com - munion with God, and regularly proves beneficial at a conscious level, bringing relief of tension, a certain inner exhilaration and a strengthening sense of God's presence and blessing.

v) Glossolalia represents, focuses and intensifies such awareness of divine reality as is brought to it; thus it becomes a natural means of voicing the mood of adoration, and it is not surprising that charismatics should call it their 'prayer language.' As a voice of the heart, though not in the form of conceptual language, glossolalia, in Christianity as elsewhere, always 'says' something – namely, that one is consciously involved with and directly responding to what Rudolf Otto called the 'holy' or 'numinous,' which sociologists and anthropologists now call 'the sacred.'

vi) Usually glossolalia is sought, found and used by folk who see the tongue-speaking community as spiritually 'special,' and who want to be fully involved in its total group experience.

All this argues that for some people, at any rate, the capacity for glossolalia is a good gift of God, just as for all of us power to express thought in language is a good gift of God. But since glossolalists see their tongues as mainly if not wholly for private use and do not claim to know what they are saying, while Paul speaks only of tongues that are for utterance and interpretation in public and seems sure that the speaker will always have some idea of his own meaning, it is not possible to be as sure of the identity of the two phenomena as restorationism requires.

Uncertainty peaks, as it seems to me, in connection with the interpre - tation of tongues.[81] Restorationism invites us to equate both tongues and interpretation today with the charismata at Corinth which were so named

---

[79]  Cf. Kildahl, *The Psychology of Speaking in Tongues* (British ed.) 83f.

[80]  Cf. Kildahl, *The Charismatic Movement*, pp. 141f.

[81]  See on this Samarin, op. cit., pp. 162–172.

nineteen centuries ago. Paul's word for 'interpret' is διερμηνεύω (1 Cor. 12:30, 14:5,13,27), which can mean explaining anything not understood (so in Luke 24:27), but in connection with language naturally implies translating the sense that is 'there' in the words (as in Acts 9:36). Paul certainly speaks as if the Corinthian sounds carried translatable meaning (1 Cor. 14:9–13), and present-day interpreters assume this about present-day tongues (unjustifiably, as we have seen). But their performances perplex.

Interpretations are as stereotyped, vague and uninformative as they are spontaneous, fluent and confident. Weird mistakes are made. Kildahl tells how the Lord's Prayer in an African dialect was interpreted as a word on the second coming.[82] An Ethiopian priest whom I tutored went to a glossolalic gathering which he took to be an informal multilingual praise service, and made his contribution by standing and reciting Psalm 23 in Ge'ez, the archaic tongue of his native Coptic worship; at once it was publicly interpreted, but, as he said to me next day in sad bewilderment, 'it was all wrong.' Kildahl also reports that of two interpreters who heard the same tape-recorded glossolalia, one took it as a prayer for 'guidance about a new job offer' and the other as 'thanksgiving for one's recent return to health after a serious illness.' Told that there was a clash here, 'without hesitation or defensiveness, the interpreter said that God gave to one interpreter one interpretation, and gave to another interpreter another interpretation.'[83] The experience is that interpretations come to mind immediately, the claim is that God gives them directly, and as with charismatic prophecy, for which a similar claim is made, so long as what is said is biblically legitimate it is incorrigible because uncheckable. Without venturing to dismiss all interpretation as delusive on the basis of a few slips that showed, and agreeing with Samarin that the sense of group rapport which the glossolalia-plus-interpretation ritual creates may be valuable in itself,[84] I think it would be most hazardous to assume that here we have a restoring of the gift of interpretation of which Paul wrote. The evidence is just too uncertain.

Hoekema suggests that when tongue-speaking brings blessing, its source is 'not the glossolalia as such but the state of mind of which it is said to be the evidence, or . . . the seeking for a greater fullness of the

---

[82] Kildahl, *Psychology* . . ., p. 63.

[83] Kildahl in *The Charismatic Movement*, p. 136. He continues: I have gained the impression that interpreters who translate tongue-speech literally are often poorly integrated psychologically. Their view of their gift of interpretation borders on the grandiose. This impression has not been tested clinically, and I offer it to the reader simply to see whether it coincides with the general impression left by this type of interpretation of tongues.

[84] Samarin, op. cit., p. 166.

Spirit which preceded it.'[85] This suggestion seems more solid than any version of the claim that current glossolalia, in which the mind is in abeyance, is edifying in and of itself. So, too, interpretations may bring blessing, by ministering scriptural encouragement, without necessarily being God-given renderings of God-given languages, as some think they are, and as interpretations at Corinth perhaps were.

*6) Can charismatic healing ministries be convincingly equated with the healing gifts mentioned in 1 Corinthians 12:23, 30? Surely not.*

The model for healing gifts in the apostolic churches can only have been the apostles' own healing gifts, for which in turn Jesus' own healing ministry was the model. But Jesus and the apostles healed directly with their word (Matt. 8:5ff., 9:6f. John 4:46ff.; Acts 9:34) or their touch (Mark 1:41, 5:25ff. Acts 28:8); healing was then instant (Matt. 8:13; Mark 5:29; Luke 6:10, 17:14; John 5:9; Acts 3:7; once in two stages, each of which was instant, Mark 8:22ff.), organic defects (e.g. wasted and crippled limbs) were healed, as well as functional, symptomatic and psychosomatic diseases (Acts 3:2ff. Luke 6:8ff. John 9, etc.); and on occasion they raised individuals who had been dead for days (Luke 7:11ff. 8:49ff. John 11:1–44; Acts 9:36ff.). They healed very large numbers (Luke 4:40, 7:21; Matt. 4:23f. Acts 5:12ff., 28:19), and there is no record that they ever attempted to heal without success (save in the one case where the disciples failed to pray, Mark 9:17–29, and Jesus had to take over). Whatever else can be said of the ministry of Pentecostal and charismatic healers of our time, and of those whose praying for the sick has been a matter, as it seems, of specific divine calling, none of them has a track record like this. We may not therefore assume, as is sometimes done, that what charismatics have now must be what Paul was talking about in 1 Corinthians 12:28 – that, and no more. In apostolic times the gift of healing was a great deal more. The most we can say of charismatic healers is that at some moments and in some respects they are enabled to be like the gifted healers of New Testament times, and every such occasion confirms that God's touch has still its ancient power. But that is much less than saying that in the ministry of these folk the New Testament gift of healing reappears.[86]

---

[85] Hoekema, *What about Tongue Speaking?*, pp. 135f.

[86] For a positive survey of healing in Christian history, cf. Morton T. Kelsey, *Healing and Christianity* (New York: Harper & Row, and London: SCM, 1973), and Evelyn Frost, *Christian Healing: A Consideration of the Place of Spiritual Healing in the Church of Today in the Light of the Doctrine and Practice of the Ante-Nicene Church* (London: Mowbrays, 1940). For negative assessments, see Warfield, *Counterfeit Miracles* and Wade H. Boggs, Jr., *Faith Healing and the Christian Faith* (Richmond, Vq.: John Knox Press, 1956). *For a charismatic healer's perspective, see* Francis MacNutt, *Healing* and *The Power to Heal* (Notre Dame: Ave Maria Press, 1974 and 1977). For wisdom on the whole subject, see an older book written to

The operative word in all my six questions has been *convincingly*. That all these ventures of assertion and denial have been tried is not in question. My point is that no arguments to date have been cogent enough to make them stick, and it seems clear enough that none ever will be. Certainly, there have been providences and manifestations among charismatics (oth‐ ers, too) corresponding in certain respects to the miracles, healings, tongues and (more doubtfully) interpretations of tongues which authenticated the apostles and the Christ whom they preached (see 2 Cor. 12:12; Romans 15:15–19; Heb. 2:3f.; and the Acts narratives). [87] Certainly, too, both in and

---

[86] *(continued)* counter the unbalance of A. J. Gordon and A. B. Simpson, Henry W. Frost, *Miraculous Healing* (repr. with 'An Appreciation' by D. M. Lloyd-Jones, London: Marshall, Morgan & Scott, and Westwood, N.J. Revell, 1951); also MacArthur, *The Charismatics*, pp. 130–55, and D. M. Lloyd-Jones, *The Supernatural in Medicine* (London: Christian Medical Fellowship, 1971).

[87] To include prophecy among 'sign-gifts' authenticating the apostles, as is sometimes done, does not seem correct. Joel's prediction, quoted by Peter at Pentecost, was of universal prophecy as one mark of the age of the Spirit (Acts 2:17f.), thus 'every Christian is potentially a prophet' (J. A. Motyer in *New Bible Dictionary*, ed. J. D. Douglas et al., London: Inter-Varsity Fellowship, and Grand Rapids: Eerdmans, 1962, p. 1045). Though prophets both before and after Christ were inspired to foretell the future (cf. Matt. 24:15; Acts 11:28, 21:10f.; 1 Pet. 1:10–12, Rev. 1:3, 22:18), their essential ministry was forthtelling God's present word to his people. This regularly meant application of revealed truth, but not necessarily augmentation of it. As Old Testament prophets preached covenant and law, mercy and judgment, so New Testament prophets preached the gospel and the life of faith for edification and encouragement (cf. 1 Cor. 14:3, 24f; Acts 15:32), and Paul wishes all the Corinthian church without exception to share in this ministry. So a prophetic 'revelation' (1 Cor. 14–26) must ordinarily have been an inspired application of truth that in one sense was revealed already; but the application would reveal how it bore on the hearers' lives there and then. There is no indication that New Testament prophets gave their messages in the name of the Father or the Son; as David Atkinson says, 'the common use of the first person singular in charismatic congregational prophecy today . . . would not seem to be of the essence of prophecy, but rather to be a behavioural habit developed within the subculture . . . the authority of the prophetic message is not (in) its form, but its content, and to use a form like that makes the weighing of the content [as prescribed, 1 Cor. 14:29ff.] that much harder' (*Prophecy*, Bramcote: Grove Books, 1977, p. 22). The proper conclusion is that, rather than suppose prophecy to be a long-gone first-century charisma now revived, and therefore to be dressed up in verbal clothes which set it apart from all other Christian communications over nineteen centuries, we should realize that it has actually been exhibited in every sermon or informal 'message' that has had a heart-searching, 'home-coming' application to its hearers ever since the church began. The confused and confusing claim that charismatics enjoy a revived

beyond charismatic circles there have been all down church history 'second blessings' and anointings of the Spirit corresponding in certain respects to Pentecost.[88] But it cannot be convincingly concluded from any of this evidence that the archetypal New Testament realities have now, after long abeyance, been given back to the church just as they were.

We need not deny that some Christians' experience of spiritual deep - ening in all traditions since the end of the first century may have felt like the apostles' Pentecostal experience; we need only note that New Testa - ment theology forbids us to interpret it in Pentecostal terms, or to interpret any experience apart from conversion itself as receiving the Spirit of Christ in the fullness of his new covenant ministry. Nor need we express a view on the perhaps unanswerable question of whether God's withdrawing of the so-called 'sign-gifts' after the apostles' ministry, which the gifts authen - ticated, was ever meant that he would never under any circumstances restore them as they were; we need only observe that they have not actually been restored as they were, though some charismatics groundlessly claim the contrary. In short, it seems plain that restorationism as a theology of charismatic experience will not do, and if we want to discern what God is doing in this movement we must think about it in other terms. [89]

---

[87] *(continued)* prophetic ministry has focused fresh interest on prophecy as a theme of discussion, but the thing itself has been, and remains, a reality whenever and wherever the Word is genuinely preached, i.e., spelt out and applied. See Atkinson, op. cit., and David Hill, *New Testament Prophecy* (London: Marshall, Morgan & Scott, 1979).

[88] Regrettably, many charismatics have spoken and written as if these post-con- version deepenings of fellowship with the Father and the Son through the Spirit have only ever happened with any frequency in the Wesleyan-holiness tradition and then in their own Pentecostal-charismatic circles. To those who know the history of Christian devotion, patristic, medieval and modern, Protestant and Catholic, this must appear as an arrogant provincialism matching in the realm of spirituality the so-called 'Anabaptist' ecclesiology, which in effect tells us to ignore the centuries between the apostles and ourselves, and see God as starting again with us. Such an attitude suggests not only ignorance of the Christian past but also forgetfulness of the Lord's promise that the Spirit should abide with the church always (cf. John 14:16).

[89] In evaluating charismatic phenomena, it should be remembered that group beliefs shape group expectations, and group expectations shape individual expe- riences. A group with its own teachers and literature can mould the thoughts and experiences of its members to a startling degree. Specifically, when it is believed that an enhanced sense of God and his love to you in Christ and his enabling power (the anointing of the Spirit), accompanied by tongues, on the model of the apostles' experience in Acts 2, is the norm, it will certainly be both sought and found; but then it will have to be tested as an expectation-shaped experience, and the expectations which shaped it will have to be tested separately.

# V

I offer now an alternative proposal for theologizing charismatic experience – sketchy and tentative, but congruous, I think, with the Bible doctrine of humanity, of salvation and of the Spirit, and congruous too with the largely positive evaluation of charismatic spirituality reached earlier, which is not affected by the inadequacy of the theology that often goes with it. I introduce my proposal by pin-pointing some facts which by now, I think, have become clear.

The charismatic movement, like other movements in the church, is something of a chameleon, taking theological and devotional colour from what surrounds it and is brought to it, and capable of changing colour as these factors change. Everywhere it, or the older Pentecostalism out of which it grew, began with some form of restorationism which rested on the axiom of the holiness movements, that the disciples' baptism in the Spirit in Acts 2 is a model for ours; but it has not everywhere stayed with that theology.

Whereas in the USA, where holiness-Pentecostal traditions remain strong in denominations, books and teaching institutions, Protestant charismatics are mostly restorationists still (at least, their literature suggests that), in Britain at least, where Reformed soteriology, stressing the unity of salvation in Christ, has more impact than Wesleyan anthropocentrism, which parcels out salvation into a set of separate 'blessings,' charismatic leaders have mostly dropped the doctrine of baptism in the Holy Spirit as a necessary second work of grace and substituted for it the thought that the entry into a fuller experience of the Spirit which they pin-point (sometimes called the release of the Spirit) is rather the subjective realization of what initiation into Christ involves. [90]

English-speaking Roman Catholics have come to say very much the same, deprecating the older Spirit-baptism teaching, stressing the objective gift of the Spirit in water-baptism in a way that evangelicals are bound to challenge, but avoiding the Arminian model of faith, or 'openness to God,' as a trigger activating God in his character as a deliverer of goods – a model which evangelical charismatics do not always avoid. Charismatic experience, we said earlier, will consist of more than one theology; now we must observe that where charismatic teaching has been revised, the thrust of the revision has been to assimilate it to accepted 'home church' doctrine, whatever that happens to be. Charismatics, while maintaining solidarity spiritually with other charismatics, are more and more seeking theological solidarity with their own parent segment of Christendom.

Moreover, the earlier theology of the charismata which maximized their supposed discontinuity with the natural and thus their significance

---

[90] Cf. *Gospel and Spirit*, sec. 2.

as proof of God's presence and power in one's life, is being replaced by 'naturalizing' accounts of them which reflect unwillingness to oppose the supernatural to the natural as the first restorationists did. (It was this 'super-supernaturalist' view of the life of grace as characteristically dis - continuous with nature which at bottom divided original Pentecostalism from the rest of the evangelical world, and made it so unpopular: 'super-supernaturalism' frightens people, and no wonder.) But now among charismatics (not so much among Pentecostal church members, who are tied to the older tradition) spiritual gifts are increasingly viewed as sanctified natural abilities; and Bennett, as we saw, would have us know that some folk speak in tongues from childhood without realizing it; and divine healing is domesticated by being expounded as a natural element in the church's regular ministry to the whole person, rather than being highlighted, as formerly, as the fruit of a supernatural healing gift which particular Spirit-baptized individuals have from God. [91]

These emphases also have the effect of moving charismatic thought into line with the mainstream Christian tradition, which sees grace not as overriding or destroying nature but rather as restoring and perfecting it, eliminating our radical sinfulness but not our rational humanity. It seems clear that all along the line charismatics today are cultivating, in place of the sense of being different from other Christians which marked them a decade ago, a sense of solidarity with their own churches.

Formerly, there was in the movement an undercurrent of sectarian judgmentalism with regard to Christians and congregations of non-char - ismatic spirituality, but that has now gone. At leadership level, the charismatic way of life with God is recommended as vital and fruitful without censuring other forms of devotion; and if recent converts are less tolerant, the leaders know that the pendulum-swing reaction of converts against what hurt and disillusioned them before they left it is a universal human problem which only time can ever resolve. Any continuing censoriousness and divisiveness among recent converts to the charismatic way, therefore, should be seen as a special local problem, and not be allowed to blind us to the fact that charismatics today as a body, some millions strong, are seeking to deepen, their churchly identity at all points [92]

So it should not jar when I propose an understanding of their experience which turns on the assumption that what God is doing in the

---

[91] Hummel (op. cit., ch. 17) does this typically and judiciously, but in a way which makes rather obvious the difference between the miraculous healing of the New Testament and today's ministry of spiritual healing by congregational prayer, when 'nothing is promised . . . but much is expected' (p. 218).

[92] Cf. recent writings of Michael Harper, particularly *Let My People Grow* (London: Hodder & Stoughton, and Plainfield: Logos, 1977) and *This is the Day: A Fresh Look at Christian Unity* (London: Hodder & Stoughton, 1979).

lives of 'card-carrying' charismatics is essentially what he is doing in the lives of believing, regenerate people everywhere – namely, working to renew Christ's image in us all, so that trust, love, hope, patience, commitment, loyalty, self-denial and self-giving, obedience and joy, may increasingly be seen in us as we see these qualities in him.

Earlier I listed twelve points where the characteristic charismatic emphases were biblical, healthful and needed, [93] but I have also argued that at each point where restorationism strikes out on its own, affirming God's renewal of New Testament distinctives as norms for our time (Spirit-baptism as at Pentecost, with gifts of tongues, interpretation, healing, prophecy), it is wrong; and if so, charismatic experience, being shaped in part by eccentric expectations arising from eccentric beliefs, will have in it elements of distortion also. My line of thought involves that, as will be seen, though I believe that all that is central and essential in charismatic experience it affirms. Let it be tested by the facts of that experience on the one hand, and by the Bible on the other. Only if it fits the facts will it merit attention, and only if it squares with Scripture will it deserve acceptance.

Assuming, now, that the categories of New Testament theology, being God-taught, have ontological status, i.e. express the truth and reality of things as God sees and knows it, and assuming further that Christlike wholeness is God's purpose for charismatics, as for other Christians, I reason thus.

God in redemption finds us all more or less disintegrated personalities. Disintegration and loss of rational control are aspects of our sinful and fallen state. Trying to play God to ourselves, we are largely out of control of ourselves and also out of touch with ourselves, or at least with a great deal of ourselves, including most of what is central to our real selves. God's gracious purpose, we know, is to bring us into a reconciled relationship with himself through Christ, and through the outworking of that relation-ship to re-integrate us and make us whole beings again. The relationship itself is restored once for all through what Luther called the 'wonderful exchange' whereby Christ was made sin for us and we in consequence are made the righteousness of God in him (2 Cor. 5:21). Justified and adopted into God's family through faith in Christ, Christians are immediately and eternally secure; nothing can sever them from the love of the Father and the Son (Rom. 8:32–39). But the work of re-creating us as psycho-physical beings on whom Christ's image is to be stamped, the work of sanctification as older evangelical theology called it, is not the work of a moment. Rather, it is a lifelong process of growth and transformation (2 Cor. 3:18; Rom. 12:2; Eph. 4:14–16, 23f.; Col. 3:10; 1 Pet. 2:2; 2 Pet. 3:18).

Indeed, it extends beyond this life, for the basic disintegration, that between psychic (conscious personal) life and physical life, will not be

---

[93] Cf. pp. 193–4.

finally healed till 'the redemption of our bodies' (Rom. 8:23; cf. 1 Cor. 15:35–37; 2 Cor. 5:1–10; Phil. 3:20f.). Not till then (we may suppose) shall we know all that is now shrouded in the mysterious reality of the 'unconscious,' the deep Loch Ness of the self where the monsters of repression and fear, and below them the id and the arche-types, live, and in which Freud and Jung and their brethren have fished so diligently (cf. 1 Cor. 13:12). Nor, certainly, till we leave this mortal body shall we know the end of the split-self dimension of Christian experience, analysed in Romans 7:14–25 and Galatians 5:16f. whereby those whose heart delights in God's law nonetheless find in themselves allergically negative reactions and responses to it – reactions and responses which Paul diagnoses as the continuing energy of 'sin which dwells within me,' dethroned but not destroyed, doomed to die but not dead yet. But the indwelling Holy Spirit, whose presence and ministry are the first instalment of the life of heaven (Rom. 8:23; 2 Cor. 1:22; Eph. 1:13f.; Heb. 6:4f.). and who is sovereign in communicating to us the touch and taste of fellowship with the Father and the Son (cf. John 1:3 plus 3:24 with John 14:15–23), abides and works in us to lead us towards the appointed goal, and he deals with each one's broken and distorted humanity as he finds it.

So what about glossolalia? We saw that present-day tongue-speaking, in which the mood is maintained but the mind is on vacation, cannot be confidently equated from any point of view with New Testament tongues. Against the background of this perception, it is often urged that since God's goal is full integration of the individual under fully self-conscious rational control, the overall pattern of ongoing sanctification must involve steady recovery of such control as we move deeper into what Scripture calls sincerity, simplicity and single-mindedness, whereby in all my many doings '*one* thing I do' (Phil. 3:13; cf. 2 Cor. 11:3; James 1:7f.) and in that case (so the argument runs) there can be no place for glossolalia, in which rational control of the vocal chords is given up. But a double reply may be in order.

First, since the charismatic deliberately chooses glossolalia as a means of expressing adoration and petition on themes he has in mind, but on which he wants to say more to God than he can find words for, it is not true to say that rational control is wholly absent.

Second, it does not seem inconceivable that the Spirit might prompt this relaxation of rational control at surface level in order to strengthen control at a deeper level. Wordless singing, loud perhaps, as we lie in the bath can help restore a sense of rational well-being to the frantic, and glossolalia might be the spiritual equivalent of that; it would be a Godsend if it were. Also, if its effect was to intensify and sustain moods of praise and prayer which otherwise one could not sustain because of wandering thoughts, it could be a positive character-builder, and lead into what exponents of mystical prayer term contemplation. And this might be specially beneficial to folk who as victims of the bustle, superficiality and inauthentic brittleness of modern living are not in touch with themselves at a deep level, and whose Christianity is in consequence more formal, notional, conventional, stereotyped, imitative and second-hand than it should be. (The charismatic movement is, after all, a mainly urban phenomenon, and it is in towns that these pressures operate most directly.) In this way glossolalia could be a good gift of God for some people at least, on the basis that anything which helps you to concentrate on God, practise his presence and open yourself to his influence is a good gift. (For others, however, with different problems whom God already enables to pray from their heart with understanding, glossolalia would be the unspiritual and trivial irrelevance that some now think it to be wherever it appears. It would be a case of one person's meat being another one's poison.)

What, then, about Spirit-baptism? We saw[94] that testimonies to this experience, as to the other 'second blessings' of evangelical pietism – Thomas Goodwin's sealing of the Spirit, the non-charismatic Spirit-bap - tism of Finney, Moody and Torrey, Andrew Murray's personal Pentecost, the 'Keswick experience' of being Spirit-filled – and also to such experi - ences as that of Bishop Moorhouse, all have at their heart joyful assurance, knowing God's fatherly love in Christ and so tasting heaven. I suggest that all these should be theologized as in essence so many experiences of the Spirit of adoption, who prompts believers to call God 'Father,' bearing witness with, or to, our spirit that we are God's children and heirs (see Romans 8:15–17); and of the active dwelling of the Father and the Son through the Spirit in and with the obedient saint (see John 14:15–23); and of our being filled in the direction of all God's fullness as the indwelling Christ enables us to grasp the divine love more and more (see Eph. 3:16–19), and so to rejoice with joy that is ineffable and glorified, i.e. has the tang and tincture of the manifested glory of God about it (see 1 Pet. 1:8).

These are all aspects of the 'assurance-complex' which the New Testament exhibits alongside the 'conversion-complex' of calling, bap - tism into Christ, regeneration, and incorporation into Christ's dying and rising. If this is right, the experience in question is not isolated (though in narrating it the temptation will always be to isolate it, particularly if a 'second blessing' theology lies already in one's mind); it is, rather, an intensifying of the sense of acceptance, adoption and fellowship with God which the Spirit imparts to every Christian and sustains in them more or less clearly from conversion on (cf. Gal. 4:6, 3:2).

Why the intensifying – which, so far from being a once-for-all thing, a 'second (and last!) blessing,' does (thank God!) recur from time to time? We cannot always give reasons for God's choice of times and seasons for drawing near to his children and bringing home to them in most vivid

---

[94] Cf. pp. 183–5.

and transporting ways the reality of his love.[95] Later we may be able to see that in particular cases it was preparation for pain, perplexity or loss, or for some specially demanding or discouraging piece of ministry, but in other cases we may only ever be able to say: God chose to show his child his love simply because he loves his child. But there are also times when it seems clear that God drew near to people because they drew near to him (cf. James 4:8; Jer. 29:13f. Luke 11:9–13, where 'give the Holy Spirit' means 'give experience of the ministry, influence and blessings of the Holy Spirit').

Different concerns drive Christians to renew their vows of consecration to God and seek his face – that is, to cry in sustained prayer for his present attention, favour and help in present need (cf. Ps. 27:7–14). The occasion may be guilt, fear, a sense of impotence or failure, discouragement, nervous exhaustion and depression, assaults of temptation and battles with indwelling sin, ominous illness, experiences of rejection or betrayal, longing for God (all these are instanced in the Psalms), and many other things. And when God reveals his love to the hearts of such seekers, putting into them, along with joy, new moral and spiritual strength to cope with what weighed them down, the specific meaning of the experience *for them* will relate to the needs that it met. So one will identify with those who theologize it as an enduement for holiness, another with the theology which views it as an empowering for service, and so on.

It looks in fact (though this is not the place to give the evidence) as if all the 'second blessing' theologies, Pentecostal Spirit-baptism included, owe at least as much to the experience of their exponents as they do to biblical exegesis. However, the biblical reality to which they all testify, each in its own partly perceptive and partly misleading way, is God's work of renewing and deepening assurance.

Let Pentecostal and charismatic testimonies to Spirit-baptism, along with testimonies to being Spirit-filled at Keswick and entirely sanctified in conservative Wesleyan circles, be weighed in the light of this hypothesis. Let the correspondence between the teaching and expectations which preceded the blessing and the testimony subsequently given to it be measured. Let physical adjuncts of the blessing – shouting, glossolalia, physical jerks, trance-phenomena and other hysterical symptoms – be discounted, for the view being tested (not to mention sober common sense) sees all these things as reflecting our own more or less idiosyncratic temperament and psychology rather than any difference between God's work of deepening this as distinct from that man's assurance and sense of

---

[95]　Cf. John Owen: 'Of this joy there is no account to be given, but that the Spirit worketh it when and how he will; he secretly infuseth and distils it into the soul, filling it with gladness, exultations, and sometimes with unspeakable raptures of mind.' (*Works*, ed. W. Goold, Edinburgh: Banner of Truth, 1967, 11:253).

communion with himself. I think it will be found that the theology proposed fits the facts.[96]

# VI

Some conclusions are now in order.

1) The common charismatic theology of Spirit-baptism (common, at least, in the worldwide movement as a whole, if not in particular segments of it in Britain and Germany) is the Pentecostal development of the two-level, two-stage view of the Christian life which goes back through the last-century holiness movements (Keswick, Higher Life, Victorious Life), and the power-for-service accounts of Spirit baptism that inter-twined with them, to John Wesley's doctrine of Christian perfection, otherwise perfect love, entire sanctification, the clean heart, or simply the second blessing. This charismatic theology sees the apostles' experience at Pentecost as the normative model for transition from the first and lower level to the higher, Spirit-filled level.

But this idea, though put forward in good faith, seems to lack both biblical and experiential justification, while the implication that all Chris-tians who are strangers to a Pentecostal transition experience are lower-level folk, not Spirit-filled, is, to say the least, unconvincing. Yet the honest, penitent, expectant quest for more of God, out of which has come for so many the precious experience mis-called Spirit-baptism, with all that has followed it, is always the tap-root of spiritual renewal, whether impeccably theologized or not; and so it has been in this case.

2) The restorationist theory of 'sign-gifts,' which the charismatic movement also inherited from older Pentecostalism, is inapplicable; nobody can be sure, nor does it seem likely, that the New Testament gifts of tongues, interpretation, healing and miracles have been restored, while Spirit-given prophecy, which in essence is not new revelation (though in biblical times this was often part of it), but rather power to apply to people truth already revealed, is not specially related to the charismatic milieu

---

[96] Charismatic theologians such as Harper and Smail, to whom the 'second-blessing' view of Spirit-baptism seems unacceptable, theologize the experience as one aspect of a unitary initiation into Christ of which water-baptism is the outward sign. But Christian initiation is essentially the establishing of a relation-ship with God and God's people in and through Christ, and the essence of Spirit-baptism, so called, as we saw, is the vivid realization (God-given, as I hold) that you have been initiated into Christ, i.e. that you are his and he is yours. Surely it is not very plausible to call this a part or aspect of God's initiating work, especially when it comes to a Christian many years after his conversion, as on Harper's own showing it did to him. The more straightforward thing to say is that it presupposes initiation, being in fact the Spirit's witness to it.

but has been in the church all along. Yet the movement's accompanying emphasis on every member ministry in the body of Christ, using ordi - nary(!) spiritual gifts of which all have some, is wholly right, and has produced rich resources of support and help for the weak and hurting in particular.

3) The charismatic stresses on faith in a living Lord, learning of God from God through Scripture, openness to the indwelling Spirit, close fellowship in prayer and praise, discernment and service of personal need, and expecting God actively to answer prayer and change things for the better, are tokens of true spiritual renewal from which all Christians should learn, despite associated oddities to which mistaken theology gave rise.

4) Charismatic glossolalia, a chosen way of non-verbal self-expression before God (chosen, be it said, in the belief that God wills the choice), has its place in the inescapable pluriformity of Christian experience, in which the varied make-up of both cultures and individuals is reflected by a wide range of devotional styles. It seems no less clear that as a devotional exercise glossolalia enriches some, than that for others it is a valueless irreverence. Some who have practised it have later testified to the spiritual unreality for them of what they were doing, while others who have begun it have recorded a vast deepening of their communion with God as a result, and there is no reason to doubt either testimony. Glossolalic prayer may help to free up and warm up some cerebral people, just as structured verbal prayer may help to steady up and shape up some emotional people. Those who know that glossolalia is not God's path for them and those for whom it is a proven enrichment should neither try to impose their own way on others, nor judge others inferior for being different, nor stagger if someone in their camp transfers to the other, believing that God has led him or her to do so. Those who pray with tongues and those who pray without tongues do it to the Lord; they stand or fall to their own master, not their fellow-servants; and in the same sense that there is in Christ neither Jew nor Greek, bond nor free, male nor female, so in Christ there is neither glossolalist nor non-glossolalist. Even if (as I suspect, though cannot prove) today's glossolalists do not speak such tongues as were spoken at Corinth, none should forbid them their practice; but they should not suppose that every would-be top-class Christian needs to adopt it.

5) Two questions needing to be pressed are whether, along with a sense of worship and of love, the charismatic movement also fosters a realistic sense of sin, and whether its euphoric ethos does not tend to encourage naive pride among its supporters, rather than humility.

6) Though theologically uneven (and what spiritually significant movement has not been?) the charismatic renewal should commend itself to Christian people as a God-sent corrective of formalism, institutionalism and intellectualism; as creatively expressing the gospel by its music and worship style, its praise-permeated spontaneity and bold ventures in

community; and as forcing all Christendom, including those who will not take this from evangelicals as such, to ask: What then does it mean to be a Christian, and to believe in the Holy Spirit? Who is Spirit-filled? Are they? Am I?

With radical theology inviting the church into the barren wastes of neo-Unitarianism, it is (dare I say) just like God – the God who uses the weak to confound the mighty – to have raised up, not a new Calvin or John Owen or Abraham Kuyper, but a scratch movement, cheerfully improvising, which proclaims the divine personhood and power of Jesus Christ and the Holy Spirit not by great theological eloquence, originality or accuracy, but by the power of renewed lives creating a new, simplified, unconventional and uncomfortably challenging life-style. O *sancta simplicitas!* Yet the charismatic life-stream needs an adequately biblical theology and remains vulnerable while it lacks one. The present essay has been written in the perhaps audacious hope of helping at this point.

# Evangelism

# Chapter 13

# Is Christianity Credible?

## I

In the same way that beauty is in the eye of the beholder, so questions sound different in different ears, according to what each hearer brings to them. When the Editor asked me for a contribution to the 'Is Christianity Credible?' series, he almost apologized that the question sounded defeatist and reductionist.[1] But to me it did not sound like that at all; it came, rather, as a welcome opportunity to say two things which in these days I find myself wanting to shout from the housetops. The first thing is that the intellectual credentials of thorough-going Christianity are very strong, much stronger than is often allowed, and it is only when Christians cease to be thorough-going that their faith ever sounds or looks forlorn. When it *feels* forlorn and dubious (and I suppose all Christians know such feelings on occasion), it is because, for whatever reason, relevant facts are not making their proper impact.

The second thing is that if thorough-going Christianity be thought incredible, it is a case of pots calling the kettle black, for the rival convictional systems which present themselves are less credible still. Scepticism, solipsism and nihilism, being philosophies of ultimate negation, cannot be refuted in the ordinary way, but can yet be shown to be paradoxical and unnecessary, while affirmations of alternative absolutes, Marxist, humanist, Freudian or whatever prove on inspection to be inadequate to fit all the facts. What I mean by 'thorough-going' I will try to say in a moment, but let me first state my conviction that the difficulties which much contemporary Prot-estantism finds in commending Christianity as a believable option for folk today springs directly from the way in which, following in the methodo-logical footsteps of Schleiermacher, we habitually scale Christianity down so as to represent it to its cultured despisers as the fulfilment of their own best thoughts, instincts and longings. Scaled-down Christianities are both

IS CHRISTIANITY CREDIBLE? was originally published in *Is Christianity Credible?* (London: Epworth Press, 1981), pp. 64–72. Reprinted by permission.
[1] What I said was, 'You may think the question smacks of reductionism.' I assumed wrongly – Ed.

the fruit and the root of uncertainty, and the supposition that the less we commit ourselves to maintain the easier it will be to maintain it never proves true. To be sure, Schleiermacher did not see himself as reducing Christi - anity, but rather as interpreting and indeed rejuvenating it in the cultural milieu of his time; reduce it, however, he did by the anti-transcendent, anti-revelationary, anti-Trinitarian thrust of his phenomenalist method of theologizing, and the problem with both him and his spiritual descendants is that their reduced creeds (for each has his own) seem arbitrary to a degree. In every case the question presses: why, if this man believes so much, does he not believe more? but if he believes so little, why does he not believe less? Thinkers in this tradition who, like Schleiermacher himself, have not been muddle-headed (and there have been many such, whose mental rigour merits deepest respect – Ritschl, Harnack, Troeltsch, Wiles for starters) might well seek to parry the pincers effect of this double question by saying that what determined their conclusions was strict application of their method. But since each person's method is their personal mix of pheno - menalism (learning what Christianity is by inspecting it as a human phenomenon) and positivism (sieving the witness to Christian origins through the meshes of a uniformitarian world-view), the problem of arbitrariness comes up again at a deeper level, where it is not so easily banished; for why embrace such methods in any form, when the revela - tion-claim that is integral to biblical religion points a different way? Stimulating notions and insights have certainly sprung from surveying Christianity by the light of Schleiermacherian methods, but the inescapable plurality of them has spawned so wide a range of diverse beliefs about Christian essentials (God, Jesus Christ, salvation) as to make anyone who wants to communicate Christianity to the wider world feel completely stymied. Looked at from this standpoint, the Schleiermacherian tradition of theological subjectivity has much to answer for.

It was, perhaps, no wonder that Karl Barth, in his zeal to speak the word of God and the reactionary passion of his love-hate relationship with Schleiermacher, not only refused to scale down what he took to be the biblical faith but rejected the whole apologetic enterprise of showing faith reasonable and unbelief unreasonable as a misguided exercise which leads only to truncated Christianities pandering to unbelievers' intellectual conceit and unable to follow Paul in diagnosing the world's wisdom as folly (1 Cor. 1–2). Barth's emphasis was timely and invigorating in the academic theological world of the twenties and thirties, where Kant's ghost still walked and the unholy league between idealist philosophy ('the rational is the real') and liberal theology ('what is real in Christianity is rational') still stood in older men's minds; had Barth not taken this line, the recovery of confidence in the biblical message which he sought to midwife might never have come to birth. But in the long term to have no apologetic – that is, no 'natural' or, as John Macquarrie urges us to say, 'philosophical' theology that roots the God-referring language and the God-affirming content of

Christian faith in the world of everyday reality – makes against credibility no less than does the solvent effect of Schleiermacherian subjectivism. Paul van Buren's switch from Barthianism, allegedly revelation-based but epistemologically uncertain, to the linguistic relativism, indeed scepticism, of *The Secular Meaning of the Gospel* is a cautionary tale showing what sort of recoil methodological contempt for philosophical theology may prompt.[2] Such contempt cannot establish credibility; rather the reverse.

## II

What, then, will confirm credibility? By what tests can a faith like Christianity, a total world-and-life view, be shown to be believable? Four tests, at least, are relevant.

First comes the test of *historical objectivity*. Christianity in all its forms claims to be a faith based on historical events. It will not, therefore, be credible unless its factual historical assertions are based on cogent evi - dence, and not significantly undermined by contrary evidence. For two centuries now much Western Protestant thinking about Christian origins has been shaped by the uniformitarian *a priori* wished on it in the name of Newton, plus the Romantic stress on the decisiveness of personal factors when men reconstruct and interpret the past, and it has become almost a shibboleth to say that everything important concerning Christian origins is shrouded in deep uncertainty. If that is just a way of saying that there is always some scholar around who will challenge his colleagues' claims, let the statement stand, for it is true; but if what is meant is that, this being so, nobody is entitled to be certain about Christian origins, I for one must demur. By 'cogent' evidence I mean evidence of the flow of events which prompts the conclusion (of the Sinai covenant-making, or Elijah's triumph at Carmel, or Jesus' bodily resurrection, or Paul's conversion, to take a selection of key items), 'however strange and mysterious, it must have happened, for what followed is inexplicable without it.' Without denying for a moment the findings of modern historiographical analysis about the complexity of historical judgments and the variety of cultural and presuppositional factors that enter into them, I wish to record my conviction that cogent evidence of this kind is in fact available to us, and supremely so in connection with the life, death and resurrection of Jesus Christ.

Second comes the test of *rational coherence*. Christianity in all its forms says that God the Creator transcends man's understanding, but insists in the same breath that what we know about him through revelation makes good sense. For credibility, substance must be given to this claim. So the various assertions made, historical, convictional and interpretative, of

---

[2]  Paul van Buren, *The Secular Meaning of the Gospel*, (London: SCM Press, 1963).

present realities under God must demonstrably hang together as a mean - ingful, workable and wise philosophy of life. Also, the logic of, and rules for, our speech about the incomprehensible Creator must be clearly explicable, as must our speech about human decisions and actions, which Christianity sees as both free *and* controlled, self-determined *and* over- ruled at the same time. These are the two areas where Christianity's logical coherence is, and in fact has always been, most suspect. Down the centuries, however, Christian spokespersons have set themselves to make evident the coherence that is claimed, and I judge that where Christianity is consistently formulated the job can still be done.

Third comes the test of *explanatory power*. As the higher can explain the lower, and the more complex the simple, but not vice versa, so one test for any position claiming, as all forms of Christianity do, to embody final truth about life is its power to account for actual human behaviour and states of mind, including denial or disregard of its own claims, and preference for other options. Also, it must give good answers to human - kind's inescapable questions about life's meaning, purpose and value, including the question of what death means, both others' death and our own, and whether the certainty of death does not render life senseless – the question with which Woody Allen, surely the shrewdest and most serious comedian of our time, as well as perhaps the funniest, is confessedly preoccupied. I would maintain that consistent Christianity, with its radical doctrines of this life as a preparation for the next, and of sin as touching the mind no less than the heart, and of the working of God's wrath and grace side by side in our fallen world, does not lack credibility here either.

Fourth comes the test of *individual experience* in relation to the expec - tations which Christian claims raise – perhaps the most sensitive area of evaluation today. All versions of Christianity claim that personal knowl - edge of God through Jesus Christ is life-transforming: for people in Christ are new creatures, and response to the gospel fulfils human nature in such a sense as to transmute realistic acceptance of what comes (to which the only alternatives are fantasy and suicide) from stoical endurance into a life of love and happiness. On this basis, Christianity claims to be the truest humanism, by comparison with which godless prescriptions for living do not merit that name at all. Such claims invite and indeed require inspection of Christianity's track record over two millennia, and their credibility will depend in measure on the credibility of Christians past and present. But the biblical call to *witness*, and the old truth that the proof of the pudding is in the eating, make the inspection appropriate from every standpoint. When someone like Don Cupitt concludes that incarnational faith must be queried because its moral effects have been so largely bad, we may disagree with his judgment on the facts, but on the relevance of his appeal to them there can be no argument. Nor, surely, has a faith adorned by men like Origen, Augustine, Francis of Assisi, John of the Cross, Luther, Baxter, Wesley, John Newton, Hudson Taylor, George

Muller, Sundar Singh, Charles de Foucauld and C. S. Lewis, plus countless lesser lights whose lives Christ has made new for all to see, anything to fear from this appeal. Nor (to anticipate an objection) are bad Christians a significant counterweight in this assessment; that people can profess Christianity without being transformed by it is not disputed; the question is, whether faith in Jesus Christ when taken seriously has a moral and spiritual transforming effect which is characteristic of it and is not naturally explicable in naturalistic terms. The devoted love of God and humanity, expressed in what might seem extravagances of prayer and service, in such lives as those cited seems to show quite decisively that it does, however many may profess faith while their lives and characters remain unchanged.

It should be added that the full force of Christianity's capacity to pass each of these tests will be felt only when related to its capacity to pass the other three also. The significance of these criteria of credibility is cumulative. If Christianity showed up badly in relation to any one of them, its credibility would remain uncertain, no matter how adequately it met the other three. But if, as I believe, it passes all four tests impressively, its overall credibility is established beyond doubt.

## III

Now the question I begged when speaking of 'consistent' and 'thorough-going' Christianity must be faced. That I have in mind a particular understanding of essential Christianity which in my view passes the credibility test better than its rivals must by now be obvious; that I hold to it because of its supposedly superior apologetic strength (in other words, on grounds less rational than rationalistic) is a suspicion to which I may have laid myself open. So I turn to ask what procedures and criteria should decide for us what is an adequate account of authentic Christianity, where various accounts are canvassed and doctors disagree? At the risk of sounding old-fashioned and cavalier, I urge that the method which is in principle decisive is that which the 'biblical theology' movement of the past half-century has aimed to follow, the method sometimes described as reading the Bible from within. In its twentieth-century form it is a reaction against imposing on Scripture alien presuppositions, but in essence it is the method of much Patristic and all Reformation theology, updated for our times.

This method takes seriously the claims of biblical authors to be witnesses to and messengers from the living God of whom they speak. Intellectually, imaginatively and existentially it seeks to identify with their faith and to see reality through their eyes, not only because their meaning and thrust is otherwise likely to be missed, but also and basically because the truths about God which they voice and apply come from God himself and are the normative word through which he speaks to us here and now. Thus the method views the teachings of each biblical author as all Christians view the recorded sayings of Jesus Christ, and seeks to comprehend, relate and apply them in their character as divine instruction.

For various reasons this method is today under a cloud. It has been thought to be tied to Barth's biblical positivism and Christological hermeneutic (which, however, it would if followed consistently have amended). Some of its practitioners, by ignoring philosophical theology, have made it seem that the method confines us to articulating biblical thoughts in biblical language of uncertain logical status. In stressing that God speaks in and through Scripture, they have appeared to minimize the cultural gap between the Bible world(s) and ours, leaving the impression that the method itself is intrinsically insensitive and naive at this point. We may query Dennis Nineham's belief that conceptual communication across a two- or three-millennia gap is not possible, but recent hermeneutical study has shown that getting into the mind of an Old Testament prophet or a first-century apostle is a very tricky business, and it is not clear that exponents of 'biblical theology' to date have sufficiently noted its complexity. As once James Barr convicted some of them of semantic naïvety, so now they are suspected of cultural naïvety, and also of theological naïvety, for not having done justice to the conceptual pluralism (not, I think, pluralism of substance, though some today argue otherwise) of the biblical material. But these shortcomings can all be corrected – as rigour in applying the method requires that they should be without any doubt being cast on the method itself.

Two of the conclusions to which this method leads may be stated here. The first is that acknowledgment of God as the self-revealed Triune Creator and Redeemer, and of Jesus Christ as our divine human mediator and sin-bearer, risen, reigning and in due course returning, and of salvation as a new reconciled relationship with God in which the believer has been made a new creature in Christ by the Spirit, are basic and indispensable elements in any adequate account of Christianity; for these things – not as Bultmannian myths, but as revealed truths – are the core of New Testament Christian belief. The second conclusion is that the criterion whereby to test our own theological theories must be this: would the New Testament writers, were they here today, recognize these constructions as being in line with what they themselves said? This is just a way of articulating the old truth that we must test all things by the written word. Thus the contents and boundaries of thorough-going Christianity may be discerned.

## IV

One last word in this all-too-brief farrago. The question, 'Is Christianity credible?' prompts the retort, 'credible to whom?' If we are thinking of the person who does not yet believe, we should remind ourselves that in New Testament evangelism and exposition the Christian gospel is always presented as God's solution to our problem – the problem, that is, of our lostness, our separation from our maker through our sins – and the good news of the solution is preceded by the bad news of the divine rejection set forth in the law under which we all naturally stand. In post-biblical Christian evangelism, whether by the apologists or Athanasius ( *Contra Gentiles* and *De Incarnatione*) or Savonarola or Luther or Baxter or Whitefield or Wesley or Spurgeon or John Sung or Billy Graham, this pattern of exposition has regularly been followed, for it is observable that the dawning of a sense of personal spiritual need makes a vast difference to one's capacity to find the gospel believable. When at Corinth Paul resolved to stick to plain unvarnished proclamation of Christ crucified, 'not in plausible words of wisdom, but in demonstration of the Spirit and power, that your faith might not rest in the wisdom of men but in the power of God' (1 Cor. 2:4f.), it looks as if this was precisely his strategy; he looked to the Spirit to make folk realize that the needs of which he spoke were real for them, and the crucified Messiah whom he proclaimed was God's merciful provision for them. We should not forget that through the Spirit there is self-evidencing, convincing force in the gospel, over and above the force of any arguments to confirm its credibility; and that the New Testament approach to the problem of human incredulity is not that the gospel needs to be changed from one generation to another so as to make it more believable, but that human beings in every generation need to be changed by the Holy Spirit so that they may be able to believe it as undoubtedly God's truth. So in seeking to commend Christianity as credible to unbelievers we should not stop short at going over the kind of thing covered in this essay; we should speak to them also, and very fully, of the spiritual predicament of humankind and the abiding problem of unforgiven, unmastered sin, and we should look to the Holy Spirit as we do so to work once more as he worked in Corinth long ago.

# Chapter 14

# A Christian View of Man

In the days when theology was thought of as Queen of the Sciences, Christian concepts were treated as ultimate principles of explanation for everything – or maybe I should say, principles of ultimate explanation – since the claim was that though secondary causes operate throughout created reality, everything must be explained ultimately in terms of God, inasmuch as it exists ultimately by the will of God and not otherwise. At present, however, the Queen is exiled from most of the kingdoms of higher learning, and has been so for the best part of a hundred years, and palace revolutions have set secular world views and ideologies on her throne, to rule in her place.

One result is that in those interdisciplinary discussions of life's great issues which every college and university worth its salt maintains, theo - logians often find themselves in the position of would-be immigrants denied entry at the border because their academic passports show them to be coming from the wrong quarter of the intellectual world. I wish therefore to begin by putting on record my delight that Hillsdale College, for one, keeps a place in its curriculum for Christian studies, and still allows that the Christian view of things might throw light into perplexing areas where, for lack of it, there is at present only ominous darkness.

Now let me tell you what I plan to do. My place in this series requires me to talk about man, and my role as a theologian commits me to talk about man in relation to God. That, however, tells you nothing about my method, and these are days in which you need to watch theologians like hawks because of the extraordinary madnesses of method in which as a fraternity we get enmeshed. So let me come clean about my own present purpose and procedure right away.

The array of intellectual enterprises which nowadays call themselves theology prove on inspection to be of two opposite sorts, each with its own set of mutations within the type as it interacts with the modern world. Some theologies start by taking from current culture fashionable hypotheses about

A CHRISTIAN VIEW OF MAN was originally published in *The Christian Vision: Man in Society*, ed. Carl F. Henry (Hillsdale, Mich: Hillsdale College Press, 1984), pp. 101–119. Reprinted by permission.

the human race, hypotheses philosophical, physiological, psychological, anthropological, historical, and socio-economic; then, treating these as fixed points, they spend their strength editing and recasting the Christian tradition so as to make it fit these secular frames of reference. Other theologies take the Christian tradition itself as their frame of reference, within which they relativize, interpret and critique the secular hypotheses and the evidence on which they are based. Though the two-way traffic of mutual interrogation flows constantly between theologians of each camp, they cannot come very close to each other because their fixed points are so different. Those of type one usually label themselves liberal, those of type two, conservative. Both groups are what they are because of what they believe to lie at the heart of the Christian tradition.

Liberals find there noncognitive religious feelings or urges which for self-descriptive purposes clothe themselves in whatever verbal forms each culture may at any time provide; conservatives find there knowledge of facts about God and men which God himself has given by what he has told us or shown us. Alongside these two mutually exclusive approaches to the question of revelation (for that is what we are talking about here) there is no third option, though there are many confused and confusing compromises littering the theological scene. But every theologian – indeed, every Christian – does in fact come down on one side or other of this fence, even those who are sure they are sitting on it.

Now I am a theologian of the second type. I would rather call myself conservationist than conservative, lest I seem to embrace a closed-minded, change-resisting ideology as I fear my fundamentalist friends sometimes slip into doing. But I shall not fuss about words; you may call me a conservative, and I shall not complain! What I perceive at the heart of Christianity is God revealing himself in saving love by word and deed within mid-Eastern history, supremely in the incarnation whereby the second person of the Godhead walked and talked as a man among men, but also in the ministry of prophets and apostles and in the Scriptures which are the literary deposit of that ministry; and I perceive the historic Christian tradition, within which I stand and out of which I speak, as a sustained struggle to grasp and apply this uniquely given revelation. So I want to bring this revelation into the present, as best I can, for the light it throws on our perplexities about ourselves, and my hope, as you would expect, is to persuade you to embrace it as the guiding light for your life.

After that, it will not surprise you that I introduce what I have to say by an extract from the Bible. It comes in fact from the Old Testament, which Christians claim as Christian Scripture. We do that because Christ and his apostles, the founders of Christianity, did it before us. It is a Christian heresy to discount or drop the Old Testament, to which Christ appealed as the unchallengeable word of his Father which he had come to fulfil. Here, now, is the passage, Psalm 8, a song of praise to God for the way he has made man.

O Lord, our Lord,
     how majestic is your name in all the earth!
You have set your glory
     above the heavens.
From the lips of children and infants
     you have ordained praise
because of your enemies,
     to silence the foe and the avenger.

When I consider your heavens,
     the work of your fingers,
the moon and the stars,
     which you have set in place,
what is man that you are mindful of him,
     the son of man that you care for him?
You made him a little lower than the heavenly beings
     and crowned him with glory and honour.
You made him ruler over the works of your hands;
     you put everything under his feet:
all flocks and herds, and the beasts of the field,
the birds of the air, and the fish of the sea,
     all that swim the paths of the seas.
O Lord, our Lord,
     how majestic is your name in all the earth!

Well, what is man? I start my argument by picking up that question as it relates to each human individual. It is an inescapable question which no one who thinks at all can avoid asking about himself or herself. We find ourselves to be self-transcendent, because we are self-conscious and self-aware. We can stand back from ourselves and look at ourselves and judge ourselves and ask basic questions about ourselves, and, what is more, we cannot help doing these things. The questions ask themselves, unbidden; willy-nilly, one finds oneself wondering what life means, what sense it makes, what one is here for. And such questions must be squarely faced.

Usually when we talk about man we are generalizing about mankind, and regularly we exempt ourselves from our own generalizations. We speak of the human race as if we were God looking down on it and not ourselves part of it. But that will not do. The acid test of our generaliza - tions is whether we can apply them to ourselves, and live in terms of them as truths about ourselves. No generalizations about others which you are not prepared to apply to yourself have any claim to respectability, for you cannot contract out of the human race; and the moment you start applying them to yourself you abandon the impersonal, collectivist standpoint so beloved by human scientists, Western as well as Marxist, and come back to the problem of the individual – yourself – and the meaning of your own life.

Maybe you recall the scintillating speech in which Shakespeare's Hamlet says, 'What a piece of work is man! how noble in reason! how infinite in faculty (i.e., ability)! in form, in moving, how express and admirable! in action how like an angel! in apprehension how like a god! the beauty of the world! the paragon of animals!' Here Hamlet says brilliantly what Psalm 8 adumbrates and Christians have always said about man: namely, that he is a kind of cosmic amphibian. He has both a body and a mind and so has links with both apes and angels; he stands between animals who have no minds like his and angels who have no bodies like his.

This is the classic Christian hierarchical view according to which the creatures are ranked in tiers, so to speak, below the Creator, at different levels of intrinsic complexity and significance in the cosmic order. Human beings are thus below angels but above the rest of the animate creation, over which mankind has actually been set to rule (Psalm 8:4–8, echoing Genesis 1:26–28). Each human individual, therefore, is wonderful, mysterious, resourceful, glorious.

But now, do you recall the plot of *Hamlet?* The quiveringly intelligent prince of Denmark is more than a mouthpiece for oracles; he is an individual in his own right, and an individual put on the spot, caught in a web of circumstances like a rat in a trap. Hamlet is charged by his father's ghost to take vengeance on the unspeakable Claudius; he cannot find a situation in which he can effectively do it, and ends as a victim of the malice that his efforts have aroused. That is the real plot of the play and the real agony of its hero, and it is this that makes *Hamlet* a tragedy in Aristotle's definitive sense – a pitiful, terrifying, cathartic story of destruc - tion and waste, the waste of a good man and a potentially fruitful life, and the dragging down of others with him.

Some tragedies (*Macbeth, Othello, King Lear* and most of Ibsen's plays, for instance) hinge upon a moral flaw or lapse which interacts with unfolding circumstances to bring about the protagonist's downfall. Other tragedies, however, like Sophocles' *King Oedipus*, Hardy's *Tess*, and *Hamlet*, work without this; they simply show us a noble person against whom the cards are stacked. The chilling fascination of their story then lies in the empathy we feel with the victim as the trap closes. For so much of life as we know it is like that! And this brings us right back to the enigma of the individual, the problem of what it means to be me. Am I a hero, a victim, or just a nonentity in the world of which I am consciously part? How should I value myself? And how should I direct myself? How should I make decisions at such crunch points in life as the tragedies portray?

> The play is the tragedy, 'Man',
> And its hero the conqueror Worm.

Is that all that can be said? Does life's ultimate frustration and waste consist in the fact that none of the things that seem important to us really mean anything? Is life, after all, 'a tale told by an idiot, full of sound and fury, signifying nothing'? Is nobility, after all, a non-issue, as so many modern writers seem to think? Again I ask: what is man? For thinking people, as I said above, the question is inescapable.

More questions arise: the question of identity, for instance. Who are you? You don masks, you play roles; how, amid all that, can you identify, and identify with, the real you? Again, there is the question of goals. Has life a purpose? If so, which way should I go to fulfil it? That raises the question of destiny. What am I here for? What can I hope for? Intimations of immortality come to us all; the atheist resolutely squelches them, dare we trust them? If we do, we next must ask whether what we do now will affect what we experience then. In any case, we all have to die some day, and that brings up the question whether my future death will make nonsense of my life, as existentialists believe it will. Can I make sense of death? I think it was Dag Hammarskjöld who said that no philosophy which will not make sense of death is fit to be a guide for life, and surely he was right. With all this comes the question of life's inner contradictions. Why do I so often feel lonely and unfulfilled and impotent and frustrated when I am doing things that I expected to enjoy?

Take the matter of relationships. Life, we know, is essentially relation - ships, and the rich life is the life enriched by one's relationships. But how do enriching relationships happen? How are they achieved? And why do I seem to myself both to want them and not to want them? If close relationships are essential to my fulfilment, why do I shrink from them, as I seem to do? If however they are not essential to my fulfilment, why do I desire them, as again I seem to do? I am a human being in contradiction, a problem and a perplexity to myself. And aren't you the same?

Look at this quote:

Always I have seen around me all the games and parades of life and have always envied the players and the marchers. I watch the cards they play and feel in my belly the hollowness as the big drums go by, and I smile and shrug and say, Who needs games?

Who wants parades? The world seems to be masses of smiling people who hug each other and sway back and forth in front of a fire and sing old songs and laugh in each other's faces, all truth and trust. And I kneel at the edge of the woods, too far off to feel the heat of the fire. Everything seems to come to me in some kind of secondhand way which I cannot describe. Am I not meat and tears, bone and fears, just as they? Yet when most deeply touched, I seem, too often, to respond with smirk or sneer, another page in my immense catalogue of remorses. I seem forever on the edge of expressing the inexpressible, touching what has never been touched, but I cannot reach through the veil of apartness. I am living without being truly alive. I can love without loving. When I am in the midst of friends, when there is laughter, closeness, empathy, warmth, sometimes I can look at myself from a little way off and think that they do not really know who is with them there, what strangeness is there beside them, trying to be something else.

Once, just deep enough into the cup to be articulate about subjective things, I tried to tell Meyer all this. I shall never forget the strange expression on his face. 'But we are *all* like that!' he said. 'That's the way it is. For everyone in the world. Didn't you know?'

That soliloquy comes from John D. MacDonald's heroic anti-hero Travis McGee, a modern Robin Hood with clay feet whose James Bondish exploits in paperback may or may not interest you. But I think you will agree that it pinpoints brilliantly this contradictory core of human experience, our recurring sense of isolation within togetherness and of alienation within community. 'That's the way it is. For everyone in the world. Didn't you know?' But how should we account for this universal state of affairs? Again we have to ask: what is man? I am sure that, as members of the human race, you have been with me in judgement and analysis thus far; I hope you will stay with me as I proceed. For now I shall try to state the Christian answer to some of these questions.

Perhaps I had better be more precise, and say: the *mainstream* Christian answer, as given in the Bible and maintained in the church against eccentric extremes ever since Christianity began. Essentially it is as follows. Every human individual has infinite worth, being made by God for nobility and glory; but every human individual is currently twisted out of moral shape in a way that only God can cure. To put it in standard Christian language, each of us by nature is God's image-bearer, but is also fallen and lives under the power of sin, and now needs grace. Sin, the anti-God allergy of the soul, is a sickness of the spirit, and the tragic sense of life, the inner tensions and contradictions just surveyed, plus our inveterate unrealism, egoism, and indisposition to love God and our neighbour, are all symptoms of our disorder.

Sometimes Christians have expressed this thought by saying that man though good is terribly weak. That however seems hardly adequate, and I side with those who speak more strongly and say that each of us is radically bad, though providentially kept from expressing our badness fully. But in human nature, viewed morally, as God views it, everything is out of true to some extent. And though we have technology for straightening roads and integrating information, it is beyond us to straighten and integrate the human character. Man needs God for that.

This in a nutshell is the view I shall develop. But since a contrasting background makes things stand out more vividly, I shall before going further remind you of the main alternative views that are current in our culture. They each offer them selves in the name of humanism, a familiar word signifying the affirmation, celebration and attempted realization of human potential; from my standpoint, however, animalism would be a better name for them, since they all invite us to live as the lower animals do, without knowledge of, or regard for, the Creator – which in the theologically definitive sense of the word 'human' is a sub-human state for a man to be in. Here, now, they are.

First comes *evolutionary optimism*, which is a secular version of the Christian heresy of self-salvation called Pelagianism. This is the view that our race and our world are actually and necessarily getting better as time goes by. This seems to me a forlorn idea which history and experience have comprehensively falsified; only a kind of faith that is impervious to facts and better society. In each case, of course, one group has to be excluded from the process, namely the manipulators them selves. Orwell imagined the result in his 1984. Any who doubt whether infallibly wise philosopher-kings, such as Plato dreamed of, can actually be found to play the role of Big Brother, or who doubt the validity of the materialist and behaviourist assumptions on which this manipulative ideology rests, or who are old-fashioned enough to believe that God alone is lord of the conscience, will understandably be less than enthusiastic.

Against the background of these alternatives, I now proceed to elucidate the classic Christian answer to the question: what is man? I have four double-barrelled points to develop, and the first thing to say is that for each of them Jesus of Nazareth, the Jesus of the four gospels, the perfect man who was God incarnate, is my center of reference. It cannot be said too strongly or too often that for Christians Jesus is both the model and the means of true and total humanness in a world where, as was said above, our own human nature has in every case been distorted and diminished by sin. Incarnation means that Jesus, who was one hundred percent divine, was also one hundred percent human, and it is supremely by observing his divine humanity that we learn what constitutes full and authentic humanness for ourselves. In Jesus we see what humanity is meant to be and what through Jesus' own mediation our flawed humanity may become. Now to my analysis.

### The first point concerns the **dignity and** dependence *of the individual*

Human dignity, yours and mine, and that of every human being without exception, flows from the fact that we are made in the image of God, as Genesis 1:26 and 5:1–2 affirm.

What does that mean? we ask. Clearly, the basic idea is that human beings are like God in a way that other animate creatures are not. How in detail to conceive this likeness is, however, a question that has exercised exegetes and theologians throughout the Christian era. The mainstream line of exposition is as follows. The *imago Dei* relationship relates not to our physical but to our personal nature, and this at four levels.

First, God, whom Genesis 1 and all Scripture presents as rational, made us rational, able to form concepts, think thoughts, carry through trains of reasoning, make and execute plans, live for goals, distinguish right from wrong and beautiful from ugly, and relate to other intelligent beings. This rationality is what makes us moral beings, and it is the basis for all other dimensions of Godlikeness, whether those given in our creation or those achieved through our redemption.

Second, God the Creator made us sub-creators under him, able and needing to find fulfilment in the creativity of art, science, technology, construction, scholarship, and the bringing of order out of various sorts of chaos.

Third, God as Lord made us his stewards, that is, deputy managers – bailiffs, as the English say, or factors, to put it in Scotch – to have dominion over the estate which is his world. This role, which presupposes our rationality and creativity, is the special theme of Psalm 8. Man's unique privilege is to harness, develop and use the resources of God's world, not only making animate creatures and vegetation his food, but tapping the resources of raw materials and energy, in order to create culture for two ends which God has inseparably linked – his honour, and our joy. Such cultural activity is natural and instinctive to us.

Finally, God who himself is good (truthful, faithful, wise, generous, loving, patient, just, valuing whatever has moral, intellectual or aesthetic worth and hating all that negates such worth) originally made man good in the sense of naturally and spontaneously righteous. Righteousness in man means active response to God by doing what he loves and commands and avoiding what he hates and forbids. God has a moral character, as you and I have, and there are specific types of action which he approves and others which he disapproves.

Human nature as created has a teleological structure such that its fulfilment (which subjectively means our conscious contentment and joy) only occurs as we consciously do, and limit ourselves to doing, what we know that God approves. Unhappily, no one naturally lives this way; in terms of our Maker's design we all malfunction on the moral level, and need both his forgiveness and his inward renewing (new creation).

What Christians say about the image of God in mankind, therefore, with some variety of vocabulary but substantial unity of sentiment, is that while we retain the image formally and structurally, and in terms of actual dominion over the created order, we have lost it materially and morally, and in terms of personal righteousness before our Creator.

Our dependence, which is the other half of my heading, has to do with our creaturehood. Because we depend on God for all good things, and indeed for our very existence moment by moment, we are obligated both to be grateful and to recognize ourselves as claimed by our Creator with absolute authority. The prevalent modern mood is certainly very different: in our fallenness and folly we crave independence of God as sovereign states crave independence of their neighbours – a syndrome which according to the Bible goes back to the Garden of Eden. But the result is enslavement to our own technology and skills, which instead of being our servants become our masters. The only way human beings can avoid bondage to things (objects, institutions, processes) and dreams (either of pleasure or of profit or of position) is by conscious subjection to the will of the living God 'whose service is perfect freedom.'

The Christian, giving his account of man, rests everything that he has to say on these basic facts of our dignity as God's image-bearers and our dependence as his creatures; and he sees both this dignity and this dependence archetypically embodied and expressed in the life of Jesus Christ.

### My second point concerns the **delight** and **development** of the individual

These are two more realities that belong together, as we shall see. Christianity views mankind as made for delight, but by reason of our fallenness missing it. Joy is never the habitual experience of those who are not right with God: instead, they feel the pressure of the questions posed at the start of this paper, and this makes full and constant joy impossible. Shelley, himself an unbeliever, testified on behalf of all such when he said, 'Rarely, rarely comest thou, Spirit of delight.' For God has sovereignly linked happiness with holiness and sin with misery, and to break these links is beyond our power. Only as life becomes love and worship of God, and love and service of our neighbour, in the knowledge of sins forgiven and heaven to come, does joy become unqualified and unending for us, as by Jesus' own testimony it was for him. But knowing God brings joy that grows, and this is the sort of development that matters most. And clearly, it is something which outward development in the form of increased wealth, skills, comfort, respect from others and range of choices cannot of itself guarantee.

The word *development is* most commonly used nowadays in an external sense and with a corporate reference-point. Thus, we speak of industrial, political and economic development of communities, and of the development of this or that communal enterprise. Mainstream Christianity in principle backs development of this kind, for it belongs to culture-building, which as was noted above is both our instinct and our appointed task. But mainstream Christianity has always attached more importance to the inward, individual development of persons in the way that brings delight even where outward deprivations per force continue. That way is the way of spiritual development, the way of personal faith and practical godliness. While not refusing interest in external community development as Eastern religion has historically done, and while welcoming and indeed fostering such development, Christianity has always held that what matters most is the welfare of the individual in his or her relation to God. Thus, when William Booth's task force set out to bring the three S's (soup, soap, salvation) to the deprived poor, there was no question which was of first importance, and so they called themselves not the Soap or Soup Brigade but the Salvation Army.

It is true that a politicized, secularized version of Christianity, animated by an abstract egalitarianism, is abroad today, calling on churches to back rebellions and revolutions all around the world in the name of compassion for the poor. But this is, to say the least, eccentric by mainstream Christian standards. Historically, while calling for Samaritanship (the relief of others' needs) and aid for development (the creation of physical well-being), the church has for the most part remembered that nothing matters more than the spiritual welfare of individuals, and that its own first task is to spread the gospel, and that it must try to keep free of socio-economic and socio-political entanglements that would make this harder to do than it is already. Jesus Christ was poor, and most Christians to date have been poor too (it was not always and everywhere as it is in today's United States); but Jesus' delight in knowing, loving and serving the one whom he called Father did not depend on his becoming part of any process of community development, nor has the joy of any Christian heart ever sprung from such a source. In an era like ours which idolizes material development this needs to be underlined.

The point can be sharpened if we focus for a moment on the question of freedom. The world assumes that the essence of freedom is to be free *from* this or that external pressure: poverty, race prejudice, economic exploitation, political injustice and the like. But that is only freedom's outward shell; it is not the real thing. The essence of true freedom is being free *for* what matters most – free, that is, for God and godliness, and so for the delight which grace and godliness together bring. The only way into that freedom, however, is to be set free from the egocentricity which binds us by nature, and that is something which Jesus Christ himself alone can do. Which leads to my final points.

### Third, I want to add to what I have already said about the design and deformity of the individual

Christianity sees each person as designed for a life beyond this life – an endless life which for those who know God will be far richer and more joyous than our present life can be, and for which life in this world was always meant to be a preparation. The Christian valuation of personal spiritual welfare as more important than any socio-economic benefit depends ultimately on the knowledge that this world passes away, while the world to come is eternal. We were never intended to treat this world as home, or live in it as if we would be here forever; Jesus pictured the man who lives that way as a fool.

But, whether or not it is true, as is often affirmed (though I am not convinced), that belief in heaven may discourage Christians from doing all the good they can on earth, it is beyond doubt that mockery from Marxists and other skeptics at the idea of 'pie in the sky, by and by, when you die' has made today's Western church feel embarrassed at having a hope of heaven, fearing lest it be howled down as a cop-out from social responsibility; so in fact very little gets spoken about that hope at the present time. (It was different, be it said, in Uganda under the Moslem butcher Amin, and in Kenya in the Mau Mau days, just as it was for the first three Christian centuries, during which time Christianity was offi - cially outlawed and any believers might find themselves facing lions in the arena at any time.) Yet it is the way of human nature as God designed it to live in and by one's hopes, and part of the real Christian's joy, increasing with age, is to look forward to eternal life in resurrection glory with the Father and the Son. Christians have sometimes described this present life, first to last, as preparation for dying, which might sound to modern ears like a gruesome and neurotic fancy; but in light of God's design of us as hoping animals the statement is really no more than a matter-of-fact indication of the truly natural outlook for us all.

But the children of our secular, materialistic culture decline to live, even to think of living, in terms of the world to come, and this, along with actual irreligion and egocentric immorality, constitutes the inward deformity which Christianity sees in fallen human beings. However handsome the face and however beautiful the body, the soul – that is, the real person – is out of shape and ugly. This deformity leads to a constant diffused discontent with things as they are, a miserable old age (because one has less and less to look forward to) and, one fears, a yet more miserable eternity. The Christian vision of each unregenerate person is accordingly of a tragic ruin – a noble creation originally, but one now spoiled and wasted, and tragically so by reason of the great potential for good and for joy that has thus been lost.

This shows why thoughtful Christians have always seen missionary ministry as the church's top priority in this world. Since it is only as individuals become Christians that the ruins of their lives get rebuilt, evangelism is service of each person's deepest need, and is thus the truest love of one's neighbour. The compassion that drives Christians at this point was verbalized thus in Old Testament times:

Come, all you who are thirsty, come to the waters; and you who have no money, come, buy and eat! Come, buy wine and milk without money and without cost. Why spend money on what is not bread, and your labour on what does not satisfy? Listen, listen to me, and eat what is good, and your soul will delight in the richest of fare. . . . Seek the Lord while he may be found; call on him while he is near. Let the wicked forsake his way and the evil man his thoughts. Let him turn to the Lord, and he will have mercy on him, and to our God, for he will freely pardon.[1]

### Fourth, I want to say a little more about the **delivering** and **deprogramming** *of the individual who is found by God's grace*

The heart of the Christian message is that the Christ who exhibited in himself true and full humanness according to the Creator's intention, and who diagnosed the spiritual deformity that sin brings, and the personal disasters to which it leads, more trenchantly than was ever done before or since, died sacrificially to redeem us from sin; rose triumphantly from death; and now lives to forgive and remake us, and turn us by his power from the travesties of humanity that we really are into authentic human beings who bear his moral image. By his death and the forgiveness that flows from it he delivers us from God's condemnation; by leading us through his word in Scripture into the paths of discipleship, and by the transforming work of his Spirit at the level of our instincts, inclinations, insights and attitudes (what Scripture calls our *heart*), he deprograms us from the game plans of our former ungodly self-centredness, teaching us to look at everything through His eyes and literally to live a new life.

His word to the world is still: 'Come to me, all you who are weary and burdened, and I will give you rest. Take my yoke upon you and learn from me . . . and you will find rest for your souls.'[2] Through Scripture and the Spirit he still fulfils this promise. In this sense Christianity is, and always will be – Christ himself.

Whether you who read these words will believe them and turn to Christ accordingly is something that I cannot arrange on your behalf, much as I wish I could. But at least I can require you to take proper note of the fact that this, and nothing less than this, is the message of biblical and historic mainstream Christianity. The widespread idea that Christi - anity celebrates the value of the individual by affirming his natural goodness and then teaching him how to do even better is false. Christi - anity diagnoses the individual as morally distorted and spiritually ruined, as we saw, and against that dark background points to Christ as the only one who can straighten out our twisted natures.

That task is like re-railing a derailed train; passengers pushing will not suffice to get it back on the track; a crane must do what is beyond the power of human muscle. I am saying that Jesus Christ remakes us in his own moral and spiritual image, and that this is something which we cannot do for ourselves by our own resources. I am further saying,

---

[1] Isaiah 55:1–2, 6–7.
[2] Matthew 11:28–29.

therefore, that at some point along the line each of us must come to the point of admitting that we need to be saved, since we cannot save ourselves. We have not got what it takes to re-order our disordered lives; we need to be saved by Jesus Christ. It is those who in humble honesty reach that moment of truth who become Christians.

And this, so I urge, is the true humanism, the true formula for human fulfilment. It is a humanism which has the Creator at its center and, as I said before, Christ as its model and means. It is the true freedom, freedom for God and goodness, which is only found under authority – the personal, unqualified authority of the living Christ. It is the freedom which Solzhenitsyn found in the Gulag where, stripped of all he had and of all his dignity in human terms, he put his faith in Jesus Christ. It is, to be sure, a life of compassion and distress; looking through Christian eyes at the way in which your fellow men ruin their lives, and involve others again and again in their own disasters, will drive you to tears.

Your understanding of the nature, value and needs of individuals will make much in our society abhorrent to you – the disrespect for God-given life, and for God its giver, that is involved in abortion on demand and in the advocacy of euthanasia and suicide, for instance; plus the frivolity of so many towards marriage vows, the cruelty of so many towards parents, spouses and children, our indifference to the needs of lonely elderly folk, the inhumaneness of our prison system, and a great deal more. The Christian will be for justice, but as he will not equate this with egalitari - anism, so he will not regard callousness towards those who offend both him and society at large as part of what justice requires. Perhaps the most authentic expression of Christian humanism will be the devotion which the believer, following his Master, will show to meeting the needs of his fellow men as they confront him. He will not be passive. He will be like the Samaritan in Jesus' parable, seeing others as comparable to the beaten-up Jew in the gutter and seeing himself as obliged to stop and help. Most of all will he try to help them, with all other forms of help that he offers, to listen to God, to take note of Jesus Christ, and to find their way into a living relationship with him, for he knows that their spiritual need is their greatest need of all. And in doing so he will be endlessly hopeful, for he knows that he works with God.

Such, then, in outline is the Christian view of man, and the root principles of the humanism that is based on it. As I close I feel bound to express my conviction that the health of Western society is directly bound up with a return to it; not only do I see it as a constructive alternative, but the dominant secular view of man, the creation of the Enlightenment, of Darwin and of Freud, whether in its optimistic, pessimistic, or deterministic mold, appears to me to be utterly bankrupt, with its insolvency showing more clearly every year. Therefore I hope with all my heart that in our time the Christian vision of godly humanness will catch hold of the Western imagination once more. I hope you may share that hope with me.

# Chapter 15

# The Word of Life

Here is St. Paul, the elderly Apostle, writing to Timothy, his junior: 'You know how from infancy you have known the Holy Scriptures, which are able to make you wise for salvation through faith in Christ Jesus. All Scripture is God-breathed and is useful for teaching, rebuking, correcting, and training in righteousness, that the man of God may be thoroughly equipped for every good work' (2 Tim. 3:15–17).

It is a tragedy that with our Christian heritage there are so few young adults today to whom one could speak in those terms, and so few teenagers and children of whom it will ever be possible to speak in such terms. The Bible no longer has the place in the homes of our country that once it had, and ignorance of the Bible confronts us today not only in the secular world but in the churches as well. That is thoroughly bad news.

I am thankful to be able to speak and write out of over fifty years of experience with the Bible since the Lord called me to faith. I can tell you frankly that I am more excited about the Bible now than I was when I started. The Bible does that to you. It proves itself over and over again to be in very truth the Word of Life to one's soul.

## The Word of Life

You meet that phrase, the 'Word of Life' in Philippians 2:16, describing the witness the Philippian Christians bore to those around them. Paul speaks of them as 'holding forth the Word of Life,' and rejoices that they did so. So the phrase there means 'the message through which divine life comes.'

But in the first verse of the first letter of John the phrase is used in a different sense: 'that which we've seen, which we've heard, which we've touched, of the Word of Life is our theme; the Life was manifested and we've seen it, and we bear witness to you of that Word of Life which we

THE WORD OF LIFE was the keynote address at the 'Word of Life' conference of the Episcopal Synod of America, held in Anaheim, Calif., in May, 1992. Originally published in *The Evangelical Catholic*, vol. IV, number 4, July/August, 1992, pp. 1–8. Reprinted by permission.

saw and heard.' There we have the Apostle John using the phrase for our Lord Jesus Christ, the incarnate Son of God.

Christ is the Word of the Father, the One in whom all the Father's thoughts and purposes find their embodiment. He is the *personal* Word of Life, for he came into this world in incarnate form to bring life with God to us who needed it. The Scripture which testifies to him is the *written* Word of Life in the sense of being the God-given message about him.

Jesus himself established the link between the personal and the written Word in another way when he said to his disciples: 'the words I speak to you are Spirit' – meaning that the life and power of the Holy Spirit of God operates through them – 'and they are life' – meaning that they are life-giving just because of the ministry of the Spirit through them (John 6:63). We do well to get clear in our minds that Word and Spirit belong together, and that the Spirit's appointed task is to impart personal knowledge of the Word himself.

The Scripture brings no life save as the Spirit uses it and the Spirit brings no life save as he applies the Word of God, the truth of the Gospel, the testimony of Jesus to our hearts. After all, as Jesus himself defined it at the beginning of his high priestly prayer, divine life means knowing the Father and the Son: 'and this is eternal life, that they should know thee, the only true God and Jesus Christ [me] whom thou hast sent' (John 17:3). God's verbal Word is the means to this knowledge.

When we talk of the Word of Life, let us be clear in our minds as to what constitutes that life. It is a relationship: it is communion and fellowship with the Father and the Son. Christianity is a pattern of discipleship to Jesus Christ and worship of the Triune God that is grounded in and controlled, informed, and shaped by the written Word. The place and function of the written Word is as the canon of Christianity – the rule, the standard or measuring rod which determines for us what's straight and what's crooked, what's right and what's wrong.

So we see that the Bible has authority, but not an authority distinct from the divine authority of the Father, Son, and Holy Spirit, nor from the royal authority of Christ the living Word. A lot of debating points have been made in the past by claiming that since the living Word has ultimate authority, the Bible, the written Word, cannot have authority in any final sense. The truth is that the authority of Jesus and the authority of Scripture are one, just as the authority of Jesus and the authority of his Father and the authority of the Spirit are one. What God has joined, let not person put asunder.

I am now going to say seven things about the Bible. I hope you are not allergic to 'apt alliteration's artful aid,' because I am going to affirm that the Holy Scriptures constitute seven realities all beginning with the letter 'L': the Bible is a library, a landscape, a letter, and a listening post, and in all these frames it proves itself to be law, light, and life.

## A Library

First, the Bible is a Library. It consists of sixty-six separate pieces of writing, some of them composite in themselves, one of them actually consisting of 150 separate items. Thirty-nine of these pieces of writing we call the Old Testament, the other twenty-seven we call the New Testament. From a literary standpoint they are all sorts: history books, visions, sermons, poems, philosophical reflections, genealogies, statistics, and much else.

But the books are bound together by a common purpose. And bound together too, as one soon discovers when one begins to read, by an extraordinary unity of subject matter as they fulfil this common purpose. The common purpose is to give us information about God and godliness. And the sixty-six books do this with marvellous consistency. Although they were written over a period of probably 1,500 years in a number of different cultures, the unity of their presentation of God and his ways is just stunning.

Early in his career as a theologian, Karl Barth spoke of the 'strange new world of the Bible,' so different from the world modern human beings – like human beings in the days when the Bible was being written – think they occupy. In this strange new world of the Bible, God the creator is actively in charge, working to carry out a great plan of redemption. As the books make clearer and clearer, this plan is to centre on a particular person, a Messiah, a Saviour whom in due course he will send.

That history, which begins in Genesis and runs on all the way through, is the backbone of the Bible. The rest of the material in Scripture is attached to this backbone, just as the rib cage and other bits and pieces of your skeleton are attached to your backbone. The prophetic books, wisdom books, and epistles explain and apply the truths about God that are made known in the history.

So in Scripture you have history – the narrative of the Creator becoming the Redeemer – and with it a great deal of explanatory and applicatory and responsive material, expressing the faith of God's people as they apprehend the message of the history and showing the right way to respond in praise and obedience. And all of this is revelation, God telling us things in order to make himself known.

So the books themselves teach us to see it. God is revealing himself as Redeemer. He is not the dumb God of philosophers since Kant, nor the impotent God of modern process theology. He is the sovereign Lord, the vocal Lord, the God who speaks.

## God Speaks

Yes, God speaks. He condescends to employ human language; the language he gave to his human creatures so that they might talk with each other, he now uses to talk with us. And he also teaches us to use it to respond to him in our praises and prayers. He is thus the God who speaks, just as he is the God who acts.

God is not, you see, one who simply speaks and teaches but otherwise does nothing – words without actions – nor is he playing a celestial game of charades – actions without words – on the stage of history, leaving us to guess what the actions mean. Words and deeds belong together in God's self-revelation.

For the last hundred years, it has been all too popular a view in Anglican circles that though God is indeed the mighty God who acts, he doesn't speak. What he does is to illuminate the minds of good people so that they are able to guess more or less correctly the meaning of what he has been up to. So, say, we should read the Scripture as embodying a series of fairly good guesses about God – guesses which, however, are not necessarily definitive, and from which we may allow ourselves to depart if we have reason, for after all a guess has no final authority.

But God is not like that. Here is a truer analogy. In England there is a qualification called the advanced driving test. When you are taking that test you have to make a running commentary to the examiner, telling him just why you are speeding up, why you are slowing down, what hazards you see, what avoiding action you are taking, and so on. God acts like that. God is active in history establishing justice and redeeming sinners, and as he works in power so he speaks by way of narrative and commentary explaining to us what he is doing and why he is is doing it.

We should read Holy Scripture, I believe, as did the Reformers four hundred and more years ago. John Calvin had a Latin phrase for the right way to talk of biblical material. It is, he said, *doctrina Dei*, teaching given by God. God has spoken to tell us what he is doing and why, and Scripture is the transcript of God's own testimony. It is God's own commentary on his actions, God's own declaration of his ways and his works.

I may say these things to Anglicans with the more confidence because the Lambeth Conference of 1958 reviewed the contents of Scripture in essentially this way. A long and inspiring memorandum titled 'The Drama of the Bible' set forth the story of God's doings as explained to us by God himself, as the revelation of his work calling for the response of our worship.

The Bible is, as was stated, a Library. Over forty human writers contributed to its composition, but expressing itself through all that they wrote is one single mind, the mind of God. God the almighty Agent is telling us what he has done and is doing and why. So there is a God-given unity of subject in the Library, as well as a diversity of backgrounds, literary styles, and casts of mind among the different writers. The Library is thus a divine-human product, the Word of God in the form of the words of humans.

## A Landscape

Second, the Bible is a Landscape, a Landscape of Life. I have spoken of it so far as teaching from God about God. But that is only half the story. The Bible is as truly a people-book as it is a God-book, and one of the most interesting and fruitful ways of reading it is to study what it has to say about life.

In the Bible you meet all sorts of people, some of them the most vital, virile, forthright, fascinating people you can imagine. And as you read their stories, you learn a great deal about the right way to live and the wrong way to live (or the many wrong ways to live) – both the pitfalls of which life is full and the triumphs in God that those who live rightly may experience.

The Bible is very much a people-book. I want to underline that, because when people hear that the Bible is God's teaching, they imme - diately assume that it must consist of the abstract formulas you meet in textbooks of systematic theology.

The Bible isn't like that in the least. I believe it is part of the wisdom of God that it shouldn't be. The Bible is focused on people: people to whom God spoke, who either did or did not respond, who obeyed or disobeyed, who found life, who missed life, who entered into spiritual triumph, who experienced spiritual disaster. But people, people, people, all the way through.

The truth is that the Bible is overflowing with humanity, full of wisdom about the business of living. There is in fact a whole section called the Wisdom Literature: Psalms. Proverbs, Job, Song of Solomon, and Ecclesiastes in the Old Testament and James in the New. In the Psalms, you have a hymn book and prayer book, a divine liturgy, for human response to the Word of God. The heartbeats of human beings in triumph and in trouble, in delight and in distress were never so vividly portrayed as they are in the different psalms.

What seems to me the wisest thing ever said about the five Wisdom books of the Old Testament is this: the Psalms teach you how to pray, Proverbs how to live, Job how to suffer, the Song of Solomon how to love, and Ecclesiastes how to enjoy. That's good philosophy given under God for our learning and our blessing. And then up comes James, the New Testament Wisdom writer, who strikes all these notes together within the compass of his five brief chapters.

Yes, the Bible is a Landscape of Life, full of wisdom about living. It is a people-book, full of fascinating people from whose behaviour and expres - sion of feelings, from whose wisdom and faith, and from whose follies and disasters there is a great deal to be learned. I said at the beginning that the Bible tells us about God and godliness. Now I can say that the Landscape of Life in Scripture inculcates lessons about godliness the whole time. Study the Bible, and you will learn how under all circumstances to serve God.

## A Letter

Now to a third and a rather different point, having to do with the personal application of Scripture to every single person who reads it or hears it read. The Bible is a Letter. This is not soft sentimentality, this is hard theology. What is a letter? It is writing addressed by a particular person, the composer, to the particular person or persons who read it.

Not everything that is written is a letter. That is to say, not every document is addressed to particular people. What we must understand about Scripture is that not only were all sixty-six books written by human authors who had an intended readership in their mind (like Paul writing to the Thessalonians or the Philippians or the Corinthians, whom he knew well), but the Bible is God's letter, consciously addressed by him in his wise providence to every single person who ever reads it, whether yesterday, today, or tomorrow.

That rather takes one's breath away, doesn't it? But this is the measure of the foreknowledge and wisdom of God. Holy Scripture in its entirety and in each of its parts is the Word of God addressed personally to everyone to whom it comes.

You have a Bible. Your name is written in the front of the Bible. Think of it as if the Lord himself had written it there. Your Bible is his Word addressed to you. In the first edition of one of my own books, there was a delightful misprint on the contents page: 'RSVP means Revised Standard Version.' Of course RSVP does not mean Revised Standard Version. It is an admonition in French: *répondez s'il vous plaît*, reply if you please.

But the misprint was a reminder to think of your Bible as if the Lord himself had written the letters RSVP at the top and bottom of each page. Everything you find in your Bible is addressed to you, and the Lord, in whose presence you read it, wants to know your response to it. It is simply staggering to think of all the millions of Christians there are and have been and will be and to reflect that God in his wisdom has adapted the Bible for the instruction of each one. But that is the truth.

The thought of personal address is already there in Paul's words to Timothy with which I started: 'you have known the sacred writings [the Holy Scriptures] which are able to make you [singular] wise for salvation.' Paul is saying: 'Timothy, think of those Scriptures that you have, and which you were brought up on, as the Lord's personal word to you, as given you to make you personally wise for salvation through faith in Christ Jesus.'

Then he goes on, still in the singular: 'All Scripture is God-breathed and is useful for teaching, rebuke, correction, and instruction in right - eousness, that the man of God [that means you, Timothy] might be equipped for every good work.'

Paul is saying to Timothy: 'God wrote the Scriptures for you, Timothy, as much as he wrote them for anybody.' (Paul was speaking, of course, of what we call the Old Testament, which was all the Bible he and Timothy had, but we may properly apply his words to the New Testament also, and to our Bible as a whole.)

So think of the Scriptures as a Letter from the Lord, a composite letter or series of letters if you like, written by divine prompting and overruling of the human penman. That's really what Paul is pointing to when he says, 'All Scripture is *God-breathed.*' The Greek word there means 'all Scripture is the product of God's creative breath.'

Psalm 33:6 says: 'By the word of the Lord were the heavens made, and all the host of them by the breath of his mouth.' Paul is declaring the same is true of the Bible. Breath means Spirit, and Psalm 33:6 is referring to the work of the Holy Spirit in creation. So we may truly say the Scriptures are God's creation, 'made by the breath of God's mouth.'

They are the product of the prompting and overruling, the guidance, direction, and sovereignty of the Holy Spirit. All Scripture is breathed out by God and as such in its divine character it is in very truth what the twentieth of our Anglican *Articles of Religion* calls it, namely 'God's Word written.' It is totally human, certainly, but it is totally divine also. It is analogous only to the incarnation, where total humanity and total deity are together in personal union.

This means that every time we read the Bible, the thought in our minds should be: this comes from the Lord through human writers, through the Holy Spirit prompting and guiding and inspiring each one of them. So let us read it first and foremost in terms of its primary authorship, in terms of its true source. Let us read it as the Word of God, as the Church has done from the very beginning.

I like the Presbyterian way of introducing readings from Scripture in public worship. I wish we Anglicans said the same. 'Hear the Word of God,' they say, 'as it is written in' and then the location of the passage is announced. The formula reminds everyone that it is the Word of God that is being read, and it must be listened to as such. 'Here beginneth' (the classic Prayer Book formula) is not as challenging as 'Hear the Word of God'!

## Its Divine Origin

Where did I get this idea of divine origin from? I got it from the Lord Jesus and his Apostles. The Lord himself expressed it when he put a question to the scribes and Pharisees, quoting Psalm 110 as an authority (Mark 12:36). The passage is one of many expressing Jesus' own testimony to the divine origin of Scripture under which he fulfilled his own ministry.

He said of Scripture 'Don't think I came to cancel the law and the prophets; I came not to destroy them but to fulfil them' (Matt. 5:17). We can see why he said that. He recognized in his Bible the utterance of his heavenly Father through the Holy Spirit, and received it as divine instruction addressed to him as to anyone. One gets the same insight in the writings of the Apostles.

In Acts 4, we read of Scripture being quoted at the first Christian prayer meeting recorded for us. The disciples have just come back from being given a hard time by the Sanhedrin, who told them that they must not preach about Jesus any more. When the church heard how Peter and John had been treated, they raised their voices together in prayer to God, quoting Psalm 2.

> 'Sovereign Lord,' they prayed, 'you made the heaven and the earth and the sea, and everything in them. You spoke by the Holy Spirit through the mouth of your servant, our father David: Why do the nations rage and the peoples plot in vain?'

Nor is that way of quoting Scripture unique, or even rare. There are many more places in the New Testament where Old Testament Scripture is quoted as the utterance of God, the product of the work of the Holy Spirit. Time doesn't allow me to go through them. Let me simply say that every single one of the hundreds of Old Testament quotations and allusions in the New Testament implies a divine origin and authority for the material referred to. The Apostles' view of the nature of Scripture should be seen as no less authoritative than the rest of their teaching. It is certainly every bit as clear.

I have called the Bible a Letter, and pictured it, not just as an open letter to all the world, but as a letter specifically addressed by God to everyone who is confronted with it. I will now round off the thought by calling it a love letter. Yes, a love letter in which God speaks of his redeeming love to draw faith and love from us in response.

You take love letters very seriously. You read them over and over. You try to squeeze out of them all the meaning that the lover put into them. So we should do as we read the Bible, treasuring it as the love letter of the Lord written to each one of us to show us the path of salvation through grace and to lead us into the life of responsive love to the God who has so wonderfully loved us.

## A Listening Post

That leads to the fourth 'L.' The Bible is a Listening Post. You read about them in spy stories: the places where the hero goes in order to listen to the bug placed in the villain's hotel room, or to get a message on his private telephone which nobody knows about except himself. Think of Scripture as the Listening Post where we go to hear the Word of God for our instruction and guidance.

I have spoken of the *inspiration* of Scripture, meaning by that its divine origin and source. I am now speaking of the *instrumentality* of Scripture as the means whereby God enables us actually to hear and receive his Word, that is, the message he addresses to our hearts.

It is our privilege to be as flies on the wall as we hear God dealing with the Israelites of old and the Roman church and the Corinthian church and the Philippian church, and Jesus dealing with the Pharisees and needy folk in his day. It is our privilege as we see and hear these things to ask, and by the help of the Holy Spirit to answer, the questions, 'If that was how the Lord viewed and spoke to those folk where they were in their situation, how must he see me, how must he see us? What must he think about us? What must he have to say to me in my own situation?'

Of course, Holy Scripture must be interpreted, and interpreted rightly, if we are to hear its message. Just as in the spy stories you can't get a message from a phone that is being scrambled, so you cannot get a message out of a Bible that is being misinterpreted. But then Holy Scripture is in itself very clear, once we get the hang of it: after all, it was written to be understood. Every one of its sixty six books, I am bold to say, was written to be understood.

Even the more enigmatic ones like Daniel and the visionary parts of Revelation, which seem to us to be written in code, are in fact written in a style that was well understood when these books were first written. It is the style scholars call 'apocalyptic,' a highly imaginative, highly imagistic, highly visionary, highly symbolic way of expression meaning.

But the symbols are relatively standard and the first readers of Daniel and Revelation knew the lingo and would not have been puzzled the way you and I are. Once you and I take the trouble to learn the lingo, our puzzlement will be dispelled. There are plenty of good, simple commentaries to help us do that.

For the rest, however, the Bible doesn't even appear to be written in code. It is written in ordinary, straightforward language with a logical flow, the same sort of language in which we write today for each other's information. The Bible was, I say again, written to be understood.

What it has to say about the things that abide – about the unchanging God; about the unchanging reality of human nature made in God's image but very much defaced and needing a total reconstruction; about the life that pleases God, the life of faith, righteousness, and morality; about the activities of godliness, praise, worship, adoration, communion – all these are clearly and consistently set forth. If these are the things we want to know about, Scripture will not present us with major problems.

In saying this, I assume a willingness to invest time and labour in getting to know one's way around the Bible. Given that investment, however, Scripture may be trusted to make itself plain to us. There is a great deal of Scripture to get acquainted with – I expect like mine your Bible has 1,300 to 1,500 pages – and I can sympathize with anyone's fear of getting lost in it. One soon finds, however, that what is referred to briefly in one place is expounded more fully in other places, and that the important things stand out.

## Ignorance or Blockage

There is, as I said, a great deal of material that God in his mercy has given us and the big things within this mass are brought out by being repeated and presented over and over in many different ways. So if you find the Bible obscure, it has to be said that you are either ignorant of the text or have some sort of blockage in your mind, not that there is anything intrinsically puzzling about the Bible as a whole.

In the days before the Reformation, the unreformed Church thought it a dreadful thing to let layfolk read the Bible because they were bound to get it wrong. The Bible, it was said, is a very difficult book; you can't get it right without the Church to guide you. The Reformers bluntly replied: 'If you find the Bible difficult, the darkness is not in the Word, but in you. You need to go to God and acknowledge that sin has blinded your mind, and humbly ask the Lord to take away that blindness and enable you to see what is there plain and clear before you in the pages of God's Word.'

Don't mishear me, now! I don't wish to imply that the historic wisdom of the Church as guardian and interpreter of Scripture is not worth bothering with. Like you. I thank God for that heritage of wisdom and understanding. I know, as you know, that the Holy Spirit of God has been active among God's people, giving understanding of Scripture and teaching wisdom from the Scripture, for almost 2,000 years. I know, as you do, that it would be stupid as well as ungrateful to ignore the value of that heritage of teaching.

But tradition is not infallible. Neither intellectual nor moral sanctifi - cation is perfected in this life, and in the corporate discernment of the Church it is possible for slippage to take place and something less than perfect wisdom to be put down on paper. Councils and synods, like individual theologians, can go wrong, and the Church's expository heritage must constantly be assessed and checked by the Scripture that it seeks to expound.

But I say again, anyone who makes light of the help that the Church's heritage can give in understanding the Scripture, anyone who doesn't weigh the witness of tradition with full seriousness, is very foolish and is bound to end up with a narrowed understanding of things. And if I may talk the language of the nursery, 'serve him right.'

Holy Scripture, then, is the Listening Post where through right interpretation of the text we come to hear and see what is God's Word to us, in the sense of how what is written applies to us. That's the 'fly on the wall' approach to biblical interpretation, and it's the safe, rational, wise, and sound way to proceed for a true understanding of the Bible.

In all teaching of Scripture and meditating upon the Scripture, this is what must be done. We should be listening to hear what the Lord has to say to us and as he enables us to see the application, so his Word can truly be said to open our eyes and touch our hearts.

## Law

Fifth, Holy Scripture is not only a Library, a Landscape, a Letter, and a Listening Post, but it is Law. I mean Law in the sense of Torah, the Old Testament word that is usually so translated. But Torah really means fatherly instruction. When you think of Holy Scripture as the Law of the Lord, don't think in terms of what is legislated by such remote bodies as Congress and the Supreme Court. Think rather in terms of the admonitions given by a wise father to his family in the intimacy of the home.

This is how the authority of Scripture is to be understood. Our heavenly Father tells us what we need to know in order to trust him aright and obey him as we should. He tells us how we are to please him and honour him by our response to him. In that sense, Holy Scripture is indeed law, law for our lives.

The Prayer Book catechism tells us that one of things required of us by the first table of the Law is to 'Honour God's name and his Word.' We honour his Word by treating it as God's Torah, his fatherly instruction having authority for our lives, showing us what to believe and what to do.

And if as we apply Scripture to ourselves, we find that the Bible is saying something other than we have supposed, contradicting what we would like to think, so much the worse for our uninstructed thoughts. As with children in the family, when father tells you something, that's the way it is! If you thought differently before, change your mind and agree with father! In that sense Holy Scripture is Law for all God's children, and that leads on to the sixth point.

## Light

Holy Scripture, which is Law, is also Light. It is a source of illumination for those who have to take a journey in the dark. That is pictured very vividly in Psalm 119:105: 'Thy word is a lamp for my feet and a light to my path.' Do you see the picture? I have to take a journey across open country. I have to find my way and it's dark. Travelling in the dark across rough country, I am at risk.

The easiest thing in the world will be for me to stumble and fall over some obstacle I simply can't see. Traversing the country in the dark, I'm likely to lose the way, miss the path, and get into big trouble. I need a light, a light that will enable me to see the path in front of my feet. God in his mercy has given me such a light. 'Thy word is a lamp to my feet and a light to my path.'

One of the museums of biblical archaeology displays a little lamp with a hook in its base, so that it cannot stand upright. It seems that the archaeologists puzzled over the construction of the lamp for quite some time before it struck someone that the purpose of the hook was to fasten the lamp into the strap of a sandal, so that the traveller would have the lamp at his feet to guide his steps.

But why, you ask, is the Word pictured as a Lamp and not a sun? Because walking by the light of Scripture is not like walking by daylight. Walking by lamplight, you see very little scenery. You can't see every -thing; in fact, you're often in the dark in every sense and can hardly understand anything of what goes on around you. But Scripture enables you to see the one thing you need to see, namely each next step you must take, so on you are able to go.

We have to be prepared to walk through life with a quiverfull of unanswered questions about the ways of God. Why this? Why that? We simply don't know. God doesn't tell us. All that God tells us is how to cope Christianly with this and that as it comes. It's like driving a car. You don't know why people behave on the road in the crazy way they do. But you do know the principles of taking avoiding action and driving correctly amidst strange and bewildering hazards. The Bible guides us in our journey across the rough country of life in the just the same way.

It is well to remind ourselves that without biblical truth and wisdom we would be absolutely lost, and so learn to come to Scripture in that healthy frame of mind in which we are very, very conscious of how much we need the light of God to guide us through life's problems. A sense of one's need of God's instruction is the best possible frame of mind for Bible study. And that leads on to the last thought.

## Life

Holy Scripture, which is Law and Light, is also Life, in the very precise sense that it bestows life through the Holy Spirit because the Holy Spirit writes it in our hearts. James 1:21 actually gives us this thought. 'Receive with meekness the implanted word,' says James. God implants the Word in our hearts, just as we implant bulbs and seeds in our flower pots.

The implanted Word, continues James, 'can save you.' The Word takes root in our hearts, and changes us in ways of which we are not at first conscious; in due course, however, we become aware that we are different from the way we were. Once I didn't see Jesus in his glory and now I do. Once I didn't love my heavenly Father or my Saviour, and now I do. Once I didn't honour the Holy Spirit and now I do. Once I didn't find worship a joy and now I do. Once I didn't desire to please God more than I desire anything else in the world, once I didn't desire God's fellowship at all, but that has changed.

What's happened? What has happened is that the Word has been implanted and taken root, and through the Holy Spirit it has become the means of life to my heart; yours too, I trust. It's the fulfilment of the new covenant prophecy of Jeremiah. 'I will write my words in their hearts.'

Well might the open air preacher of legend gather a crowd by putting his hat down on the sidewalk and walking around it, pointing to it and saying, 'It's alive, it's alive!' When the crowd was standing round him, wondering what he had got under the hat, he picked it up and there was his Bible, and away he went preaching the Word of Life.

I leave you with that thought. Bible truth imparts spiritual life, and we need to soak ourselves in Scripture if we are ever to learn how to know and love and serve and honour and obey our Lord. You see how excited I am about the Scriptures. God grant you a share of that same excitement, and a full measure of that divine life to which the love of God's Word opens the door.

# Chapter 16

# To All Who Will Come

My text is John 6:35–37. 'Then Jesus declared, "I am the bread of life. He who comes to me will never go hungry, and he who believes in me will never be thirsty. But as I told you, you have seen me and still you do not believe. All that the Father gives me will come to me, and whoever comes to me I will never drive away." '

The theme of these verses is the greatest, sweetest, most glorious theme any preacher can ever handle: the love of God in Jesus Christ our Lord. It is the theme which Reformed people love to refer to as sovereign grace.

In the New Testament, *love* and *grace* mean just about the same thing. Both are key words, and both have a significance far in excess of any meaning either of them had in secular Greek literature. A new thing had come into the world with Jesus Christ, knowledge of divine love such as no man had ever imagined. So old words had to be polished up, redefined, and used with a new weight of meaning in order to express the new thing. In the New Testament the words *agape* (love) and *charis* (grace) are so used. They are focal words, for they express the heart of this glorious message.

These particular verses highlight the greatness, richness, sweetness, and glory of the truth of the love of God in Jesus our Lord because they show that the love of God not only makes salvation possible but actually saves. It does more than create a possibility. It actually does the job. Reformed theology has always stressed this, and rightly so, because our Lord himself stresses it in this and other texts. I hope that by stressing it myself I may be able to show that the love of God is a far bigger, greater, and more wonderful thing than some Christians have yet seen.

## Redeeming Love

Let us work our way into the subject like this: How would you define the love of God if I put you on the spot and asked you to do so with

---

TO ALL WHO WILL COME was originally published in *Our Saviour God*, ed. J. M. Boice, (Grand Rapids: Baker Book House, 1980). Reprinted by permission.

reference to a text? I guess that you would go to John 3:16. I suppose that is about the best known text of the New Testament, and it does speak of the love of God in glowing terms. 'God so loved the world that he gave his one and only Son, that whoever believes in him shall not perish but have eternal life.' If you thought of quoting from the passage I am taking, you would perhaps cite verse 35, where Jesus says, 'I am the bread of life. He who comes to me will never go hungry and he who believes in me will never be thirsty.' This too is a wonderful exhibition of the love of God. So we ask: What do these two texts show us?

First, they show the love of God in *redemption*. In the sentence 'God so loved the world that he gave,' 'gave' has reference to the cross of Christ. The words come just after Jesus has said to Nicodemus, 'As Moses lifted up the snake in the desert, so the Son of Man must be lifted up.' Once when Israel was traveling in the wilderness, snakes entered the camp, and the people were being bitten and were dying. God told Moses to make a brass snake, set it up in the middle of the camp, and tell any who were bitten by the snakes to look at the brass serpent and they would be cured. And so they were. This was a wonderful foreshadowing of the way in which we sinners may look to the representative 'sinner' – yes, allow me to use that phrase, the One, I mean, who acts as a substitute for us sinners under the judgment of God – and be saved. There he is, lifted up on the cross. He is dying in our place. We look, see our sins judged there, and live. This is the beginning of the story of the love of God: redemption.

The second element in the love of God as revealed in Christ is *invitation*. These verses, John 3:16 and 6:35, also have this element, showing us that Jesus Christ, who died for sin, now opens his arms and invites us to come to him and promises to receive us as we come. 'Come to me,' he says, 'and I will give you the fruits of my redemption. Come to me, and you will find through me the life you need. I am the bread of life. He who comes to me will never go hungry.' The second half of verse 35 links up with that: 'And he who believes in me will never be thirsty.' Coming to Christ and believing on Christ are one thing. Each phrase explains the meaning of the other. In heart, one approaches him. In heart, one trusts him. In heart, one relies on him. In heart, one casts oneself upon him. This is believing. This is coming. 'Closing with Jesus Christ' – that is the way Luther put it. He meant that one stretches out one's arms and embraces Christ.

So the second element in the love of God in Christ our Lord is the risen Savior's invitation to those who need him and who know they need him to come, trust, and receive him and thereby to find life. Behind verse 35 one can hear the echo of the opening words of Isaiah 55: 'Come, all you who are thirsty, come to the waters' – you who have no money, never mind – 'come, buy and eat! Come, buy wine and milk without money and without cost.'

## Electing and Preserving Love

Now see what Jesus has to say in verse 36. He has been talking to the great crowd of five thousand whom he fed with bread in the wilderness. They have come across the lake of Galilee to meet with him again. What are they after? They say, 'From now on give us this bread.' They are thinking of another meal of the kind they had the day before. They are thinking of material bread. So when Jesus said, 'I am the bread of life,' they looked at him and frowned. They did not understand. They wanted physical bread, and what Jesus was saying seemed irrelevant.

In some circles there is a strong body of opinion which urges that the church must 'let the world write the agenda.' The church is to see what hopes of 'humanization,' as it is called, non-Christians have and then help them achieve those hopes. Learn from John 6 what happens when you let the world write the agenda. Does the world want Jesus as the bread of life? No. The world wants something else: material advancement of one kind or another. So the world will harness the church if it can. It will give the church a bad conscience in order to persuade Christian people to expend their energies in giving the unconverted world what it wants. What a pathetic mistake!

Of course, Jesus does not yield to this request. He has to say sadly as he looks at this crowd, 'You have seen me, and still you do not believe.' But what happens now? Is this the end of the story? Shall Christ and the world simply part company? No. For see now what Jesus goes on to say in verse 37, saying it, I believe, for his own encouragement as well as to instruct those to whom his invitation seemed irrelevant. 'All that the Father gives me will come to me; and whoever comes to me I will never drive away.' What is he doing here? He is showing us that there is more to the love of God than the achieving of redemption and the inviting of needy sinners to receive Jesus Christ as their Savior.

More yet? What more could there be? Well, this: *election, vocation, reception,* and *preservation.*

*Election is* the Father giving to the Son a great company whom the Son will certainly save. Jesus refers to it in the phrase 'all that the Father *gives* me.' *Vocation* is what we term 'effectual calling.' Jesus refers to it when he says, 'All that the Father gives me *will come to me.*' Then there is *reception.* However slow a person may be in coming to Christ, however long he may have held out in unbelief, however long he may have been distracted from seeking the Savior by his desire for this world's goods – like Jesus' congregation who were distracted from seeking him by their desire for another free meal – nonetheless when that person begins to come to Christ, Jesus is there is receive him. Jesus refers to this when he says, 'Whoever comes to me, I *will never drive away.*' Finally, there is the thought of *preservation.* For when Jesus says, 'Whoever comes to me, I will never [in any way] drive away,' he is referring not only to the moment of the person's coming but to the whole of that person's life on earth. He means, 'I will *never, at any stage*, drive that person away.' This becomes plain when he goes on to say in verse 39, 'This is the will of him who sent me, that I *shall lose none* of all that he has given me, but raise them up at the last day.'

So here you have not only those items in the love of God with which we began – redemption wrought on the cross and the Savior's invitation to all to come to him – you also have election, vocation, Jesus' glad reception of those who come (however slow they have been in getting the message), and the promise of preservation as well. These are all from first to last expressions of the love of God.

Now you are beginning to see what I meant when I said at the beginning that the love of God is a bigger thing than some Christians are aware of. Charles Spurgeon, that great evangelist of a hundred years ago, was once asked to reconcile the two halves of verse 37: the first half, speaking of election ('all that the Father gives me will come to me'), and the second half, speaking of reception ('whoever comes to me I will never drive away'). Spurgeon said, 'Why are you asking me to reconcile the two halves of this verse? I don't understand your problem. *I never reconcile friends.*'

One can guess what was going on in the mind of the man who had asked the question. He thought of the truth of divine election as in some way a threat to the person who wants to be a Christian. He saw it as a hindrance to the person who wants to come to Christ, but who perhaps will find that because their name is not written in the Book of Life, Christ is not interested in them and will not receive them. He wants to come, but the door is slammed in his face. What Spurgeon knew (and this explains Spurgeon's answer) is that so far from the truth of election excluding anybody who wants to come to Christ, which it does not do, it is only election which causes any fallen man or woman in this world ever to want to come to Christ at all.

## Totally Adequate Love

Most of us know the little acrostic we use to summarize the Reformed way of declaring God's work of salvation: TULIP. Each of those letters points to an important Reformed doctrine. Four of these items are explicit in these verses which we are studying, and the fifth is implicit.

*T* stands for total inability or depravity. It is total twistedness in God's sight. Put in words of one syllable, total inability means that you and I do not have what it takes to respond to the Word of God, whether his law or his gospel. He speaks, but we do not respond. As Jesus says in verse 36, 'You see me, and you don't believe.' Seeing is not believing for the natural man. On the contrary, as Jesus goes on to say in verse 44, 'No one can come to me unless the Father who sent me draws him.' Sin has robbed us of our ability to respond to God, and that is where we all start. This is why election shuts nobody out: the reason is that nobody would be interested in coming to Christ at all were it not for the active love of God expressed in election.

*U* stands for unconditional election. It is God's giving to the Son his choice of some – indeed, many – out of this mass of fallen humanity. There is nothing in them to prompt his choice. All he saw when he foresaw you and me in our sin was twistedness, guilt, disobedience, and uncleanness. The natural thing to expect God to do was simply to pass sentence of rejection. But God does not leave the matter there. Out of this mass of a fallen humanity he gives a great multitude to his Son to save. You say, 'Who started all this talk about election? Was it John Calvin?' No. 'Was it Augustine?' No. 'Was it Paul?' No, again. It was the Lord Jesus Christ himself and none other. Here in John 6 he is talking about it very freely. 'The Father has given to me a great multitude,' says our Lord, '*and they will come to me.*' This is the reality of unconditional election, without which there would be no salvation for anyone.

The *L* of TULIP stands for limited atonement, a not altogether happy phrase. The thought which the phrase is expressing is simply that Christ's death on the cross guarantees the salvation of those whom the Father has given to him. He says in chapter 10 of John's Gospel – speaking of himself as the Good Shepherd who knows his sheep and is known by his sheep – 'the Good Shepherd' lays down his life '*for the sheep,*' specifically, definitely, and effectively to save them (v.15). That is what this phrase 'limited atonement' is pointing to. Christ died on the cross specifically for those whom the Father had given him. It is true that by virtue of his death an invitation goes out to the world. But a further part of the truth is that Christ by his death on the cross has ensured that those whom the Father gives him will respond to that invitation when it reaches them. That is what limited atonement, or better, *definite, particular, effective redemption*, as I prefer to call it, is really saying.

Then there is the *I* of TULIP. This stands for irresistible grace, which again is not a very happy phrase. It is the way in which theologians in the past have expressed the idea of what I earlier called vocation or effectual calling. What does that mean? It means that God works in people's hearts by sovereign grace, taking away their imperviousness to his Word, taking away their inability to respond to that Word, and changing the disposition of their hearts so that instead of saying 'Nonsense' when they hear the word of Christ, they say, 'That's just what I need.' And they come. 'All that the Father gives me will come to me,' says our Lord, because, as he said in verse 45, 'it is written in the Prophets, "They will all be taught by God." ' And he continues, 'Everyone who listens to the Father and learns from him comes to me.' So there is such a thing as divine teaching in the heart. There is such a thing as God enlightening people so that they receive and respond to Jesus' invitation. This is irresistible grace, irresistible because it takes away the disposition to resist. As the Westminster Confession puts it, those who are the subjects of God's teaching, calling, drawing work come to Christ 'most freely, being made willing by his grace.'

Are you a Christian? A believer? Then you came to Christ because you found yourself willing, longing, desirous, wanting to, as well as, perhaps, not wanting to but knowing you must. How was that? It was because God worked in your heart to give you this desire. He changed you. It was his irresistible grace that drew you to the Savior's feet. Praise him for it! It was one expression of his love to you.

The *P* of TULIP stands for preservation, that preservation of the saints of which our Lord is speaking when, having said, 'Whoever comes to me, I will never drive away,' he goes on to explain it as a word for the future as well as the present: 'I shall lose none of all that he has given me, but raise them up at the last day.'

In the English university system – maybe here in the States also – you can be thrown out at the end of any particular year if you have not done well enough in your exams. But it is not so with the Lord Jesus. People come to Christ, trembling, disobedient, stumbling, and they are received. Then as Christians they lapse most grievously. Again and again they feel, 'Oh, I've made such a mess of my discipleship, surely there'll be no mercy for me.' But there always is. You have fallen, no doubt, and badly, but Christ is there to lift you up and assure you once again that he is still with you and is keeping you. So learn from your mistakes, and try again and go on in his strength.

This is the TULIP, the precious message of the love of God in all its length, breadth, height, and depth. And now note the adequacy of this love. Love needs to be adequate to the need of the one loved. Think of it in human terms. Think of a mother's love for a child, a husband's love for his wife, a wife's love for her husband – love always wants to be adequate to the need which it sees in the beloved person. The same is true of God's love, and it is adequate. Let us dwell on this for a moment.

## Three Views of Salvation

Long ago, when I was an undergraduate, I had an experience on one of the rivers in Oxford where students love to pole themselves around in flat-bottomed boats called punts. I do not know if undergraduates do it in the universities of this country, but we do it in Oxford. The experience was my falling into the river. I can still remember the surprise I had when I suddenly found myself upside down in the water and that there were strands of green weed around my head and the light was up at my feet. You do not forget that sort of thing quickly, and on the basis of that experience I construct for you the following illustration.

Imagine a man who has fallen into a river. He cannot swim. The weeds have caught his feet. He is threshing around, but he cannot get free and will not be above the surface for very long. His state is desperate. Three people come along on the bank. One looks at him and says, 'Oh, he's all right; if he struggles he'll get out; they always do. It's even good for his character that he should have to struggle like this. I'll leave him.' The second person looks at the poor struggling man and says, 'I'd like to help you. I can see what you need. You need some tips about swimming. Let me tell you how to swim.' He gives him a great deal of good advice, but he stops there. Then there is the third man who comes along and sees the measure of the trouble. He jumps in, overcomes the man's struggles, gets him free from the weeds that have caught him, brings him to shore, gives him artificial respiration, and puts him back on his feet. Which of those three men is the truest illustration of what God does to save us?

These three views have theological names. The first corresponds to what is called Pelagianism: its only message is self-help. A hard and unfeeling form of Christianity it is. The second corresponds to what is called Arminianism: God tells us how to be saved, but stops there. The third corresponds to Calvinism. And you can see how the illustration fits. God takes the initiative. Christ comes right down to where we are, enters into our trouble, and does all that has to be done. He breaks the bonds of sin that bind us, brings us to land (that is, to God), restores life, and makes us believers, all this by his sovereign grace which saves absolutely and wonderfully from first to last.

## For Our Encouragement

'All right,' you say, 'I know you're an Episcopalian, but you're talking like a good Presbyterian, and I'm a good Presbyterian too. I've met this doctrine before. I know it's true. I wouldn't dispute it. But, honestly, it all sounds to me very far away, and I'm a little frightened by this talk about election. I don't feel it says anything to me where I am.' If that is your feeling, let me round off by trying to show you the relevance of this message of sovereign grace in three ways.

First, it is a truth full of joy to believers. I asked a moment ago, 'Why have you and I come to Christ?' Answer: because of God's eternal love in election, which is going to keep us to the end. This is expressed in the words of Toplady's great hymn.

> The work which his goodness began
> The arm of his strength will complete;
> His promise is Yea and Amen,
>     And never was forfeited yet.
> Things future, nor things that are now
> Not all things below or above,
> Can make him his purpose forego
>     Or sever my soul from his love.

If you can say that, you have a fount of joy in your heart that will never fail you. It is marvelous assurance to be able to say that and know that it is true. Now the truth of the love of God, as I have been spelling it out, enables us to say that every day of our lives. Do you know the joy that this truth brings? If you are a believer, you know this joy is for you. Take it. Make it your own, and let it flow in your heart every day of your life.

Second, this truth is full of hope for evangelists. It tells the evangelist that even though by human standards of reckoning no one can come to Christ when the gospel is preached, yet some will, because the Father will draw them to Christ through our words. Seeking to make disciples of the nations would be the most hopeless, pointless, fruitless activity the world has ever seen were it not for the sovereign love of God which opens eyes and hearts and draws people to the Savior's feet through the stumbling, fumbling, inadequate words of Christ's human witness.

Look at it this way. Was Jesus a good evangelist? Was he talking clearly when he said, 'I am the bread of life. He who comes to me will never be thirsty'? I do not think any of us will hesitate to say, 'Yes, he was a fine evangelist, the perfect evangelist. He was the ideal communicator. There was nothing wrong with the way he was putting it.' Yet even this faultless evangelism was not enough to induce faith; even he had to say sadly of his congregation, 'But as I told you, you have seen me and still you do not believe.' But then what? Was he discouraged? No. He knew the answer. 'All that the Father gives me will come to me,' he said. 'Some of you will be enlightened by my Father through the word I have spoken. The crowd as a crowd may not come, but one and another of you will come. This is my sure and certain hope as an evangelist.'

As with Jesus, so also with you and me as we seek to bear our witness to Christ. Fruit does not depend on our being brilliant evangelists. It depends on the Father enlightening and drawing. So when we preach this Christ, relaying his promises and inviting people to his feet, there is hope. With the Word goes the Spirit, and the Spirit teaches, enlightens, and instructs. You and I may have to say, 'I'm no Paul, I'm no Spurgeon, no Whitefield, no Billy Graham.' Maybe we are not. But who are they? They are merely spokesmen and mouthpieces through whom the Father drew men to Christ yesterday. The same God will draw people to faith through our and others' witness to Jesus Christ tomorrow. It is all his doing. The knowledge that he is going to do it should give us hope.

Third, this is a truth full of encouragement for seekers. The Greek participle translated in our Bibles by the words 'whoever *comes* to me' (v.37) would better be translated 'whoever *is coming*' or 'whoever *is in process of coming* to me.' The promise is that such a one will not be cast out. There were some in the crowd listening to Jesus, and there are many more in our churches today, who were and are seeking Christ. The folk I think of are coming to church, reading the Word, praying day by day, trying to get the doctrines of grace clear – and they are finding it hard to do. Somehow things are not coming clear for them in the way things are coming clear for others. Around them various individuals are being converted suddenly and dramatically, like a cork being pulled out of a bottle. These folk of whom I am speaking are glad, and think it is marvelous, but it makes them frightened about their own situation. They ask, 'May it be that there is no mercy for me? May it be that I shall be too late because I'm so slow?' No! This is the precious truth this participle is teaching. Jesus says, 'However difficult the journey to the foot of my cross, I will wait for you. And you will find that I shall go on helping you and will receive you when you do come.' You can miss a plane by being too late at the terminal. You will not miss Jesus Christ by coming slowly, if you are seeking him with all your heart and in all your slowness are coming as fast as you can.

You may be one who has heard the gospel for years and has not bothered about it. You see now that you need Christ and must set yourself to seek him. But you feel, 'With half my heart I want to come to Christ, yet with the other half I'm holding back.' Let me ask you: Are you willing to be made willing to come to Christ? Then go to him and talk to him about that. Ask him to work in your heart and make you willing to come to him. There is time. He is the Lord of time. Ask him to begin with you where you are and draw you. You will find as you are drawn that Christ is there in his patience, love, and forbearance to meet you.

To you seekers, then, I offer this word of encouragement. Go on seeking. As you seek you will find the Lord waiting for you. May the Lord Christ draw us all to his feet, bring us all into the knowledge of the richness of his love, and lead us all into that joy of assurance which is every Christian's birthright.

# Chapter 17

# A Calvinist – and an Evangelist!

## I

Why the dash and exclamation mark in my title? Why should it be thought strange for a Calvinist to be an evangelist, or an evangelist a Calvinist? That the two things seem incongruous to very many is beyond question; but why should they? Whence comes the expectation that Calvinism will distract a man from evangelism, or make him ineffective in it?

Before tackling these questions, let the present writer come clean. He is one of those who, if accused of being Calvinists, have no choice but to plead guilty – though he would wish to add that, in his case, at any rate, it is the Bible, not Calvin, that must be blamed for this state of affairs. He is not, however, writing this article to commend Calvinism (he has done that elsewhere), but to clear away misunderstanding. The widespread suspicion that Calvinism is inimical to evangelism has done much harm; it has led to coolness, distrust, and actual quarreling among many Bible-believing Christians; and it is high time it was nailed for the falsehood it is.

We may grant at once that if this suspicion were well founded, it would show at once, in the clearest possible way, that Calvinism is a theological perversion. Any point of view which makes evangelism unnecessary or unimportant thereby discredits itself. 'I haven't the faintest interest in a theology that won't evangelise,' said James Denney – and so say, or should say, all of us! We do not blame those who imagine that Calvinism and evangelism will not mix for disliking Calvinism on that account, but the fact of their dislike makes us very anxious to put the record straight.

George Whitefield and the Wesley brothers, and again C. H. Spurgeon and D. L. Moody, could love and honour and trust each other as brothers in evangelism, even though Whitefield and Spurgeon were Calvinists in a way that the Wesleys and Moody were not. It is hoped that this article may do something to promote a similar spirit among some Calvinistic and non-Calvinistic evangelicals today.

A CALVINIST – AND AN EVANGELIST! originally appeared in *The Hour International* (London), No. 31, August, 1966 pp. 25–27. Reprinted by permission.

## II

We begin by asking: what is a Calvinist? – or rather, since this article is concerned with people, not just abstract positions, what are those Chris - tians who, like the present writer, plead guilty to being Calvinists, concerned to stand for?

First and fundamentally, they stand for pure and consistent theism. Deistic thinking sets God apart from his world, making his relation to it one of transcendence without immanence: pantheistic thinking absorbs God in his world, making his relation to it one of immanence without transcendence; Robinsonian radicalism uses the language of transcen - dence to express the thought of immanence, and so muddles us all up; but theism holds fast to the Biblical teaching that God's relation to his world is one of complete transcendence and complete immanence at the same time. Paul taught this at Athens. 'The God that made the world . . . being Lord of heaven and earth, dwelleth not in temples made with hands; neither is he served by men's hands, as though he needed anything.' (Acts 17:24f.). That is God's transcendence. He is not far from each one of us: for in him 'we live, and move, and have our being' (verse 28). That is God's immanence. Paul held both together, and Calvinists seek to do likewise.

Calvinists, then, worship a God who, as the world's creator, is distinct from it, greater than it, and independent of it, but who, at the same time, as its governor, is completely involved in it, upholding it in being and controlling all that happens in it. 'The whole earth is full of his glory' (Isa. 6:3), and he 'worketh all things after the counsel of his will' (Eph. 1:11). All truth, goodness, beauty, pleasure, and human life itself, are his gifts, and the very existence of things from one moment to the next is due to his active energy. If the Calvinist is accused, as Spinoza was, of being a 'God-intoxicated' man, he takes it as a compliment. The basic thing to grasp about him is that he is a man who believes in God with all his might, and who, in order that his thinking may be true and honouring to God, seeks to keep the thoughts of God's universal *sovereignty*, and his *glory* as the end of all things, always uppermost in his mind.

Believing in such a God, Calvinists have no difficulty with the idea of miracles. Why should not almighty God use his creative power, which upholds all things every moment, to produce effects which go beyond what the observed regularities of the created order could have led one to expect, or ultimately can enable one to explain? Therefore Calvinists accept whole-heartedly such basic Christian facts as the incarnation, Christ's bodily resurrection, man's inner re-creation by the new birth, and an inspired Bible whose words are God's own words, and stand out against any watered-down versions of these facts, insisting that the desire to dilute these fundamental doctrines shows nothing more respectable than an incapacity to believe properly in God. Calvinists thus appear as thoroughgoing theists and whole-hogging supernaturalists, aiming to be no less consistent and uncompromising in their Christianity at the intellectual level than at the levels of personal devotion and moral conduct.

This leads on to the second thing, for which Calvinists stand – sovereign grace, God's Lordship in salvation. Their emphasis here reflects not only their principle of acknowledging God's sovereignty everywhere, but also their certainty that sinners cannot do anything to save themselves. This certainty, under the technical name of Total Inability, is the first of the famous 'five points of Calvinism' – actually, the five points of Reformed teaching which were reasserted at the Synod of Dort (1618) in face of the denial of each by the school of Arminius. The other four points are Unconditional Election, Limited Atonement (better, definite atonement or particular redemption), Irresistible Grace (better, effectual calling), and Preservation of the Saints, through the covenanted persever - ance with them of their Saviour. These points, the so-called 'doctrines of grace,' block in the shape of the sovereign action whereby God is held to save sinners. A handy way of remembering the 'five points' is to realize that their initial letters spell the word TULIP.

## III

By an evangelist we mean a person who, by whatever means, seeks to preach the good news of Christ and the promise of salvation, and to bring men and women to repentance and faith in him.

Is there anything in Calvinism to discourage or distract a Christian from being an evangelist?

It is worth noting at once that the most distinguished Calvinists always rejected as slanderous the suggestion that there is. To take just one example: on Thursday, April 11, 1861, at the newly opened Metropolitan Tabernacle, C. H. Spurgeon introduced a day conference on the doctrines of grace by an address entitled 'Misrepresentations of true Calvinism cleared away', and in the course of it he said this:

> A yet further charge against us, is that we *dare not preach the gospel to the unregenerate*, that, in fact, our theology is so narrow and cramped that we cannot preach to sinners. Gentlemen, if you dare to say this, I would take you to any library in the world where the old Puritan fathers are stored up, and I would let you take down any volume and tell me if you ever read more telling exhortations and addresses to sinners in any of your own books. Did not Bunyan preach to sinners? . . . Did not Charnock, Goodwin and Howe agonise for souls, and what were they but Calvinists? Did not Jonathan Edwards preach to sinners? . . . The works of our innumerable divines teem with passionate appeals to the unconverted . . . Was George Whitefield any the less seraphic?

Did his eyes weep the fewer tears or his bowels move with less compassion because he believed in God's electing love and preached the sovereignty of the Most High? It is an unfounded calumny. Our souls are not stony; . . . we can hold all our views firmly, and yet can weep as Christ did over a Jerusalem which was certainly to be destroyed.

Again, I must say, I am not defending certain brethren who have exaggerated Calvinism. I speak of Calvinism proper . . . as I find it in *Calvin's Institutes*, and especially in his Expositions. I have read them carefully. I take not my views of Calvin from common repute, but from his books. Nor do I, in thus speaking, even vindicate Calvinism as if I were concerned for the name, but I mean that glorious system which teaches that salvation is of grace from first to last. And again, then, I say, it is an utterly unfounded charge that we dare not preach to sinners.

Has the Calvinist a gospel for everyone? Yes, they have. They proclaim a Saviour who is able to bring pardon to the worst and eternal security to the weakest. They proclaim invitations to come to Christ, and promises of forgiveness to those who repent and believe, which are addressed by God to everyone who hears them, and to which God will stand in every single case where they are accepted. The Calvinist's gospel centres, not on the mystery of election, but on God's universal offer of Christ to all who will receive him. Nobody who hears this gospel is excluded from salvation unless by unbelief they exclude themselves. 'He that will, let him take of the water of life freely' (Rev. 22:17). 'Whosoever shall call upon the name of the Lord shall be saved' (Rom. 10:13).

Has the Calvinist a reason for preaching the gospel to others? Yes, they have. They know that salvation is through faith, not apart from it, and that no one will be saved at all who does not hear and believe the message of Christ. They know that God brings his elect into a state of grace through the gospel, and recognizes in consequence that the gospel must be made known to all and sundry if anyone is ever to be saved.

Has the Calvinist a motive for preaching the gospel to others? Yes, they have. God's love towards them, the Father's love in electing them and the Son's love in redeeming them and the Spirit's love bringing them to faith, has been shred abroad in their hearts and thrilled them to the marrow. Now it overflows in compassion to those who are as yet strangers to it. They love sinners; they want to see God glorified in their salvation; so they take the life-giving gospel to them.

Has the Calvinist a hope when they preach the gospel to others? Yes, they have, though apart from his knowledge of God's sovereignty in grace he could have no hope whatever. They know that sinners are by nature blind and deaf to God, so that were evangelism a matter merely of someone bearing testimony to Christ it would be foredoomed to fail. But they know too that evangelism is never a matter of human testimony alone. Where God sends the Word he also sends the Spirit, and through the Word the Spirit opens the hearts of God's elect and brings them to faith. The Calvinist's confidence as they proclaim Christ, therefore, lies in their certainty that God in sovereign grace can and will use the message to save some, and hence they expect results.

The truth thus seems to be, not that Calvinism inhibits evangelism, but rather that it provides a spur to it. Other things being equal, a Christian should evangelize better – more earnestly, more tirelessly, more expec - tantly – for being a Calvinist! Nor is this a matter of theory alone. Many, if not most, of the greatest evangelists that the Church has seen – men like Whitefield, Berridge, Rowlands, Grimshaw, Baxter, Bunyan, Ed - wards, Spurgeon, Brainerd, McCheyne, Brownlow North and many more – were Calvinists, and their record is magnificent. In them one sees the theory which we have sketched out here incarnated in flesh and blood, and translated into glowing action. These are the men to study, if one wants to know whether Calvinists can really be evangelists.

But if all this is so, whence comes this pervasive notion that Calvinism makes against evangelism?

It seems to spring from the following two sources.

## (1)  The infection of 'hypercalvinism'

Since the seventeenth century, a steady trickle of professed Calvinists in England have found difficulty with the free and inclusive character of God's promises to sinners in the gospel. Some have held that they should only be offered to sinners under conviction, or sinners who had already repented; others, that they should not be offered to the unconverted at all, nor should unbelievers be told that they have a duty to receive them. Only a minority have ever held such views, and 'mainstream' Calvinists, in company with Spurgeon, quoted above, have always rejected them as a perversion; nonetheless, critics have persistently tarred all Calvinists with this particular brush.

## (2)  The Calvinistic critique of 'Finneyism'

The gifted and godly C. G. Finney did more than anyone else to found modern fashions in evangelism. He first devised the evangelistic campaign ('protracted meeting'), the penitent form ('anxious seat') from which comes the modern missioner's counselling room, and the idea of the freelance professional 'evangelist' whom the churches should call in when they need his special skill. He believed that the anointing of the Spirit which God gives to an 'evangelist' is specifically intended to equip him to act as a spiritual battering-ram, using argument and appeal to bludgeon his unconverted hearers into submission to the gospel by sheer force of his own sanctified personality.

Calvinists have questioned these methods and notions. They have objected to the Arminian, indeed Pelagian, assumptions behind the battering-ram conception (Finney himself was an avowed anti-Calvinist); they have deplored the detaching of evangelism from the regular rhythm of the Church's life which was implied by the 'protracted meeting' ideology; they have criticized the importance which 'Finneyism' imparts to the personality of the evangelist; they have complained of the glamour, ballyhoo, and irreverent sentimentality, which, as they felt, came to mark evangelistic occasions planned in terms of Finney's ideas, in which every thing was directed to securing the sinners' capitulation at the end of the meeting. This is not the place to discuss the rights and wrongs of these criticisms. Our only point here is the factual one, that, since 'Finneyism' has in the past century, become so standard, through Moody, Torrey, and their successors, as to constitute in many minds almost a definition of evangelism, Calvinists who venture to criticize it are often taken to be criticizing and opposing evangelism as such.

It should by now be clear, however, that this is unfair. What Calvinists have practised in the past and seek to re-establish in the present is a type of evangelism which does justice to the truths that God himself is the true evangelist, that it is he who brings souls to new birth, that the local churches are the basic evangelizing units, that evangelism must be fully integrated into local church life, and that evangelistic practice must be reverent, worshipful, and worthy of God. What modifications of the Finneyite pattern as we know it today are required to this end, and what new a departures this ideal might call for in our time, are matters which many are debating, and it would be pre-mature to suggest conclusions here, even if space allowed, which it does not. If, however, parties to these debates will fully trust each other, we may hope that the way forward will soon become clear to all. It is certainly of vital importance that it should.

# Chapter 18

# Understanding the Lordship Controversy

If, ten years ago, you had told me that I would live to see literate Evangelicals, some with doctorates and a seminary teaching record, arguing for the reality of an eternal salvation, divinely guaranteed, that may have in it no repentance, no discipleship, no behavioural change, no practical acknowledgement of Christ as Lord of one's life, and no perseverance in faith, I would have told you that you were out of your mind. Stark, staring bonkers is the British phrase I would probably have used. But now the thing has happened. In *The Gospel Under Siege* (1981) and *Absolutely free!* (1989), Zane Hodges, for one, maintains all these positions as essential to the Christian message, arguing that without them the gospel gets lost in legalism. Wow.

Nor is this all. Hodges lashes the historic reformational account of the gospel, which he labels 'Lordship salvation,' as a form of works-righteousness, because it affirms that repentance – turning from sin to serve Jesus as one's Lord – is as necessary for salvation as faith – turning from self-reliance to trust Jesus as one's Saviour. Such repentance, says Hodges, is a work, and justification is through faith apart from works. To preach and teach in reformational terms is to compromise the grace of the gospel. It is vital, says Hodges, to see that there is no necessary connection between saving faith and good works at any stage.

Hodges comes out of that branch of the dispensationalist stable which has consistently assured everyone that by biblical standards Reformed theology is systematically off-centre and misshapen. Hodges' argumenta - tion had already in essence appeared in the Schofield Bible and the writings of Lewis Sperry Chafer and Charles Ryrie. He might not have attracted much notice had not a distinguished fellow-dispensationalist with a Reformed soteriology, John MacArthur, Jr., attacked his view in *The Gospel According to Jesus* (1988), a strongly worded book with forewords by Boice and Packer. *Absolutely Free!* was Hodges' reply to MacArthur.

UNDERSTANDING THE LORDSHIP CONTROVERSY was originally published in *Tabletalk*, Ligonier Ministries, Orlando, Florida, May, 1991. Reprinted by permission.

It is an odd situation. Both sides proclaim that God's grace is absolutely free, that justification is absolutely central, that faith is absolutely necessary for salvation – and that the other side's account of what it means to be a Christian is absolutely wrong. Hodges calls MacArthur's position 'a radical rewriting of the Gospel,' 'Satanic at its core,' which has 'turned the meaning of faith upside down,' destroying the ground of assurance and producing doctrine that the New Testament writers would find unrec - ognizable. MacArthur calls Hodges' position a 'tragic error' that 'destroys the Gospel,' 'promises a false peace,' 'produces a false evangelism,' and 'offers a false hope.' What, we ask, is the point of cleavage that so drastically divides men who seemed to agree on so much? The question is not hard to answer. It has to do with *the nature of faith*.

Hodges defines faith in exclusively intellectual terms, as mental assent to what God tells us in the gospel. This intellectualism recalls the old Roman Catholic conception of faith as believing what the church teaches. It corresponds exactly to that of the eighteenth-century Scottish eccentric Robert Sandeman, who affirmed that 'every one who . . . is persuaded that the event [Christ's atoning death] actually happened as testified by the apostles is justified.' It corresponds also to the view of Karl Barth, for whom faith is simply believing that because of Christ's death and resurrection one is already justified and an heir of eternal life, as is everybody else.

By contrast, faith according to reformational teaching is a whole-souled reality with an affectional and volitional aspect as well as an intellectual one. It is, as the seventeenth-century analysts put it, *notitia* (factual knowledge), *assensus* (glad acceptance), and *fiducia* (personal trust in a personal Saviour, as well as in his promises). It is a principle of new activity, as the Westminster Confession brings out:

> By . . . faith, a Christian believeth to be true whatsoever is revealed in the Word . . . yielding obedience to the commands, trembling at the threatenings, and embracing the promises of God . . . But the principal acts of saving faith are accepting, receiving, and resting upon Christ alone for justification, sanctification, and eternal life, by virtue of the covenant of grace (XIV. 2).

Clearly, if the intellectualism of Hodges, Sandeman, and Barth is right, Westminster confuses, misplacing the emphasis. Equally clearly, if West - minster is right, what Hodges, Sandeman, and Barth define is less than faith, and will not of itself bring salvation.

As is apparent, I think Hodges is wrong, and ruinously so. I find his doctrine of faith involving four major errors.

### *The first is* an error about Christ

Is Christ divided, or divisible? Has not God joined the three roles of prophet (teacher), priest (atoner), and king (Lord and Master) in the mediatorial office of his Son? Does he not in Scripture require mankind to relate positively to each? Does not Christ's own Gospel teaching, well set out by MacArthur, show that he himself does not accept the separating of salvation from discipleship, whereby he is acknowledged and taken as Saviour but rejected as Lord? My answer is not Hodges' answer, and his teaching does not seem to me to honour my Saviour.

### The second is **an error about works**

Hodges equates faith as a psychological act ('closing with Christ,' as the Puritans put it) with faith as a meritorious work, and so argues that to call for active commitment to discipleship as part of a saving response to the gospel is to teach works-righteousness. But this is a confusion. Every act of faith, psychologically regarded, is a matter of doing something (know - ing is as much a mental act as are trusting, receiving, and resolving to obey); yet no act of faith ever presents itself to its doer as anything but a means of receiving undeserved mercy in some form. Hodges' inability to distinguish faith as an act form faith as a work makes him increase, rather than dispel, the confusion about the terms of the gospel that he rightly sees as bedeviling us today.

### The third is **an error about repentance**

In Scripture, repentance and faith go inseparably together; repentance means turning from sin, faith means turning to Jesus. Dispensationalists do not always observe this connection. Some, fastening onto the etymol - ogy of repentance in Greek (*metanoia*), explain it as merely a change of mind about who Jesus is; Hodges, seeing that repentance means in Scripture a change of life, detaches it from the way of salvation (thus contradicting the Westminster Confession, which on the basis of Luke 13:3,5, says that 'none may expect pardon without it') and depicts it as a voluntary adjustment to God that may come before salvation or after salvation or never at all. To say the least, he fails to convince.

### The fourth is **an error about regeneration**

When Scripture speaks of regeneration, which it represents as a new birth, a quickening of the dead, what is in view is an inner transformation of one's being, or 'heart,' which makes it impossible for one to go on living under sin's sway as one lived before. The effect of regeneration is that now one *wants*, from the bottom of one's heart, to know, love, serve, trust, obey, and honour the Father and the Son, so that obedient devotion and discipleship spontaneously spring up where there was only resentful hostility to God before. Hodges' account of Christian discipleship as a prudent and fulfilling, though not a necessary, option shows that he does not understand this at all. In particular, he does not see that the faith that justifies only appears as an expression of a regenerate heart.

The pastoral effect of this teaching can only be to produce what the Puritans called 'Gospel hypocrites' – persons who have been told that they are Christians, eternally secure, because they believe that Christ died for them, when their hearts are unchanged and they have no personal commitment to Christ at all. I know this, for I was just such a gospel hypocrite for two years before God mercifully made me aware of my unconverted state. If I seem harsh in my critique of Hodges' redefinition of faith as barren intellectual formalism, you must remember that once I almost lost my soul through assuming what Hodges teaches, and a burned child always thereafter dreads the fire.

# Chapter 19

# The Gospel – Its Content
# and Communication:
# A Theological Perspective

Let me speak first of three specific benefits which reflection on our theme – the content and communication of the Gospel, related together as a single topic – may yield.

First, it will serve to remind us of the obvious but ever-relevant truth that *the content of the Gospel must always control the method of its communication* , and that we must judge the value of the various techniques proposed for use in evangelism by asking how far they can and do succeed in getting the message across.

The modern communications industry, and the theoretical studies which guide it on its way, tend always to detach questions of method from those of content, and to treat the task of communicating as if its dimensions were constant, irrespective of what it is that is being put over. But this is not so, and an inappropriate technique may limit understanding by inhibiting challenge at depth even while at surface level it enlarges understanding by bringing conceptual clarity. In the case of the Gospel, the content includes a diagnosis of the hearer's state and needs before God, value-judgements on the life they live as compared with that which might be theirs, and a call to judge themselves, to acknowledge the gracious approach and invitation of God in Christ, and to respond by a commitment more radical and far-reaching than any other they will ever make; and the Gospel is not fully communicated unless all this comes over.

---

THE GOSPEL – ITS CONTENT AND COMMUNICATION: A THEO-LOGICAL PERSPECTIVE was originally published in *Gospel & Culture: The Papers of a Consultation on the Gospel and Culture, convened by the Lausanne Committee's Theology and Education Group* John Stott and Robert T. Coote, eds. (Pasadena: William Carey Library, 1979), pp. 135–153. Reprinted by permission.

So the Gospel must be *verbalized* (for none of this *ad hominem* address can be communicated otherwise, just as the truths on which it rests cannot otherwise be explained), and in its verbal form it must be *preached*, that is, set forth by a messenger who, whether *viva voce* in the flesh or on film or tape or radio, or in print, interprets and applies it to those whom they address in a way which makes its existential implications for them plain. Such media of expression as instrumental music, pictures, sculpture or dance may reinforce the Gospel by the mood or vision they express, but they cannot, strictly speaking, communicate it; only preaching can do that. Similarly, teaching the Christian faith as an academic discipline (as is done in English state schools and universities) is not strictly communi - cating the Gospel, for although the relevant themes are analyzed the thrust of the application is not present. It cannot be too strongly stressed that since the Gospel is a personal message from God to each hearer, the only appropriate and effective way of communicating it is for a messenger to deliver it on God's behalf, ambassador-style (cf. 2 Cor. 5:20) – that is, identifying with God's concerns and expressing by the way they use words the mind and heart of God, how he hates sin and loves sinners, and what he has done, is doing and will do for the salvation of those who turn to him.

God has shown us that preaching is the only natural and adequate way to communicate the content of the Gospel by himself actually commu - nicating it this way. 'Truth through personality,' which was Philip Brooks' definition of preaching has been the principle of God's commu - nication throughout, first through the prophets and then climactically through his own incarnate Son. It is noteworthy that the writer to the Hebrews introduces the Son as a God-sent preacher of the Gospel before saying anything about his role as priest, sacrifice and mediator.

> In many and various ways God spoke of old to our fathers by the prophets; but in these last days he has spoken to us by a Son . . . Therefore we must pay the closer heed to what we have heard . . . how shall we escape if we neglect such a great salvation? It was declared at first by the Lord . . . (Heb. 1:1f., 2:1,3).

This chimes in with the evangelists' highlighting of the preaching of the Gospel of the kingdom as the initial and basic activity of Jesus' public ministry (cf. Mark 1:14f.; Matt. 4:17, 23; Luke 4:16–21; John 3:3–15). When Thomas Goodwin the Puritan wrote, 'God had but one son, and he made him a preacher,' he was echoing an authentic note in the New Testament witness.

The Gospel can be preached both formally and informally, both to crowds, congregations and to single individuals (cf. Acts 8:29–35), but preached it must be, or its full content as a message from God will not be passed on. This is surely undeniable, and from it two far-reaching conclusions clearly follow. First, whatever experts in contemporary communication may urge to the contrary, preaching must continue as a main activity of the church until the Lord comes. Second, whatever technical skills a Christian communicator may command, what will count ultimately is what he is in himself, whether his manner backs up his matter in making God's mind and heart known or not, and we shall be dealing with Christian communication, intra-cultural or cross-cultural, in a way that is shallow and inadequate, wrong-headed indeed, if we leave this personal dimension out of account.

Second, our reflections may serve to remind us that *problems in communicating the Gospel raise questions about its content*: questions which it will be ruinous to answer wrongly, but which when answered in the right way can be a source of much help in our communicative task.

It is natural that those who find that they cannot convince others of the truth and relevance of the message which they announce as offering life to all, should ask themselves whether they have yet understood it correctly. The question is a proper one, but wrong turnings are easily taken when answering it. First example: Rudolf Bultmann saw the biblical miracle-stories, and the supernaturalist view of the cosmos which they implied, as an obstacle to acceptance of the Gospel by contemporary Germans, and so in 1941 he proposed his demythologizing program, which removes the stumbling-block of miracles by abolishing the divine and miraculous Christ who performed them. (One thinks of the man who, having bought ointment to cure a wart on his nose, later telephoned the vendor to say that his wart had gone, but could he please have his nose back.) Bultmann's program appears to have been double mistaken. Hermeneutically, it went wrong in holding that the New Testament witness to Jesus as divine Saviour and risen, reigning, returning Lord is myth in a sense which excludes its space-time factuality; theologically, it erred by assuming that the Creator cannot or will not work miracles in the world external to us, but limits his work to the sphere of our self-consciousness and self-understanding, which notion brings an arbi - trary and anti-biblical dualism into our thought about God and his world. Second example: in *Honest To God* (1963), J. A. T. Robinson posited 'the end of theism' because, as he urged, 'supranaturalism,' i.e. the idea of transcendent personhood, could no longer communicate any sense of God's presence to modern Western man, and he offered instead a notion of God formed in terms of depth, immanence, love and moral claims. Here, too, there seemed to be two mistakes: a hermeneutical error, in not seeing that the biblical writers offer their account of God not as a human projection but rather as a revealed description, and a theological error, in shrinking God by letting go of the Triune aseity which (as I continue to think though Robinson has explicitly denied it) is central to the biblical disclosure of who and what God is. I cite these familiar examples as cautionary tales. Both Bultmann and Robinson aimed at effective communication, but their way of getting around the stumbling-blocks was to reduce the message in a way that lost the baby along with the bath-water. It is never safe for the Christian communicator to conclude that the less you commit yourself to assert, the easier it will be to assert it, or to treat objections to a particular tenet as a sign that it is dispensable.

But for communicators who hold to historic Christianity problems in making it seem true and relevant can be salutary. What they may show is that, as a J. B. Phillips' book-title once told us, *Your God is Too Small*, so we must see our presentation of the Gospel as being too limited, taking too much for granted and not digging deep enough. What we may be failing to do, or at least to do clearly and thoroughly enough, is to highlight those absolutes of God's self-disclosure which show up the preconcep-tions and preoccupations that impede communication as being themselves relative, and therefore arbitrary to a degree and open to question and revision. The Western skepticism about the supernatural which sparked off Bultmann's demythologizing program and Robinson's journeyings beyond theism would be a case in point; so would the Latin American and Black American preoccupation with personal freedom and social betterment which has produced the politically angled 'liberation theol-ogy,' in which seemingly on a universalist basis, political action does duty for evangelism; so would any movement which thinks of our humanness, freedom and dignity as conditional upon our not being exposed to social, political or economic manipulations by folk for whom we are merely means and not ends.

These perspectives need relating to the true absolutes which our self-announcing God has made known in Christ – the sovereign omnipo-tence of his work in creation, providence and grace; more specifically, the terms of his plan of salvation; most specifically of all, the paradigm of humanness, freedom and dignity in the life of Jesus Christ, not excluding the hours of his betrayal, show trial, torture and death on the cross. It is a question whether in cross-cultural communication today Christians are always careful enough to establish these absolutes as the frame of reference within which all human preconceptions must be set for checking and correction and any circumstance which goads us to think and work harder here will be a blessing in disguise.

For certainly, if this is not rigorously done, the result of not doing it is predictable from the start. Sooner or later, the biblical Gospel, in which God the Creator appears in judgement and mercy reconciling the world to himself, will itself be relativized and thereby distorted through being assimilated to man's prior interests. The world will write the agenda – and it will be man's agenda rather than God's. This seems to be what happened at Bangkok in 1973, where the word 'salvation' became the label for many things that men desire, but which are not salvation in the revealed and regulative Bible sense. It happened before in old-style liberalism, which turned the kingdom of God preached as Gospel by Jesus into the kingdom of ends taught as ethics by Kant. It will no doubt happen again, if allowed to. There is no way to stop it happening save to assert the true frame of reference effectively – if we can. So running up against ideas about God or the world or man which challenge the Gospel can be good for us, by prompting us to anchor our message more explicitly and robustly in the divine ultimates and absolutes (as did Paul when on the Areopagus, facing polytheism, he spelled out basic Christian theism at length and with emphasis). Thus, through being stirred to strengthen the foundations, we may end up presenting the Gospel a good deal more adequately than before.

Third, our reflections may alert us to the fact that our *own assumptions about the content of the Gospel can themselves become an obstacle in communicating it*; for we all tend to equate our own culture-bound understanding of Christ with the Gospel itself, and this way trouble lies.

All understandings of the Gospel, whether British, North American, Latin American, African, Indian or what have you, are in the nature of the case culturally conditioned. I cannot jump out of my own cultural skin, nor can you, nor can anyone. Equally, of course, the presentations of the Gospel in the New Testament itself are culturally conditioned; but there we may believe that the Palestinian and Hellenistic cultural settings, so far from being distorting or limiting or obscuring factors, were providentially shaped so as to be wholly appropriate vehicles for express - ing and exhibiting God's last word to the world – the word spoken once for all in the Jew who was his incarnate Son and through his chosen witnesses, the apostolic theologians, in whose minds Rabbinic and Hellenistic culture so remarkably met and blended. That God's revelation of himself in Christ is culture-bound only in the sense of being culturally particularized, as being historical it had to be, but net at all in the sense of being culturally distorted, seems to me to be a crucial truth for hermeneutics today, and one which urgently needs some fresh exposition and defense; but here I only asset it in order then to make the point that there is no other culture of which this can be said.

We may be sure, therefore, before ever we sit down to look, that any version of Christianity produced anywhere at any time will bear marks of one-sidedness or myopia, not only because of imperfect exegesis and theologizing but also for reasons of cultural limitation. A culture operates as both binoculars and blinkers, helping you to see some things and keeping you from seeing others. So we shall need to be consciously critical of whatever form of the Christian tradition – in our case, the evangelical tradition – we have inherited; just as we shall need to be aware that from the great smorgasbord of international evangelical tradition no two of us are likely to have ingested quite the same meal. Being the fallen creatures we are, we shall always find it easier to see motes in others' traditions than beams blocking vision in our own, and, being unaware of our own blind spots, we shall be tempted to ascribe to those expressions of the Gospel in theology, liturgy and behaviour patterns which we know best a finality, fullness and universality which may only be claimed for the gospel itself, and the Christ of whom it speaks, Then the danger will be that in seeking to proclaim the Gospel in cross-cultural situations we shall impose on people our own cultural forms for expressing the Gospel, forms which to them are alien and unauthentic, and which when accepted become badges of a dependence that is not wholly healthy. My knowledge here is limited, but I think as I write of the zeal of some African clergy for Anglican clerical uniform, and of a Japanese seminary for instilling the Westminster Confession.

When a version of Christianity developed in one cultural setting is exported in this way to another, the major trouble is likely to be not that it includes idiosyncrasies but rather that it ignores matters of importance. As in our personal discipleship sins of commission are usually less grievous than our leaving undone so much that we ought to have done, so the chief defects of this or that version of Christianity are likely to be the things that, unwittingly, we leave out − as, for instance, medieval Christianity left out all sense of history. To give one example, which comes near home for us all: the Western evangelical tradition is weak on the doctrine of creation. Following the almost mortal second-century conflict to establish against the Gnostics that God the Redeemer is also God the Creator, the conflict in which Irenaeus achieved so much, belief in creation, and in the Creator's direct, immediate and particular provi - dential control over all that he had made, became a Christian theolo - goumenon which, since the Reformation, evangelicals, concentrating all attention on the doctrines of grace, have simply taken for granted. The result is a five-fold weakness.

First, we still lack any magisterial counter to the deist, pantheist and materialist versions of the uniformitarian myth of the universe which grips so many minds these days, and which modern technology is widely though erroneously thought to confirm. Second, evangelical discussions of the appropriate way to relate the witness of holy Scripture to that of natural science on, for instance, creation (including evolution), the flood, and the constitution of the human organism remain almost discreditably naive. Third, we regularly ignore the cosmic dimensions of God's reconciling work in Christ, and of the renewal that is promised at Christ's return. Fourth, an atomic individualism, really a product of European rationalism and romanticism two centuries ago, has crept into our thinking about individuals before God, making us unable, it seems, to take seriously enough the family, racial, national and Adamic solidarities which Scripture affirms as part of the created order, and which the so-called 'primitive' mind grasps so much better than most of us do. Hence come theological fumblings when interpreting the faith. Fifth, we are short of a theology of nature and the natural, and so we have constant

difficulties in convincing our critics that the biblical positivism which is
our regular theological method as evangelicals is in fact genuinely attuned
to the nature of things as God made them. Now should anyone take over
any version of the Western evangelical tradition in theology as a final
standard, he would be buying along with many strengths this chronic and
often overlooked weakness on creation. It is important that such purchases
should be outlawed, lest in retrospect someone should feel himself to have
fallen victim to a confidence trick.

So in cross-cultural Christian communication the right course will be
neither to impose on folk of other cultures forms of Christian expression
belonging to our own, nor to deny them access to our theological,
liturgical, ethical and devotional heritage, from which they will certainly
have much to gain, but to encourage them once they have appreciated
our tradition to seek by the light of Scripture to distinguish between it
and the Gospel it enshrines, and to detach the Gospel from it, so that the
Gospel may mesh with their own cultures directly. Thus among younger
nations with distinct cultural styles, and, perhaps, some touchiness about
cultural imperialism, the Gospel may be set free to do its job, running and
being glorified without hindrance. If it is true (as I for one believe) that
every culture and sub-culture without exception in this fallen world,
whether primitive or tribal or Hindu or Christian, or a form of the
constantly shifting 'pop' youth culture which affluent nations develop
these days, is a product not just of human sin but also of God's common
grace (which means, biblically speaking, of the work of the life- and
light-giving Word of John's prologue), then respect for other cultures as
such, and desire to see them not abolished but reanimated by Gospel grace
in their own terms, must undergird all particular criticisms of ways in
which, missing the good life, they embrace the not-so-good life instead.
This practice of respect will set us all free for critical dialogue with all
forms of human culture Christian and non-Christian alike, while safe -
guarding us against both the appearance and the reality of cultural
imperialism while we engage in it.

Putting the point positively, we shall urge Christians of other cultures
to use the resources of our own heritage in the way that Barth urges us
all to use the creeds, namely as a 'preliminary exposition' of the faith, by
which they may be helped to subject their own culture to the corrective
and directive judgement of the Word of God. Long ago that Word
'Christianized' Greco-Roman culture very thoroughly; a century ago it
was Alexander Duff's vision that a similar thing might happen in India;
today, as we face the global cultural imperialism of Marxists, active
attempts to Christianize or re-Christianize all cultures is much to be
desired. And if in the process Christians of other cultures criticize sub-
and post-Christian elements in our own heritage, we must not mishear
this as cultural imperialism in reverse. The *koinonia* which is the church's
proper life is two-way traffic, taking as well as giving, and it requires us

both to share what resources of Christian insight we have and to take gratefully any further insights that others offer us. Only so can we avoid canonizing the clumsinesses, blind spots and poverties of our own tradition, and thereby actually misrepresenting the content of the Gospel which we seek to make known.


## The Content of the Gospel

Thus far we have explored in general terms three preliminary points: first, that the Gospel, being what it is must be communicated by preaching; second, that establishing its truth and relevance involves not diminishing it at the points of difficulty, but countering directly any preconceptions which oppose it; third, that the Gospel may not be equated with any post-apostolic formulation or cultural embodiment of it, but must be distinguished from them all. Now we move on to look at its content in more precise terms.

'Content' could be a misleading word here; not because the implica - tions of givenness and fixity which follow from its dictionary meaning, 'that which is contained' as in a book or box or cupboard, are in any way misleading (they are in fact absolutely correct: remember Paul, in the first paragraph of Galatians), but because it conveys the idea of something passive and inert, something that is 'there' on a take–it–or–leave–it basis, and thus fails to suggest the dynamism which the New Testament associates with the Gospel, on the basis that whenever it comes before anyone God actually preaches it in the power of the Holy Spirit. But this point, once noted, need not detain us.

A glance at the relevant lexicography shows that the Gospel ( *euaggelion*, good news: sixty times in Paul) is the message that God has acted and acts now in and through Christ for the world's salvation. God's saving action was the burden of 'the Gospel of the kingdom' which Jesus preached (*euaggelion* appears seven times in Mark), and Jesus' incarnation, death, resurrection, reign and return was the theme of the Gospel according to Paul. Sometimes 'the Gospel' in Paul seems to signify the evangelistic *kerygma* which C. H. Dodd isolated long ago in Acts, sometimes it embraces the whole Christian message as such. To make this Gospel known is God's work through man: God appoints Christians to be his heralds, ambassadors and teachers ( *keryx, presbys, didaskalos*) taking the message to the world. This task is regularly described by the use of three verbs: *euaggelizomai* (tell the good news, *euaggelion), kerysso*: (utter an announcement, *kerygma*), and *martyreo* (bear testimony, *martyria*). The aim is to persuade (*peitho*), to 'disciple' (*matheteuo*, Acts 14:21, cf. Matt. 28:19), and so to turn men to God (*epistrepho*).

Laying out the contents of the Gospel in full is a complex task, for the material is abundant, varied and occasional. There is the *kerygma* of the speeches in Acts and such passages as Romans 1:3f. and 1 Corinthians 15:3f., detailing the fulfilment of prophecy in Jesus' life, death for sins, resurrection and kingdom, and the promise of pardon and the Spirit to those who repent and believe. There are the four accounts of Jesus' ministry, each highlighting his death, resurrection and expected return in glory, and each so angled as to present a different facet of his identity and role (in Mark, God's toiling, suffering servant; in Matthew, Davidic king and new Moses; in Luke, God's prophet; in John God's eternal Son, the life-giver, full of grace and truth); each account is called (presumably by its author) 'the Gospel.' There are also many presentations of Jesus Christ in the epistles, with the thematic changes rung according to what the writers thought their readers needed to hear. All this material has a 'between-the-times' perspective, looking back to Christ's first coming, forward to his reappearing, and upward to his present heavenly reign. Perhaps the clearest way to analyse it is in terms of six distinct (though overlapping and complementary) 'stories,' each of which is the Gospel just as all six together are the Gospel. Two of the stories are about God, two about Jesus Christ, and two about man, thus:

## A. Stories about God.

### (i) God's purpose: the kingdom

The Creator has judicially subjected all mankind to sin and death, and the rest of this creation to 'futility' and 'corruption' (*mataiotes, phthora*), in consequence of the guilty disobedience of the 'first man Adam,' in whom all now die. But from all eternity it has been his gracious plan, purpose and pleasure to restore this situation and bring the cosmos to perfection at the end of the day through the mediation of the 'last Adam,' the God-man Jesus Christ. All the decisive events in God's plan save the last have now been played out on the stage of world history. The key to understanding the plan, as it affects mankind, is to see that by God's appointment each man's destiny depends on how he stands related to the two representative men, Adam and Christ. What God planned was to exercise his kingship (sover - eignty, an ultimate fact) over his rebel world by bringing in his kingdom, that is, a state of bliss for sinners who, penitently returning to his obedience, should find under his sway salvation from sin's guilt, power and evil effects. In this kingdom Jesus Christ should be God's vice-regent, and trusting and obeying Christ should be the appointed way of returning from sin to God's service. God prepared the way for the kingdom by making himself king of a national community created out of the family of Abraham: to this community he gave territory, his law, a national life, prophets and kings as his spokesmen and deputies, and promises of the Messiah who would come to reign over them in the new era of peace (shalom) and joy. When at the appointed time Christ came, Israel the prepared nation rejected him and compassed his crucifixion; but God, having achieved world redemption according to his plan through Christ's death, raised him to life and set him on the throne of the universe, where now he reigns, furthering his kingdom by sending the Spirit to draw men to himself and by strengthening them for faithful obedience in face of mounting opposition till the day dawns for his return to judge all men and finally to renew all things.

In this story, the goal of God's action is to glorify himself by restoring and perfecting his disordered cosmos, and the Gospel call is to abandon rebellion, acknowledge Christ's lordship, thankfully accept the free gift of forgiveness and new life in the kingdom, enlist on the victory side, be faithful in God's strength, and hope to the end for Christ's coming triumph. New Testament passages of special relevance for this story include Acts 2:14–36, 3:12–26, 10:34–43, 13:16–43, 17:22–31; John 3:3–15; Romans 1–3, 5, 8:19ff.; 1 Corinthians 15; Rev. 4–5, 17–21.

## (ii)  God's people: the church

In this fallen world where people are alienated through sin from both God and each other, God has acted to create for himself a new people who should live with him and with each other in a fellowship of covenant love and loyalty. He acted thus. First, he made a covenant with Abraham and his descendants, thus binding himself to them to bless them and them to him for worship and service. When later he brought Abraham's family out of Egypt he renewed the covenant and gave them, along with the law which showed what behaviour would please and displease him, a cultus which had sacrifice at its heart, whereby sin might be put away and communion between him and them maintained. When subsequently Israel fell into unfaithfulness, a recurring pattern of divine action emerged, judgement on all, followed by deliverance and renewal for a faithful remnant. When Christ came to set up a new and richer form of the covenant relationship by his priestly sacrifice of himself, Israel spurned his ministry, and he was then the true Israel, the faithful remnant, in his own person. In him God's Israel was reconstituted out of believers as such, and in it Jew and Gentile are together as fellow-citizens, branches of one olive tree and brothers in one family. Thus reconciliation to both God and each other takes the place of the alienation that was there before. In glory the church will remain one city, family and flock together.

Christ's death as sin-bearer under God's judgement, followed by God's affirmation of him in resurrection, was the definitive fulfilment of the judgement-and-renewal pattern, and resurrection out of death in one sense or another, in union with Christ's dying and rising, is the appointed and abiding shape of life for God's people, as the symbolism of their baptism shows. It is a pattern which their physical resurrection at Christ's return will finally complete.

God's covenant people, the church, lives a public life of humiliation, dispersion, opposition and distress, but its inner, hidden life is one of union and communion in the risen Christ with him and each other, as the Lord's Supper regularly proclaims. Loving ministry to one another and to needy folk everywhere is the life-style which properly expresses the hidden reality: in which connection Paul pictures the church as Christ's body, with each limb animated and equipped by his Spirit for the service which he through it will render.

In this story, the goal of God's action is to have a people who live with him in love, and whose corporate life, by uniting the seemingly incom - patible in sharing Christ's unsearchable riches, shows forth to the watching angels the 'many-stranded wisdom of God' (Eph. 3:10). The Gospel call, from this standpoint, is to accept a share in the life and hope of God's forgiven family by bowing to the Lord whose death redeemed the church and whose risen life sustains it. This is not (be it said) to put the church in Christ's place, but to preach Christ as the answer, through the church, to everyone's problem of isolation and alienation from God and human - kind. The church does not save, but as the redeemed society it is certainly part of the Gospel. New Testament passages especially relevant for this story include John 17; Romans 6:9–11; 1 Corinthians 11–14; Gal. 3–4, 6; Ephesians; Colossians; Hebrews; 1 Peter.

## B. Stories about Jesus Christ

### (iii) The grace of Christ

In Jesus Christ God has given the world a Saviour whose great salvation more than matches man's great need, and whose great love (which should be gauged from the cross) will not be daunted or drained away by our great unloveliness. Jesus is set forth as prophet, priest and king – teacher and guide; mediator and intercessor; master and protector – and the focal point of his saving work is identified as his cross, concerning which each Christian can say 'he loved me, and gave himself for me' (Gal. 2:20). Christ's death was an act of righteousness, for he endured it in obedience to his Father's will. As such, it wrought redemption, freeing us from the curse of God's law, i.e. exposure to divine judgement, at the cost of Christ's own suffering. His death was redemptive because it achieved an act of propitiation, quenching God's wrath by dealing with the sin that evoked it. It propitiated God by being an act of substitutionary sin-bearing, in which the judgement which our sins deserved was diverted onto Christ's head. From the cross to the risen Christ's gift of a permanent new relationship with God, which Paul analyses as justification (pardon plus a righteous man's status) and adoption (a place in the family with certainty of inheritance), and the writer to the Hebrews calls sanctification (acceptance by God, on the basis of consecration to him). With this new status is given new birth, the indwelling Spirit, progressive transformation into Christ's image, and glorification – in short, comprehensive subjective renewal. God's goal in all this is the perfect bliss of sinners, and the Gospel call is an invitation to faith in Christ, through which all these gifts come to us, from the Saviour's own hand, 'for free.' New Testament passages of special relevance for this story include Romans 3, 5, 8; 2 Corinthians 5:14ff. Hebrews.

### *(iv)  The glory of Christ*

From eternity the Father loves the Son, and delights to give him glory and see him honoured (cf. John 5:20–22). The Son, for his part, loves the Father and delights to do his will. As the Father gave honour to the Son in the work of creation and providence, so he has now resolved to make him pre-eminent in the economy of redemption (cf. Col. 1:13–20; John 1:1–5, 14). So he has rewarded the Son's obedient self-humbling to the point of death by not only restoring to him the glory that was his before the incarnation (cf. John 17:1–15, 24), but also by making him head of the church and lord of the worlds, giving him 'the name which is above every name [i.e., *kyrios*, Lord], that at the name of Jesus every knee should bow . . . and every tongue confess that Jesus Christ is Lord, to the glory of God the Father' (Phil. 2:9ff.). Though Christ's mediatorial kingdom as such will end when the work of grace is done (cf. 1 Cor. 15:24ff.), the doxology, 'worthy is the Lamb,' shall be sung forever (cf. Rev. 5:12ff.). In this story, God's goal is the praise and glory of Jesus Christ his Son, and the Gospel call is a summons to join those who, acknowledging that all their hope is in Christ, are already resolved to spend all eternity honouring his name.

## C.  Stories about man

### *(v)  God's image restored*

Briefly: humans are made to display God's image and likeness by practising righteousness in fulfilment of his creaturely vocation. God's image is more than the rationality which makes such righteousness possible; it is the actual achievement in human life of that which corresponds to God's own moral goodness and creativity. But full God-likeness failed to materialize in Adam personally, and the same is true of all who are in Adam. Thus we fall short of our true human destiny, as God planned it, so now he restores the image in his disciples, by leading us through his word and Spirit into the life that actualizes it – the life, that is, of active, habitual, creative response to the calling of God. This is what Paul refers to when he says that we are being renewed in knowledge (of God) after the image of the One who first led us to 'put on the new man' (Col. 3:10, KJV). In this story, God's goal is to see his own character fully reflected in us, and the Gospel call, quite simply, is to let ourselves be remade so that we at last become human.

### (vi) Humanity's joy begun

Briefly again: humankind without Christ is in a pitiable state, whatever may or may not appear on the surface of life. We are guilty, lost, without hope as death approaches, short on self-mastery, pulled to and fro by conflicting allurements and distractions; there are skeletons of sensuality, callousness, arrogance and other unlovely things in our cupboard; we regularly find frustration and discontent, partly because our reach exceeds our grasp, partly because we feel thwarted by circumstances, partly because we are so largely unclear what is worth our endeavour anyway. The various things wrong with the folk to whom Jesus is seen ministering in the Gospels – hunger, chronic illness, fever, epilepsy, blindness, deafness, dumbness, lameness, leprosy, lunacy, organic deformity and in three cases actual death – vividly picture these spiritual needs (and were undoubtedly included in the Gospels for that purpose). But Jesus Christ gives peace – with God, with oneself, with circumstances and with other people – plus his own presence and friendship, plus a call to witness and service as the priority concerns of life in this world, plus a promise of enabling by the Holy Spirit, plus an assurance of final glory in the Saviour's own company, and this brings integration, purpose, contentment and joy such as one has not known before. And the promise is that as one travels the road of discipleship, so these things will increase. In this story, God's goal is a purpose of compassion, namely to impart to us by this means the joy for which we were made; and the Gospel call is a summons to enter through faith and obedience into the joy that Christ gives.

As each strand of a rope is a little rope in itself, so each of these six stories is itself authentic Gospel, though the fullness of the message only appears when all six are put together. (The six 'stories' cited are not necessarily exhaustive. One could add, for example, 'God's Promise – The Renew - ing,' which would deal with the new heavens and new earth.) But what precisely are we to suppose that these biblical declarations are telling us? There is widespread agreement today that such notions as we have been reviewing – God's purpose; God's people; the cluster of images expressing different aspects of salvation; the Father exalting the Son; God's image in man; peace, contentment and joy as divine gifts – should be seen as theological 'models,' on the analogy of models in physics. This is to say that they are thought-patterns which function in a particular way with their own particular 'logic,' helping us to focus one area of reality (relationships with God) by conceiving of it in terms of another, better known area of reality (relationships with each other). This gives us an idea of *how* they mean, but does not begin to tell us what they mean. And if we press that question, sharp disagreement appears, for modern theolo - gians fan out across a broad spectrum between two extremes. The one extreme is to say that the models are humanly devised for focusing empirical apprehensions of ourselves and our position in God's presence (*coram Deo*), and cannot be trusted to yield any definitive truths about God. The other extreme is to say that they are divinely revealed anthropomorphisms which God uses to tell us facts about himself in terms meant to be normative for our subsequent thinking. Bultmann and exponents of the 'new hermeneutic' like Fuchs and Ebeling stand at the one extreme, evangelical and Catholic conservatives stand at the other, and there are many half-way houses.

The choice as to where to stand in this spectrum will be determined for us by our Christology. If we accept as true anything like the Johannine Christology, we shall treat the things Jesus tells us about God as normative revelation, and we shall treat Jesus' own revelatory words as our paradigm for both the Old Testament (to which, as all scholars today seem to agree, Jesus listened as to his Father's voice), and also the New Testament (to whose authors the Johannine Christ promised authoritative inspiration explicitly, and who often claim to speak to Christ's Spirit and with his authority). We cannot here enter into the modern Christological debate, so I simply put on record that for me, at least, the Johannine Christ is 'for real' (a conviction which can, I think, be compellingly justified), and that hence I view the models of the six-fold Gospel story as revealing factual truths about God, not of course exhaustively (that would be impossible) but truly and trustworthily so far as they go.

I urge, therefore, that these models should never be treated, as some treat them, as contingent conceptualizations in ancient cultural terms of a non-verbal sense of God which we would today do well to unshell and repack in other terms. Rather, the conceptualizations themselves should be seen as divinely given modes of instruction. Hence it should be a matter of conscience to us, if we attempt 'cultural transposition' of them for some didactic purpose (e.g., to secure 'dynamic equivalence' in a free-flowing Bible translation), to explain at some point that the transposition merely *illustrates* what the original means and does not strictly speaking *translate* it at all. (I am thinking here of concepts with logical substance, as distinct from conventional verbal forms like the three-decker universe and diffused-consciousness psychology, which are used for expressing other truths without being asserted as normative themselves.) When it comes to the substance of teaching, we may not cut loose from the biblical categories in which God teaches us to think.

So if asked the content of the Gospel for today in England, Chile, Borneo, Bermuda, Tibet or wherever, I shall offer a formula based on the six-theme analysis above, and urge that there are five points to be taught.

First, the Gospel tells us *of God* our maker, in whom we live and move and are, and whom we have been made to worship and serve, and in whose hands, for good or ill, we always remain, and whose will and purpose should always determine ours. Like Paul at Athens, we must introduce folk to the Creator whom they have forgotten to remember, and go on from there. Not till the Creator's claim is seen can we ever grasp the sinfulness of sin.

Second, the Gospel tells us of *sin*, defining it as failure to meet the holy Creator's claim first by aping him and then by fighting him, and depicting it as rebellion against his authority, lawlessness in relation to him as our lawgiver, missing the mark which he gave us to aim at, and becoming guilty and unclean in his sight in consequence. The Gospel tells us that we are the helpless slaves of our own rebelliousness and cannot put ourselves right. Not till we begin to grasp these things can we ever appreciate the dimensions of the declaration that Jesus Christ saves us from sin.

Third, the Gospel tells of *Christ*, and we must teach both the facts and the meaning of his life, death, resurrection and reign. We must spell out who he is and what he has done, and we must teach folk to interpret the meaning and purpose of human life in terms of him. It is sometimes said that it is the presentation of Christ's person, rather than of doctrines about him, that draws sinners to his feet, and it is certainly true that a theory of atonement, however orthodox, is no substitute for the Saviour: it is the living Christ who saves, not any theory about him. But Jesus of Nazareth cannot be known as the living Christ unless we are clear that he was eternal God and his passion was really his redeeming action of bearing away men's sins; nor shall we know how to approach him till we have learned that he is now God's king on the throne of the universe. Not till we are aware of these things can we see what the response for which Christ calls really means.

Fourth, the Gospel tells of *faith, repentance and discipleship*, and so must we. Faith is credence and conviction regarding the Gospel message, and a consequent casting of oneself on the promises of Christ and the Christ of those promises as one's only hope. Repentance is a change of heart and mind, leading to a new life of denying self and serving the Saviour as king in self's place. Discipleship is a matter of relating oneself to the living, exalted Christ as both learner and follower, and to the rest of Christ's disciples as one who longs both to learn from them and to give to them, and who knows that his master's will is for him to be in their company. These things must be clearly taught, or the nature of the Christian life will surely be misunderstood.

Fifth the Gospel tells of *newness*: new life in the Spirit, who assures and enables; new relationships in the body of Christ, where love expressed in fellowship through mutual ministry is the rule; new goals in the world for all disciples, who find that, though they are no longer of it, Christ leaves them in it to render service to it; and new hope for both one's personal future and that of the world as such, inasmuch as Christ is publicly coming back. When in 1948 at the first World Council of Churches assembly at Amsterdam Karl Barth led off with a paper entitled 'The Return of Jesus Christ the Hope of the World' he struck a most proper note; one wishes that over the past 30 years the W. C. C. had managed to stay with it. When, where, how and with what measure of discontinuity with what has preceded Christ will come back we should not claim to know, but the certainty that he who now reigns invisibly will one day show himself and in doing so create new heavens and a new earth, wherein dwells righteous - ness, and that meantime he stands at the end of the road of each Christian's earthly life to meet him or her and take him home, brings a radiancy of hope to which secular optimism, however starry-eyed, cannot hold a candle. These points, too, must be clearly taught, as must the ethical demands of discipleship in terms of love to God and neighbour, the sanctifying of relationships, and the imitation of God and of Christ.

Some brief points about the communication of the God-given Gospel may now be made to round off. They draw together threads that hung out at various points in our earlier argument.

First, the key to persuasive Christian communication lies less in technique than in character. Paul was a great communicator, not because he was eloquent (by the standards of his day he was not, as he tells us in 2 Cor. 10:10, cf. 1 Cor. 2:1–5, and reading his letters with all their verbal roughness one has to agree), but because he knew his own mind and had a great capacity for identifying with the other person. It is clear that though he has looked to the Holy Spirit to make his communicating fruitful (cf. 1 Cor. 2:1–5), he knows that the Spirit works through appropriate means, and so was very conscious of the human factors in persuasion, namely cogency of statement and empathetic concern, and was always most conscientious in labouring to achieve them. He set no limit to what he would do, however unconventionally, to ensure that he did not by personal insensitiveness or cultural inertia set barriers and stumbling-blocks in the way of men coming to Christ. 'I have made myself a slave to all, that I might win the more. And to the Jews I became as a Jew, that I might win Jews . . . to those who are without law, as without law . . . that I might win those who are without law. To the weak I became weak, that I might win the weak; I have become all things to all men, that I might by all means save some' (1 Cor. 9:19–22). It was to remove possible stumbling-blocks for Jews that Paul had Timothy circumcised (Acts 16:3) and also, it seems, Titus, though as he insisted he was under no obligation to do this (see Gal. 2:3). His loving, imaginative adaptability in the service of truth and people is a shining example to all who engage in evangelistic communication, and cannot be pondered too often or taken too seriously.

Paul was a man who could, and did, share himself without stint. From his letters we know him well, and we can appreciate the trauma that lies behind the autobiographical passage of Philippines 3, where he tells us how Christ stripped him of cultural pretensions. 'Here was a man,' F. W. Dillistone comments,

> who possessed all the marks of privilege within a particular historical tradition. His pedigree, his tribal status, his religious dedication, his formal education, his personal commitment had been such that by every standard of Jewish orthodoxy and by every sanction of national tradition he was justified in regarding himself as successful, superior and secure. He was surely in a position, if ever a man was, to communicate religious truth to the ignorant and under-privileged. Yet he had submitted every part of his historical inheritance to the judgement of the Cross. Nothing could be removed but everything could be re-interpreted. Those things which seemed positive gain could be judged as of no account in the service of Christ: those things which had seemed to be hindrances and handicaps might well prove positive assets in the new order of living. In any case there was henceforth to be no final confidence in the heritage from personal and past history . . . [Then Dillistone continues] The missionary today cannot escape from his own history, national, social or individual. But it is his duty, as far as possible, to become aware of that history and to bring it under the judgement of the central touchstone of history. Only so can he dare to approach those who belong to a different historical tradition and whose personal histories are very different from his own. He will become aware of their own pride of history, their own aspirations for a richer historical destiny. He will judge these not solely in the context of his own historical framework but in the light of that history held under the judgement of the Cross and the promise of the resurrection. It goes without saying that this is no easy task . . .[1]

For all who, with Paul, enter the world of cross-cultural communications these are surely wise and weighty words.

Second, there are procedural guidelines in communicating Christian - ity which cannot be ignored without loss. If we do not stay with the biblical story, and the scriptural text, and most of all with the person of the Saviour; if, while observing the distinction between milk and meat, foundation and superstructure, we do not labour to make known the whole revealed counsel of God; we do not seek, as part of our commu - nicative strategy, to show the Gospel shaping relationships in home and family, in imaginative gestures of neighbour-love, and so on, and to ring

---

[1] *Christianity and Communication*, pp. 106f.

the changes on *both* the 'Christianizing' of existing culture and the forming of an alternative culture as modes of Christian expression; if, finally, we decline to show any respect for cultures, however pagan, other than our own; then there is no reason to expect communication to proceed well in any context whether in our local church down the road or on the other side of the world.

Third, Christian communication cannot be made easy, and there is not necessarily anything wrong with what we are doing if in a particular situation at a particular time the task proves cruelly hard. Our Lord Jesus Christ was a prince and a paragon among communicators (nobody, I think, can ever dispute that) yet even he failed constantly to anchor his message in men's hearts, as his own parable of the Sower declares. His mighty works were clear proof in themselves of his messianic identity (cf. Matt. 11:1–6), yet Chorazin and Bethsaida saw them and did not repent. In a world satiated with communication of one sort and another, as today's world is, and with human hearts no less hard than in Jesus' day, the same negative response can be expected again in very many cases.

> A great deal of research, [writes Dillistone], waits to be done on the whole subject of 'communications-fatigue.' What produces maximum or minimum response? When is the limit to effective response reached? What are the relative values of variations and repetition? These questions need further investigation, but what is certain is that in a world in which information of every kind is being poured through channels of every kind it is becoming increasingly difficult for the distinctively Christian communication to gain a hearing or to win any response . . . Today, as in Jesus' day, there is no *guarantee* that the exhibition of or the witness to the mighty works of God will not be either ignored or misunderstood.[2] There is no expeditious road to pack and label men for God. There is likewise no guaranteed form of effective communication. Always the struggle must continue. The end is never in sight.[3]

On which sobering note we close.

---

[2]  op. cit., p. 147.
[3]  op. cit., p. 149.

# Chapter 20

# The Message is Unchanged

*And I, brethren, when I came to you, came not with excellency of speech or of wisdom, declaring unto you the testimony of God. For I determined not to know anything among you, save Jesus Christ, and him crucified.*

*And I was with you in weakness, and in fear, and in much trembling. And my speech and my preaching was not with enticing words of man's wisdom, but in demonstration of the Spirit and of power: that your faith should not stand in the wisdom of men, but in the power of God (1 Corinthians 2:1–5 KJV).*

Basic missionary, evangelistic and pastoral policy has to do in the first instance not with programs – though programs have their place – nor with institutions – though you cannot get far without institutions – but with the message.

That is what Paul is saying to us in 1 Corinthians 2:1–5. That is the fundamental fact to which he would recall us. The first maxim for those who engage in missionary work, pastoral care or evangelism is: Trust your message. Your message is God's own witness to reality. And God can be trusted to honour it.

Paul's words come directly out of his own experience. That makes them much more powerful. Truth in life is always more impressive than truth in formula. Paul came to Corinth with the aim he had wherever he went: to communicate the gospel with a view to converting his hearers. He unites these two concepts in the single word he often uses to describe his ministry: *persuade*. 'We persuade men' (2 Corinthians 5:11). We persuade men to receive and respond to God's truth.

Communication with a view to conversion ought never to be a matter of dispute among evangelicals. Beyond all question, this is our given task.

---

THE MESSAGE IS UNCHANGED was originally published in *The Alliance Witness*, June 23, 1982, pp. 11–14. Reprinted by permission.

# The Mind Barrier

Corinth was a large Greek city, cultured, sophisticated, decadent, a city devoted more than most to the pursuit of pleasure. Paul tells his readers, 'I came having made a decision that I knew would at first disaffect you, because it meant that I would not be measuring up to your expectations.'

Paul had decided on a policy that excluded eloquence and the parading of wisdom. 'I did not come to you with any of that,' he says. His words give us a hint of the cultural expectations of those first-cen - tury Corinthians. As inheritors of the Greek philosophical culture they appreciated argument, they esteemed eloquence, they delighted in debate. They were much more interested in discussion than they were in truth. They were more concerned about the skilful presentation of a point than they were about whether what was being talked of was real or not.

By his very style at Corinth Paul challenged their frame of mind. 'I did not come with eloquence,' he said. Nor did he speak with what the Corinthians, with their cultural expectations, could recognize as wisdom.

Why not? Here we must fill in Paul's thought, but certainly it went something like this: 'I saw that those expectations of yours were conceited expectations. And if I had conformed to them, I would have been pandering to your conceit and flattering you.' If people look for cleverness of argument and you make your presentation of Christianity to them by means of clever arguments, what you actually are doing is affirming their intellectual excellence. You are saying to them in effect, 'This is the only way that is appropriate for presenting the message to cultured, thoughtful people like you.'

Paul believed that by reason of sin the human mind was blind to divine things. The minister of the gospel has to humble people at this very point, where they assume that they are intellectually competent and wise. To rely on cleverness is not simply to trust the arm of flesh – my own human resourcefulness as a communicator – but it is also to give up any attempt to convince people that their minds have been blinded through sin and that what they must do is humble themselves and accept what God tells them.

And yet that is what the evangelist has to do. His or her technique of presentation must humble the self-assertive intellect of conceited people and make them realize that the gospel comes to them not as something for them to discuss and debate as if they could judge it, but as a word from God that judges them. So Jesus dealt with Nicodemus, and so did Paul deal with the Corinthians.

I suspect that cleverness is becoming a curse in Christian communication today. We are laying too much stress on our apologetics and our supposedly cogent arguments for proving the truth of Christianity. I suspect that in our concentration on fleshly, showy, salesmanlike methods we are catering to today's cultural expectations in a way that really cannot be defended.

To catch people's attention and get them listening is one thing. That of course is good and right and necessary, and Paul himself would adapt his style of presentation in order to do that. But the further element of cultural and intellectual flattery that so easily enters into our communication is what bothers me.

Paul says, 'I came to you . . . declaring unto you the testimony' – some manuscripts say 'mystery' – 'of God.' In either case, Paul is saying that his business as a messenger of God was not to feed God's Word into the arena of debate, but simply to proclaim it with the authority of the Lord himself from whom it comes. Whether his listeners will hear or whether they will turn away, Paul sets himself to announce, to explain and to enforce what God has said. But to be clever? No. Not at any point at all, and for a very good reason.

## Paul's Policy

James Denney, a Scottish theologian of the turn of the century, said, 'You cannot at the same time give the impression that you are a great preacher – or theologian or debater or whatever – and that Jesus Christ is a great Saviour.' If you call attention to yourself and your own competence, you cannot effectively call attention to Jesus and his glorious sufficiency.

By the way in which you present the faith you do in fact determine whether people attend to Christ or to you. So Paul did not preach to the Corinthians with lofty words of wisdom. His policy excluded that and demanded something quite different. In verse 2 he tells us what this was. 'I determined,' Paul says, 'not to know anything among you, save Jesus Christ, and him crucified.' 'You would invite me to talk to you about all the things in which you were interested,' Paul was saying in effect. 'I resolved that I would not do that. Rather, I would insist gently but firmly on talking to you always about the thing I have been sent to declare.'

I do not think Paul meant that he would not talk about anything except the atonement. Luther was right in saying to Erasmus, 'There is more involved in preaching Christ crucified than going up and down saying simply, "Christ was crucified." '

So I think that at Corinth, as everywhere else, Paul would have expounded the whole counsel of God. He would have talked about the whole of God's purpose for man and the whole of God's gift to man, and he would have talked about the moral and spiritual realities of Christian living. But he would have done it in such a way that the cross was always his centre of reference.

He would never have allowed himself, or those to whom he was speaking, to get out of sight of the hill called Calvary. That is the point. And in the message that we take to our modern world we must be equally clear that the creative, redeeming love of God on the cross, whereby sins were borne and new life was won, is the hinge on which everything turns.

As you study your New Testament you will find that in fact everything there is related to the cross and everything is seen in light of the cross. That is how Paul presented the whole counsel of God at Corinth. And why? He had two reasons for adopting this policy. First, his commission required it – 'Christ sent me . . . to preach the gospel' (1 Corinthians 1:17). He was a man under orders.

If the question is the one Paul himself raises – 'Do I seek to please men?' (Galatians 1:10) – there is no question what his own stance was. He was done with man-pleasing. He was concerned to please God always and only and in this instance to do so by faithfully delivering the message with which he had been entrusted.

## God's Adequacy

But there was a further reason why Paul cheerfully and wholeheartedly adopted the policy of knowing nothing among the Corinthians except Christ and him crucified. Paul knew that human need dictates this policy. For it is only through the knowledge of Christ – his Person and his work – that human need at its deepest level is ever met.

Let me try to state this theologically. The wisest thing ever said to me was the word of an old minister years and years ago. It was no more than a throwaway line in a conversation about something else. But it seems to me still the most pregnant sentence I have ever heard.

'Remember,' he said, 'God is sovereign in all things, and all problems find their solution at Calvary.'

'All problems' in that statement was shorthand for all *spiritual* problems. But, mind you, most human problems are spiritual in the final analysis. That is, they have in them a dimension that has to do with one's relationship with God, and you cannot get the human part of the problem right until the relationship with God has been put right as well.

Paul was very clear on this. Let me just mention some examples to illustrate what this means. Guilt is a very fundamental problem, and people who deny God are still hung up with it today. The psychiatrists tell us that. Paul knows that the problem of guilt finds its solution at Calvary, in the knowledge of Christ, who 'made peace through the blood of his cross,' as Paul puts it in writing to the Colossians (1:20). This is the way, the only way, into God's peace.

Or take the pervasive modern problem of *forlornness*, as I like to call it – or loneliness. But it is a little more than loneliness, really. It is the sense that in this great bustling world I am on my own and I am lost. I have no one to turn to, no one to help me, and I do not know where I am going.

To this forlornness there is no answer save to know the love of God personally directed to me.

But how does a person come to know that love? Paul tells us: 'God commends his love toward us, in that, while we were yet sinners, Christ died for us' (Romans 5:8). Take people to the foot of the cross and tell them of Jesus Christ and him crucified and what his death means, and at once a solution to the problem of forlornness begins to appear. Yes, God loves you and he did this for you. He cares for you. He wants you as his child. He adopts you into his family by virtue of what Christ has done for you. He will be with you and love you forever. Now you are no longer lost; you are found.

The cross is also the answer to the heartaching problem of *fear*. Fear takes many forms. There is fear of the consequences of the past. There is fear of the unknown future. There is fear of the relationships in which one is involved, and of the people to whom one has to relate. And some are afraid of what it will cost them to follow God. They realize that God is calling them, and his call requires them to break with the way they have been living. They see that they are going to lose on the deal, at least in human terms. They are not quite sure they can face it.

What people facing the problem of fear need to know is the adequacy of God to support, to help, to strengthen them for his own service, to carry them through pressures, strains, pains, whatever, and to turn their material loss into spiritual gain. The adequacy of God is the issue.

Paul preaches the adequacy of God from the cross. Did you ever notice it? 'He that spared not his own Son, but delivered him up for us all' – see the logic – 'how shall he not with him also freely give us all things?' (Romans 8:32).

What does that mean? All *good* things, Paul means; and *all* good things. All the good things *we* can think of? No, better than that. All the good things *God* can think of!

The fact that he has given us the greatest gift at the cross, His own Son, to die for us guarantees that he will give us 'all things' – everything else that we need, and everything he can devise that makes for our ultimate happiness. This is the final answer to the problem of human fear.

Or maybe the problem is plain, straight, ornery *self-will*, the inclination to do what I feel like doing, whether right or wrong. Again, Paul takes this problem to the cross of Christ and deals with it there. 'Know ye not,' he says, 'that . . . ye are not your own? For ye are bought with a price' (1 Corinthians 6:19–20). So – 'glorify God in your body.'

C. T. Studd, a great missionary of two generations ago, once said, 'If Jesus Christ be God and died for me, no sacrifice is too great for me to make for him.' The logic is plain: sacrifice must answer sacrifice, love answer love. But it is also plain, is it not, that none of us can evade the constant problem of self-will? Solve it where alone it can be solved – at the foot of Christ's cross.

Paul knew that the message of Christ and him crucified has *power* – power to touch the human heart at the level of its deepest need, power to provide a new dynamic for a new kind of living, power to evoke loyalty and commitment, power to make men new.

Paul wanted to see lives transformed by that power. He knew that was what God purposed. So, understanding these things, he formed the policy of preaching only Christ and him crucified, testifying rather than debating, and never getting away from the theme of redemption.

## Results

What were the results of Paul's decision? There were two.

On the one hand, it obliged him to trust God. He knew he was going to look a fool in the eyes of the Corinthians. All right! He was prepared for that. He was going to rely on the Lord to honour his own Word.

'I was with you,' he says, 'in weakness, and in fear, and in much trembling. And my speech and my preaching was not with enticing words of man's wisdom, but in demonstration of the Spirit and of power' (2:3–4). By this Paul means that he looked to the Holy Spirit to demonstrate, confirm and authenticate the divine truth of the message that he had brought. He was not seeking to do it himself; he was leaving space for God to do it.

But Paul did feel a bit of a fool. That is what the words 'weakness' and 'fear' are pointing to. He felt silly and expected ridicule.

'All right,' he is saying, 'I knew that faithfulness required this of me, but I knew I could trust God to honour my faithfulness to him.' So Paul trusted in the Holy Spirit to authenticate the Word.

The second consequence of Paul's policy follows right on from this. The policy produced the Corinthian church, for the Spirit did as Paul had hoped. And so there was now a church at Corinth for Paul to write to. God does honour faithfulness to his truth, which includes presenting it in God's own chosen way, as a witness which can only be received through the enlightening that the Spirit gives.

Do you remember how in Acts 18 we read that at a certain point in the Corinthian mission, when Paul had been, I suppose, somewhat discouraged by the way people had been reacting to what he was saying, a vision came to him? The Lord spoke to him by night, saying, 'Be not afraid, but speak, and hold not thy peace: for I am with thee, and no man shall set on thee to hurt thee: for I have much people in this city' (18:9–10).

God was telling Paul, 'Through your witness, out of your preaching, I am going to call forth a church. You will see it! You carry on with the work and you will see the fruit. Speak and do not hold your peace, for I have many people in this city.' So Paul continued with the mission, and the Corinthian church was born by the mighty power of the Spirit of God through the faithfully spoken word.

People today are suggesting that we should feel free to amend the message, modernize it, move its centre of reference, give to the cross of Christ a different significance from that which Paul saw in it. They want us to shift attention from the cross to other emphases about Jesus, or even to shift attention from Jesus to Christlike things in other faiths.

Our response ought to be a courteous but firm 'No!' This is not the way. This is not the message.

Altering the gospel in the manner described is a disastrous mistake which, if not challenged, is going to ruin souls. It will reduce to the vanishing point zeal for missions – indeed, I fear that is happening in some places already. And where missionaries go out with an altered message, there will be very little real fruit.

Stay with the Paul of 1 Corinthians 2:1–5! Only so can we meet the deepest needs of man, and only so can we hope to see God calling forth men and women and building his church in these days. Major on your message, then, and learn under God to be rich and tireless communicators of the good news of Jesus Christ, the living Lord, and him crucified.

If he is the One about whom you are constantly talking, you need not be too anxious about your communicative techniques. They will almost look after themselves. They really will.

If you and I should parade our own guesses and fancies, folk would soon be bored and turned off, and no skills in communication could stop it happening. But if we testify to Jesus the Saviour, the Jesus of Scripture, sharing him as we have him in our hearts, we shall appeal to the deepest human needs, and people will come to recognize him as the reality that they desire. God the Holy Spirit can be trusted to see to that!

May we be found doing our part, and seeing the Spirit do his, in these dark and confusing days.

# Chapter 21

# What is Evangelism?

## Evangelism and Theology

'Most evangelists,' writes Michael Green, 'are not very interested in theology: most theologians are not very interested in evangelism.' [1] This testimony, alas, is true. Evangelism and theology for the most part go separate ways, and the result is great loss for both.

When theology is not held on course by the demands of evangelistic communication, it grows abstract and speculative, wayward in method, theoretical in interest and irresponsible in stance. When evangelism is not fertilized, fed and controlled by theology, it becomes a stylized perform - ance seeking its effect through manipulative skills rather than the power of vision and the force of truth. Both theology and evangelism are then, in one important sense, *unreal*, false to their own God-given nature; for all true theology has an evangelistic thrust, and all true evangelism is theology in action. That this double unreality exists today needs no proof from me.

Seventy years ago, a generation after evangelism and theology had parted company in Scotland, James Denney pleaded for a reuniting of the two interests. 'If evangelists were our theologians or theologians our evangelists, we should be nearer the ideal,' he wrote; for 'the evangelist is in the last resort the judge of theology. If it does not serve his purpose it is not true.' For himself, he declared, 'I haven't the faintest interest in any theology which doesn't help us to evangelize.' [2] But Denney's words

WHAT IS EVANGELISM? was originally published in *Theological Perspectives on Church Growth*, ed. Harvie M. Conn, Den Dulk Foundation, (Phillipburg: Presbyterian and Reformed, 1976), pp. 91–105. Reprinted by permission.

[1] Michael Green, *Evangelism in the Early Church* (London: Hodder & Stoughton, 1970), p. 7.

[2] The quotations are from *The Death of Christ* (London: Hodder & Stoughton, 1902), p. vii; *The Expositor*, June, 1901, p.0; and James Moffatt's 'Introduction' to *Letters of Principal James Denney to his Family and Friends* (London: Hodder & Stoughton, 1921), pp. xiif.; all cited by John Randolph Taylor, *God Loves Like That! The Theology of James Denney* (London: SCM Press, 1962), pp. 29f.

went unheeded, and the separation of theology and evangelism remains a characteristic fact of the late twentieth-century world.

It has been a fact of unhappy consequence for evangelism in several ways. First, it has led to evangelism being equated with revivalist proce - dures, or, at any rate, revivalism being regarded as evangelism *par excellence*.

The revivalist pattern, with its special meetings and preachers, its aura of romance and excitement, its claims to supreme spiritual importance, and its methods and techniques for 'drawing in the net' was created by such men as the 'new school' Pelagian, Charles G. Finney,[3] and that much-loved exponent of the 'simple gospel,' Dwight L. Moody.[4] That God has worked, and worked wonderfully, through men who have used this pattern is undoubted, but one can still ask whether he has done so because of, or despite, this or that feature of it. Unfortunately, however, there is no agreed answer to such questions, for evangelical theology has done so little to evaluate the revivalist pattern in a theologically disciplined way. Pietistic and revivalist norms of 'gospel preaching' and Christian conversion have tended either to be accepted uncritically or to be criticized undiscerningly.

Revivalism has come under the hammer often enough from sacra - mentalist, liberal, radical and secularist standpoints, but these critiques, being shaped by doubts as to whether a definite conversion experience is valid or valuable, have not helped evangelicals who see this experience as biblical, beneficial and a privilege to assess what they say and do to induce it. Puffs for revivalism and squibs against it have come from evangelical sources, but little more; and meantime the updated revivalism of Dr. Billy Graham's crusades and organization continues as the greatest single force (so it would seem to the casual observer) in evangelism today.

Through revivalist crusades, and smaller ventures modelled on them, men and women are finding salvation, and for this one thanks God. Yet it cannot be denied that the situation as described has its problems. To his own embarrassment, the evangelist finds himself regarded as a nobler and wiser person than any theologian, and his methods viewed as a kind of sacred cow, which none may touch and against which none may speak. Also, those who evangelize by other than revivalist means (e.g., through the structures of Christian nurture in church and home) find themselves constantly under suspicion of neither understanding nor practising evan - gelism at all. Also, such discussions of evangelism as arise under the shadow of revivalism regularly centre upon the methods to employ rather than the message to convey; and this is most unhelpful, because it is in connection with the message that the deepest disagreements about

---

[3] B. B. Warfield comments on Finney's Pelagian doctrine of plenary ability in *Perfectionism* (New York: Oxford University Press, 1931), 11, pp. 173ff.

[4] On Moody, cf. W. G. McLoughlin, *Modern Revivalism: Charles Grandison Finney to Billy Graham* (New York: The Ronald Press Company, 1959).

evangelism emerge. For if you are (say) a universalist, construing the gospel as a call to wake up to the fact that we are all in a saved state; or a Tillichian, understanding 'God' as the name for whatever is our 'ultimate concern;' or an old-style liberal, for whom the good news is that we are God's children by nature and can never be anything else; or one who thinks that to join the visible church is to enter the sphere of actual salvation automatically – then your evangelistic message, to which you invite response, will be significantly different from that of the man for whom the gospel is God's call to sinners to turn to Christ for shelter from the wrath to come (cf. 1 Thess. 1:9f.). To argue about methods while agreement on the message is lacking is inept; but revivalism, with its stress on techniques, has unfortunately encouraged this kind of ineptness.

The confusions indicated above have been augmented in recent years by the radical reconceiving of evangelism to which, as it seems, the World Council of Churches has now given its blessing. [5] Rejecting as paternalistic all idea of 'propaganda' and 'proselytizing' – that is, of making disciples and planting new churches – this novel concept identifies the church's evangelistic task as one of exhibiting the *shalom* (peace, harmony, human community, integrity and justice) which Jesus brought into the world, and of labouring to extend it where it is lacking. Evangelism thus ceases to be primarily a matter of speaking and becomes instead primarily a matter of practising a serving presence among men.

The true task of mission (it is said) is one of 'entering into partnership with God in history to renew society,' [6] and for this task the world must be allowed to write the agenda. In this context of a humanizing commit - ment, dialogue with men of other faiths and of no faith will certainly occur, but its aim will be to achieve mutual understanding and respect within the bonds of our common manhood rather than to persuade anyone to become a Christian. Thus evangelism is radically secularized. As C. Peter Wagner correctly puts it:

> Whatever good works the church does, become evangelism, according to this definition. Harvey Cox says, for example, 'Any distinction between social action and evangelism is a mistaken one.' Colin Williams agrees that 'the distinction between individual evangelism and evangelism calling for (social) changes is a false one'. This is 'presence evangelism.' A silent Christian presence, characterized by good works and charity, is called 'evangelism'. [7]

---

[5] For evidence of this, see *Eye of the Storm: The Great Debate in Mission* , ed. Donald McGavran (Waco: Word Books, 1972), and *The Evangelical Response to Bangkok* , ed. Ralph D. Winter (South Pasadena: William Carey Library, 1973).

[6] J. G. Davies, *Dialogue with the World* (London: SCM Press, 1967), p. 15.

[7] C. Peter Wagner, *Frontiers in Missionary Strategy* (Chicago: Moody Press, 1971), p. 126.

This is as far as possible from the revivalist idea of evangelism as the attempt to induce one-by-one personal conversion. One understands the desire of ecumenical missionary strategists to avoid giving any impression among the younger nations of ideological imperialism, and one applauds all who for Christ's sake seek to humanize a brutal and oppressive world; but one still has to ask, is there any correspondence between this essentially non-communicative program and *evangelism*, as the Bible presents it? If revivalist evangelism needs a little correction from Scripture, surely radical evangelism needs far, far more.

## The Concept of Evangelism

If, now, we turn to the Bible and allow it to instruct us, we find that it yields a concept of evangelism that is trinitarian and theocentric. Evan-gelism is usually defined as man's work, and this man-centredness leads to many mistakes about it; but the basic biblical perspective is that evangelism is *a work of God*. God the creator, in the glory and power of his tri-unity, is both God the redeemer and God the evangelist.

God's world lies under judgement because of mankind's apostasy and sin; 'the wrath of God is revealed from heaven against all ungodliness and unrighteousness of men, who suppress the truth in unrighteousness' (Rom. 1:18). But God loves the world to which, because of sin, he is hostile; 'God so loved the world, that he gave his only begotten Son, that whoever believes in him should not perish, but have eternal life' (John 3:16). He is the God who in love *sends*: The Father 'loved us and sent his Son to be the propitiation for our sins' (1 John 4:10); the Son brought us knowledge of the Father (John 14:9); now the Father and the Son have sent the Spirit to testify and give knowledge of the Son (John 14:26; 15:26; 16:14), and of his Father as our Father through him (cf. John 20:17).

It is through the Spirit's agency that blind eyes and hard hearts are opened, so that Christ is acknowledged in his divine glory as our Saviour and Lord. 'God, who said, "Light shall shine out of darkness," is the One who has shone in our hearts, to give the light of the knowledge of the glory of God in the face of Christ' (2 Cor. 4:6). 'No one can say, "Jesus is Lord," except by the Holy Spirit' (1 Cor. 12:3) – but when the Spirit enlightens, this is precisely what men do say.

Thus God in sovereign love overcomes the spiritual paralysis and perversity of the fallen human heart, and through this inward teaching by the Spirit draws us to himself (John 6:44f., cf. 1 John 2:27). 'If one may employ an anthropopathism and ascribe human feelings to God,' wrote R. B. Kuiper – and surely he was right to think that one may – 'God has a passion for souls,'[8] and this is how God expresses and satisfies it. He

---

[8] R. B. Kuiper, *God-centered Evangelism: a Presentation of the Scriptural Theology of Evangelism* (Grand Rapids: Baker Book House, 1963), p. 95.

made us; he loved us; he ransoms us; he reclaims us. 'Salvation is from the Lord' (Jonah 2:9).

But this is not the whole story. In the Bible evangelism is not only a work of God, it is also a work of man or rather *a work of God through man*. As God sent his Son to become man and so to 'explain' him (cf. John 1:18), so now, adhering to the incarnational principle, if we may so speak, he sends Christian men to be heralds, ambassadors and teachers in his name and on his behalf. (These are the three main words that Paul uses to express his office as God's spokesman κῆρυξ, πρέσβυς, διδάσκλος.)

The task which God gives to his messengers is primarily and essentially one of proclamation, which the New Testament expresses chiefly by the use of three verbs with their cognate nouns: εὐαγγελίζομαι (tell the good news, εὐαγγέλιόν); κηρύσσω (utter an announcement, κήρυγμα, and μαρτυρέω (bear witness, μαρτυρία. The proclamation is not, however, to be made on a casual, take-it-or-leave-it basis; the end in view is to 'persuade' (πείθω, 2 Cor. 5:11 etc.), to 'disciple' (μαθητεύω, Acts 14:21), and so to 'turn' or 'convert' ἐπίστρεφω a verb which in this sense is used with the evangelist or the sinner, not God, as its subject, as when Paul tells Agrippa that Christ sent him to the Gentiles 'to open their eyes so that they may turn (or, to turn them) from darkness to light' (Acts 26:18, cf. Luke 1:16; James 5:19f.). Evangelism, as I wrote elsewhere, is 'communication with a view to conversion.'[9]

Those who evangelize, then, are 'working together' with God (2 Cor. 6:1), and if they follow Paul's example they will never allow themselves to forget that all the power that comes through their witness, and all the fruit that results from it, are from God and not from themselves. 'I preached Christ crucified to you,' wrote Paul to the Corinthians, in such a way that 'your faith should not rest on the wisdom of men, but on the power of God . . . I planted, Apollos watered, but God was causing the growth' (1 Cor. 2:5; 3:6, cf. Acts 19:9f., where the 'many people' in verse 10 are those Corinthians whom the Lord purposed to call to himself through Paul's preaching).

Our gospel came to you, wrote Paul to the Thessalonians, 'in power and in the Holy Spirit and with full conviction' (1 Thess. 1:5); that explains why they received it 'for what it really is, the word of God, which also performs its work in you who believe' (2:13). Paul sees their conviction as the fruit of their election, and so thanks God for their faith, which was God's gift to them (1:2–5; 2:13). Luke shows the same perspective when he says of Lydia, 'the Lord opened her heart to respond to the things spoken by Paul' (Acts 16:14).

---

[9] J. I. Packer, *Evangelism and the Sovereignty of God*, (London: Inter-Varsity Fellowship), 1961, p. 85.

Recognition that all the power and fruit of the word is from God and not from any human source does not, however, mean that the evangelist may disregard the human factors in persuasion. The ordinary principles of effective persuasion are not changed just because in a special way God is working through them. Paul was very conscious of the human factors in persuasion (cogency of statement, and empathetic concern), and he was most conscientious in observing them. He set no limit to what he would do to ensure that he did not, through personal insensitiveness or cultural inertia, set barriers and stumbling-blocks in the way of men's coming to Christ.

> I have made myself a slave to all, that I might win the more. And to the Jews I became as a Jew, that I might win Jews . . . to those who are without law, as without law . . . that I might win those who are without law. To the weak I became weak, that I might win the weak; I have become all things to all men, that I may by all means save some (1 Cor. 9:19–22).

It was to remove possible stumbling-blocks for Jews that Paul had Timothy circumcised (Acts 16:3) and also, it seems, Titus, though as he stressed he was under no compulsion to do this (Gal. 2:3). Paul's loving, imaginative adaptability in the service of truth and people is a shining example to all who engage in evangelism, and it cannot be pondered too often or taken too seriously.

But what in the last analysis determined Paul's view of his role as a 'Christian persuader'[10] was his awareness that his ministry, like all Chris-tian ministry, was both the form and the means of Christ's. It was Jesus Christ himself, the risen Saviour and enthroned Lord, who in and through Paul's evangelism 'preached peace' (Eph. 2:17), and made his voice heard (Eph. 4:21; cf. John 10:16,27), and drew men to him (cf. John 12:32). The faith that sustained Paul in evangelism was that Christ would continue to do this, as in fact he had been doing everywhere that the gospel went (cf. Col. 1:6); and when Paul thought of his achievements in evangelism, his way of describing them was as *'what Christ has accomplished through me*, resulting in the obedience of the Gentiles by word and deed in the power of the Spirit' (Rom. 15:18f.). To say that Paul, and all others who evangelize, work for the Lord is not untrue, but to speak of them as working together with him is truer, and to speak of him as working through them is the most profound and precise truth of all.

There is one further way in which the concept of evangelism which we are building up needs extension, namely by reference to the message proclaimed. In the Bible, evangelism appears as *a work of God through men proclaiming Jesus Christ, and the new community in him*. Christian

---

[10] Title of a perceptive book by Leighton Ford on the work of a professional evangelist (New York: Harper & Row, 1966).

communication is not evangelism unless the full truth about Jesus is set forth. It is not enough to speak of the attractiveness of his person while omitting reference to the atoning significance of his work, as old-style liberals did. Nor is it enough to speak of his death as a sacrifice for sin if one declines to confess his deity, as Jehovah's Witnesses do. Nor will it suffice to dwell on his earthly life and impact while remaining agnostic about his physical resurrection, present reign, and approaching personal return, as is the common radical way.

It is not adequate to point to Jesus' personal relationship with his disciples two millennia ago if we do not also declare that the glorified Jesus, though temporarily withdrawn from our sight, offers us just such a personal relationship today. For it is essentially this relationship that the Christian gospel is about. Jesus lives, and personal discipleship goes on. This, which from one standpoint is the central meaning of Jesus' resur - rection and the outpouring of the Spirit, is from that same standpoint the evangelist's central message. And the new community belongs to this central message, for the call to become a disciple is also a call to become a partner with all other disciples.

The question whether the church is part of the gospel used to be debated with some heat. If 'church' is taken to mean a particular denomination or organization, viewed as an institute of salvation through its established channels of grace, the answer is certainly no. But if 'church' means the brotherhood of God's children by adoption, into which all believers come and in the fellowship of which they find their God-intended fullness of life, then the answer must be yes. When John Wesley said that there is nothing so un-Christian as a solitary Christian, he spoke a profound truth. The gospel invites to fellowship, not merely with the Father and the Son, but with the saints too. What God calls us to is not 'flight of the alone to the Alone,' but life as a son in his worldwide family, where the rule is that our Father provides for each of us through the ministry of our brothers.

By the light of our concept of evangelism as a work of God we can now assess definitions of evangelism as a human activity. There is no reason why we should not define evangelism in this way, so long as subordination to God's purpose and dependence on God's power are duly stressed. Perhaps the best-known definition of this kind is that of the Archbishops' Committee on evangelism in the Church of England, which in 1918 stated that to evangelize is 'so to present Christ Jesus in the power of the Holy Spirit, that men shall come to put their trust in God through him, to accept him as their Saviour, and serve him as their King in the fellowship of his Church.'

In my book, *Evangelism and the Sovereignty of God*, I applauded this definition in all respects save its consecutive-clause wording, 'that men *shall* come,' which implies that the criterion of whether a particular activity is evangelism or not is whether or not it succeeds in converting anyone. The wording needed, I urged, was 'that men *may* come,' so that evangelism as an activity is unambiguously defined in terms of purpose rather than of consequence.[11] The resultant definition would then correspond exactly with the crisper formula of Michael Green: 'Evangelism . . . is proclaiming the good news of salvation to men and women with a view to their conversion to Christ and incorporation in his church.'[12] However, C. Peter Wagner takes me to task for making this proposal, in a rather muddled section of his otherwise stimulating book, *Frontiers in Missionary Strategy*.[13]

The thesis Wagner wants to establish is that it is insufficient to conceive of evangelism as 'presence' if this does not lead on to proclamation, and that proclamation in turn is insufficient if it does not issue in attempts at persuasion. This is certainly right. The need for positive attempts to persuade was one of the points which my own book most laboured (see pp. 48–53, 75–82, 85, 92f., 99f., 103–106, 119–121). It is, therefore, disconcerting to find Wagner (who, incidentally, quotes Green's definition with warm approval) calling me 'one who has considered the options and come out on the side of proclamation evangelism' – i.e., a view of evangelism which sees proclamation, not as a *means*, but as an *alternative* to persuasion.[14] I can assure Wagner (and my book is evidence) that that is an option I *never* considered!

Wagner seems to be pleading for two things. One is, uninhibited though non-manipulative attempts to persuade unbelievers to turn to Christ. He wants to see a vigorous pressing of 'the well-meant gospel offer,' the 'free offer' of Christ, the invitation to 'whosoever will' to take the water of life, the call to that exercise of faith which is at once the sinner's need and his duty. With this, in principle, I hope everyone will agree; certainly, as an admirer of Richard Baxter, Joseph Alleine, George Whitefield, Jonathan Edwards and C. H. Spurgeon, I do.

---

[11]  Packer, op. cit., pp. 37ff.

[12]  Green. op. cit., p. 7. My definition tallies also with that of the World Congress on Evangelism in Berlin, which is an expansion of that given by the Archbishops' Committee: 'Evangelism is the proclamation of the Gospel of the crucified and risen Christ, the only Redeemer of men according to the Scriptures with the purpose of persuading condemned and lost sinners to put their trust in God by receiving and accepting Christ as Saviour through the power of the Holy Spirit and to serve Christ as Lord in every calling in life and in the fellowship of his church, looking towards the day of his coming in glory' (quoted from Wagner, op. cit., p. 133).

[13]  Ibid., pp. 124–134.

[14]  'Proclamation evangelism,' Wagner explains 'measures success against the yardstick of how many people hear and understand the gospel message. This is often reported in terms of how many people are reached by attending a certain evangelistic campaign listening to a certain radio broadcast or reading a certain piece of evangelistic literature' (ibid. p. 132ff.).

The second thing Wagner advocates is the use of a pragmatic, short-term calculus of 'success' in church-planting and church-growth as a guide to where it is, and is not, right to deploy further missionary and evangelistic resources. This is much more disputable, but we cannot pursue discussion of it here.

Let me round off this section by quoting one further definition – Dr. George W. Peters' analysis of 'evangelization' as 'the authoritative pres - entation of the gospel of Jesus Christ as revealed in the Bible in relevant and intelligible terms, in a persuasive manner with the definite purpose of making Christian converts. It is a presentation-penetration-permeation confrontation that not only elicits but demands a decision. It is preaching the gospel of Jesus Christ for a verdict.'[15] Though there is no explicit reference here to the power and purpose of God or the church of Christ, the central emphasis on persuasion and conversion is in itself entirely right.

## Educational Evangelism

One recurring problem when revivalist patterns of evangelism are fol - lowed, whether in single churches or in the 'mass evangelism' of city-wide campaigns, is that they allow so little room for instruction. From this it follows that where people are ignorant of biblical basics, these methods become inappropriate. Wisely did R. B. Kuiper say:

> Historically the appeal of mass evangelism has been largely to the will and the emotions. That holds of the evangelistic preaching of both Wesley and Whitefield, to a limited extent to that of Jonathan Edwards, and most certainly to that of Dwight L. Moody, Charles G. Finney, Billy Sunday, and the Gypsy Smiths of more recent times. There was some justification for the nature of that appeal. All the aforenamed evangelists had good reason to assume on the part of their audiences a measure of knowledge of the basic teachings of Christianity. Today that assumption is no longer valid . . . The general populace is well-nigh abysmally ignorant of Bible history and Bible doctrine, as well as Bible ethics. In consequence, evangelistic preaching must today be first of all instructive.[16]

Paul spoke of the 'the gospel, for which I was appointed a preacher *and a teacher*' (2 Tim. 1:10f.), and said of Christ, 'we proclaim him . . . *teaching every man* with all wisdom' (Col. 1:28). In both texts the reference to teaching is explanatory of the reference to preaching; Paul saw himself as a teaching preacher, an educational evangelist, and it is vitally important

---

[15] George W. Peters, A *Biblical Theology of Missions* (Chicago: Moody Press, 1972), p. 11.

[16] Kuiper, op.cit. p. 163.

at the present time that we should confine ourselves to patterns of evangelistic practice which allow for thorough instruction, after Paul's example. For there is in fact a good deal to be conveyed.

If we ask, What is the evangelistic message?, the New Testament seems to show that there are essentially five points on which instruction must be given.

First, the gospel is a message about *God*; telling us that he is our maker, in whom we exist and move each moment and in whose hands, for good or ill, we always are, and that we, his creatures, were made to worship and serve him and to live for his glory. These are the foundation-truths of theism, and upon them the gospel is built. The Jews of New Testament days, with Old Testament faith behind them, knew these things, and when the apostles preached to Jews they could take them for granted. But when Paul preached to Gentiles, whose background was polytheistic, it was with theism that he had to start.

So, when the Athenians asked him to explain his talk about Jesus and the resurrection, he began by telling them about God the creator. 'God . . . made the world . . . he himself gives to all life and breath and all things . . . and he made . . . every nation . . . that they should seek God' (Acts 17:24–27). This was not, as is sometimes supposed, a piece of philosophi-cal apologetic which Paul afterwards regretted, but the first and basic lesson in theistic faith. Modern people are for the most part as ignorant about creation and creaturehood as were the ancient Athenians; like Paul, therefore, we must start in evangelizing them by telling them of the Creator whom they have forgotten to remember, and go on from there.

Second, the gospel is a message about *sin*. It defines sin as failure to meet the Holy Creator's total claim, and it diagnoses sin in us, telling us that we are helpless slaves of our own rebelliousness, showing ourselves under the righteous judgement of God, and assuring us that nothing we do for ourselves can put us right. Not until we have begun to grasp these things can we see what it means to say that Jesus Christ saves from sin. All sorts of awarenesses of need are symptoms of sin; much of the task of evangelistic instruction is to take occasion from these symptoms to diagnose the real disease, and thus bring to light 'the problem behind the problem,' our fundamental wrongness with God.

Third, the gospel is a message about *the person and work of Christ*; an interpreted story of the earthly life, death, resurrection and reign of God's Son. Both the facts and the meaning must be given. Whether or not we use the technical terms, 'incarnation,' 'atonement' and so forth, we must teach what they express – who Jesus was, in relation both to the Father and to us, and what he did as his Father's will for us. It is sometimes said that it is the presentation of Christ's person, rather than of doctrines about him, that draws sinners to his feet, and it is certainly true that it is the living Christ who saves, and that a theory of atonement, however orthodox, is no substitute for a saviour. But Jesus of Nazareth cannot be known as the living Christ if we are unaware that he was eternal God and that his passion, his judicial murder, was really his redeeming action of bearing away men's sins. We cannot see Jesus as a personal saviour till we see this, nor can we know how to approach him till we have learned that the man of Galilee now reigns as God's king, and must be hailed as such.

Fourth, the gospel is a message about *new birth*, telling us that our plight in sin is so great that nothing less than a supernatural renewing of us can save us. There has to be a wholly new beginning, through the power of the Holy Spirit.

Fifth, the gospel summons us *to faith, repentance and discipleship*. Faith is not a mere feeling of confidence, nor repentance a mere feeling of remorse; both are dynamic states of the whole person. Faith is credence and conviction regarding the gospel message, and it is more; born of self-despair, it is essentially a casting and resting of oneself on the promises of Christ and the Christ of those promises. Repentance is a changed attitude of heart and mind, leading to a new life of denying self and serving the Saviour as king in self's place. And discipleship is a matter of relating oneself to the living, exalted Christ as a learner and a follower, and to the rest of Christ's disciples as one who longs both to learn from them and to give to them, and who knows that his master's will is for him to be in their company.

This, in outline, is the evangelistic message, and it needs to be thoroughly taught everywhere where it is not already thoroughly known. It is the Holy Spirit's work to make sinners repent and believe, but it is our task and responsibility to make sure that they are clear what the gospel is, how it affects them, and why and how they should respond to it; and until we are sure that a person has grasped these things, we are hardly in a position to press him to commit himself to Christ, for it is not yet clear that he is in a position really and responsibly to do so.

Whatever means and structures we use in evangelism, all the points listed must be taught. If we tried to short circuit the process of instruction and to precipitate 'decisions' without it, we should merely produce psychological upsets; people would come to our vestries and counselling sessions in an agitated state; they would go through motions of commitment at our bidding, but when the shock wore off it would appear that their decision meant nothing save that now they are to a greater or less extent 'gospel-hardened.' And if a few proved to be truly converted, that would be despite our methods rather than because of them.

It is no part of my present task to attempt judgements on any particular ways of evangelism that are practised today, but it is surely plain from what has been said that there can be no safer or more natural milieu for evangelism than the steady teaching, witnessing and nurturing of the local church.

## Response to the Gospel

This essay is seeking to spell out a normative theological concept of evangelism, by which any attempted reformation of evangelism in our day will need to be controlled. One further matter requires discussion for the clarifying of this concept, namely the nature of the response which evangelism requires. So far, we have spoken of it as conversion, involving faith, repentance and discipleship; but this formula is not clear enough in its meaning, and we must take the analysis further.

The common pietistic and revivalist understanding, present at presup - positional level even when it is not made theologically explicit, is that the gospel of God is meant to induce a characteristic *conversion-experience*. This is conceived as a compound of two elements: the experience of receiving, and committing oneself to, the God and the Christ of the gospel, and the experience of receiving assurance from that God, so that one knows oneself pardoned and accepted by him. The relative emphasis on these two elements has varied: in the eighteenth century, for example, the stress was on assurance ('finding peace'), in the twentieth it has been on commitment ('decision for Christ'); but it is constantly assumed that where there is one there will also be the other. In the pietistic revivalist tradition, evangelistic procedures (meetings, sermons, tracts, conversa - tional techniques) have all been shaped by the desire that God should use them to induce conversion-experiences, and the belief that this is precisely what he wills to do. But here some comments must be made.

First, it must be said that while a conversion-experience, like any other particular conscious encounter with a gracious God, is a precious gift, and while no adult can turn to God and live to God without some experiences of this encounter (the Holy Spirit will see to that), the Bible teaches no doctrine of God-given experiences as such. It defines God's purpose and work in men's lives in terms, not of experiences, but of relationships, and though relationships issue in experiences, the two things are not the same.

God's work in our lives, whereby he creates and deepens our love relationship with himself, is more than experience (for it is an actual transformation of our being, in ways which do not yet fully appear), and it is beyond experience (for the experiences which are its product are far less than its measure; much of what God does in us is not directly experienced). To say, then, what is true – that God wills through our evangelism to work in unbelievers and call them effectually to himself – is something bigger than, and somewhat different from, saying that God will through our evangelism induce conversion-experiences.

Second, it must be said that this particular concept of a conversion experience, while its ingredients are biblical in themselves, is a construct from these ingredients in the light of much Protestant Christian experience since the Reformation, rather than being a biblical norm.

Third, it must be said that what the Bible looks for in Christians is not the consciousness of a conversion-experience, but the evidence of a converted state; and its angle of interest when dealing with actual conversions is motivational rather than psychological – that is, its purpose is not to tell us what men who turned to God felt like, so that we can imaginatively put ourselves in their shoes, but to show us how God actually met them and moved them to go his way. The signs of convertedness are simply the marks of discipleship, the marks, that is, of being one of the Lord's *learners* – namely, a structured knowledge of God in Christ, which the learner seeks constantly to deepen and augment; a practical recognition of total and controlling commitment to God and his will, and to Christ and his people; and an awareness that knowing and enjoying God is man's true life (just as it is his chief end), which leads him to press on resolutely to know his Lord better, at any cost and by any road, and to look ahead with eagerness to the glory that is promised when Jesus comes again.

Fourth, it must be said that the more we concentrate on inducing, isolating and identifying conversion-experiences, the more risk we run of misunderstanding and misrepresenting the course of actual experience. For it is not always possible to isolate the moment of conversion. God leads some into a firm faith-relationship with himself by a series of imperceptible steps, so that the precise moment of passage from death to life cannot be picked out for inspection. (This is the case in many Bible biographies.) Conversely, it is only too possible to induce in the suscep - tible experiences of supposed conversion which do not develop into discipleship or a meaningful church commitment, but issue in nothing – as happened in the Cornish revivals of the last century, in which folk 'got converted' time and again without any real change of heart; and as seems to have happened during the first decade of Evangelism in Depth in Latin America.[17]

What this means is that in all evangelism our aim must be nothing less than to make men Christ's disciples in the community of disciples; that we must constantly check our evangelistic structures to ensure that this aim comes through clearly; and that we leave people in no doubt that the response we hope to see in them is convertedness rather than a particular conversion-experience. Also, the question arises whether, instead of isolating individuals in order to pursue with them the issues of personal commitment, which is a basic revivalist technique, we should not give priority to evangelizing them in their natural human groupings – in the West, for instance, the nuclear family; in other countries, the extended family (the clan), or the tribe – seeking a discipleship commitment from the group, and from individuals as members of it. This would be a step back towards the evangelistic style of the apostolic age, which, as Harry

---

[17] Cf. Wagner, op.cit., pp. 139–160.

R. Boer notes, was marked by 'the conversion of *families* or *households*. The Church was not built up of so many individual Christians but of *basic social units*, of *organic wholes*, and these units, these wholes, were the fundamental cells of society, namely *families*.'[18] Is this part of what the reformation of evangelism in our day might mean?

The view of evangelism put forward in this essay is conceived in terms of God and his message primarily, and of man and his methods only secondarily. It affirms that what man says and does in evangelism must be determined by what God is doing, and that the divine message itself must determine the aims and methods of the human messengers. To discuss in detail how this approach might bear on contemporary evangelistic practice is beyond my scope – and, I think, my competence. I limit myself to offering an overall concept of evangelism, crystallized from Scripture as best I can; and I hope it may make some small contribution towards the reform and renewal of evangelism which, on any showing, is a major need at this time.

---

[18] Harry R. Boer, *Pentecost and Missions* (London: Lutterworth Press, 1961), p. 165.

# Chapter 22

# Evangelical Foundations for Spirituality

## I

For Christians in the historic main stream, *theology* means thinking and talking about God and his creatures in the light of God's own self-disclosure in history and Scripture; *ethics* means determining what types of action and qualities of character please God; and *spirituality* (which has also been called spiritual, moral, ascetic, devotional, and casuistical theology in its time) means

> enquiry into the whole Christian enterprise of pursuing, achieving, and cultivating communion with God, which includes both public worship and private devotion, and the results of these in actual Christian life[1]

– or, more briefly, mapping what Henry Scougal labelled 'the life of God in the soul of man.'[2] One could fairly characterize spirituality as the study of godliness in its root and its fruit.

These definitions show that, on the one hand, ethics and spirituality should be viewed as departments of theology and be controlled by the truths of theology and, on the other hand, theology should always have an eye to the ethical and devotional implications of its theses, since God's truth is given to be practised.

But it does not always work out this way. Because theology is commonly anchored in universities and similar academic settings, where the advancement of learning rather than the direction of life is the goal, some theologians never see ethics and spirituality as their business, and

EVANGELICAL FOUNDATIONS FOR SPIRITUALITY was originally published in *Gott Lieben Und Seine Gebote Halten*, ed. M. Bockmuehl, and K. Burkhardt (Geissen: Brunnen Verlag, 1991), pp. 149–162. Reprinted by permission.

[1] Henry Rack, *Twentieth Century Spirituality* (London: Epworth Press, 1969), p. 2.
[2] Scougal's work under this title was published in 1677, and was much appreciated by the Wesleys and Whitefield.

limit their interest to abstract and formal truth in a way that ultimately trivializes theology itself; while some exponents of spiritual life, not seeing themselves as theologians or theology as basic to their task, let their wisdom appear as comments from experience for those who care rather than as elucidation of the summons to commune with God that the gospel issues to every believer.

Since the age of the great Puritan and Pietist theologians ended, this disjunction between theology, ethics, and spirituality at the conceptual level, and the consequent distribution of their study between three different groups of specialists, have brought great weakness into the churches. This distribution is now, however, firmly institutionalized in the course structures and syllabi and in the make-up of teaching faculties in most centres of Christian learning, and hence cannot easily be changed. In practice, it is only when individual instructors labour of set purpose to bring the three fields of concern together in their own teaching that the disjunction is ever nowadays overcome.

Perhaps the most memorable feature of Klaus Bockmuehl's career as a professional theologian was that he set himself to do precisely that. He saw ethics and spiritual life as branches of theology, just as Augustine and Luther and Calvin and Wesley and Edwards had done before him. He kept the three together in the classroom, and in two small books, the latter finished only weeks before his death, he highlighted some of the deepest roots of discipleship.[3] He saw his teaching role as requiring him to be transparently a believer, letting his own evangelical spirituality appear, and the renewing of a literate, honest, childlike evangelical spirituality in others was a matter of constant concern to him. In this respect he was a shining example of a theologian, so to speak, in the round.

As a former colleague, I would now pay tribute to his memory and his purpose by offering a sketch of what seem to be key perspectives for the realizing of authentic evangelical spirituality in our time.

## II

By addressing two preliminary questions I can clarify my standpoint and thrust.

### First: is evangelical spirituality distinctive? If so, how?

For me, as for Klaus Bockmuehl, 'evangelical' means, not Lutheran, Reformational, Pietistic or Baptistic as distinct from Catholic, Orthodox,

---

[3] Klaus Bockmuehl, *Living by the Gospel* (Colorado Springs: Helmers & Howard, 1986); *Listening to the God Who Speaks* (Colorado Springs: Helmers & Howard, 1990).

or post-Enlightenment, but relating and witnessing biblically to Jesus Christ. An evangelical is one who honours and proclaims the Christ of the Scriptures, who is Jesus of Nazareth, God incarnate, humankind's crucified and risen Saviour and reigning Lord, Son of the Father and way to the Father, focus of Christian faith, hope, love, worship and service. Christ, for the evangelical, is not just the potent memory, kept alive in the church, of a good man long gone, as he is for so many post-Enlightenment thinkers; rather, he is the one slain Lamb of God now alive from the dead, the Master and Friend of each believer for time and eternity, the divine Redeemer who with the Father and the Holy Spirit is to be adored for ever and ever. It is common nowadays to define an evangelical in terms of a methodological commitment to the divine truth and trustworthiness of the canonical Scriptures, and there are good historical reasons for starting the definition there; [4] but the heart of the matter is devotional and doxological commitment to the Christ of those Scriptures, in the terms adumbrated above.

What follows, then? This: that from the perspective of individual identity, all who understand Christianity as faith in, love for, and worship of Jesus Christ as their sin-bearing Saviour are evangelicals; all who affirm his sufficiency to save sinners are proclaiming evangelical theology; and every projection of trustful, grateful Christ-centredness as the true and only path of life for sinners is evangelical spirituality, even when justifi - cation by faith, salvation by grace, and Christ's threefold office as prophet, priest, and king are not articulated in an adequately biblical way. Theo - logical deficiency here certainly needs correction, but the pattern of piety itself is already evangelical in type before the conceptual corrections take place. If 'catholic' is taken in a theological rather than denominational sense as signifying commitment to the universal over the local, occasional, eccentric and sectarian, then evangelical spirituality appears as authenti - cally catholic, inasmuch as it represents the devotion of what has always been the central Christian flow.

Conscious acknowledgment of Jesus Christ as one's Saviour, of his Father as one's own Father through the grace of adoption, and of the Holy Spirit as Sustainer of this twofold fellowship, is of the essence of evangelical spirituality, and this Trinitarian framework sets it apart from anything else that is called spirituality anywhere in the church or in the world.

### Second: is the study of evangelical spirituality important? If so, why?

Competence in the field of spirituality is always important as a basis for pastoral care and direction, whereby penitents are pointed along the path of growth in Christ. Pastors, as the Puritans in particular never tired of

---

[4] See my *'Fundamentalism' and the Word of God* (London: Inter-Varsity Press, 1958).

insisting, are called to be physicians of the soul, promoting and guarding the spiritual health of God's people, and their work requires them to understand what it means for individuals to love and enjoy God through Jesus Christ. As physicians need knowledge of physiology in order to detect and treat pathological states, so pastors need insight into spirituality in order to teach and advise for the furthering of spiritual health and the overcoming of sin and folly in their many forms. Excellence in spiritual direction has been rare on both sides of the Reformational divide, and this seems to reflect the fact that studies of the dynamics of spiritual life have too often been crudely, simplistically, and carelessly done – a state of things that had to change, and has perhaps started to change already. Clearly, however, more competence in spirituality is being currently called for than is currently available.

Furthermore, a competent understanding of the spiritual life is needed today in order to vindicate in face of secular scepticism and post-Christian humanism the historic Christian contention that a life of faith, hope, love and worship, of fighting sin, struggling to pray, and denying oneself across the board, is our only true fulfilment in this world. That thesis has doubtless never sounded more paradoxical anywhere than it does in the permissive, materialistic modern West; yet it never was more true, and skill in spirituality is required in order to state it well, as it deserves to be stated, in our present world.[5]

# III

All I can attempt in this brief essay is to specify three basic theological perspectives and three basic biblical themes that in my view need fresh attention if a fully evangelical spirituality is to flourish in our time.

The three theological perspectives are as follows:

## (1)   *Thoroughgoing theocentricity*

It is often and truly said that the gospel message, through the power of the Spirit of Christ that it mediates, turns people's lives upside down. Less frequently it is noted that the anti-God syndrome in our system called original sin has turned our lives upside down already, so that this inverting change of heart by the Spirit, commonly called conversion, actually sets us right way up, to live in the way truly natural to us for the first time ever.

What happens is that in a sovereign act of grace that the New Testament theologizes as birth from God (John 1:13; 13:5–8; James 1:18; 1 Peter 1:23; 1 John 3:9; 5:1, 4), co-resurrection with Christ (Rom.

---

[5]  J. I. Packer and Thomas Howard, *Christianity the True Humanism* (Waco: Word Books, 1985), is a first attempt.

6:4–11; Eph. 2:1–10; Col. 2:13; 3:1–11), new creation in Christ (2 Cor. 5:17; Gal. 6:5) and regeneration (Titus 3:5), and that Pietism highlights as *die Wiedergeburt*, God unites the individual to the risen Lord in such a way that the dispositional drives of Christ's perfect human character – the inner urgings, that is, to honour, adore, love, obey, serve and please God, and to benefit others for both their sake and his sake – are now reproduced at the motivational centre of that individual's being. And they are reproduced, in face of the contrary egocentric cravings of fallen nature, in a dominant way, so that the Christian, though still troubled and tormented by the urgings of indwelling sin, is no longer ruled by those urgings in the way that was true before.

Being under grace, the Christian is freed from sin (Rom. 6:14–7.6; Gal. 5:13–25; cf. John 8:31–36); the motivational theocentricity of the heart set free will prompt the actions that form the habits of Christ-likeness that constitute the Spirit's fruit (Gal. 5:22f.), and thus the holiness of radical repentance (daily abandonment of self-centred self-will), childlike humility (daily listening to what God says in his Word, and daily submission to what he sends in his providence), and love to God and humans that honours and serves both, will increasingly appear. This thorough-going intellectual and moral theocentricity, whereby Christians come to live no longer for themselves but for him who died and rose to save them (cf. 2 Cor. 5:15), is first God's gift and then the Christian's task, and as such it is the foundation not only of sound ethics but also of true spirituality.

Not surprisingly, the crusading secular humanists of the past hundred years have seen this self-abandoning theocentricity of faith, hope, and love as unnatural and impoverishing. Christians, however, experience it, despite the inward and outward conflicts in which it involves them, as joy, so long at least as their commitment to it remains clear-headed and whole-hearted, and the natural, Spirit-sustained functioning of their regenerate hearts is not inhibited by psychological blockage, hurt, or disorientation.[6] The knowledge that they live under the guarding, guiding, protecting and empowering hand of a loving almighty Creator, with a hope of glory assuring them that however good anything has been so far there is better to come, and that it will eternally be so, yields joy without end. In face of today's hedonistic secularism the 'solid joys' (John Newton's phrase) of thoroughgoing Christian theocentricity need to be stressed.

## (2) Thoroughgoing Trinitarianism

In contemporary reflection on the Christian life, lack of a rigorous biblical Trinitarianism is a great and widespread weakness – though there are signs

---

[6] Some of these inhibiting factors are dealt with in James Houston, *The Transforming Friendship* (Oxford: Lion Publishing, 1989); *In Search of Happiness* (Oxford: Lion Publishing, 1990).

that God is blending post-Barthian theology with charismatic experien-tialism in a way that should bring improvement here.[7] The weakness seems due to four causes. The first is an unawareness of the relevance of the Trinity for evangelical life as a result of rating it a theologoumenon of orthodoxy, to be upheld against heretics, and not seeing it as the structural frame of godliness itself.

The second cause is the 'humanitarian' Christology of liberalism, which sees Jesus as an exemplary God-filled man rather than a gracious divine Saviour,[8] plus the practical demythologizing of the Holy Spirit that was almost standard in the medieval doctrine of grace (maintained by Roman Catholics into this century) and that still breaks surface wherever the Spirit is referred to, whether by liberals or by conservatives, as 'it' (a supernatural influence) rather than 'he' (a personal agent).[9] Liberal theology, which was always implicitly unitarian, has had a baleful influence here.

The third cause is failure to appreciate what Trinitarianism actually means – that, so far from being a kind of conundrum devised at Nicaea and Constantinople in order to squelch Arianism, it is in fact the joyful proclamation that, as a Puritan somewhere put it, and as John's gospel shows, 'God himself is a sweet society,' and that the purpose first of creation and then of redemption was to extend that fellowship of love by bringing creatures into it.

The fourth cause, linked with the third, is unawareness that the essence of the Christian life is involvement in the relational life of the triune Godhead, knowing the Father of the Son as one's own heavenly Father, knowing the Son of the Father, who reigns, as one's own Saviour and Lord, and knowing the Holy Spirit, really though indirectly, as imparting vision and empowering devotion from which none should ever have lapsed. These causes have long combined to keep the church from seeing that a truly theocentric spirituality will be truly Trinitarian. It is a happy thing that now at last, it seems, this obstacle to devotional right-mindedness is being overcome.

To say that sound spirituality must be fully Trinitarian is to say that in our fellowship with God we must learn to do full justice to the part that each of the divine Three plays in the team job, as we may venture to call

---

[7] See three books by Thomas Smail: *Reflected Glory* (London: Hodder & Stoughton and Grand Rapids: Eerdmans, 1976); *The Forgotten Father* (London: Hodder & Stoughton and Grand Rapids: Eerdmans, 1979; [reprinted Vancouver: Regent College, 1995]; *The Giving Gift* (London: Hodder & Stoughton, 1988).
[8] I have discussed this in 'Jesus Christ the Lord', in *The Lord Christ*, ed. J. R. W. Stott (London: Collins, 1977), pp. 32–60, and in 'The Uniqueness of Jesus Christ', *Churchman*, 1978/2, pp. 101–111. Both included in this collection.
[9] One cannot but regret that Alistair Heron, *The Holy Spirit* (Philadelphia: Westminster Press, 1988), vii, pp. 173–76, argues for the impersonal usage.

it, of saving us from sin, restoring our ruined humanness, and bringing us finally to glory. Should we neglect the Son, whether through some doctrinaire revisionist Christology or simply by lapsing into natural religion with Islam, so that we lose our focus on the Son's mediation, blood atonement, risen life, royal glory, and heavenly intercession, we shall slip back into legalism, a version of the treadmill religion of works, probably linked in these days with a syncretist theology.

Should we neglect the Spirit, losing our focus on the fellowship with Christ that he creates, the renewing of nature that he effects, the assurance and joy that he evokes, and the enabling for service that he bestows, we shall slip back into formalism, a version of the religion of aspiration and perspiration that lacks both inspiration and transformation, a religion of mechanical observances, low expectations, deep ruts of routine, and grooves that quickly turn into graves.

Should we neglect the Father, losing our focus on the tasks he sets and the disciplines he imposes (cf. Heb. 12:5–14), we shall become soft, lazy, self-absorbed, unsteady and erratic, with a dull and sleepy conscience – spoiled children, in the most literal sense, in God's family. As in human families, so in the divine: children who, for whatever reason, do not experience, along with love, moral strength and precision in their fathers carry character weaknesses with them throughout their lives. God's spoiled children will reveal themselves as exploitative egoists who make heavy weather of any troubles and setbacks that come their way, thus failing spectacularly to live out the self-denying theocentricity to which they pay lip-service.

True Trinitarianism in the head and the heart can take us beyond these pitfalls; but anything less virtually guarantees a spiritual development that is one way or another stunted and deformed.

### (3) Thoroughgoing two-worldliness

New Testament Christianity is essentially two-worldly: not other-worldly in the sense of lacking interest in this world, but seeing life here as travel to, and preparation for, and indeed as a foretaste of, a life hereafter in which all without exception will reap what they sowed here in terms of their attitudes and decisions God-ward. Those who are Christ's will receive infinite enrichment in terms of joy in their God and Saviour; others face infinite loss, first of God's active kindness and then of all the good and pleasant things that this kindness brings now.

Death, or the return of Jesus Christ, whichever comes first, will effect a transition from the world of life-choices to the world where our Maker gives us what, fundamentally, we have chosen concerning him – either to be eternally with him, or eternally without him. And since our experience of the destiny we chose will be unending, and will in fact grow directly out of our life now, the whole of this present life should be lived in light of the future – which means, for Christians, living in the power of the magnificent hope of glory with Christ that the Father has given them.

Here is a further aspect of the naturalness to which regenerating grace restores us; for whereas the proverb says, while there's life there's hope, the deeper truth is that only where there is hope is there life. Man is a hoping animal, who lapses into gloom and apathy when he has nothing to look forward to. So Christ, who diagnoses living in the present with never a thought about death and the life to come as supreme folly (cf. Luke 12:5–21), directs us to lay up treasure, not on earth, but in heaven (Matt. 6:19–21; Luke 12:32–34) – in other words, to live, not in this-worldly, but in two-worldly terms, facing up to the issues of eternity as we have stated them. All Christians seem to have understood this, and laboured to act on it, until relatively recently.

But nowadays Christians have largely lost the two-worldly perspective of the Scriptures and have embraced for all practical purposes the Marxist, materialist, secular humanist assumption that this life is all that matters, because it is all there is. Creative Christian thought about spiritual life is now funneled almost entirely into exploring spiritual and relational enrichment in this world, and Christians generally seem to have internal - ized the Marxist mockery of 'pie in the sky when you die,' so that they feel deep down, just as Marxists do, that any serious reflection on the life to come is uncouth and unhealthy.

So we preach to each other, and write books for each other, about the path to present blessings in its various forms, and heaven and hell hardly get a mention. We treat any call to think seriously about the world to come, not as a sober Christian realism, based on Scripture, but as a sign either of escapism, if the focus is on heaven, or of vindictiveness, if it is on hell; and in both cases we see it as something regrettable. The wisdom, received from the Christian past, that only when one is ready to die is one ready to live, is forgotten; with the world, we treat continuance of life, as such, as the supreme value. Death finds us unprepared, and in daily life it is observable how little strength we have for the practice of detachment or renunciation in any form at all. Authentic spirituality, however, requires of us that we re-learn the discipline of sitting loose to everything here in order to lay hold of glory hereafter, and our living cannot be in shape, Christianly speaking, until we have recovered the two-world perspective, with its attendant recognition of the eternal significance of all present action, that the New Testament exhibits to us.

## IV

To these three basic theological perspectives for spirituality I now add three basic biblical themes, from which, as I see it, all that is essential for understanding what godliness is may be drawn. I merely point to, and generalize about, the wealth of material that awaits exposition under each head; this is, after all, no more than a brief programmatic essay. There will be some formal overlap with things already said, but they will be approached from a different angle.

### (1)  The new relationship: the Christian under God's covenant

All biblical religion has a royal covenantal form: that is, it is a matter of pledged mutual commitment, in which two parties give themselves to each other in total love and loyalty on the basis of promises, stipulations and requirements imposed by the superior party on the inferior, in this case by the divine king and benefactor on those he has saved. Every Christian believer, Jew and Gentile alike, lives under God's new covenant by virtue of being united to Jesus Christ, the specific seed of Abraham to whom specific promises were given when God covenanted with Abra - ham in the patriarchal age (see Gen. 12–13; chs. 15, 17, interpreted by Gal. 3). The contrast between 'new' and 'old' covenants has to do with the greater range of God's promises, and the greater adequacy of his mediatorial arrangements in and through Christ, as compared with the provisional, typical arrangements that had gone before (see Heb.1–31, and Jesus' words at the Last Supper: Matt. 26:28; Luke 22:20; 1 Cor. 11:25); it does not bear on Paul's insistence that the establishing of those who are in Christ as Abraham's seed and heirs of all that God's blessing of Abraham embraced was God's plan throughout (Gal. 3:14, 26–29).

Under the old covenant, the spiritually alive person trusted God and lived by faith in his promises, just as New Testament believers were later to do, and godly character, as seen and modelled for us in the Psalms, had in it at least the following dispositional qualities: responsive attention to God's words of self-revelation, with loyal conformity to his commands and trustful hope in his gracious purposes (Ps. 119); adoring admiration of God's works in creation and providence (Ps. 46, 104, 107); submissive patience under God's afflictions (Ps. 102; cf. Job; Lam.); hearty gratitude for God's gifts (Ps. 118); active identification with God's cause (Ps. 101; 139:19–24); constant desire for God's fellowship (Ps. 16, 42) and joy in it as it is experienced (Ps. 23); committed solidarity with God's people (Ps.7); prayerfulness at all times (Ps. 63); and neighbourliness with all one's fellows (see Lev. 19:13–18).

Under the new covenant none of this changes, and these qualities remain integral to godliness still. The profiles of New Testament saints, however, embody four further behavioural characteristics, each shaped by the enrichment of God's present grace to his people that the new covenant has brought. These characteristics are as follows: a personal relationship of faith and love towards Jesus Christ, the risen Saviour and Lord; a responsible use of the freedom from subjection to legal codes that

God's gift of justification and adoption into his family has conferred; an active involvement in the church's every-member ministry, through receiving, discerning, and using the gifts (*charismata*) bestowed by the Holy Spirit; and a resolute detachment from pursuing this world's allurements of pleasure, profit, and position, a detachment maintained through the power of one's new-found love for God and one's hope of future glory with Christ (1 John 2:15–17; 3:2f.).

All this yields a basic definition of Christian spirituality as recognition of and response to the reality and power of God through Jesus Christ in the covenant of divine grace. This covenantal basis for communion with God was central to the Puritan understanding of the Christian life, and was spelt out clearly in the Westminster Confession, but less has been heard of it recently, and renewed exploration of it is currently needed. God's covenant with each Christian is a covenant of permanent friend - ship, like that between Jonathan and David (cf. 1 Sam. 1:3; 20:2), and of abiding fidelity, like that between husband and wife (cf. Ezek. 16:8; Mal. 2.14), and it defines the relationship in a definite way that has to be clearly grasped if the relationship itself is to grow and deepen. Here, then, is a major biblical agenda item for the renewing of evangelical spirituality today.

### (2) The new creation: the Christian sharing Christ's life

The New Testament speaks emphatically of the 'newness' ( *kainotes*, from *kainos*, meaning 'of a new kind': see Rom. 6:4; 7:6; cf. 12:2) of the Christian's life in Christ, as compared and contrasted with all that went before. John, Peter and James, as we saw, present the start of this newness as a new birth, and Paul presents it as a new creation, as co-resurrection with Jesus, and as putting off the old person and putting on the new one (Eph. 4:4; Col. 3:10).

Putting off and putting on is the language of changing clothes, and when the NIV renders 'man' as 'self' it misses some of the meaning; what the Christian has put off is solidarity with Adam, and what he puts on is Christ, or solidarity with Christ, as the source and principle of his new life (cf. Rom. 13:14; Gal. 3:28).

Each image entails the thought of a totally fresh beginning: one has ceased to be what one was, and has commenced to be what previously one was not. Paul then charts the course of this newness in terms of being restored as God's image (Col. 3:10), serving righteousness and God as bondslaves of both (Rom. 6:16–23), and bringing forth the fruit of the Spirit (Gal. 5:22–25); John speaks of walking in the light (1 John 1:7); and indeed the whole body of New Testament writers labour the thought that Christians are called to live in a radically different way from those around them, and from the way they themselves lived before. The proclamation of newness as both a divine gift and a Christian obligation is loud and clear.

We glanced earlier at the theological and psychological reality of this great change, which the dying-and-rising symbolism of baptism proclaims (cf. Rom. 6:3f.; Col. 2:12) and the Holy Spirit, by uniting us to the risen Christ, actually effects. Intellectually the change is an opening and enlightening of the blinded mind to discern what previously we could not discern (2 Cor. 4:3–6; Eph. 1:17f.; cf. Luke 24:25, 31, 45) – namely, the spiritual realities of Christ and his salvation. Motivationally, within the heart, the change is an implanting in us of the inclinations of Christ's perfect humanity through our ingrafting into him: this produces in us a mind-set and lifestyle that is not explicable in terms of what we were before. The Spirit-born person, as Jesus indicated, cannot but be a mystery to those who are not born again themselves; they can form no idea of what makes him tick (cf. John 3:8).

The New Testament enables us to form some idea of the characteristic exercise of heart that marks those whom God has thus brought into newness of life. Knowing the truth of the gospel, each will adore Christ as, in Newton's words,

> Jesus, my Shepherd, Husband, Friend,
> My Prophet, Priest, and King,
> My Lord, my Life, my Way, my End,

and will feel inwardly what Charles Wesley expressed when he wrote:

> Jesus, my all in all Thou art;
> My rest in toil, my ease in pain,
> The medicine of my broken heart,
> In war my peace, in loss my gain,
> My smile beneath the tyrant's frown,
> In shame my glory and my crown:
>
> In want my plentiful supply,
> In weakness my almighty power,
> In bonds my perfect liberty,
> My light in Satan's darkest hour,
> In grief my joy unspeakable,
> My life in death, my heaven in hell.

Seeing themselves as travellers on the way home, they will live by hope – hope, quite specifically, of meeting their beloved Saviour face to face, and being with him for ever. Discerning sinful desires in themselves despite their longing to be sin-free, and finding that in their quest for total righteousness their reach exceeds their grasp, they will live in tension and distress at their frustrating infirmities (cf. Rom. 7:14–25). They will call on God as their heavenly Father, glorify and love him, honour and love other people, hate and fight evil in all its forms, grow downwards into a deeper and more childlike humility, and practise patience under pressure. All this is at the same time determined obedience to God's law, conscious imitation of Christ in attitude and purpose, and satisfying fulfilment of their own new instincts – in other words, naturalness in expressing their own new selves.

A further biblical agenda item for the renewal of spirituality in our time, in face of the misunderstandings of human nature that secular humanism sponsors and the whole Western educational system assumes, is the study of the newness of the Christian person, and the naturalness of godliness when one is a new creature in Christ.

### (3) The new community: the Christian in God's church

The gospel fosters individuality, in the sense of realization that as regards the present decisions that determine eternal destiny one stands alone before God; no one can make those decisions for someone else, and no one can enter the kingdom of God by hanging on to someone else's coat-tails. The individuality that consists of a sense of personal identity and responsibility Godward is a Christian virtue, making for wise and thoughtful behaviour, and is a necessity for mature life and growth in Christ. But it has nothing to do with individualism, which is actually a proud unwillingness to accept a place in a team of peers and to be bound by group consensus. The gospel condemns individualism as disruptive of the life of the divine family, the new community of believers together that God is building in each place where individual Christians have emerged. Harmonious consensus, undergirded by brotherly love, is to be the goal for every church, and individualism is to be overcome by mutual deference. So, at least, says the New Testament.

But the necessary protests of Pietism in continental Europe and of Puritanism and evangelicalism in Britain against unthinking conformity to the routines of a state church on the supposition that this is all there is to Christianity have brought to birth not only much biblical individuality, but a great deal of unbiblical individualism as well. The latter is still with us, constantly spawning parachurch organizations accountable to no one but their founders, and nowadays it is almost expected that persons of intense piety will want to sit loose to the structured life of the organized churches.

The modern lay movement, expressed in *cursillo* ministry, small groups, accountability and discipling relationships, and all that goes with these, seeks to curb this individualism, but often falls victim to new forms of it, and the same has to be said of the charismatic renewal. The study of biblical principles and patterns for the involvement of the individual Christian in the worshipping and serving human units that, locally and ecumenically, make up the body of Christ is a further agenda item for a renewed spirituality.

The corporate aspect of Christian spirituality can be defined as practising mutual love and care in God's family on the basis that this is the life to which we are called and for which Christ equips us: each believer must be ready to lay down his or her life for Christ in others, and must be duly grateful when others lay down their lives and bear burdens for Christ in his or her own self. This is not, however, so well understood, nor so well practised, as it needs to be.

## V

Though a gentle, patient, and tolerant person in himself, Klaus Bock - muehl saw contemporary Christians as called to battle − for truth in theology, for faithfulness in the churches, and for the wisdom and glory of God in a secular, apostate, and now mad world.

> Under the perspectives of good and evil, God and secularism, there is more drama in the twentieth century than would ever be necessary to give profile to our lives. Sometimes our days get dull, because we forget the perspective of the battle that is often waged so invisibly and silently. But it is above all in these struggles that we today find the concrete concerns for our prayer, intercession, proclamation, and teaching.[10]

The quest to recover true spirituality, which from another standpoint is the quest to recover authentic humanness, is part of this battle, both in the church and outside it, where secular humanism stands entrenched. I hope that Klaus would have approved my suggestions as to where we shall find resources for the fight.

---

[10] *Living by the Gospel*, 119.

# Christian Living

# Chapter 23

# The Christian and God's World

I am not an American. I am British by birth and Canadian by choice. But though I am not an American, I feel it to be an enormous privilege, as well as a tremendous responsibility, to be addressing Americans on the theme of the guidance that a trusted Bible gives for action – corrective, visionary, reforming, prophetic, evangelical, salt-and-light action in community life today.

## The Battle for America's Soul

Why do I feel this so strongly? Why, because of the uniquely significant vocation that God appears to have given to the United States of America in the modern world.

Theologians, as you know, distinguish between *special* grace, the grace that saves sinners by turning them to Christ and that builds up the church in and through Christ, and *common* grace, the grace of providential action – sometimes kindly, sometimes severe – that restrains sin, maintains some order and some justice in our fallen communities, and so provides a milieu in which the gospel and the work of special grace can go forward. When Paul directs Christians to pray for rulers 'that we [believers] may live peaceful and quiet lives in all godliness and holiness' (1 Timothy 2:2), his words clearly express this view of common grace serving the interests of special grace.

I see the United States as having at this time a unique role in the world at both levels of divine operation. I might perhaps be able to see this more clearly than a native American ever could, simply because I look at it from outside. As a non-American, I do not endorse any form of that utopian triumphalism, the secular counterpart of the Pilgrims' hope of building new Jerusalem in Massachusetts, that periodically breaks surface in the American mind and that looks to outsiders so ominously like the pride

THE CHRISTIAN AND GOD'S WORLD was originally published in *Transforming Our World* (Portland: Multnomah, 1988), pp. 81–97. Reprinted by permission.

that goes before a fall. The idea that America is God's most favoured
nation and always will be is a snare and a delusion that can only sap
America's spiritual strength in the way that Aleksandr Solzhenitsyn and
Malcolm Muggeridge think has happened already. Do not, I beg you, fall
victim to any such notion as that.

Nonetheless, I want to go on record as saying to you, and about you,
the two things that now follow, and I ask you to hear me well.

First, as regards *special grace*. The United States of America is a nation
of almost a quarter of a billion people. Of these, 65 per cent claim a church
connection, and something between twenty and forty million – maybe
one in ten, maybe one in five profess to be born again evangelical
Christians. The United States has a conversionist folk religion that gives
great support to evangelism. (I say that with feeling, as I think any Western
European would, for in our native countries the folk religion is formal
and formalistic, and greatly obstructs evangelism.)

During the forty-three years of my Christian life, the work of
evangelism in America, both in local churches and in larger crusades, has
been advancing apace, and the fruit of this advance now shows in many
striking ways. Evangelical churches and seminaries, many of them
founded within the past generation, are crowded out. Evangelical litera -
ture has never sold so well. At no time for more than a century has the
evangelical profile been higher. Impressive young people keep emerging,
on the way to leadership in tomorrow's church. Also, a great deal of
money constantly becomes available to finance evangelical churches, plus
a vast array of evangelical parachurch ministries and overseas missions too.

Of no other human unit of comparable size anywhere in the world
can these things be said. In Britain and Australia, it is estimated that 1 to
2 per cent of the population are evangelical Christians – certainly not
more – and the supply of manpower for missionary work has dwindled
to a trickle. In continental Europe, things are on the whole worse. In
Africa and Latin America, the number of professed Christians grows by
the million, but inner instabilities, political agonies, and grinding eco -
nomic hardships make it impossible for the Christian communities to
become a major missionary force beyond their own doorsteps. The
evangelical church in China – whether computed at ten or fifty million,
or somewhere between those two extreme estimates – lives under
permanent political threat and, in any case, is too poor and too geographi -
cally static to be able to spread the gospel in any significant way outside
its own country. The same seems to be true of the big evangelical
constituency in Korea and the smaller one in India.

What it boils down to is that among the larger nations, only the United
States has both the manpower and the money to sustain evangelical world
mission for the next generation, and this gives America a uniquely
important role in the global strategy of the kingdom of God at the present
time.

Then, second, as regards *common grace*. The United States of America has in the providence of God effectively become, since World War II, both the police force and the defence force of the entire non-Communist world. Whether this role is always fulfilled in the best way is something about which we can argue. But there can be no argument about the fact that the role now exists, and that the American people have accepted it. The isolationist noises that floated across the Atlantic when I was a boy are no longer heard, for today's Americans see themselves as having an obligation – many would soberly say, a God-given obligation – to try, at least, to be the world's peacekeeper and a bulwark against Marxist advance. In light of the typical hostility of Marxist regimes to the Christian gospel, the importance of America's role for preserving religious liberty and an open arena for worldwide evangelism is too obvious to need discussion.

From these facts, I conclude that America has a central and crucial place, at two levels – not just one, in the contemporary Christian world mission.

How important it is then that America's inner spiritual resources be strong enough to sustain this dual role. And how certain it is that Satan will seek by every means in his power to undermine America's spiritual resources, so that the nation falls down on the job. And how inescapable, to me at least, is the conclusion that the capture over the past half-century by the imperialist ideology called 'secular humanism' of America's media establishment, its educational establishment, its literary and artistic estab - lishments, its medical, socio-economic and legal establishments – in short just about all its character shaping and opinion-making structures apart from the evangelical church itself – has been one of Satan's strategic manoeuvres, a well-conceived and sadly successful one, against the kingdom of God.

A few days ago, a European colleague of mine at Regent College said to me, in words that I find prophetic, 'the battle for the soul of America is just about to begin.' I took his thought to be that all the separating out of Christian and post-Christian standpoints during the last several decades (which in this regard have felt tense enough, God knows, to many of us) has been merely preliminary to the really decisive encounter – a clash that remains future but cannot now be far off. Hitherto, the forces of secularism and humanism, on the one hand, and of biblical Christianity on the other, have been positioning themselves – more truly perhaps than either side has yet realized – for direct confrontation.

The clash will be between the uninhibited materialistic egoism of the full-blown secularist, in which the only values recognized are one's own pleasure, profit, and power ('the lust of the flesh, and the lust of the eyes, and the pride of life,' as the King James Version of 1 John 2:16 called them) and the consistent theocentric altruism of the thoroughgoing Christian, in which the supreme value of my neighbour to God, and therefore to me, determines all personal relations and all social policy.

Outsiders see American society as prone to push ideas to extremes, and there is no question that materialistic pragmatism, based on relativistic morals, is being pushed to extremes in the United States today. Hence - forth, it would seem, sustained ideological conflict must be expected, assuming as I do assume that biblical Christians in the United States will not raise their hands in meek surrender before the secular humanist juggernaut.

When I posit as one of the contending viewpoints a consistent theocentric altruism – that is, a God-honouring concern for the welfare of all other human beings before oneself – I am not, I confess, looking in the direction of neoliberal Protestantism or neomodernist Catholicism, free though both those movements have been with that sort of language. Both lose touch, more or less, with the biblical view of my neighbour's nature and need. Both as a result become half-way houses to humanism of the secular sort. And on moral questions in society, both tend to end up kicking the ball through their own goal. (Think of neoliberalism's support of violence in the name of peace and of its expressed views on, for instance, divorce and remarriage, abortion, and homosexuality.)

No, what I have in mind is a realistic commitment of conscience to the actual spiritual values and moral absolutes of Scripture and Scripture's Christ – a commitment, therefore, to care for my neighbour without limit because they bear God's image, even though I do not believe in their natural goodness, as perhaps they themselves do, and even though they may be weak or handicapped or sexually misaligned or guilty of major crime or as yet unborn. To be frank, it is only among those who trust their Bible absolutely that I expect ever to see commitment of this quality.

When my colleague anticipated escalating confrontations between biblical Christianity and empire-building secularism, I think he read the signs of the times correctly. They are, to my mind, ominous. I have to agree with those who see secularism as so deeply entrenched already in the places of power that loosening its grip must require at least a generation of all-out argument, no matter how right-minded and God-blessed that arguing may be. I have to agree also with those who doubt whether evangelicals generally have perceived the gravity of the issues that are currently at stake, or the extent of the pressure (mostly indirect as yet) that society is in the process of mounting against nonrelativist biblical belief. Chesterton's words express what I am forced to say as I look at the big picture of North America:

> I tell you naught for your comfort,
> Yea, naught for your desire,
> Save that the sky grows darker yet,
> And the sea rises higher.

From all that I have said, you can see why, at just this moment in the battle for the soul of the most influential nation on earth, I count it a huge privilege, as well as a huge responsibility, to be speaking to you about these things.

My subject is 'The Christian and God's World.' But although this has been a long introduction, this is, in fact, what I have been discussing from the start. So far I have offered only contemporary analysis and comment, however. What I aim to do now is to set my mapping of this field of Christian responsibility on a directly biblical basis. In what follows, I shall be discussing in order each of these four alliterated realities: the *concept* of God's world, the *creation* of God's world, the *corruption* of God's world, and the Christian's *calling* in God's world. By this means, I seek to deepen our insight into the present-day tensions upon which I have been dwelling thus far.

## The Concept of God's World

I speak first, then, of the concept of God's world, that is, of the world *as God's*. My point here is simply that in the sense in which it is God's, it is not ours, and we must not slip into the bad habit of supposing that we own it and may therefore deal with it any way we like.

When we say 'world,' it is clear that we are referring in a general way to all that surrounds us – spatially, temporally, and relationally. But what do we mean when we add the possessive adjective and speak of '*our* world'? If we are thinking in physical and geographical terms, 'our world' will signify this planet, with its chemical structure, climatic laws, limited resources, vast population and so on. If we are thinking in racial and anthropological terms, 'our world' will signify people of all nations. If we are thinking historically and culturally, 'our world' will signify the state of things in this particular era. If our focus is personal and subjective, 'our world' will signify things as they appear to each of us from the vantage point (or through the blinders) of each one's private knowledge, beliefs, and interests, so that each of us truly lives, as we say, in a 'world' of our own. But whichever of these specific meanings is in view, the use of 'our' is man-centred and, therefore, from one standpoint at least, dangerously improper. Why? Because it is not really our world in any sense at all. God made it, God sustains it, God owns it, God keeps it, God rules it, and we are part of it.

Between them, the biblical words for 'world' cover approximately the same range of meanings that our English word does, but always with a theological, God-centred perspective. The biblical vision is of the world as belonging to God and of ourselves as, at most, his stewards, bailiffs, agents, lieutenants and trustees – his regents, as we say at Regent College – charged to manage God's world for him according to his revealed will.

God putting Adam to tend a garden perfectly pictures our God-given cultural task. We are to see the entire created order, including, of course, our neighbours and ourselves, as the estate that we, as God's gardeners, are responsible for cultivating.

Sometimes this responsibility is called the 'cultural mandate,' meaning mankind's obligation to develop a pattern of corporate life that honours the Creator by embodying true moral and spiritual values and so furthers the realizing of all the joyful potential of human life in God's world.

Never forget that the glory of God and the happiness of man were always meant to go together! Where you truly have the former, you will truly have the latter also. A necessary element in any realistic plan to reduce the sum of present human misery is a return to the cultural mandate.

The humanism that we face treats the world and everything and everyone in the world irreligiously, and sees this as a mark of maturity, as if by deleting the divine you come of age. We must be clear that this attitude expresses not maturity but apostasy and needs to be challenged at every point. After all, were God not upholding the world in being, no humanist would exist to deny him. It cannot be said too often that this world is in every sense God's world, which his human creatures must learn to handle reverently, for his praise.

## The Creation of God's World

Now to my second topic, the creation of God's world. Here my purpose is to plead for a worthy testimony to the wonders of the Creator's work.

Come with me, then, to the first chapter of the Bible, and observe that there we are shown God bringing into being a world-order. The achieving of order out of dark and formless chaos is the central story line of Genesis 1:1–2:3. It is natural to conclude that the 'goodness' that God tells us he saw in each thing he formed and in the finished work of creation as a whole (Genesis 1:4,10,12,18,21,25,31) lay partly, at least, in the fact that every item represented a step forward in the excluding of chaos and the establishing of order. A further natural conclusion is that God gave us Genesis 1 as the highly formalized narrative it is partly, at least, to underline for us the fact that he loves order and sees beauty in it, and is in every sense a God of order, as opposed to randomness and confusion.

Beyond this very basic point, Genesis 1 is tricky ground for interpreters to walk on, as we all know. But I will venture a little further. The following observations should surely command general assent.

First, *the chapter celebrates the fact of creation and the power, wisdom, and goodness of the Creator, on whom attention centers throughout* . Though many of God's creatures are mentioned by name as the narrative unfolds, what is being said at each stage is not 'meet the *creation*' (as if we had never met it before), but rather 'meet the *Creator!*' From our knowledge of the marvellous complexity of all the creatures that are listed we are to gauge their Maker's glory and adore him accordingly.

Second, *the style of the chapter is imaginative, pictorial, poetic, and doxological* (glory-giving, in the manner of worship), rather than clinically and prosaically descriptive in the deadpan scientific fashion. It is, after all, as we said, ceremonial celebration, telling us who made the world and each item within it, rather than how in detail he produced each effect.

Third, *the Earth-centeredness of the presentation reflects theological interest in man's uniqueness and responsibility under God on this planet*, not scientific naiveté . . . about the solar system.

Fourth, *the pastoral and edificatory purpose of the narrative is to show its readers their own place and calling in God's world* and the abiding significance of the sabbath as a memorial of creation – not to satisfy academic or technical curiosity about the distant past.

No interpretation of Genesis 1 that ignores these built-in perspectives can be right, nor can it be other than a majoring in minors, for these are the angles that are important. Within them, to be sure, it is legitimate to ask how the six days of creation relate to shifting scientific theories of origins. Various hypotheses are offered. None of these, however, is more than an educated guess. So none should expect ever to have the field to itself, and each should be put forward with modesty and tolerance toward other views.

It is another victory for Satan when Bible-believers go for each other's throats over their rival notions of what the sciences say about the six days of creation and what the text says about the ideas of the scientists. Such infighting is a luxury that, pressed as we are by the secularist squeeze of which I spoke earlier, we can neither justify nor afford. Tenacity of belief that all the Bible is true does not require equal tenacity in believing that all one's own ideas about its meaning in disputed areas are true also. And in the case of Genesis 1, a worthy echo of its witness to the Creator's glory becomes impossible if all we let ourselves think about when interpreting it is Bible-and-science questions. A worthy witness to the reality of the Creator, one that links up compellingly with the sense of creatureliness that is indelibly inscribed on every human heart, is what we most need today.

## The Corruption of God's World

My third theme, the corruption of God's world, requires me to narrow my focus from the world in the sense of the entire cosmos to the world in the sense of our race in rebellion, organized without God and indeed against God, and hence unfriendly to basic biblical values. 'The world' in this sense of hell-bent humanity is (of course!) a frequent focus of the New Testament, where Christian conflict with the world is a recurring theme. My purpose here is to do just one thing, namely, to spotlight the motivation that drives the world in its self-affirming, anti-God courses of action. For that, I take you to the story of the tower of Babel in Genesis 11:1–9, where the totalitarian dynamics of the fallen human collective are pictured with supreme starkness.

What drives the world? Pride, plus pride's daughter, paranoia – the sense of being constantly threatened unless one can collar more power than one has at the moment. Augustine analysed 'original sin' as pride (*superbia*), the passion to be 'top person,' independent, self-sufficient, big, strong and, thus, secure. And surely he was right. No profounder analysis is possible, for this is the very heart – the heart of the heart, we might say – of the 'play-God, fight-God, kill-God' syndrome that infected our race in Eden and rules the unregenerate still.

The project planned on the plain of Shinar illustrates this perfectly: 'Come, let us build ourselves a city, with a tower that reaches to the heavens, so that we may make a name for ourselves and not be scattered over the face of the whole earth' (v.4). There was bravado here. The project was grandiose to the point of goofiness. They were going to build a great city and a skyscraper tower within it as a symbol of its strength, and all they had to work with was crude makeshift materials – home-made bricks instead of quarried stone, and bitumen (surface tar) instead of proper mortar. But the prospect of power intoxicated them, so that they lost the capacity to calculate what was realistically possible and what was not. (One thinks of Hitler's boast that his Third Reich would last a thousand years. It actually staggered along for twelve before defeat in World War II put an end to it.) Buoyed up by the feeling that if everyone pulled together there was no limit to what they could do, these starry-eyed devotees of earthly glory set themselves to establish the greatest power base ever.

The pride that spawns all centralized collectivism and all totalitarian empire building was never more clearly expressed. Scattered, we stumble and suffer, they reasoned. But by our solidarity, we stand and are safe! The world still thinks in these terms.

In due course, we read, 'The LORD came down to see the city and the tower that the men were building' (v. 5). He gave the project a run for its money, so that its perversity might clearly appear before he finally frustrated it by confusing the builders' language, making it impossible for them to cooperate any more and so bringing about the very scattering that they had hoped to avoid (cf. vv.4 and 8).

Such is still his way. To preserve an environment in which gospel godliness is at least possible, he regularly breaks up ungodly unions, brings down power blocs, and causes the same pride that first drew sinners together in empire building to push them apart in misunderstanding and mistrust of each other. This pattern of divine action, which from one point of view is merited judgement – dealing with sin as it deserves – is from another point of view common grace, restraining sin from doing as much damage as it otherwise would. God will not let his world be spoiled or his Word suppressed beyond a certain point, and his partial, if not total, restraint of sin in the structures of society will continue to operate till Antichrist comes.

Meantime, it remains a natural urge in fallen humanity to band together to create units of power and to require unqualified commitment and total loyalty to those units. That is both the proof and the measure of the world's corruption. Those who direct the world's political, economic, and ideological power plays may be expected constantly to feel that the biblical Christian's loyalty to Scripture and its God is a threat to them. Paranoia will then take over, and what the Puritan, Richard Baxter, in the title of one of his books, called *Cain and Abel Malignity*, will express itself against faithful believers over and over again. We must be prepared for this.

## The Christian's Calling in the World

My fourth theme is the Christian's calling in the world. How should the Bible-believers of the secularized West respond to the pressures under which the world puts them? How should they position themselves in relation to politics, economics, poverty, the arts, conservation, education and the many other spheres of human concern in which sub- and anti-Christian attitudes have become dominant?

Let me clear the ground by dismissing at once three inadequate responses to such pressures, all of which were embodied in persons whom we meet in the gospel story and none of which was endorsed by Jesus himself. Palestine was enemy-occupied territory, just as this world is, the Romans being the enemy in the one case and Satan in the other, and different Jews responded to the dominance of the Romans in different ways.

The Zealots embraced the way of *confrontation:* they sought the over-throw of Rome in holy war and the replacing of Rome's rule by a kingdom of saints, in which only loyal Jews would find a place. They showed no interest in the non-political kingdom of God that Jesus preached.

The Sadducees took the way of *compromise:* they reasoned that since they could not beat the Romans, they had better join them. So they greedily grasped and hung onto such crumbs of power as the Romans threw them and cynically settled for liquidating Jesus, lest he so disturb things that their little bit of power would be forfeit.

Finally, the Pharisees followed the path of *separation:* they withdrew from all associations that they thought defiled them and would not touch any sphere of life in which the Romans were publicly in control.

Thus, the Zealots never made common cause with the world, the Sadducees never challenged the world, and the Pharisees never got involved with the world. All three attitudes have their counterpart today, as you know.

But Jesus and the apostles saw none of these paths as proper for Christians in this fallen world. Rather, they set before us in essence the original cultural mandate, pointed up by the four imperatives that follow:

*Discern what is good and what is bad about the world*. As we saw earlier, God made the cosmic order genuinely good. When Paul says, 'Everything God created is good' (1 Timothy 4:4), he is merely echoing Genesis 1. It is the Manichaean heresy to affirm that the world of matter, physical life, and sensory pleasure is valueless and evil. Down the centuries that heresy has haunted Christian minds and produced many ugly things: a false antithesis between the material and the spiritual; false guilt about enjoying food, physical comfort, and sex in marriage; glorification of dirt, seediness, and uncouthness; pride in one's world-denying asceticism; contracting out of the arts and all cultural endeavour ('not spiritual, you know'); and so on. But the truth of the goodness of creation teaches us to negate all such nastiness (for such it really is), and that we must learn to do.

However, the other side of the truth here is that the world of humankind has become genuinely bad through the moral and spiritual twisting of human nature. 'The play is the tragedy Man,' and the tragedy centers in the fact that our sinfulness is precisely good gone wrong, nobility befouled, real value really wasted. The bitter fruit of the fall is that now human relations are disrupted (Cain kills Abel, and Lamech proclaims jungle law as early as Genesis 4); people exploit and swindle each other and enjoy inflicting cruelty and violence; community struc - tures are disrupted by self-seeking; science is made to serve selfish ambition; the fine arts are used to undermine morality; and the nightmar - ish state of things summarized in Romans 1:26–31 is found to be a realistic description of all societies at all times.

The created values of human life must not be confused with its acquired corruptions, nor must the requirements of righteousness be forgotten as we focus on the habits of fallen humankind – or we shall never know how to act rightly in God's world. Unprincipled acquies - cence in corrupt manners and customs, based on the assumption that whatever is, is right, is not the way to be, and we must not allow thoughtless empathy to make us imagine that it is.

*Understand Christian liberty and responsibility in the world*. The freedom of the Christian was a New Testament and Reformation emphasis that is often obscured today. What it meant was that Christians are not bound to the law in any form as a system of salvation, nor to any of the typical rites and restrictions that God imposed under the old covenant (cf. Galatians 4:21–5:1,13), and that no use of created things for enrichment and enjoyment is defiling, provided the user shows gratitude to the God from whom these benefits come (1 Timothy 4:3–5).

But this privilege of drawing joy from what one now knows to be one's Father's world must be exercised responsibly; otherwise, we sin. Responsible use of freedom limits one's action to what is helpful spiritually to oneself and others (1 Corinthians 6:12; 8:9, 13; 10:23, 31–11:1). It restricts one to what best serves the glory of God and the good of others, and forbids one to let the merely permissible become the enemy of that best, elbowing it out for the sake of a lesser good. It will often be a more responsible use of freedom to say no to the permissible, just because it would not have a good effect on others, than to say yes to it just in order to make the point that it is indeed permitted under the gospel. Christian liberty must never be swallowed up by subcultural legalism, but neither may it ever degenerate into sub-Christian license. We shall never know how to act rightly in God's world until we are clear on this.

*Distinguish the use from the misuse of the world*. 'Using' the world (Paul's phrase, 1 Corinthians 7:31) means dealing constructively with the people and the resources that constitute one's personal environment. It means involvement, planning, and toil in the task of creating wisdom, welfare, and wealth for oneself and others. Misusing or abusing the world means being enslaved by these activities so that, in effect, they become our idols and we live for them as activities, rather than seeing them as means of honouring and praising the God who led us to them.

Enslavement to activities is worldliness in its purest form: the compul - sive workaholism that I described is as worldly as is any form of laziness. It needs to be better understood than it sometimes is that whether persons are worldly or not depends not on how much pleasure they take from life, but on the spirit in which they take it. If we let pleasant things engross us so that we forget God, we are worldly. If we receive them gratefully with a purpose of pleasing God by our appreciation and use of his gifts, we are not worldly but godly. Worldliness is the spirit that substitutes earthly goals (pleasure, profit, popularity, privilege, power) for life's true goal, which is the praise of God. For a human being to receive praise is not worldly, but it is worldly to angle for praise and applause, to find one's highest happiness in having people compliment and admire you and to lose sight of the fact that the ultimate recipient of praise for all the good things humans are praised for should always be the Creator himself. Only when the peril of worldliness is truly understood and avoided, and the nonworldly use of the world is truly practiced, can our commerce with the created order become a fulfilment of the Creator's calling to Christian believers.

*Value the people as distinct from the ways of the world*. Society's ways are bad, due to sin, and people need to be rescued from them. Jude was making this point very bluntly when he said: 'Snatch others from the fire and save them; to others show mercy, mixed with fear – hating even the clothing stained by corrupted flesh' (Jude 23). Redirecting the misdirected lives of those whom our grandfathers called 'precious souls' belongs to the work of evangelism, which is always the first and basic form of social service and the first item of the Christian calling in the secular community.

Loving sinners and hating their sins, sharing our faith with them to save them from the fire while feeling awed horror at the despite done to God by the filthy things they have dabbled in, is the prime task that God sets his people in every age, and no amount of concern for wider cultural involvements must be allowed to displace it from its priority.

Cultural endeavour without evangelism is one stage worse than evangelism without cultural endeavour, for the concentration on evan - gelism does at least put first things first. But evangelism with cultural endeavour, making common cause with others when they fight for what is right in society, while mounting opposition against them when they go after what is wrong, is the proper formula for fulfilling the Christian's calling in God's world.

I do not say that the discharge of this dual mandate can be made easy or straightforward. I know that in our day at least, it cannot. The Western societies in which we are called to serve God as his stewards of creation and his Samaritans to those in spiritual and material need are whirling maelstroms of sectional selfishness, economic exploitation, utopian un - naturalism, crushing collectivism, rival power plays, moral cynicism and manipulative corner cutting at every turn. Such conditions are bound constantly to hamper and thwart us, but they must never induce us to stop. It is our business to persist faithfully in our God-given role in the world as the salt that preserves it and the light that guides it, and not to be daunted if our labour feels like a drop in a bucket that makes no difference at all. One day our Master's 'Well done' will more than make amends for any discouragements that we may suffer here and now.

And should not that be enough for us? Let us, like Nehemiah, first pray, and then give ourselves to our task.

# Chapter 24

# The Means of Growth

Last words are ordinarily solemn words. Here are Peter's last recorded words at the end of his second letter: 'Grow in the grace and knowledge of our Lord and Saviour Jesus Christ. To him be glory both now and forever! Amen.'

This gives us our subject: growing in grace and the means of growth. I expect that you speak of spiritual growth often and that you think it is important. You are right. It is important. Why? This is not only because personal growth has become of great concern in the secular world these days, but chiefly because, as we know from the Bible, the growth of God's children is a central concern of God himself. The Christian life begins with new birth, and birth is meant to issue in growth.

In the New Testament growth in grace is a *fact*. Here, for instance, is Paul at the beginning of 2 Thessalonians praising God for the way in which the Thessalonian believers had grown: 'We ought always to thank God for you, brothers . . . because your faith is growing more and more, and the love every one of you has for each other is increasing' (2 Thess. 1:3).

We find further that growth in grace is a *goal* for which the apostles prayed and to which they gave direction. Thus Paul, in 1 Thessalonians 3:12, had prayed exactly for that for which he was praising God at the beginning of the second letter, as we have just seen. He prayed, 'May the Lord make your love increase and overflow for each other and for everyone else.' He prayed that they might increase in love, and he was seeing the answer to his prayers when he later praised God that they were, in fact, so increasing. Colossians 1:10 and Philippians 1:9–11 show Paul praying that believers might grow in faith and love and abound in good works. Peter, from whom we took the words with which we started, gave directions for growth at the beginning of his first letter, saying, 'Like newborn babes, crave pure spiritual milk [that is, the Word of God], so that by it you may grow up in your salvation' (1 Pet. 2:2).

Growing in grace is also *commanded*. 'Grow in grace!' says Peter using the imperative mood. To grow in grace is not an option, but an order.

THE MEANS OF GROWTH was originally published in *Tenth*, (Philadelphia: Tenth Presbyterian Church), July, 1981, pp. 2–11. Reprinted by permission.

The wife of one of my colleagues recently had a baby. You know what joy it is to parents for the first few weeks to have a baby. But just imagine, if the months and years went by and the baby never grew. Imagine that at the end of, shall we say, five or ten years the baby was still eighteen inches long, lying helpless in a cradle, not having grown. No one would be rejoicing then. It would seem a tragedy. It is equally horrible when the children of God, newborn babes in Christ, fail to grow toward the stature of their Savior. As Arthur Pink once said, 'It brings no glory to God that his children should be dwarfs.'

## Foundations for Growth

I have four things to speak about in trying to spell out the meaning of spiritual growth: its foundations, some mistakes about it, its dimensions, and its means. Let me speak first of the foundations, the presupposed realities which determine the shape and nature of the growth process.

Three basic facts constitute the foundations of growth in grace. Fact number one is *regeneration by the Holy Spirit's new birth*, what Paul in Titus 3:5 calls 'rebirth and renewal by the Holy Spirit.' When people turn to God we call it conversion. But we know that God works in people to make them will and do of his good pleasure, and it is only because he so works that we do turn to God. So our turning to God in repentance and faith is equally God turning us to himself by the sovereign work and power of his Holy Spirit. When we think of this great change as our turning to God, we call it conversion. When we think of it as God turning us to himself, we call it regeneration or new birth.

Conversion and regeneration are then the same great change of direction, viewed, however, from two different angles. Not all Re-formed theologians have said it quite like that. But John Owen, the Puritan, who of all English-speaking theologians seems to me the greatest, saw and expounded it that way. He has convinced me. He said that conversion is my action, psychologically speaking. But he added that it is equally God's work in me and that he must have all the praise and glory for it.

God's work of regeneration then, of which conversion is the psycho-logical form, is the first foundation of growth in grace. Through regen-eration we become new creatures, indwelt by the Holy Spirit who wrought this great change in us. Growth in grace means going on from there; it is the living out, maturing and ripening of what God wrought in us when he turned us to himself.

Alongside this first foundation is a second: *justification by grace*. Regeneration and justification — that is, our pardon and acceptance by God — are two facts which go together. The passage from which I took the phrase, 'rebirth and renewal by the Holy Spirit' is really on justification. It begins in Titus 3:4.

> When the kindness and love of God our Savior appeared he saved us, not because of righteous things we had done [there were no such deeds], but because of his mercy. He saved us through the washing [that consists] of *rebirth and renewal by the Holy Spirit*, whom he poured out on us generously through Jesus Christ our Savior so that, *having been justified by his grace*, we might become *heirs* having the hope of eternal life. This is a trustworthy saying (vv.4–8).

You see the links here. With new birth goes justification. And with justification goes adoption into God's family and our instatement as God's heirs. Now, therefore, we are God's children. His law is now our family code and no longer an oppressive burden as it was before we were converted. It is now an expression of our Father's will which we delight to keep because we want to please the One who loved us and saved us. So it is for all who are justified, and growth in grace is growth into this glad obedience.

The third fact, which goes with the first two, is: *incorporation into* Christ. As Paul says in Galatians 3:27: 'All of you who were baptized into Christ have been clothed with Christ.' Now we are in Christ, united to him for time and eternity. Again, he says in 1 Corinthians 12:13: 'We were all baptized by one Spirit into one body [the body of Christ, which is the fellowship of all believing people].' Now we are members of Christ's body in the basic scriptural sense of being his limbs, for that is what 'members' means in the New Testament: limbs, organs, parts in the body of Christ. The head, Christ himself, animates and nourishes the whole so that the whole fellowship, as Paul said in Ephesians 4:16, 'grows and builds itself in love.' Our growth in grace is growth within the overall growth of the body. Christians ordinarily grow in a context of fellowship, not apart from that context.

Our individual growth in grace, which rests upon these three things, is that work of God in our lives that is pictured in 2 Corinthians 3:18 – our being changed from glory to glory by the Lord who is the Spirit. We call it sanctification, but growth in grace is an equally proper name for it. This is the 'good work' which Paul says he trusts God to complete in the lives of those in whom he has begun it (Phil. 1:6).

From another standpoint, it is the work of God in bringing forth in us what in Galatians 5:22 is called 'the fruit of the Spirit . . . love, joy, peace, patience, kindness, goodness, faithfulness, gentleness and self-control.' As we look at those qualities we realize that they are a profile of Jesus Christ in the lives of his followers. Growing in grace means that this profile of the Savior, this reflection of his lovely and glorious character, becomes more and more what we are in our character, attitudes and conduct.

## Mistakes About Growth

God's people sometimes make mistakes when thinking about spiritual growth, mistakes which can be a source of real trouble unless one is aware of them and takes care to avoid them. Here are three.

*Mistake number one: to suppose that growth in grace is measurable in the way that physical growth is measurable.* My son, when he was fifteen, liked from time to time to stand against the post of one of the doors in our home, level a pencil across the top of his head and mark his height there. The post now bears a series of different marks, each dated, showing how he has been growing over the years. Again, if you have a scale, you can use it to check how your children are increasing in weight from one month to another. That is how it is in our physical lives. But what we are talking about is a work of God which centers in our hearts at a level deeper than consciousness will take us.

There is a divine mystery in the work by which God makes us grow in grace. We cannot measure it by any simple, regular technique of assessment like measuring height or checking weight. What Scripture shows is this. Growth in grace is known by the way we behave under pressure, when times of testing and temptation come, when the heat is on and there is a crisis. Then our reaction and behavior show whether we have been growing in grace or not.

Let me show what I mean from Scripture. Here is Abraham. At the age of seventy-five he was promised a son. He and his wife were childless, but God undertook to give him an heir. He has waited eleven years, and now is eight-six and his wife is only a few years younger. They cannot wait any longer. Their faith cracks. Sarah says to Abram, 'Look, I shall never have a child. You have a son by Hagar, my maid, and then that child will count as ours, and thus the promised heir will appear.'

Thus Abram and Sarah conspired together to play the amateur providence and bring God's promise to pass by unhallowed means. And they did it! Ishmael was born. But God never accepted Ishmael. It was just a sad mistake, a testimony to immaturity in the life of faith.

But follow the story on a little. Isaac has arrived – his parents about one hundred years old at the time – and Isaac is now a teenager, and Abram is a very elderly man indeed. Now we read in Genesis 22: 'God tested Abraham. He said to him, "Abraham . . . take your son, your only son Isaac, whom you love, and go to the region of Moriah. Sacrifice him there as a burnt offering" ' (vv.1,2). Do you suppose that ever a father's heart hurt more than Abraham's heart hurt as he tramped up the mountain with Isaac? Do you suppose that any servant of God has ever felt more strongly, 'This word from God is crazy'? Hardly. But Abraham had grown over the years, and this time he trusted God to know what he was doing. He was prepared at God's command to endure even the death of his son. This is the behavior of a man who has ripened in grace. It is our behavior under pressure that shows whether we have been growing in grace or not.

I remember some years ago talking to a clergyman friend of mine who only two days before had been confronted by a woman in a counseling appointment in his vestry. She had tried to seduce him there, and he was still literally shaking as he thought of it. He had resisted. But it was a shattering temptation, a real trauma for him. That is what I mean when I speak of crisis times, sudden testings, which show whether we have got our roots well down into the grace of God or not. Just as the high winds show whether trees have a good root system or not – if they have not, they get blown over – so do the times of testing show whether we have a good, strong, spiritual root system anchored firmly in our Lord Jesus Christ.

Let us not make any mistake here. Growth in grace cannot be measured by any simple process of assessment, but it will be tested, as sure as eggs are eggs. It is for us to seek to walk with God in a way which guarantees that when the temptation comes it will find us rooted firmly in him. Then we shall find with the temptation 'a way of escape,' just as Abraham, in fact, found that he was not required to kill Isaac after all.

*Mistake number two is to suppose that growth in grace is a uniform process* . It is not so. There are growing times, when a person grows in the Lord much more rapidly than at other times. God, who finds us all different from each other when his grace first touches us, deals with different Christians in different ways.

Let me illustrate this from Scripture. Consider Peter. When Jesus called Peter he was a bluff, hearty, warm-hearted, open-handed leadership type, as we would say. But he had one area of weakness. He was impulsive, headstrong and unstable. Thus he suffered from what I call 'foot-in-mouth' disease, frequently saying foolish things which he had not thought out, and then not standing by them. On the evening of Jesus' betrayal he said to the Lord, 'Though they all forsake you, I won't.' But within a few hours of saying that, he was thrown into panic by a servant girl's questions and denied his master three times. That was the blackest moment of Peter's pilgrimage. He went out, it says, and wept bitterly.

But now the crucified Jesus rises, ascends to heaven and pours out the Spirit. What happens? From the day of Pentecost onward Peter is a transformed man. Very suddenly, at the point of his greatest weakness, he has grown. Now what he says is wise and weighty, and he is the anchor-man of the early church, the real rock-man. ( *Petros* means 'rock.') Now he is fulfilling the role to which the name Jesus gave him had pointed. Oh, he still made mistakes. Paul calls attention to one of them in Galatians 2. But in the making of his character there had been a sudden and dramatic advance.

Now think about John. When Jesus first knew John, John was a fierce fellow. Jesus nicknamed him Boanerges, 'the son of thunder.' I guess John was one of those men with great, black, bushy eyebrows that meet in the middle. He had zeal, but it was a savage, fierce zeal. At the end of John's life, however, we find him writing three letters into a situation in which some folks were claiming to be more spiritual than others and had split a church. He writes to folk who had remained loyal to the apostolic teaching to reassure and encourage them. In this situation, where we might have expected John to knit his brows and speak very fiercely about those who had left, we find in him instead the gentleness and restraint that mark him out as the apostle of love. He still sees spiritual issues in black and white. There is still a zeal for the Lord in everything he says. But the gentleness of love marks his spirit.

What happened? Over the years, gradually, one would suppose, John has been transformed so that no longer is he a son of thunder but he breathes instead the very spirit of Christlike affection and concern. This is growth in grace, but it is a different process from the sudden transformation that took hold of Peter.

Those who compare themselves with each other, says Paul in one place, are not wise. One reason why this is so is that God does not deal with us all at just the same points, at just the same time, nor at just the same pace. If we want to measure ourselves, let us rather ask: What am I able to do because I am a Christian living in the faith and strength of Christ today that I was never able to do before I was a Christian?

It is no great thing if a person who was nice before he was converted remains nice afterward. But it is a triumph of grace when a person like Peter, who was unstable as water before Pentecost, is suddenly turned into a strong, steady man. What do you find yourself able to do through Christ today which you were never able to do before? If you have an answer to that question, you have a testimony to a real measure of growth in grace. You are not assessing it in any absolute way, but you are finding in yourself the proof that God is indeed at work in you.

*Mistake number three is to suppose that growth in grace is automatic*; to suppose that it is something you need not bother about because it will look after itself, something which is guaranteed, particularly if you are a professional minister, missionary or church officer. The enemy wants to encourage all who seek to serve God to take it for granted that as we do our job we shall automatically grow and mature in Christ and therefore need not bother about sanctification at all. He wants to encourage us to think this way because, if we are not striving to grow, we are actually in danger of doing the very opposite, namely, shrinking as a person behind the role we play.

Growth in grace means, among other things, that you are becoming more richly and robustly *human* than you were before. That is what it means to be changed from one degree of glory to another, so that more and more you will bear the image of Jesus Christ, the perfect man. Those of us who minister, I think, have over the years erred greatly here. We have concentrated on our role, and as individuals we have so often shrunk. My wife has sometimes had to say to me, 'I don't want your ministry; I want you.' What she is telling me when she says this is that I have been treating her in an official way rather than leveling with her and letting her level with me as spouses should. She is right to insist on that.

Here is a limerick which calls attention in a rather jocular way to the sad fact that many Episcopal clergy (of which I am one) fall short of this increasing humanness:

> To his bishop a rector once said,
> 'May I take off my collar in bed?'
>    His bishop said, 'No,
>    You may not do so,
> You must wear it until you are dead.'

I feel that this is what some of my Episcopal brethren are clearly resolved to do. I say this as a warning: growth in grace has to do with your personal life as distinct from the role you play in the church. We must not assume that growth will look after itself and proceed automatically if it is not our conscious concern.

## Dimensions of Growth

Now a word about some of the dimensions of growth, those Christlike qualities which will increasingly appear in us if we are growing in grace.

Quality number one: *praising God*. Those who are growing in grace increase in the spirit of doxology and worship. They are less and less self-absorbed and self-concerned. There is a kind of balance effect that operates here. If your pride and conceit are rising, your concern about praising God will be diminishing. But if your passion for praise is growing, then your sense of your own dignity will decline. You will be following in the footsteps of Paul who, writing to the Corinthians about A.D. 57 or 58, spoke of himself as the 'least of the apostles'; who, writing to the Ephesians about A.D. 61 or 62, spoke of himself as 'less than the least of all saints'; and who, writing to Timothy about A.D. 65 or 66, spoke of himself as the 'chief of sinners.' These phrases show that his estimate of himself was going down. As a result, in his letters he increasingly breaks out into doxology, which shows how passionately his heart longed to exalt and praise God. There is no growth in grace without increase in the spirit of humble praise.

Second, one grows in the spirit of *enduring*. Or, as the English Bible has for centuries rendered it, one grows in patience – steady endurance when the pressure is on. You see it in the Savior as his enemies closed in on him and the opposition increased toward the end of his ministry. That did not stop him. He endured. You see it in the apostles and in everyone else who is growing in grace. Hebrews was a letter written to Christians under pressure, Jewish Christians who were running the gauntlet of persecution from unconverted Jews. The writer says to them, 'You need to persevere so that when you have done the will of God, you will receive what he has promised' (Heb. 10:36). There is no growth in grace without increase in power to endure.

Third, growth in grace means an increase in the spirit of *loving* whereby you care for others and actually lay out your time, trouble, strength, prayers and every other resource to help them. The Lord is our model here. This was the kind of ministry he had throughout. He ever lived in terms of the principle that it is God first, others second, oneself last. Even on the cross, in his final agony, he was still concerned for others. When they nailed him to the cross he prayed for the soldiers who were doing it. As he hung on the cross he saw his mother and told John to look after her. When the penitent thief spoke to him he said, 'Today you will be with me in Paradise' (Luke 23:43). This was love – self-giving to the uttermost. There is no growth in grace without an increase of Christlike love.

The fourth dimension of growth, which we see also in the Savior and in the apostles, Paul in particular, is *contending*, contending for God's truth against error. The one who grows in grace learns to fight for God's truth for the sake of people, and to do it in love, yet with firmness against the error itself, as Paul did when he wrote to the Galatians and the Colossians. His was a fighting spirit – not, however, the spirit of the firebrand who fights irresponsibly and cantankerously and disrupts churches, not the spirit of the cross-grained man you can never get along with – but a spirit of pastoral contention fighting for truth for the sake of people and their spiritual welfare.

## Means of Grace

Finally, what are the means of growth, the means whereby this work of God is carried on in your life and mine? Theological text books normally speak of 'the means of grace,' a medieval phrase that the Reformers held on to in order to express the thought that through these particular activities God does work to transform our lives.

The means of grace are usually listed something like this: *Bible truth*, preached and received through preaching, studied in the text, meditated on, applied to oneself, taken to heart, laid up in the memory, taken as a guide for life; *prayer*, the regular exercise of communion and fellowship with God; *worship* with the Lord's people, particularly at the Lord's Supper but also in hearing the Word regularly proclaimed and joining in the prayers and the vocal praise; and the *informal fellowship* and interchange of the Lord's family as one stands by and ministers to another.

As we approach the study of these growth activities, we need to remember first that growth which comes from God through these means comes only as in using them we look beyond them to the Lord himself, asking him to bless for our spiritual welfare what we are doing. If we suppose that sharing in these activities, 'using the means of grace,' as we say, has a magic of its own, if, that is, we suppose that we can trust the means of grace to guarantee our growth automatically, we will be off the track and will not grow in grace, however much we listen to sermons, pray and go through the motions of fellowship with God and our Christian brethren. We must use the means of grace spiritually, as opposed to using them superstitiously. We are to grow precisely *in the knowledge of our Lord and Savior Jesus Christ* to whom our eyes and our trust must be directed in everything. This is what it really means to grow in grace – that you do have your eyes on the Lord and your hope in the Lord all the time, and so are coming constantly to know him better.

Second, growth in grace is always growth by grace and under grace, never beyond grace. And grace means God enriching sinners. That is who we are. We do not grow beyond grace. We never get to a point where we can cease to thank God for Calvary on a day-to-day basis and humble ourselves before him as hell-deserving sinners. There is no sinless perfection in this life. Sinless perfection is part of the hope of glory. Here, the best the Lord enables us to do is less than perfect, and we must constantly ask God to forgive what is defective. Can you receive that insight? It is basic, I believe, to a true view of this matter. If you have understood the second half of Romans 7 where we see Paul at his best, reaching out after perfection and then lamenting that his reach exceeds his grasp, you will appreciate what I am saying. However much we use the means of grace, we shall never cease to be in this life hell-deserving sinners living daily by pardon. And God forbid that we should ever be found thinking in any other terms!

Real growth in grace will bring you consciously closer to Jesus Christ day by day, and that indeed will be one of the signs that God really is at work in your life. As you see him more clearly, love him more dearly and follow him more nearly, you will grow in the knowledge of your Savior, sin-bearer, example, master, and source of all the strength and power you need to follow in his steps.

God grant that we may grow in the grace and knowledge of Christ more and more every day of our lives.

# Chapter 25

# Seeing God in the Dark

## How do you Find Strength in God
## when your World is in Ruins?

The scene is familiar: You see it with heartbreaking regularity on TV. A strong, rugged man stands beside a pile of burnt-out rubble that was once his home. He is in tears. He does not know where his family is or even if they are still alive. He has nowhere to turn for food or help. We find him pitiful and pathetic, but we are glad we are not in his shoes.

Where is this scene? Beirut? Baghdad? Dubrovnik? No, we are in Ziklag, a little Philistine town some forty miles southwest of Jerusalem. It is just over three thousand years ago, about 1015 B.C. The man is David, who later will be Israel's king. But at this point he is in his late twenties – a refugee, an outlaw, and a failed leader who seems doomed.

What has happened? The story is this. (See 1 Samuel 30:1–6.) David, fleeing for his life from King Saul, had offered his services and those of his six hundred men to King Achish, a local Philistine potentate, as a kind of Foreign Legion. Achish had given them Ziklag for their home, and they had all brought their families and settled there. They had marched with the rest of Achish's troops to a pan-Philistine muster against Israel. But Achish's colleagues had refused to trust David and his men in a battle against their own people and had sent them packing.

Already depressed (for no army can be told it is not trusted without damage to its morale), they had trekked back to Ziklag and found it a smoking ruin. Desert raiders, Amalekites, had sacked it, burned it, and taken captive as slaves everyone they had found there. Six hundred homes and families were simply gone; hence, the tears of fury and pain. 'David and his men wept aloud until they had no strength left to weep' (1 Sam. 30:4).

SEEING GOD IN THE DARK was originally published in *Discipleship Journal*, Vol. 69, 1992. Reprinted by permission.

When people are smarting under an unexpected hurt, they want to relieve their feelings by finding a scapegoat, someone to blame. It was so here. David's men got ugly and turned on their leader. They blamed him, one supposes, for being so preoccupied with pleasing Achish that he had marched every single able-bodied man to the muster, thus failing both them and their families by not leaving a guard to fend off raiders. Think of living in the old Wild West where Indians and bandits roamed; men went armed, and women and children never traveled save in the company of someone with a gun. It was that sort of world, and David's error of judgment had been real. So we move to the point where 'David was greatly distressed because the men were talking of stoning him; each one was bitter in spirit because of his sons and daughters' (v.6).

## Despair among the Ruins

We can see what was going through David's mind as he stood, alone and tearful, by the ruins of his house. His great distress was compounded by several things.

There was personal loss: His own home and his own two wives were gone. But that was only the start of it.

There was, for sure, the recognition that through lack of forethought he had indeed failed his men and their dependents. Nothing is more distressing to a good man or a real leader (David was both) than knowing you have let down those who trusted you.

There was his total isolation. Now not only Saul and the Philistines but his own men, too, had turned against him. Universal hostility, leaving you with no one to whom you can even talk on equal terms, is hard to bear.

There was the apparent hopelessness of the situation. The Amalekites had come on camels, and David and his men were on foot. They were already exhausted from their three-day, forty-mile march. What hope was there of catching the raiders, even if David could be sure where they had gone?

Also, there was, quite certainly, a crushing sense of God's judgment. For David had played a double game with Achish. To curry favour with his Philistine patron, he had plundered villages, massacred their inhabi-tants, given Achish the booty, and told him the raids had been made in Israelite territory. In fact, the raids had been against people who had nothing to do with Israel, including – yes! – Amalekites (1 Sam. 27:8). While the deception prospered, David had doubtless assured himself that he was being super-smart and that killing Amalekites was the Lord's business anyway (see Deut. 26:17–19). But deep down, he knew that this callous, Machiavellian banditry – for banditry is what it was – merited God's vengeance. And when he saw what the Amalekites had done to

Ziklag, his conscience told him that this poetic justice was in fact the vengeance he had provoked.

David, then, was in a state of distress of a kind that might well have destroyed him. The shock of disaster, grief at one's loss, collapse of one's life-strategy, and a sense of undergoing just retribution can each of them have paralyzing effects, and here they were all together. 'Heartache crushes the spirit' (Prov. 15:13); 'a crushed spirit who can bear?' (Prov. 18:14).

Misery is the natural consequence of calamity, and paralyzing despair is the natural child of misery. David's surrender to grief was an entirely natural reaction to what had happened. In his shoes, we would have done the same, and many can testify that in similar circumstances they did exactly that. Distress – depression – desperation is a natural downhill slide.

Had David stopped there, it would have been the end of his career as a leader and probably of his life. But he did not stop there. Challenging and finally overcoming the paralysis that grief was generating, we now see in David the spiritual reaction of faith. 'But' – it is one of the great Bible 'buts' – 'David found strength (*RSV*, "strengthened himself") in the LORD his God' (v.6).

How did he do it?

## The Secret of Strength

'He prayed,' suggests someone. Yes, in due course, he did. But that, I am sure, was not what came first. When feelings of despair overwhelm you, rational prayer is beyond you. You are like a person being swept downstream towards the falls; you must recover your footing on the stream bed or you are lost. The secret of recovering your footing spiritually at such a time lies in the little word *think*, and that was undoubtedly where David began. He thought. He did not wait to feel better, but argued with the emotions that were telling him all was lost. He made himself recall what he knew of God and thought out how it all applied to him at that moment. Thus he 'found strength' in the Lord; thus he calmed his soul; thus he prepared himself to pray.

'Strengthened by thought' is the formula that fits. The medievals would have called David's action meditating, and the Puritans would have described it as preaching to oneself. Less important than deciding what to call it is learning to do it. It is a discipline we all need to master.

Every time we pray, it is wise first to remind ourselves, deliberately, of who and what God is and how we stand related to him through his covenant love. Never is this more necessary than when we are reeling under the impact of some shock or being deafened by the inward screams of desire or panic or pain. David acted on this wisdom. Setting himself to think he made his rational faith reassert itself over his runaway feelings.

He let his faith tell him what to think, and when he knew what to think, he could see what to do. He was in this a model of godly wisdom.


## Five Steps to Recovery

I now offer a reconstruction of the series of thoughts that he forced into his disoriented, despairing heart as he stood in lonely isolation in ruined Ziklag, surrounded by men who, he knew, had mutiny and murder in mind. It is, of course, guesswork but it is not wild guesswork. The psalms show us the logic of David's faith clearly enough to warrant every suggestion I shall make.

I believe that David ran before his mind five thoughts, as follows:

### 1. My God reigns

He thought of God's sovereign power. He reminded himself that God is in total control of all that happens on earth, and that having brought him into this extremity, God was certainly able to bring him out of it. Remembering God's omnipotence was the first step in recovering his footing.

The psalms are strong on God's sovereignty and dominion. 'The LORD does whatever pleases him' (Ps. 135:6; cf. 115:3). 'The seas [emblem of chaos] have lifted up O LORD . . . their voice . . . their pounding waves. Mightier than the thunder of the great waters, mightier than the breakers of the sea – the LORD on high is mighty' (Ps. 93:3–4). Or, more simply, 'The LORD reigns' (Ps. 93:1, 96:10, 97:1, 99:1, 146:10). All Scripture agrees that a God who is only in control of things half the time is a figment of a disordered imagination. The beginning of stability for us all is to know that God is on the throne, that his eye is on us and his hand over us all the time. Nothing comes our way apart from his will. In the deepest sense everything is under control.

### 2. My God forgives

David thought of God's pardoning mercy. He recalled that 'with you there is forgiveness, therefore you are feared.' In other words, right-minded reverence is rooted in a knowledge of God's mercy in the remitting of one's sins (Ps. 130:4). My guess is that David's first breath of prayer was a plea for forgiveness for the callous killings involved in his bamboozling of Achish. Certainly, he dwelt on the truth that it is God's glory to forgive the penitent and that no sin is too great to be forgiven. He knew that no chastened transgressor need ever forfeit his hope of restoration and a future with God. And as David thought along these lines, his footing grew firmer.

All Scripture confirms what David knew. 'The blood of Jesus . . . purifies us from all sin . . . If we confess our sins, he is faithful and just [in keeping his word both to us who sinned and to the Son who died to save us] and will forgive us our sins and purify us from all unrighteousness . . . He [Jesus] is the atoning sacrifice for our sins' (1 John 1:7,9; 2:2). For any who feel themselves under God's judgment, there is forgiveness just as soon as they confess and forsake the acts that provoked the judgment.

### 3. My God cares

David thought, too, of God's covenanted protection. 'The LORD is my shepherd' (Ps. 23:1). Himself a shepherd, David knew that the shepherd's job is precisely to look after the sheep, keeping them well-fed and safe at all times. So he must not suppose that men's alienation from him meant that God had abandoned him. Even in ruined Ziklag, God was with him to love and bless him. As David dwelt on this, his despair (I am sure) dissolved like melting snow.

All Scripture confirms what the Shepherd Psalm proclaims, namely the covenant care of God for his servants. 'In all things God works for the good of those who love him, who have been called according to his purpose' (Ro. 8:28). God's shaping of all that happens to believers so as to promote their 'good' – that is, their holiness and joy – is a fact, even when it does not look or feel so. 'Surely goodness and love will follow me all the days of my life' (Ps. 23:6). God's commitment to me, to be my God who shepherds me home, guarantees that.

### 4. My God is consistent

Is God unstable? Certainly not! So it may safely be inferred that, having proved his love to me in the past, he will do so again. David thought of his previous experiences of God's goodness and reasoned that, as John Newton puts it in his sublimely straightforward way,

> His love in time past
> Forbids me to think
> He'll leave me at last
> In trouble to sink;
> Each sweet Ebenezer
> I have in review
> Confirms his good pleasure
> To help me right through.

David had reasoned this way before Saul – 'the LORD who delivered me from the paw of the lion and the paw of the bear will deliver me from the hand of this Philistine' (1 Sam. 17:37). So now he told himself that his God, who saved him from the lion, the bear, Goliath, and Saul's spear (1 Sam. 19:9–10) would surely act again on his behalf in his present nightmare situation. For God does not lose interest in those he has once begun to love and bless.

Ebenezer was the name of a stone memorializing God's past help (1 Sam. 7:12). Every Christian should live by the Ebenezer principle – storing up memories of past mercies and bringing them to mind whenever reassurance about God's love is needed, as does the exile of Psalm 42:4–6 and the invalid of Psalm 77:4–12. In this way David found strength to face the pressures of the present, and so may we.

### 5. My God is faithful

Unlike humans, who from time to time let each other down, God always keeps his word. David must have called to mind God's explicit promises, such as (perhaps) Psalm 91:14–15:

> 'Because he loves me' says the LORD, 'I will rescue him;
> I will protect him, for he acknowledges my name.
> He will call upon me, and I will answer him;
> I will be with him in trouble,
> I will deliver him and honour him.'

David, we may confidently say, found strength in trusting the fidelity of his promise-keeping God.

Mapping the Christian life in *Pilgrim's Progress*, Bunyan pictures despair as giant imprisoning believers in Doubting Castle; but the Christian gets out of despair by using 'a key called Promise.' Exactly! Knowing that God's promises to us in Scripture are certain of fulfillment frees us from doubt and gives us strength to face the future.

## God My Strength

The strength (power) of God (Ps. 24:8, 31:2, 62:11) is what theologians call a communicable attribute – that is, a quality of God that in exercise imparts its own analogue or image to man. Thus, God's wisdom makes us wise; God's strength makes us strong. 'The LORD gives strength to his servants' (Ps. 29:11, cf. 84:5). The strength given is a capacity 'to do and to endure,' as the hymn puts it; a capacity that without God's empowering we would not have. As Giver of this strength, God is called 'my' or 'our' strength (Ps. 28:7, 46:1, 59:17, 73:26, 118:14, cf. Is. 12:2).

We have been watching God give David strength at Ziklag by stirring him to the resolute thought through which he 'found strength.' It was gratitude for such experiences that David was expressing when he declared, 'I love you, O LORD, my strength' (Ps. 18:1). And one way in which we today learn to love God is through our own experiences of being strengthened at crisis times in this same manner.

Just for the record, after David had 'found strength,' he prayed and got guidance that enabled him, against all expectations, to restore the situation completely (see the rest of 1 Samuel 30). To be sure, God does not always resolve our crises this way, but he always gives strength to cope to those who will learn to think as David thought. And that, for us, is what really matters.

# Chapter 26

# Westminster and the Roller Coaster Ride

When a Presbyterian tells you that the Westminster standards – that is, the Confession of Faith, the Larger and Shorter Catechisms, and the Directory for Public Worship drafted by the Westminster Assembly in the 1640s – are classics, you may not be very impressed. After all, these documents have become foundational for Presbyterian churches; would you not expect a Presbyterian to say they were good?

When, however, an Episcopal clergyman says the same, and gleefully points out that most members of the Assembly were Episcopal clergymen, and bewails the self-inflicted weakness of the Episcopal church through ignoring this part of its heritage, I hope you sit up and take notice. For I am that clergyman, and I come not to bury Westminster, as many do, but to praise it, and my present task is to draw out of the Confession wisdom that we need.

We experience life as a roller coaster ride – up, down, jolt, drop, lurch sideways, swing and sway, never steady – and a recurring syndrome nowadays is the feeling that whenever something we planned and counted on goes wrong, whenever (for instance) death claims one or someone becomes chronically ill, and whenever miraculous deliverances from disaster fail to materialize, this is a problem for faith. 'Can God be real and good when such things happen?' we ask; and we find ourselves doubting it.

Why do we feel this way? The source of our feeling is the idea that God ought to keep the Christian's life as trouble-free in this world as it will be in heaven; that in this fallen world he ought to stifle sins at birth so that society may enjoy the justice and peace at which lawmaking in democratic communities always aims; and that if he does not do these things it argues that he is either not fully in charge of his world or not really a God of love. So when trouble comes we feel deep doubts about God; and that, of course, makes handling the trouble twice as hard.

WESTMINSTER AND THE ROLLER COASTER RIDE was originally published in *Tabletalk* (Orlando: Walk Thru the Bible Ministries), Vol. 14, No. 3, March, 1990, pp. 6–10. Reprinted by permission.

I sympathize with the feelings – after all, I am a late twentieth-century human being myself – but I see them as utterly at variance with the facts, and I do not know a better way to show this than to quote, with minimal comment, the Westminster Confession's masterly Chapter 5, 'Of Provi - dence.' The Scripture proofs that bulk it up to five pages of close print in my copy have to be left out for space reasons, but the 500 words of the seven paragraph chapter itself shall be cited in full.

> *I. God the great Creator of all things doth uphold, direct, dispose, and govern all creatures, actions, and things, from the greatest even to the least, by His most wise and holy providence, according to His infallible foreknowledge, and the free and immutable counsel of His own will, to the praise of the glory of His wisdom, power, justice, goodness, and mercy.*

In other words, God exercises purposeful management and control over everything everywhere all the time, and nothing happens without his being involved. 'The LORD *reigns*.' We should believe, even when we cannot as yet see, that all events will eventually appear to us, from one standpoint or another, as matter for praise. God knows what he is doing, and is in the process of achieving something wise and good every moment. The glory of God through praise for his manifested praiseworthiness is God's goal throughout, and is guaranteed to be the final result.

> *II. Although, in relation to the foreknowledge and decree of God, the first cause, all things come to pass immutably and infallibly, yet, by the same providence, He ordereth them to fall out, according to the nature of second causes, either necessarily, freely, or contingently.*

This is saying that within the created world-system, everything operates according to its own built-in nature, and God keeps it that way (which is why it is possible to do as many do, and imagine the universe as a closed box of forces with God shut out, or perhaps not existing at all). In our case, God maintains in us the power of decision and action that he gave us when he made us. 'Free agency' is a better name for this power than 'free will,' because 'will' is such a slippery abstraction. (No, Virginia, we are not robots 'really.' Robots are not answerable for their actions as humans are. Biblical belief in God's lordship over our doings does not mean that our actions are really his and not really ours. Don't ever get mixed up about that.)

> *III. God, in His ordinary providence, maketh use of means, yet is free to work without, above, and against them, at His pleasure.*

So God can work miracles, today as yesterday, and doubtless sometimes does; though mostly he sustains rather than suspends the regularities of created nature, and therefore miracles can never be counted on.

*IV. The almighty power, unsearchable wisdom, and infinite goodness of God so far manifest themselves in His providence, that it extendeth itself even to the first fall, and all other sins of angels and men; and that not by a bare permission, but such as hath joined to it a most wise and powerful bounding [setting of limits], and otherwise ordering, and governing of them, in a manifold dispensation, to His own holy ends; yet so, as the sinfulness thereof proceedeth only from the creature, and not from God, who, being most holy and righteous, neither is nor can be the author or approver of sin.*

The point here is that in overruling and using moral evil for his own good ends, and so making it part of his plan, God remains innocent of blame for the evil itself. Guilt and blame belong to the rebel creatures who deliberately defy their Creator. So much Scripture makes clear, though without attempting to tell us all that was and is involved in God's sovereign decisions concerning sin – his decisions, that is, that have allowed and do allow to happen that which he hates and forbids. (You need to remember, Virginia, that we only know about God what he tells us; speculation gets us nowhere except into bewilderment, confusion, and error, so don't indulge in it. Just bear in mind, as you think about this, that God is now at work in and through Christ to eliminate the evil that for the moment he permits, within set limits, to exist, and he will not give up until all evil has become a thing of the past.)

*V. The most wise, righteous, and gracious God doth often times leave, for a season, His own children to manifold temptations, and the corruption of their own hearts, to chastise them for their former sins, or to discover unto them the hidden strength of corruption and deceitfulness of their hearts, that they may be humbled; and, to raise them to a more close and constant dependence for their support upon himself and to make them more watchful against all future occasions of sin, and for sundry other just and holy ends.*

So the inward aspect of the roller coaster ride turns out to be a preplanned maturing discipline to make us grow into a truer godliness and holiness. We might call it God's Upward Bound course, whereby he licks us into shape for future joys. Holiness here, happiness hereafter, is the principle that prompts his procedure. God does not shield us from trouble, but helps us in trouble and through trouble as he carries out his plan for our moral and spiritual growth. 'Before I was afflicted I went astray, but now I obey Your word . . . It was good for me to be afflicted so that I might learn your decrees' (Psalm 119:67, 71).

*VI. As for those wicked and ungodly men whom God, as a righteous Judge, for former sins, doth blind and harden, from them He not only withholdeth His grace whereby they might have been enlightened in their understandings, and wrought upon in their hearts; but sometimes also withdraweth the gifts which they had, and exposeth them to such objects as their corruption maketh occasion of sin; and, withal, gives them over to their own lusts, the temptations of the world, and the power of Satan, whereby it comes to pass that they harden themselves, even under those means which God useth for the softening of others.*

Keep in mind Pharaoh (Exodus 5–14) and the unbelieving Jews of New Testament times (Romans 9–11, etc.), and you will not have a problem with any of this.

*VII. As the providence of God doth, in general, reach to all creatures, so, after a most special manner, it taketh care of His church, and disposeth all things to the good thereof.*

In other words: In both the delightful and the dreadful things that happen, God preserves, protects, and provides for each believer in a way that promotes his plan for the mission and perfection of his people. To be more concerned on our roller coaster ride about the good of the church than for personal health, wealth, comfort, and convenience is thus truly godly, for it is truly Godlike. (Yes, Virginia, in God's reckoning the church matters most. Didn't you know?)

Such is Westminster wisdom on providence – concentrated biblical insight that will never go out of date. What a mercy it will be if it never any more falls out of our own minds and hearts!

# Chapter 27

# An Introduction to Systematic Spirituality

*Speaking from a newly founded Chair, I find myself freed from one embarrassment only to fall into another. I have no great predecessors to overshadow me; on the other hand, I must try (as the theatrical people say) to 'create the part.' The responsibility is heavy. If I miscarry, the University may come to regret not only my election – an error which, at worst, can be left to the great healer – but even, what matters very much more, the foundation of the Chair itself.*[1]

Thus C. S. Lewis began his inaugural lecture in Cambridge, in 1954, as the University's first Professor of Medieval and Renaissance literature; and I would make his words my own, merely substituting 'Regent College' for 'the University,' as I launch out on this, my own inaugural discourse as your first Sangwoo Youtong Chee Professor of Theology. I, too, have a part to create. Lewis' next sentence was: 'That is why I have thought it best to take the bull by the horns and devote this lecture to explaining as clearly as I can the way in which I approach my work.' With that also I identify; I propose in what follows to sketch out my own approach to my future work in the Chee Professorship; and I hope you will not take it amiss if I start anecdotally, for I think I can get furthest fastest by doing that.

## I

Moliére was the Alan Ayckbourn of his day, and in one of his comedies a character discovers that he has been talking prose all his life, and never

On December 11th, 1989, Dr. J. I. Packer was installed as the first Sangwoo Youtong Chee Professor of Theology at Regent College. This article is based on his inaugural lecture delivered on that occasion. AN INTRODUCTION TO SYSTEMATIC SPIRITUALITY was originally published in *Crux* (Vancouver: Regent College, 1990), XI, no. 1, March, pp. 2–8. Reprinted by permission.
[1] C. S. Lewis, 'De Description Temporal,' in *They Asked for a Paper* (London: Geoffrey Bles, 1962), p. 9.

knew it. When he makes the discovery he is as pleased as Punch. Some
years ago I made a similar discovery. A man said to me: 'These books of
yours, they're all spirituality, aren't they?' Up to that moment I had never
thought so; all my books had been commissioned for didactic, apologetic,
evangelistic, or controversial purposes, as their titles show. ( *Fundamentalism and the Word of God, Evangelism and the Sovereignty of God, God has
Spoken, God's Words*, do not sound like the titles of devotional books, do
they?) But when he said it I realized that he was right, and rejoiced
accordingly. I should have known all along that I was writing spirituality,
for the Puritan passion for application got into my blood quite early; I
have always conceived theology, ethics, and apologetics as truth for
people, and have never felt free to leave unapplied any truth that I taught,
whether orally or on paper; and to speak of the application of truth to life
is to look at life as itself a relationship with God; and when one does that,
one is talking spirituality. So the man spoke the truth, and I remain grateful
to him for helping me to appreciate what I was actually up to.

A definition of spirituality will help us at this point. I am using the
word in its twentieth-century Christian sense, according to which it
means, in the words of Henry Rack, 'enquiry into the whole Christian
enterprise of pursuing, achieving, and cultivating communion with
God, which includes both public worship and private devotion, and the
results of these in actual Christian life.'[2] By spirituality, therefore, I mean
the study of what Henry Scougal, in the title of his book which so
helped George Whitefield, called 'The Life of God in the Soul of Man';
or, putting it another way, the study of godliness in its root and in its
fruit. Prior to this century, spirituality went under a number of names:
Roman Catholics called it ascetic theology, from the Greek *askeo*, which
means to practise some discipline or routine; the Puritans called it
'practical divinity,' and also 'casuistical divinity,' because so much of it
had to do with 'cases,' that is, specific problems and anxieties of
conscience; mainstream Anglicans, from the seventeenth century on –
ward, called it 'moral' or 'devotional' theology; the Orthodox have
called it 'spiritual theology' or 'mystical theology' or, quite simply,
'spiritual life.'[3] Today, it is a field of specialist academic interest, with
its own journals, books, editions of key texts, and professional confer –
ences. It is also a focus of ecumenical, pastoral and devotional interest

[2] Henry Rack, *Twentieth Century Spirituality* (London: Epworth Press, 1969),
p. 2.
[3] For some historical background, see T. Wood, *English Casuistical Divinity during
the Seventeenth Century* (London: SPCK, 1952); T. McAdoo, *The Structure of
Caroline Moral Theology* (London: Longmans, 1949); V. Lossky, *The Mystical
Theology of the Eastern Church* (London: James Clarke, 1957); and ed. Gordon
S. Wakefield, *The Westminster Dictionary of Christian Spirituality* (Philadelphia:
Westminster Press, 1983), *passim*.

at lay level, hence the retreats, retreat centres, schools of prayer, and writings on the inner life that abound at the present time. All branches of the church are involved, and a great deal of wisdom is currently breaking surface. These may be lean days for some other of the church's endeavours, but they are good days for spirituality.

Back, now, to anecdote. When I came to join the Regent faculty in 1979 I was delighted to discover that my old friend Dr. Houston, who when he approached me about the job in 1976 had been Professor of Interdisciplinary and Environmental Studies, had shifted his field of interest, was in process of becoming Professor of Spiritual Theology, as he is now, and had started teaching the courses on spirituality and prayer that he teaches today. I had come prepared to offer Regent my own foundation course on the theology of the Christian life that I had been teaching in a British theological college since 1970, but now there was no need. It is a pleasure to contemplate, and celebrate, Dr. Houston's achievements in this field – his series of Classics of Faith and Devotion; [4] his recent book, *The Transforming Friendship*;[5] and the enormous influence that his classes and counselling have had on successive generations of Regent students. Regent has, in fact, set an example to other theological teaching institutions by its emphasis on spirituality, and its unwillingness that theology should ever be taught and learned in a way that, however much it enriches the head, impoverishes the heart. When people ask me, as they sometimes do, why I feel I belong at Regent, this emphasis on spirituality always bulks large in my answer.

What gives spirituality its special importance in the educational organism offered by Regent College? Regent is committed to two principles that mesh together – first, every-member ministry in the body of Christ; second, the priority of person over function (in other words, that what you are matters more than what you do and does in fact determine and delimit what you can do in ministry). Therefore, Regent people need wisdom and insight in the realm of spirituality for the following reasons at least:

First, as ministering servants of Jesus Christ we are required to be promoters and guardians of health and humanness among God's people, and we need spirituality for that. Let me explain.

When I say 'health,' I am thinking of spiritual health, and when I describe us as its promoters and guardians I am remembering the Puritan pastors, who saw their calling precisely as that of 'physicians of the soul.' Now, a would-be physician is set at an early stage to study physiology, so that she will understand the healthy functioning of the marvellously complex unit that we call the human body, and so become fit to move on to pathology, where she learns of the many ways in which a body that

---

[4] Portland: Multnomah Press, 1981.
[5] Oxford and Batavia: Lion Publishing, 1989.

is diseased, debilitated, or wounded can malfunction, and how to diagnose
and treat these malfunctionings. A moment's thought makes it obvious
that it has to be this way round. She cannot become competent in treating
bad health till she knows what constitutes good health, and can plot a
route for recovery of good health from the sick state in which she found
her patient. In the same way, we cannot function well as counsellors,
spiritual directors, and guides to birth, growth, and maturity in Christ
unless we are clear as to what constitutes spiritual well-being as opposed
to spiritual lassitude and exhaustion, and to stunted and deformed spiritual
development. It thus appears that the study of spirituality is just as
necessary for us who hope to minister in the gospel as is the study of
physiology for the medical trainee; it is something that we cannot really
manage without.

What has to be said about the need for spirituality in order that we
may fulfil our calling as promoters and guardians of humanness is
similar.[6] North American culture effectively lost God two generations
ago; now, by inevitable consequence, it is in the process of losing man.
What does it mean to be truly and fully human? The post-Christian
world around us no longer knows, and is being sucked down into deep
cultural decadence for lack of this knowledge. Biblical Christianity,
however, still has the answer, if anyone is still willing to listen. The
Bible proclaims that humanness is more than just having a mind and a
body; it is essentially a personal and relational ideal, the ideal of living
in the image of God, which means being like Jesus Christ in creative
love and service to our Father in heaven and our fellow men on earth.
When Scripture speaks of humans as made in God's image and thus as
being God's image-bearer, what it means is that each human individual
is set apart from the animal creation by being equipped with the personal
make-up, the conscious selfhood, feelings, brains, and capacity for
love-relationships, without which Christ-like holiness would be impos -
sible; as it is impossible, for instance, for cats and dogs. But Scripture
also speaks of the new creation of believing sinners, and defines this as
the motivational and dispositional renewing of us in Christ by the Holy
Spirit, and assures us that it is only through new creation that Christlike
holiness ever becomes actual.

We may state the matter this way: structurally, God's image in us is a
natural given fact, consisting of the rational powers of the human self, as
such; substantively, however, God's image in us is an ongoing moral
process, the fruit and expression of a supernatural character change from
self-centredness to God-centredness and from acquisitive pride to outgo -
ing love – a change that only Christians undergo. So the conclusion of

---

[6] I tried to make this point in *Knowing Man* (Westchester: Cornerstone, 1979),
and more fully with Thomas Howard in *Christianity: The True Humanism* (Waco:
Word Books, 1985).

the matter is that the true and full image of God is precisely godliness –
communion with God, and creativity under God, in the relational
rationality and righteousness that spring from faith, gratitude to one's
Saviour, and the desire to please and honour God and to be a means of
helping others; and the true goal of life is to know and receive and
cooperate with God's grace in Christ, through which our potential for
Christlikeness may be realized.

But who nowadays knows this? Secular humanism, which pretty much
controls the chief opinion making institutions in our culture – the media,
the press, the educational establishment, the arbiters of taste and fashion,
all in fact except the church itself – does not know it; secular humanism
may tolerate religion as a quaint private hobby for those who still want
it, but deep down it rejects religion in any form as dehumanizing, a
debilitating crutch that ideally no one would need because we would all
be able to stand on our own feet without it. The challenge to Christians,
and particularly perhaps to Regent people, with our announced concern
for integration of all life under God, is to show that Christianity – yes,
old-fashioned, self-denying, God-fearing, sin-hating, Christ-honouring,
Bible-believing, altruistic, monogamous, frugal Christianity – is the true
humanism, making for the authentic fulfilment and contentment of
human individuals.[7] But the making of this case is precisely a venture in
spirituality, and without some study of spirituality we are not likely to do
our job very well.

And then, secondly, in addition to needing some understanding of
spirituality – that is, of how God draws people into deeper fellowship
with himself in order that we can fulfil our purpose of witness and
ministry, we need it also for our own spiritual well-being. Not since
ancient Sparta have any people in any era shown such an obsessive
concern for physical well-being as I observe on the West Coast of North
America today. Have you, I wonder, been circularized as yet with a
request to subscribe to *The Wellness Letter*, put out from California's
Berkeley campus? Don't worry, friends, you will be, I am sure, before
very long; I have been thrice, already. *The Wellness Letter*, which is all
about physical and mental health, is a typical product of our times. Now,
should not we who are Christians be as concerned about the quality of
our relationship with God as the world is about the quality of its digestion
and muscle tone? Surely the question answers itself: of course we should!
But the resources we need for pursuing that concern are those provided
by the study of spirituality.

It appears, then, that all Regent College's characteristic interests do in
fact converge here; and for myself, as I have already indicated, I greatly
value Regent's pioneer role in setting spirituality at the centre of the
Christian curriculum, where it belongs.

---

[7]  This is the thesis which *Christianity: The True Humanism*, seeks to demonstrate.

## II

'But wait a minute,' says someone; 'your praise of spirituality is all very well, and it's nice to hear, but are you not a theologian?' (Well, yes, that is what I am supposed to be.) 'And have you not been employed at Regent these past ten years as a teacher of historical and systematic theology?' (Yes, I have.) 'And is it not in your capacity as a theologian that you have been appointed to the Chee Chair, which has attached to it a trust deed requiring you to (this is a quotation) "specialize within the area of systematic, philosophical, historical or ethical theology"? and is not this your inaugural lecture in that Chair?' (Yes, yes, it's all true.) 'Well then,' says my questioner, 'haven't you rather wandered off the point?'

Have I? Let me tell you a story. Cricket, as you know, is England's national game, and the phrase, 'the wars of the Roses,' is kept alive in England to describe the intense rivalry that marks the annual games between the counties of Lancashire and Yorkshire. At one of these encounters an enthusiast from the South of England was watching Lancashire bat well before a Yorkshire crowd. He applauded several scoring shots, with cries of 'Well played,' 'Good stroke,' and so forth, oblivious of the stony silence around him. Then he felt a tap on his shoulder, and the shoulder-tapper said: 'Art tha Lancashire?' 'No,' said he. 'Art tha Yorkshire?' 'No, I'm from London.' 'Then, lad, this is nowt to do wi' thee: *shut up*.' Have I, like the man from London, strayed into a world of concern where I have no business to be, and where my expressions of enthusiasm do not belong? Should I, as a theologian, keep clear of spirituality? Frankly, I do not think so, and the next stage in my argument requires me to tell you why. In order to make my point, however, I need now to don my professional theologian's hat in an explicit way, and back up a bit.

What is the subject-matter of systematic theology, and what is the proper method for studying it? My argument requires that I now block in my position on this pair of questions with some exactness; and the best way, I think, for me to do that is to review with you at the level of principle the two views on the subject that are most commonly met in North American Protestantism.

The first view, stated in terms of principle, is this: the proper subject-matter of systematic theology is Christian feelings and ideas about God, and the proper way of studying this material is threefold. It is partly exegetical, treating the New Testament in particular as the earliest example of Christian feelings and ideas; it is partly historical, tracing the forms that Christian feelings and ideas have taken down the centuries; and it is partly critical, letting present-day beliefs and belief-systems call in question thoughts and attitudes that belong to the Christian tradition and to suggest alternatives. This has been the generic view of Protestant subjectivists for two centuries, from the historical mysticism of Schleiermacher to the individualistic existentialism of Bultmann and the process theologians' mythology of God the poor struggler. Its basis is the belief that God's revelation, whatever else may be true of it, has no cognitive content. Bible teaching may trigger off some awareness of God, understood in more or less impersonal terms as the immanence of the transcendent and the transcendence of the immanent, and also some veneration for the more or less misty figure of Jesus; but no part of the Bible is in any sense the uttered Word of our Creator telling us things about himself and us. All theologies are therefore necessarily relative, depending for their thrust and content on the private mind-set and selective preferences of the theologians who put them together, and we may expect as many different systematic theologies to emerge in the church as there are theologians to think them up. Theological pluralism, on this view, argues theological health.

As you can see, this view trivializes theology, reducing it to a learned exercise of the religious imagination which no one is the worse for not bothering with. However, my reason for rejecting it is not that it is trivial, but that it is false. With Karl Barth, I affirm against it the reality of the God who speaks to us in and through Jesus Christ, using the words of Holy Scripture as his instrument. I go beyond Barth in affirming that the Bible is the Word of God intrinsically as well as instrumentally, and I insist that the authority of Bible teaching – the authority, that is, of the Holy Spirit speaking in Scripture, as the Westminster Confession puts it – is the authority of God himself, and specifically of Jesus Christ the Lord in person. And, though I do not join Barth in his denial of general revelation through the created order, I further affirm, as he also did, the total inability of the fallen human mind to think correctly about God, and gain true knowledge about him, apart from the instruction of Holy Scripture mediated by the illumina - tion of the Holy Spirit. The first fact to be reckoned with, so I maintain, is the reality of the self-revealed, self-revealing God who in and through the Scriptures has spoken and still speaks to make himself known, and all accounts of the content and method of systematic theology that fail to do justice to this fact are to be rejected. Discard, therefore, view number one.

View number two is that the proper subject matter of systematic theology is revealed truth about the works, ways, and will of God, and that the proper method of studying it is twofold. The first task is exegetical. Treating the biblical material as God's own didactic witness to himself, given in the form of the didactic witness to him of the Bible writers, we are to draw from the canonical text everything we can find relating to the Creator, and receive it as pure truth from God's own mouth. This view and use of Scripture, the historic mainstream view of the Christian church,[8] comes to us directly from Christ and his apostles, who, as has often been shown, both modelled and taught it,[9] and its claims on our assent, as Christ's disciples, are just the same, and just as strong, as are the claims of any other teaching that was demonstrably given by the Master. Let me say, up to this point I am in comfortable agreement with this second view, and I hope you are too.

The second task for students, on this view, is synthetic. All the data about God that exegesis has established must be brought together in a single coherent scheme, just as a historian schematizes all his facts into a single flowing narrative, or scientists observing the love-life of frogs (or, shall I say, Masters and Johnson studying human sexual behaviour in the manner of scientists observing the love-life of frogs)[10] schematize their findings into a single analytical report. This, essentially, was what medieval theologicans were doing with their data before the Reformation; this, essentially, is what the Protestant scholastics of the seventeenth century did, and it is what most of the theology teachers of the evangelical theological renaissance of the past half-century have done. The massive theological systems inherited from the Protestant past bear impressive witness to the thoroughness of these endeavours, and similar productions, written for textbook purposes, are still emerging.[11]

'Well,' says someone, 'you are called an evangelical theologian; do you not go along with this passion for system-building?' To a large degree,

---

[8] This description is sometimes disputed, on the grounds that pre-Reformation and post-Reformation exegesis were two significantly different things. In approaching Scripture as the didactic utterance of the God and Father of our Lord Jesus Christ, who is our Father in him, there was however not the least, difference or divergence in the Christian church until the days of the Enlightenment. For an overview, see R. P. Preus, 'The View of the Bible Held by the Church: the Early Church through Luther,' *Inerrancy*, ed. Norman Geisler (Grand Rapids: Zondervan, 1979), pp. 357–92; John D. Hannah, ed. *Inerrancy and the Church* (Chicago: Moody Press, 1984).

[9] See, for instance, J. W. Wenham, 'Christ's View of Scripture,' *Inerrancy*, pp. 3–36; B. B. Warfield, *The Inspiration and Authority of the Bible* (Philadelphia: Presbyterian and Reformed, 1952), pp. 51–226; Wayne A. Grudem, 'Scripture's Self-Attestation and the Problem of Formulating a Doctrine of Scripture,' ed. D. A. Carson and J. D. Woodbridge, *Scripture and Truth* (Grand Rapids: Zondervan, 1983).

[10] I do not mean to imply that the love-life of frogs is not an intrinsically interesting topic.

[11] Millard J. Erickson, *Christian Theology* (Grand Rapids: Baker Book House, 1983–85); Gordon R. Lewis and Bruce A. Demarest, *Integrative Theology*, vol. 1 (Grand Rapids: Zondervan, 1987); Paul Enns, *The Moody Handbook of Theology* (Chicago: Moody Press, 1989); Alan F. Johnson and Robert E. Webber, *What Christians Believe: A Biblical and Historical Summary* (Grand Rapids: Zondervan, 1989); etc.

I do, though I think that the older descriptions of the method of doing it were over-simplified; but I demur at one rather basic point. When Protestant scholastics of the older type insist that the didactic content of Scripture must be thought into a unity and seen as a whole, and when they refuse to allow contradictions, paradoxes, dialectical thought-forms, or any other mode of rational incoherence into their systematic syntheses, I am with them one hundred percent; I think this is the only reverent, wise, and docile way to go. But I question the adequacy of conceptual - izing the subject-matter of systematic theology as simply revealed truths about God, and I challenge the assumption that has usually accompanied this form of statement, that the material, like other scientific data, is best studied in cool and clinical detachment. Detachment from what, you ask? Why, from the relational activity of trusting, loving, worshipping, obey - ing, serving, and glorifying God: the activity that results from realizing that one is actually in God's presence, actually being addressed by him, every time one opens the Bible or reflects on any divine truth whatsoever. This second stage in theological method, as commonly practised, separates the questions of truth from those of discipleship; it proceeds as if doctrinal study would only be muddied by introducing devotional concerns; it drives a wedge between theology and doxology, between orthodoxy and orthopraxy, between knowing true notions about God and knowing the true God himself, between one's thinking and one's worshipping. Done this way, theology induces spiritual pride and produces spiritual sleep (physical sleep, too, sometimes). Thus the noblest study in the world gets cheapened. I cannot applaud this.

So now for my own view, which is a re-angling, small perhaps but (I think) significant, of the second position that we have reviewed. I put it to you that the proper subject-matter of systematic theology is *God actively relating in and through all created things to human beings* ; God, about whom those biblically revealed truths teach us, and to whom they point us; God, who lives, loves, rules, speaks, and saves sinners; God, who calls us who study him to relate to him through penitence and faith and worship as we study, so that our thinking about him becomes an exercise of homage to him. From this basis (if one accepts it) it follows that the proper state of mind for us as we come to synthesize the exegeted teaching of Scripture will be one not of detachment but of commitment, whereby we bring to our theologizing the attitude not of a critic but of a disciple; not of one who merely observes God, but of one who actively worships him. Then we shall be in less danger of speculative extrapolations that go beyond Scripture, which it is almost impossible to keep out of theologies that the detached intellect, often (be it said) aided by Aristotle, puts together. We shall be in less danger of forgetting the transcendent mystery of God's being and action, and of putting him in a box constructed out of our own concepts, which the detached intellect, longing to master that which it studies, is very prone to do. We shall be in less danger of the irreverence of treating God as if he were an impersonal object below us, frozen fast by us for the purposes of our study, and of failing to remember that he is the great personal Subject, far above us, apart from whose ongoing life we should not exist at all. And we shall be shielded from the further irreverence of allowing ourselves to grade God's work in connection with the sovereign mysteries of predestination and evil, and to conclude that if we ourselves were God we could do a better job. 'Your thoughts of God are too human,' said Luther to Erasmus. [12] He might have said, your theology has too little worship in it; whichever he had said, the point would have been the same. In short, we are called to make our study of theology a devotional discipline, a verifying in experience of Aquinas' beautiful remark that theology is taught by God, teaches God, and takes us to God. [13] So may it be, for all of us.

## III

Now do you see what I have been driving at all this time? I want to arrange a marriage. I want our systematic theology to be practised as an element in our spirituality, and I want our spirituality to be viewed as an implicate and expression of our systematic theology, just as ethics is already viewed, at least by the discerning. The current framework in ecumenical spirituality studies seems to me to need more biblical and theological control; too often the perspective remains egocentric, and the inward journey, with its rhythms of time and place and its alternations of desert and oasis, feast and fast, solitude and fellowship is expounded from the experience of saints, in whatever pattern of significance impresses the expositor, without any theological assessments being directly made. Spirituality books are written that contain no application of Scripture, just as theological tomes are written that contain no application of truth to life. As I want to see theological study done as an aspect and means of our relating to God, so I want to see spirituality studied within an evaluative theological frame; that is why I want to arrange a marriage, with explicit exchange of vows and mutual commitments, between spirituality and theology, or (if you would rather hear it put this way) between systematic and spiritual theology. That is what my lecture title was pointing to. Given the marriage, both our theologizing and our devotional explorations will become systematic spirituality, exercises in (allow me to say it) knowing God; and we shall all be the richer as a result.

Maybe you have already had enough theology for one lecture; but I thought I ought to illustrate my concern by giving an example of how

---

[12]  Martin Luther on *The Bondage of the Will*, tr. O. R. Johnston and J. I. Packer (London: James Clarke; Old Tappan N.J. Revell, 1957), p. 87.

[13]  *Theologia a Deo docta, Deum docet, ad Deum ducit* .

the spirituality of some would benefit from more solid, Bible-based theological controls. Here then is my example: Sound spirituality needs to be thoroughly Trinitarian. In our fellowship with God we must learn to do full justice to all three Persons and the part that each plays in the team job (please allow me that bold phrase) of saving us from sin, restoring our ruined humanness, and bringing us finally to glory. Neglect the Son, lose your focus on his mediation and blood atonement and heavenly intercession, and you slip back into the legalism that is fallen man's natural religion, the treadmill religion of works. Few evangelicals, perhaps, need to be reminded of this, but some do. Again, neglect the Spirit, lose your focus on the fellowship with Christ that he creates, the renewing of nature that he effects, the assurance and joy that he evokes, and the enabling for service that he bestows, and you slip back into orthodoxism and formal - ism, the religion of aspiration and perspiration without either inspiration or transformation, the religion of low expectations, deep ruts, and grooves that become graves. More evangelicals, I think, need reminders here. Finally, neglect the Father, lose your focus on the tasks he prescribes and the discipline he inflicts, and you become a mushy, soft-centred, self-indulgent, unsteady, lazy spoiled child in the divine family, making very heavy weather of any troubles and setbacks that come. This loss of focus is surely a widespread weakness in these days, and very many of us need to be admonished about it.[14]

That is my example; and now I will bring this discourse to an end. From all of that I have said you can, I trust, form some idea of what to expect from the first occupant of the Chee Chair (which, I take it, is what you wanted to know, for why else would you be reading this?). Strength - ening every way I can the links between spirituality and systematic theology will certainly be high on my agenda. I do not think I shall cramp Dr. Houston's style; what I do will be more in the nature of digging out foundations and putting in drains, leaving the air clear for him to fly in, as at present. So now you know!

At the close of the inaugural lecture from which I quoted when I began, C. S. Lewis described himself as a cultural dinosaur, and begged his hearers, even if they disagreed with his old-fashioned approach to literature, to value him as a specimen of a vanishing breed. 'Use your specimens while you can,' he said. 'There are not going to be many more dinosaurs.'[15] My theology, I know, is old-fashioned enough to be de - scribed as dinosauric in some quarters, and sociologists like Jeffrey Hunter are sure that such theology cannot survive; but I wonder. Does God change with the passing years? If the Bible is his Word for the world, will it ever go out of date? Will its meaning change with the culture? Will the

---

[14] On this latter point, see Thomas Smail, *The Forgotten Father* (London: Hodder and Stoughton, 1979 and Vancouver: Regent College, 1994).

[15] Lewis, op. cit., p. 25.

human heart change with technological advance? Will the gospel change as the world's religions talk to each other? And are the inward exercises of godliness essentially any different from what they were one, two, five, ten, fifteen centuries ago? Some things do not change; and it is out of the conviction that God and godliness are among them, and are in fact to be classed among what Carlyle called the 'eternities and immensities,' that I do my work in the way I do. The day will declare it; meantime, let us all labour to do what, as we see it, needs to be done.

# Chapter 28

# Predestination and Sanctification

My announced theme is 'Predestination and Sanctification,' but it could better have been called 'Sanctification and Predestination' – that way around – because sanctification is the central concern of what I shall be saying. Predestination, as we shall see, undergirds and gives force to what the Bible says about sanctification in the Christian life. I begin by putting everything under the judgement of God's Word. Note how God himself joins sanctification and predestination together.

*But we ought always to thank God for you, brothers loved by the Lord, because from the beginning God chose you to be saved through the sanctifying work of the Spirit and through belief in the truth. He called you to this through our gospel, that you might share in the glory of our Lord Jesus Christ* (2 Thess. 2:13, 24).

*We always thank God for all of you, mentioning you in our prayers . . . We continually remember before our God and Father your work produced by faith, your labour prompted by love, and your endurance inspired by hope in our Lord Jesus Christ* (1 Thess. 1:2–5).

*Finally, brothers, we instructed you how to live in order to please God, as in fact you are living . . . It is God's will that you should be sanctified [this is the will of God, even your sanctification,* KJV]; *that you should avoid sexual immorality . . . For God did not call us to be impure, but to live a holy life* (1 Thess. 4:1, 3, 7).

*Praise be to the God and Father of our Lord Jesus Christ, who has blessed us in the heavenly realms with every spiritual blessing in Christ. For he chose us in him before the creation of the world to be holy and blameless in his sight* (Eph 1:3, 4).

*Therefore, as God's chosen people, holy and dearly loved, clothe yourselves with compassion, kindness, humility, gentleness and patience. Bear with each other and*

PREDESTINATION AND SANCTIFICATION was originally published in *Tenth* (Philadelphia: Tenth Presbyterian Church), July, 1983. Reprinted by permission. It began as an address to the Philadelphia Conference on Reformed Theology, and bears the marks of its origin.

*forgive whatever grievances you may have against one another. Forgive as the Lord forgave you* (Col. 3:12, 13).

*I have revealed you to those whom you gave me out of the world [that is, by election]. They were yours; you gave them to me and they have obeyed your word. . . . My prayer is not that you take them out of the world but that you protect them from the evil one. They are not of the world, even as I am not of it. Sanctify them by the truth; your word is truth. As you sent me into the world, I have sent them into the world. For them I sanctify myself, that they too may be truly sanctified* (John 17:6, 15–19).

These Scriptures speak for themselves showing the link between sanctification and predestination.

## Set Apart for God

What do we mean when we use the word 'sanctification'? The diction - aries tell us that the Greek word (*hagiasmos*) means, first and foremost, being set apart for God. It means being brought near to God by being set apart from other relationships. It means being consecrated. But we must go deeper into it than that.

The New Testament seems to speak of sanctification from two complementary angles. From one standpoint it tells us that *sanctification is the work of God*, changing the Christian's nature to transform him into something which by nature he was not.

We see this in the Westminster Shorter Catechism:

*Question 35: What is sanctification?*
*Answer: Sanctification is the work of God's free grace, whereby we are renewed in the whole man after the image of God, and enabled more and more to die unto sin, and to live unto righteousness.*

As the Westminster Confession (XIII. 1) says:

They who are once effectually called and regenerated, having a new heart and a new spirit created in them, are further sanctified, really and personally, through the virtue of Christ's death and resurrection, by his Word and Spirit dwelling in them; the dominion of the whole body of sin is destroyed, and the several lusts thereof are more and more weakened and mortified, and they more and more quickened and strengthened, in all saving graces, to the practice of true holiness, without which no man shall see the Lord.

The biblical warrant for such teaching is found, for instance, in 1 Thess. 5:23, where we find Paul praying, 'May God himself, the God of peace, sanctify you through and through. May your whole spirit, soul and body

be kept blameless at the coming of our Lord Jesus Christ.' Again, in 2 Cor.
3:18, Paul says that as we behold the glory of the Lord Jesus, so we are
'transformed into his likeness with ever-increasing glory, which comes
from the Lord, who is the Spirit.' Accordingly, as Paul says in Gal. 5:22,
we who walk in the Spirit are enabled to produce the 'fruit of the Spirit,'
which is 'love, joy, peace, patience, kindness, goodness, faithfulness,
gentleness and self-control.' That is the profile of the Lord Jesus in the
lives of his disciples, effected by God.

The work of God could be compared to renovating a building while
it continues in use. The building is you and I living our lives. In those
lives of ours, God is at work demolishing bad habits, the ways of the
old person, and building up good, new habits of Christlike action and
reaction. God is making us new. This is 'the gospel mystery of
sanctification,' as Calvinists have sometimes expressed it.

In Phil. 2, Paul says, 'Work out your salvation with fear and trembling
for it is God who works in you to will and to act according to his good
purpose' (vv. 12, 13). God is doing something entirely supernatural in
our lives. God is changing us into the image of the Lord Jesus. This cannot
be explained in natural terms. It is the work of grace and of his indwelling
Holy Spirit.

This is sanctification viewed from the divine angle, and we do well to
have awe and reverence for it (which is what 'fear and trembling' really
means) and never to forget that our lives, characters and innermost beings
are the subject of this mysterious, transforming work of God. We should
look for it in the lives of our brothers and sisters in Christ and rejoice
when we see it. We should have very sensitive consciences concerning
the work of God in our own lives lest we mar it by disobedience or sinful
habits indulged.

But that is only half the story. The other angle on sanctification which
the New Testament gives us is to show it as *the quality of a Christian's life*.
From this standpoint the words which are used as close synonyms for
sanctification are 'righteousness' and 'holiness.' From this standpoint what
we are talking about is obedience to God, the effort and disciplined
activity of doing his will. This is what I call the 'resistance movement' in
the Christian life.

You know about the resistance movement in France, Holland and
other countries during the last war, in which German-occupying forces
were resisted from the inside by loyal people. Well, in the Christian life
there must also be a resistance movement, resistance to the allurements
of the world, the flesh and the devil, and to the power of bad habits still
unbroken. There must be resistance to those seductions into wrong ways
which are presented to us every day. 'Live by the Spirit,' says Paul, 'and
you will not gratify the desires of the sinful nature.'[1]

---

[1]  Gal. 5:16.

From another standpoint this involves the imitation of Christ – imitation, in fact, of both the Father and Son in the love they have shown us. 'Be imitators of God . . . as dearly loved children,' says the Apostle. 'And live a life of love, just as Christ loved us and gave himself up for us, as a fragrant offering and sacrifice to God.'[2] We are to love because he first loved us. This is the discipline of imitating our Lord.

The human side of sanctification also involves the discipline of pleasing God. I Thess. 4:1 states it: 'Finally, brothers, we instructed you how to live in order to please God, as in fact you are living.'

Sanctification is a life, then, of obedience, of resisting sin, of imitating Jesus, and of fellowship with God as one seeks to please God in everything one does. Are we living that sort of life? We ought to ask ourselves that right now, because this is what the real Christian life is all about: obeying, resisting sin, imitating Christ and pleasing God, as was said.

Sanctification, we now see, is both a gift (that is one side: God working in us to renew and transform us) and a task (the task of obedience, righteousness and pleasing God). And we must never so stress either of the two sides that we lose sight of the other. Think only of the task, and you will become a self-reliant legalist seeking to achieve righteousness in your own strength. You will not make any headway at all. Think only of the work of God in your life, and the chances are that Satan will trick you into not making the necessary effort and not maintaining the discipline of righteousness so that, in fact, even as you rejoice in the work of God in your life, you will be dishonouring it by your slackness. Hold both sides of the matter together in your mind, if you want your living to be right.

## A Neglected Priority

I am concerned about sanctification because it seems to me that today's church is very, very insensitive at this point. I put it to you that holiness is a neglected priority of the modern church. It was a priority for the Lord Jesus; he prayed that the Father would sanctify his disciples by the truth. It was a priority for Paul, as we have seen from these many texts I have quoted. Is it a priority for the people of God today? As I look around, I see a neglect of sanctification.

What has happened to produce this neglect? Two things at least have gone wrong. First, our godliness (so called) is excessively human-centred. It focuses on 'my personal satisfaction' rather than 'the glory of God.' The emphasis is all on self-fulfilment, happiness, being shielded from trouble and being enabled to succeed. Success in relationships, success in one's sex life, success in everyday activities, has become the name of the game.

---

[2] Eph. 5:1, 2.

Book after book has been written to guide us to success in these areas. But I do not see that our eyes are on the Lord and that our supreme concern, the thing that consumes us and makes us run, is the glory of God This means that at the level of motive our human-centeredness is leading us to neglect the reality of sanctification.

Second, our activity – and there is a great deal of Christian activity these days – lapses again and again into activism, so that activism almost becomes our religion. By activism I mean that self-reliant activity whereby the whole of our Christianity is a matter of running around and doing things for God – being busy, busy, busy for God. We admire the busiest Christians. We take it for granted that they are the best Christians. We admire the rush and bustle of endless Christian activity. Some of us are spiritually barren because we are too busy even to pray. I tell you, brothers and sisters, if you are too busy to pray, you really are too busy.

A nineteenth-century pastor, Robert Murray McCheyne, of Dundee, Scotland, once said: 'My people's greatest need is . . .' How would you have expected him to finish that sentence? Nowadays, I would suppose, a lot of pastors would say, 'My people's greatest need is that I should have counselling skills or expository skills or other ministerial skills.' McCheyne did not talk that language. 'My people's greatest need,' he said, 'is *my personal holiness*.' Do we think in those terms? Is that our vision? I fear not. Therefore I say, holiness seems to me to be a neglected priority in today's church, and it distresses me. I take it further. I put it to you that holiness is a fading glory in the evangelical world. I put it to you that generations ago people cared about holiness. Folks cared about sanctifi - cation in a way we do not, and at that point they were in advance of us and we are now grievously behind them.

I think of the seventeenth-century Puritans for whom holiness was the watchword of life. I think about John Wesley who, though he was a confused Calvinist, did get his priorities magnificently right. He said on more than one occasion that God raised up the Methodist movement, not primarily for evangelism – he never put it that way – but 'to spread scriptural holiness throughout the land.' I do not agree with Wesley's understanding of Christian holiness at every point. But I can only applaud him for putting holiness first and making it top priority in the spiritual movement which he sought to encourage.

A hundred years ago an Anglican bishop, J. C. Ryle, wrote a magnificent book with a one-word title: *Holiness*. I do not think any book with so forthright a title, nor certainly with such forthright contents, has been written since Ryle's.

Holiness, I repeat, is a fading glory in the evangelical world. We are preoccupied with controversy, scholarship and liberty in ethical matters, and we are disillusioned. I think, with the holiness teaching on which we were brought up. And perhaps that is not too wrong a reaction. There has been a type of holiness teaching which has been sterile and inadequate.

Yet I was a little bothered (as well as amused) at what an inner–city pastor said to me in 1979. Somebody had asked, 'What do you think of the victorious Christian life?' He replied, 'It's all right if you've got the time and the money for it.' You can see why I was amused. But can you see why I was bothered? Should Christians be able simply to shrug off the quest for holiness, as if it were a matter of secondary importance? According to the New Testament, as we saw, at the very heart of our Christian living should be a passion in all things to obey God, imitate our Saviour, resist sin and please our gracious Father. Nothing can alter that priority.

If we do not learn to adorn with good works the reformed theology as taught in Scripture, we cannot expect people around us to be impressed by it. I defend Calvinism as the purest version of Christian truth that the world has ever seen. But the only defense of it which will finally carry conviction with others is the demonstration that it produces holy lives. I want to see the reformed faith come to possess the minds of more and more of God's people in these days, and to that end I challenge you to outlive the rest of the church. Pursue sanctification, and thus demonstrate the power of reformed theology in your life.

## Five Basic Truths

Having said that, I want to set forth what I call the parameters of sanctification as I discover them in the New Testament. They are five basic biblical truths. On four of them I shall spend very little time, but on the fifth I shall elaborate.

### *Basic truth number one:* **The context of sanctification is justification by the blood of Christ**

If we would rightly understand this matter of Christian holiness, we must get it clear that in this world we shall never be more than sinners justified by the shed blood of Jesus Christ. It is very important that we remove from our minds any conceited notion that suggests that as we grow in holiness we shall need the cleansing blood of Christ less. We shall never get beyond our need of the blood of Jesus. In the sight of God we shall always be forgiven sinners – that, and no more. John Wesley on his deathbed was heard to say, 'No way into the holiest but by the blood of Jesus.' Another church leader said as he was dying, 'I never so much felt my need of the blood of Jesus, nor was I ever enabled to make such good use of it.' Whatever else the doctrine of sanctification means, it does not mean that we move out of the sphere of being sinners justified by faith. A proud holiness, which supposes that it has got beyond that, would be a contradiction in terms. It would be pharisaism. God shield us from it!

*Basic truth number two:* **The source of sanctification is union with Jesus Christ**

Co-crucifixion and co-resurrection with him is how Paul puts it in the opening verses of Romans 6. We are united with Christ at the point where our first life, the old life, ends and the new life begins. The beginning of the new life means the renewing of our hearts so that now we love what before we hated – God and his attributes, God's will, God's way, God's purposes – and the deepest desire of our heart is how to know God, love God, get close and keep close to God, serve God, please God and praise God all our days. The source of Christian sanctification lies just there, in the change of our natures. So the summons to sanctity is no more nor less than the call to be natural as a Christian and let those new instincts, impulses and longings express themselves in the way one lives. Holiness is the naturalness of the regenerate person.

I know that there has to be self-denial in relation to carnal self, the old sinful impulses which, though dethroned, have not yet been destroyed and therefore still fight back for dominance. Nonetheless, the deepest thing in you now, as a regenerate Christian, is newness of life. Let it come out. Express it. Sanctification arises from that regenerating union with Christ.

*Basic truth number three:* **The agent of sanctification is the Holy Spirit who works in us to make us will and act according to God's good pleasure**

His work in us does not, of course, mean that we do not ourselves work. It means that we work effectively, because we work in the power which the Spirit gives. When Paul says, 'Work out your own salvation with fear and trembling [awe and reverence], for it is God who works in you to will and to act according to his good purpose,' he is calling us to a life in which again and again we get down on our knees and say, 'Lord Jesus, without you I can do nothing. Gracious Father, without the help of your Spirit, I can do nothing. Help me by the Spirit to get it right.' Then, believing that God hears and answers prayer, we move into action attempting to do that very thing about which we have prayed. And we find ourselves helped. After this we thank the Lord for having worked in us to will and to do of his good pleasure. If anything is still wrong, we take the discredit to ourselves and ask forgiveness; but for all that went right we thank God. The Holy Spirit is the agent of sanctification, and it is important to remember that it is so. We cannot sanctify ourselves, and self-reliance thwarts and brings to a halt God's work.

*Basic truth number four:* **Sanctification is a battle**

The battle is described in Gal. 5:17:

> *For the sinful nature desires what is contrary to the Spirit, and the Spirit what is contrary to the sinful nature. They are in conflict with each other, so that you do not do what you want.*

This means that we never have a completely undivided mind. We never have our hearts entirely set on the things of God, so that even if our actions are right by external standards, our hearts are nevertheless never quite right. There is always some resistance from the sin that dwells in us.

So we are making headway – if indeed we are making headway – against opposition, and it is struggle and conflict constantly. Thank God, we do make headway. But it is always headway against opposition. We misunderstand radically if we allow ourselves to forget that sanctification is a battle all the way.

## Proof of Election

Against the background of these four basic, parameter truths I now set number five, the one I wish most fully to emphasize:

### One dynamic of sanctification is God's predestinating purpose

Back up for a moment and remind yourself of what election means. The reformed doctrine of election has in it two crucial points. Point one is that salvation is through election. Our salvation results from God forming and putting into action a plan to save us. He has decided upon this plan unconditionally, that is, not waiting for us to deserve it, because if he had waited until we deserved it, he would have been waiting forever. Salvation is through God's election.

Point two is that those who are saved may know their election and live in the joy of that knowledge. We find this in the first chapter of Peter's second letter where, having summoned his readers to righteous - ness in this form: 'Add to your faith goodness; and to goodness, knowl - edge; and to knowledge, self-control; and to self-control, perseverance; and to perseverance, godliness; and to godliness, brotherly kindness; and to brotherly kindness, love,'[3] he then says, 'Be all the more eager to make your calling and election sure.'[4] Labour, in other words, to get to the point where you know that you are among those whom God has called and chosen. 'Sure' in this context implies certainty of knowledge of what one's life shown to be objectively factual. How does one do that? Well, Peter has just been telling us: by pursuing sanctification, by practising that

---

[3]  2 Peter 1:5, 7.
[4]  2 Peter 1:10.

supernatural Christian life in which you are going on from one degree of Christlikeness to another.

John Owen said it in these words:

> Faith, obedience and holiness are the inseparable fruits, effects and consequences of election. In whomsoever these things are wrought, he [that person] is obliged, according to the method of God in the gospel, to believe in his own election.

Why ought he to? Because his life is showing qualities which only the lives of the elect show. Thus they may know themselves to be one of God's elect because his life has been changed. And they ought to labour to make their election sure to himself in this way because of the joy this gives and the impulse in the life of godliness which springs from it.

I realize that to some people this will sound very paradoxical, because the doctrine of election is constantly suspected of having the opposite effect, that is, of not promoting holiness but of promoting carelessness. It is supposed to be antinomian, to use the technical word.

John Wesley was all his life convinced that this is so. Here is a quotation from him, written in his last days. He poses a question and then answers it.

> Question: What is the direct antidote to Methodism, the doctrine of heart holiness?

> Answer: Calvinism. All the devices of Satan for these fifty years have done far less toward stopping the work of God than that single doctrine. It strikes at the root of salvation from sin, previous to glory, putting it [salvation] on quite another issue.

Wesley meant that Calvinism, as he understood it, says that people may be saved without holiness just by virtue of their election. It is almost pathological, it seems to me, for Wesley to have gone on cherishing that misrepresentation of Calvinism, which no Calvinist of his day would have accepted for a moment. But for whatever reason, Wesley was convinced that this was so. And many folk since Wesley's day have continued in the conviction that Calvinism, by saying that we are saved in consequence of God's election, also says that whether we are holy in life does not matter one way or the other.

The supposition is that there is no restriction placed on those who are seen as God's favourites. God indulges them in any breaches of his laws they like to commit. He does not bother about it. Therefore there is no motivation for righteousness once you know you are elect. If you are thinking along these lines, you could not be misunderstanding the reformed faith and the faith of the Scriptures more radically, as I shall now demonstrate.

Let me set against that supposition the following principles:

One: *In Scripture sanctification is a goal of God's election*. Sanctification is what he selected us for. 'He chose us in [Christ] before the creation of the world to be holy and blameless in his sight.'[5] Is that not clear enough?

Two: *Sanctification is a fruit of God's election*, because God's election issues in that work of inner renewal whereby our hearts are changed. One of the things we previously hated but now have come to love is righteousness. Saints love righteousness. Previously they did not; now they do. Let John Owen, with his own rumbling rhetoric, put this point to us in application to people who maybe have taken up with the notion against which I am arguing.

> Why, says one, if God has thus chosen me I may then live in sin as I please. All will be well and safe in the latter end, which is all that I need care for. But this is the language of a devil, not a regenerate man . . . I shall use some boldness in this matter. He that doth not understand, he who is not sensible that an apprehension by faith of God's election love in Christ hath a natural, immediate, powerful influence upon the souls of believers unto the love of an holy obedience, is utterly unacquainted with the nature of faith and its whole work and actings towards God in the hearts of them that believe. Is it possible that anyone who knows these things can suppose that those in whom they are in sincerity and power can be such stupid, impious and ungrateful monsters, so devoid of all filial affection toward God, as to cast poison into the spring of all their own mercies in this way?

When Paul says in Col. 3:12, '*As God's chosen people* . . . clothe yourselves with compassion, kindness, humility, gentleness and patience,' what he is showing is that knowledge of God's election produces new energy for holiness, motivated by gratitude and love.

Three: *Sanctification is the only proof of one's election*.[6] Making sure that in your life the supernatural. Christlike way of living is abundantly shown forth is the only proof of election you can ever have. Would you know your election? You may know it from the holiness of your life. If there is no holiness to be seen, no practice of sanctification, no supernatural living, no change in your nature, then there is no basis on which you have any right to suppose that you are one of God's chosen people.

Four: *Sanctification is advanced by the knowledge of your election*. For when you know that God has laid hold of you, taken you up as it were out of the gutter of sin, cleansed you by the blood of Christ, adopted you into his family, made you his son, justified you, forgiven you, renewed you, and is now grooming you for glory, your awe, love and gratitude for the work of God will overwhelm you. I am bold to say that if you have never

---

[5]  Eph. 1:4.
[6]  2 Pet. 1:10.

known what it is to be overwhelmed with awe, love and gratitude for the saving work of God in your life, I very much doubt whether that saving work can have started in you yet. No, if you know anything of the reality of God in your life, then awe, love and gratitude dominate your soul and you feel the force of Paul's words:

> *Therefore, I urge you, brothers, in view of God's mercy, to offer your bodies as living sacrifices, holy and pleasing to God – which is your spiritual worship. Do not conform any longer to the pattern of this world, but be transformed by the renewing of your mind [that is, your whole person, soul and spirit]. Then you will be able to test and approve what God's will is – his good, pleasing and perfect will.* [7]

You will say with Charles Wesley, who thought he was an Arminian but, in fact, ceased to sound like one as soon as he started writing his poems,

> *Oh, for a heart to praise my God,*
> *A heart from sin set free,*
> *A heart that always feels the blood*
> *So freely shed for me,*
>
> *A heart resigned, submissive, meek,*
> *My dear Redeemer's throne,*
> *Where only Christ is heard to speak,*
> *Where Jesus reigns alone,*
>
> *A heart in every thought renewed,*
> *And full of love divine,*
> *Perfect and right and pure and good,*
> *A copy, Lord, of thine.*

Sanctification is a *goal* of God's election, a *fruit* of God's election, the only *proof* of God's election, and the knowledge of election is a great *spur* to further advance in the way of holiness. Do you believe me? Then search your heart and see if you are taking this truth into your own life as you should.

---

[7] Romans 12:1.

# Chapter 29

# Conscience, Choice and Character

There are two crucial areas where anyone venturing today to write on – Christian ethics takes his life in his hands: namely, the understanding of man's nature and the analysing of moral thought. In both areas, Christian views face strong secular attack, and in neither are Christian minds always clear. But clarity here is necessary if ever we are to see how God's law should order our lives, and how law-keeping perfects our nature. The territory may not be by-passed just because it is disputed. This essay, which is a theoretical (though not on that account unpractical) study of how individuals come to discern and do God's will, takes us straight to both battlefields, and our first step must be to set up our flag on the ground we intend to occupy.

## Human Nature

'What a piece of work is man!' said Hamlet. 'How noble in reason! how infinite in faculty [capacity]! in form, in moving, how express and admirable! in action how like an angel! in apprehension how like a god! the beauty of the world! the paragon of animals!' Bang on, as a modern groundling might say. The words which Shakespeare puts into Hamlet's mouth reflect with dazzling vividness the classic Christian vision of man: namely, as a cosmic amphibian, having a body which links him with animals below him but being in himself a thinking, loving, choosing, creative, active person like God and the angels above him. It is the horse that is usually called the noble animal, but on the Christian view the description is better suited to the rider. There is no such created grandeur as that of humankind.

I am human; what, then, am I? Not, as philosophers and gnostics ancient and modern would tell me, a soul that would get on better without a body,

CONSCIENCE, CHOICE AND CHARACTER was originally published in *Law, Morality and the Bible*, G. J. Wenham and B. Kaye, eds., (Downer's Grove: InterVarsity Press, 1978), pp. 168–192. Reprinted by permission. This chapter is indebted to material by Gordon Stobart and Dennis Winter.

but a complex psycho-physical organism, a personal unit describable as an ensouled body no less than an embodied soul. Bodilessness is not a welcome prospect; after physical death I shall be incapable of that full self-expression which belongs to full personal life till a new body is given me (as, praise God, one duly will be). I am at once the highest of animals, since no other animal shares my kind of mental life, and the lowest of rational creatures, for no angel is bounded by physical limitations as I am.

Yet I, as a human, can enjoy the richest life of all God's creatures. Mental and physical awareness meet and blend in me, fearfully, wonder-fully and fascinatingly. There is far more to me than I can know or get in touch with, at least in this preliminary, probationary life, and I never reach the limits of wisdom, goodness and depth of relationship with others that open out before me. But I must keep my head. My task is not to dizzy myself by introspecting or speculating to find, if I can, what lies at the outer reaches of consciousness, nor to pursue endless, exquisite stimulation in hope of new, exotic ecstasies. It is, rather, to know and keep my place in God's cosmic hierarchy, and in that place to spend my strength in serving God and humankind.

A cool head, however, is hard to find. Having within me some thing both of ape and of angel, I can all too easily lose my cosmic balance, so to speak, and lapse into incoherent oscillation between seeing myself as no less than God, a spirit having absolute value in myself and settling the value of everything else by its relation to me, and seeing myself as no more than an animal, whose true life consists wholly in eating, drinking, rutting and seeking pleasures for mind and body till tomorrow I die. I often catch myself slipping one way or the other; I look around, and see my fellow men in the toils of this crazy oscillation all the time; I read my Bible, and find that it has been so everywhere since the Garden of Eden. Such is life in a fallen world.

### The image of God

The human animal, we said, is noble. What makes him so? Not his ambitions or achievements, which, as we have hinted, are rarely admirable and often downright discreditable, but his personal constitution. The most mysterious yet glorious truth about human nature is this: that each individual, male or female, old or young, sophisticated or rough, handsome or ugly, brilliant or slow of mind, outstanding or ordinary, bears God's image. We learn this in the first chapter of the Bible, Genesis 1, which is a majestic introduction of the Creator by means of a review of his work.

The thrust is this: 'Think of all that makes up the world you know – day, night, sky, sea, sun, moon, stars, trees, plants, birds, fish, animals, insects, big things, little things, and most of all yourself and other human beings of both sexes; now meet their Maker! and gauge the excellence of his wisdom and power from the marvellous complexity, order and goodness which you see (and he also saw) in his work.' (There is a parallel argument in Job 38–41, where God leads Job to acknowledge the fathomlessness of divine wisdom by reminding him of the wonders of the animal kingdom, especially Behemoth the hippopotamus and Leviathan the crocodile.) 'And realize too,' Genesis 1 in effect continues, 'that you, the admiring observer, were made like your Maker in a way that none of these other things are, so that you might manage the lower creation for God, as his steward, and enjoy its riches as his gift to you. That is your calling, so go to it!'

The key statements here are in verses 26 and 27: 'God said, "Let us make man in our *image*, after our *likeness* . . ." So God created man in his own *image*.' The image of God in which humankind was and is made (cf. Gen. 5:1; 9:6; Jas. 3:9) has been variously explained in detail. It has been identified, for instance, with rationality (e.g., by S. R. Driver), with moral capacity (e.g., by J. Laidlaw), with knowledge of God in righteousness and holiness (e.g., Calvin), with dominion over the lower creation (e.g., by H. Thieliecke), and with the man-woman relationship in marriage, corresponding to the inner relationships of the Three-in-One (by Karl Barth).

Von Rad urges that the phrase must refer to each human individual as a whole, in the psycho-physical unity of his being, not just to 'higher' mental and moral qualities in abstraction from his body; and P. D. Kinder, standing it seems on von Rad's shoulders, writes thus: 'When we try to define the image of God it is not enough to react against a crude literalism by isolating man's mind and spirit from his body. The Bible makes man a unity: acting, thinking and feeling with his whole being. This living creature, then, and not some distillation from him, is an expression or transcription of the eternal, incorporeal creator in terms of temporal, bodily, creaturely exist - ence – as one might attempt a transcription of, say, an epic into a sculpture, or a symphony into a sonnet. Likeness in this sense survived the fall, since it is structural. As long as we are human we are, by definition, in the image of God.'[1] This line of thought seems to win increasing scholarly assent. But however expositors differ on the nuances of the phrase, the broad theologi - cal implications of asserting that each person is made in God's image are matters of general agreement, thus:

The assertion shows each person's true *dignity* and *worth*. As God's *image-bearer, he merits infinite respect, and his claims on us (which are really the*

[1] *Genesis*, (*Tyndale Old Testament Commentaries*, Inter-Varsity Press, 1967), p. 51 On the relation between 'image' (*selem*) and 'likeness' (*d muth*), Kidner rightly comments: 'The words *image* and *likeness* reinforce one another: there is no "and" between the phrases, and Scripture does not use them as technically distinct expressions, as some theologians have done, whereby the "image" is man's indelible constitution as a rational and morally responsible being, and the "likeness" is that spiritual accord with the will of God which was lost at the Fall' (pp. 50f.).

*claims of God's image in him) must be taken with total seriousness. No man should ever be thought of as a mere cog in a machine, or a mere means to an end.*

The assertion points also to each person's true *destiny*. Our Maker so designed us that our nature (the mass of potencies, urges and needs of which each man is made up) finds final satisfaction and fulfilment only in a relationship of responsive Godlikeness – which means, precisely, in that state of correspondence between our acts and God's will which we call *obedience*. Living that is obedient will thus also be teleological, in the sense of progressively realizing our *telos* (Greek for 'end,' 'goal') as the Shorter Catechism classically defined it – 'Man's chief end is to glorify God, and [in so doing] to enjoy him for ever.' By contrast, to live disobediently is to forfeit fulfilment and to sentence oneself to a life which, however pleasure-filled, is Godless and ultimately joyless.

Finally, the assertion confirms the genuineness of each person's *freedom*. Experience tells us we are free, in the sense that we make real choices between alternatives and could have chosen differently, and theology agrees. As the Creator is free within the limits of his own nature to choose what he will do, and as his praise springs from recognition that what he chose was good, so also with us. Self-determining freedom of choice is what sets God and his rational creatures apart from, say, birds and bees, as *moral* beings. Any suggestion that this freedom is illusory and unreal, so that my choices, being somehow programmed in advance, do not matter, and I to not need to work at them, must be squashed as satanic. Granted, predisposing factors influence our choices (much more, in fact, than they should!); granted, God is sovereign in and over our choices (this is part of the mystery of the creature's dependence on the Creator); none the less, it is one aspect of God's image in us that the choices we make are genuinely ours, and are no less decisive for our future than God's choice to create and redeem was decisive for his.

### Behaviourism

The modern attack on the biblical view of humanity comes from a standpoint mainly determined by expertise in the sciences, biological and human. Sometimes this standpoint claims the name of scientific human - ism, though its appeal to speculative extrapolations beyond the evidence, and its denial of humankind's glory as bearer of God's image, would suggest 'unscientific brutism' as a more appropriate name. Purposing to affirm and exalt humanity, this view actually negates and demeans him by assimilating him entirely to the lower animals. It sees us as a 'naked ape' and an animated computer, wholly programmable by external conditioning once it is known how we work.

Concentrated, not to say mesmerized, study of physical, psychological and social factors that condition human action has bred doubt as to whether free (that is, self-determined) moral choices occur at all, and whether, if they to, it is not best to try and stop them, and train people instead into automatic behaviour patterns, by methods comparable to Pavlov's with his dogs or the brainwasher's with his victims. The pipe-dreams of popular Marxism, Aldous Huxley's *Brave New World*, George Orwell's *1984*, C. S. Lewis' *That Hideous Strength* (a flawed fairy-tale, but a brilliant analysis), and B. P. Skinner's *Beyond Freedom and Dignity*, show from different angles what the manipulations of a behaviourist utopia might amount to. Space forbids proper discussion of this viewpoint, but two quick comments can be made.

First, the basic mistake which this view makes is to overlook something quite essential to our humanness, namely our sense of being accountable (worthy of praise or blame) for what we do, and therefore answerable to anyone who has the right to take account of us.

A mature person wants to be recognized as morally responsible for their actions, and as they resent refusal to give them credit for what they say and do right, so they do not refuse blame for saying and doing what they know was wrong. They are clear that though external factors may have conditioned their action, their own decision was its direct cause – and so, we think, they should be, for that is how it really was. We are repelled by one who says they should not be blamed because they are mentally sick, or society's helpless victim, for however much we incline to say these things about them in extenuation, we know that when they say them about themselves they are making excuses and being morally dishonest, just as you and I would be if ever we acted this way. To accept accountability for one's choices is part of what it means to be truly human, and any proposal to ignore or change this, or to destroy people's awareness of it (as if we could!), is not humanizing; just the opposite! It is the most radical and grotesque dehumanization that can be imagined, as the novels of Huxley, Orwell and Lewis mentioned above make very plain. [2]

Second, the mistake comes of not distinguishing between two levels of language (two 'logical grammars,' or simply two languages, as philosophers would say) which we regularly use side by side when talking of human behaviour. They correspond to the difference within our own self-consciousness between 'me' and 'I,' the object-self I observe, and I the subject-self who do the observing. They are, first, impersonal objective language, to which belong all scientific accounts of historical, social, physical, chemical and psychological factors which condition people's acts; and, second, personal subjective language, in which all statements have to do with the individual subject-self thinking, feeling, acting, reacting and making choices. To this latter language belongs all talk about morality (moral goodness and badness, moral judgments and moral responsibilities).

---

[2] For further development of this point see C. S. Lewis, 'The Humanitarian Theory of Punishment,' in *Undeceptions: Essays on Theology and Ethics* (Collins, 1971).

The two languages cannot be reduced to one, nor can statements made in either be translated into, or explained without remainder, in terms of the other. They are distinct and complementary, and for full understanding we need both, the first supplementing the second; for the correlations between our external conditioning and our personal choices and decisions are many, and we should abuse our minds if we ignored them.

Scientific humanism, however, tends habitually to go beyond noting the correlations, and to offer explanations of what is said in the second language in terms of the first, thus in effect explaining *away* moral realities as being something else. For example, it might well explain a person's choice of burglary as a way of life in terms of a sociological description of their early life in the slums, and go on to suggest that by changing his environment and reconditioning them we can make an honest citizen out of them. This is to treat a criminal as an invalid needing cure, rather than as a responsible wrongdoer – a patronizing and dehumanizing fancy, guyed as it deserves in that blackest of black comedies, *A Clockwork Orange*.

The mistake occurs, as we said, because we so love using impersonal, objective, 'scientific' language that we treat as unreal, or less than ultimate, any realities whose nature it cannot express. A moment's thought, however, will convince us that the realities of personal motivation and purpose in our choices are quite distinct from any external factors which condition them. Should the scientific humanist invoke at this point that full-blown theoretical behaviourism which views all our conscious mental life as the accidental by-product of physical changes in our bodies and brains, the reply would be that in that case his very invoking of the theory is the accidental by-product of physical changes within them, and thus has no rational validity for them or anyone else. This is the *coup de grace* for all reasoned denials of the validity of reasoning: those who take them seriously thereby forbid others to take them seriously.

The best response to naive utopian behaviourism, with its simple animalist view of man and its simple optimism about the possibility of retraining him by skilled manipulation, will be to urge that each individual is infinitely mysterious, both to others and to himself, so that no man-made formula can in principle be adequate to produce the desired effect. Anyone who thinks and feels at all deeply finds himself a mystery to himself, fascinating and frustrating by turns, and comes to see that only omniscience would in principle suffice to sort him out.

## Conscience

One specific aspect of God's image in us is our conscience, classically defined by Thomas Aquinas as man's mind making moral judgments. As God's mind passes judgment on moral issues, so does our's, and as God's moral judgments should control our acts and will actually settle our destiny, so our conscience functions in the style of a voice within actually addressing us to command or forbid, approve or disapprove, justify or condemn. Conscience does not feel like the spontaneous working of my mind which it actually is; it feels, and is divinely intended to feel, like a monitor from above. The description of conscience as a voice from God highlights the unique character of this particular mental operation. (It should not, however, be taken to imply that divine finality attaches to all the deliverances of conscience; conscience needs educating by Scripture and experience, and to the extent that it has not been thus educated its deliverances will be deficient. From the standpoint of standards, it is truer to say that conscience is a capacity for hearing God's voice, rather than an actual hearing of it in each verdict that conscience passes.)

The experience of conscience is universal, and the operation of it, particularly when condemnatory, has an emotional dimension ('pangs'). It is not perhaps surprising that attempts should have been made to analyse conscience in emotional terms simply, as nothing but feelings of liking and disliking, on the model of my reactions to curry, which I like, and coconut, which I loathe. Critics labelled this analysis the 'Boo-hurrah' theory ('coconut? murder? *boo!* curry? promise-keeping? hurrah!').[3] Were the analysis true, moral reasoning designed to persuade to, or dissuade from, particular courses of action would be comparable to 'try this, you'll like it' and 'don't eat that, it's horrid,' and no universal moral standards could ever be agreed, any more than it could ever be agreed that henceforth everyone shall like curry and dislike coconut. But conscience itself tells us that morality is essentially a matter, not of taste, but of truth; not of feeling, in the first instance, but of judgment, based on principles which are in themselves universally valid, and claim everyone's assent.

Traditionally, and surely correctly, conscience has been held to involve two faculties, ability first to 'see' general moral truths and second to apply them to particular eases. Aquinas called the first capacity *synderesis* and kept *conscientia* for the second; Peter Martyr the reformer, followed by many seventeenth-century writers, spoke of theoretical and practical understanding, different words for the same distinction. It was unques-tioned among both Protestants and Roman Catholics till this century that the workings of conscience take the form of *practical syllogisms*, e.g. 'Stealing is wrong; taking the umbrella would be stealing; therefore taking the umbrella would be wrong,' or 'Bank robbers deserve punishment; I robbed a bank; therefore I deserve punishment'; and, despite some

---

[3] The best-known expositions of the 'Boo-hurrah' approach are by A. J. Ayer in *Language, Truth and Logic* (Gollancz, 1936), chapter 6, and by C. L. Stevenson in *Ethics and Language* (Yale: New Haven, 1944). For a candid philosophical criticism of it, see A. C. Ewing, *Ethics* (English University Press, 1953), chapter 7, especially pp. 115–126.

latter-day hesitations based on doubt as to whether God really reveals universally binding moral truths, the historic doctrine seems true, as anyone who checks his own moral reasoning will soon see. Though conscience pronounces on particular actions and cases, it does so on the basis of general principles, which, though not always explicit in the initial pronouncement, will be explicitly cited in justification if the pronounce - ment is at any stage questioned. And if no such universal principle could be produced to justify a particular pronouncement, the right conclusion would be that here is no genuine deliverance of conscience at all, but a neurotic symptom (guilt, or an obsession, in the psychiatrist's sense of those words) masquerading as the voice of conscience, and needing to be relieved and dispelled, if possible, by professional therapy.

C. A. Pierce argued that the New Testament writers who refer to conscience (Paul, Peter, Luke in Acts, and the writer of Hebrews) used the word in the limited sense that it bore in everyday secular Greek, namely a capacity for feeling pangs of remorse about past actions now seen as wrong, as distinct from a power of direction and vindication of oneself in moral matters.[4] But even were this true, which seems doubtful (note Rom. 2:15, where conscience excuses; 9:1, where it attests a right desire, expressing good will; 2 Cor. 1:12, where it approves; and Acts 23:1; 1 Tim. 1:5,19, where conscientious obedience produces a 'good' conscience; cf. Acts 24:16; Heb. 13:18), the point would be verbal only.

Scripture is clear on what we have already affirmed from experience, namely that humankind's 'heart' (in biblical usage the dynamic centre of our personal existence, including our self-conscious intellect, emo - tion and will) will not only 'smite' and 'reproach' in conviction (the bad conscience: cf. 1 Sam. 24:5; 2 Sam. 24:10; Job 27:6), but also both prompt and attest integrity (the good conscience: cf. Gen. 20:5f.; Deut. 9:5; 1 Kings. 3:6; 9:4; Ps. 119:7). The mental operation called *conscientia* in Latin and *syneidesis* in Greek (both words meaning 'co-knowledge' and signifying a second level of awareness accompanying one's primary awareness of an impulse, thought, act or possibility of action) directs (Rom. 13:5) as well as records (2 Cor. 1:12) and judges (Rom 2:15; cf. 1 John 3:19ff.), and does all three as, structurally speaking, God's monitor in the soul.[5] Yet its judgments may fall short of God's (1 Cor.

---

[4]  Pierce, C. A., *Conscience in the New Testament* (SCM, 1955).

[5]  The Puritan, Richard Sibbes, expounding 2 Cor. 1:12, gave striking substance to this thought by picturing conscience as God's court within us, thus: 'To clear this further concerning the nature of conscience, know that God has set up in a man a court, and there is in man all that are in a court. 1. There is a *register* [registrar] to take notice of what we have done . . . The conscience keeps diaries. It sets down everything. It is not forgotten, though we think it is . . . Conscience is the register. 2. And then there are *witnesses*. "The testimony of conscience."

4:4; cf. 1 John 3:19ff.); when possessed by false principles of judgment it will be 'weak' and misdirect (Rom. 14:2 and *passim*; 1 Cor. 8:7–12, cf. 10:25–29); and when moral and spiritual light has been resisted it may become 'seared' (i.e. cauterized, rendered insensitive) (1 Tim. 4:2; Eph. 4:18).

Being God's voice in and to us structurally, our conscience binds us and must always be conscientiously followed; but when through igno -rance or confusion its dictates are not God's voice substantially, our conscientiousness will not lead to our pleasing God. (Did Jephthah please God by sticking conscientiously to the vow of Judges 11:30f. when this meant killing his daughter?) So a Christian with an uninstructed con -science is in fact, whether they know it or not, in a deft stick; they cannot please God by either disobeying their conscience or obeying it. This fact shows how vital it is that Christians should study biblical morals as well as biblical doctrine, and also what a nightmare our lot would be did we not know God's daily forgiveness on the basis of his once-for-all justifi -cation of us, through the blood of Jesus Christ who is the propitiation for all our sins, known and unknown.

Freud's view of conscience has had great influence in this century, and some reference to it is desirable before we move on. Freud gives the name of conscience to the various neurotic and psychotic phenomena of obsessive restriction, compulsion and guilt to which we earlier referred. His model of man, hypothesized on the basis of clinical work with the mentally ill in *fin-de-siècle* Vienna, pictures the psyche as like a troubled home, where the ego on the ground floor (that is, the self-conscious self, with doors and windows open to the world) comes under pressure both from the id (aggressive energy rushing up from the cellars of the unconscious) and from the super-ego (an unnerving voice of command from upstairs, whereby repressed prohibitions and menaces from parents and society are 'introjected' into conscious life in portentous disguise, and

---

[5] *(continued)* Conscience doth witness, this have I done, this I have not done. 3. There is *an accuser with the witnesses*. The conscience, it accuseth, or excuseth. 4. And then there is the *judge*. Conscience is the judge. There it doth judge, this is well done, this is ill done. 5. Then there is an *executioner*, and conscience is that too . . . The punishment of conscience, it is a prejudice [pre-judging] of future judgment. There is a flash of hell presently [in the present] after an ill act . . . If the understanding apprehend dolorous things, then the heart smites, as David's "heart smote him," 1 Sam. 24.5 . . . The heart smites with grief for the present, and fear for the time to come.'

'God hath set and planted in man this court of conscience, and it is God's hall, as it were, where he keeps his first judgment . . . his assizes. And conscience doth all the parts. It registereth, it witnesseth, it accuseth, it judgeth, it executes, it doth all' (A. B. Grosart (ed.) Sibbes, *Works* (James Nichol, 1862), III, pp. 210f.

with disruptive effect). The super-ego, each person's tyrannical psychic policeman, is the culprit to which neuroses and psychoses are due, and the goal of psycho-analysis is to strengthen one's ego to unmask the super-ego and see it for the hotch-potch of forgotten traumas which it really is, thus winning freedom to discount it.

Since Freud's view equates the super-ego with conscience, it might seem to us, as it certainly did to him, directly to undermine any concept of conscience as God's voice; but in fact what Freud talks about is what Christian pastors have learned to recognize as the 'false conscience' – more or less irrational scrupulosity which shows the mind to be not so much godly as sick. The right comment here is Ronald Preston's: 'Whether, therefore, Freud's theories are sound or not, they do not contradict Christian teaching. Indeed they throw light on the well-known phenomenon of the "scrupulous conscience." He has confused the terminology by being unaware of the usual Christian understanding of the term.'[6] In other words: what Freud calls conscience is precisely not conscience on the Christian view, and what Christians mean by conscience (practical moral reason, consciously exercised, growing in insight and sureness of guidance through instruction and use, and bringing inner integration, health and peace to those who obey it) is not dealt with by Freud at all.

## Standards

Whether Christians always draw from Scripture the standards whereby they judge of moral good and evil is open to question, but it will not be disputed that this is what they should do. What criteria, then, does Scripture give for judging the morality of deeds done, and for making choices which are not merely legitimate but the best possible in each situation? By what rules should conscience go in these matters?

The first criterion that Scripture yields concerns *the nature of the action*. God loves some types of action and hates others. 'I the Lord love justice, I *hate* robbery and wrong' (Isa. 61:8). 'Speak the truth to one another . . . do not devise evil in your hearts against one another, and love no false oath, for all these things I *hate*, says the Lord' (Zech. 8:16f.; cf. Jer. 44:6; Amos. 5:21; Rev. 2:6). In the Decalogue God forbids various types of action which he hates: disrespect and distrust towards himself, in a number of forms; disrespect for parents (and by parity of reasoning other bearers of God-given authority); disrespect for human life, for the marriage bond, and for property; and disrespect for truth, especially truth about other people. Most of the Bible's ethical teaching in both Testaments is

---

[6] Ronald Preston, 'Conscience,' in John Macquarrie (ed.), *A Dictionary of Christian Ethics* (SCM, 1967), p. 68.

elaboration and enforcement of these principles, buttressed with theo -
logical reasons why some types of action are unfitting and only their
opposites can be right.

We should note that the nature of actions, as Scripture and common
sense view them, can only be made clear by speaking of them direction -
ally, that is, in terms of their object – that at which the physical movement
is aimed, and in which it naturally results. Thus, any physical movement,
of whatever sort, which puts me in possession of what belongs to someone
else, without his permission and against his presumed will, but of set
purpose on my part, would be theft. Actions have to be defined not
abstractly, in terms that are physical alone, but concretely, in terms of the
agent's aim and object, to which his physical movement is the means.
(This assumes, of course, that the agent is rational, and knows what he is
doing.)

We should note too that when Jesus linked Deuteronomy 6:4f. with
Leviticus 18:18b as the two great commandments, on which all the
specific ethical teachings of the law and the prophets depend (Matt.
22:36–40), he was focusing positively the two proper overall purposes of
actions, which the Decalogue illustrates negatively. The Decalogue said,
in effect: do nothing which in any way dishonours your God, or your
human neighbour who bears his image. Jesus' formula, in effect, says: do
everything that expresses the purpose of pleasing and exalting your God,
and benefiting your neighbour (which is what 'love' for God and
neighbour means).

That this is no cancellation of the Decalogue appears both from the
rubric Jesus gave for interpreting all his teaching (Matt. 5:17: 'Think not
that I have come to abolish the law and the prophets; I have come . . . to
fulfil them'), and also from Paul's exposition of loving one's neighbour
in terms of keeping the second table (Rom. 13:8–10: 'He who loves his
neighbour has fulfilled the law. The commandments . . . are summed up
in this sentence, "You shall love your neighbour as yourself." ') So when
good Samaritans bind up the wounded, it is proper to speak of acts of
healing (healing being their object) which express a purpose of love
(others' welfare being their designed goal). Healing is the object of the
action, love the purpose of the agent. Clarity requires the distinction.

Third, we should note that God's law in both Testaments, full as it
looks, is actually quite open-textured. It is not a minutely detailed code
of practice for all our actions every moment (the sort of code which Jewish
expository tradition produced); it is, rather, a set of broad guiding
principles with sample applications to set us going (case law for the courts
in the Pentateuch, actual or imaginary examples for individual guidance
elsewhere).

Some of the applications are couched in typical Eastern hyperbole –
for instance, Jesus' 'If any one would sue you and take your coat, let him
have your cloak as well; and if any one forces you to go one mile, go

with him two miles' (Matt. 5:40f.) – and this shows their purpose: they
are not so much models for mechanical imitation as cartoons of required
attitudes, which we must learn by experience spontaneously to express.
Cartoonists' drawings make their point by simplifying and exaggerating,
and such parabolic sayings of Jesus as I have just cited work the same way.
The cartoon is there to give us the idea, but most of the detailed applying
of the principles is left to us, to manage as creatively as we can. Four aids
are given us in Scripture for this task.

*First*, there is the calculus embodied in Jesus' so-called 'golden rule':
'Whatever you wish that men would do to you, do so to them; for this
is the law and the prophets' (Matt. 7–12). The last clause, compared with
Matthew 22:40, shows that what the 'rule' is telling us is how to work
out the way to love our neighbour as ourselves. The method is, first to
recognize that naturally, necessarily and by God's will as Creator, you do
love and care for yourself, seeking your own well-being, and to think of
all the treatment from others that you feel would conduce to this end;
and then to make that the standard for your treatment of them. Christ's
matter-of-fact appeal to self-love as setting a standard (an appeal which
Paul also makes in Ephesians 5:28f., when teaching husbands how to love
their wives) should not shock us; self-love is not sin till it becomes
inordinate, and in fact a proper self-love is a further facet of God's image
in us, for he too seeks his own felicity.

The assertion, common nowadays, that one cannot robustly love
either God or one's neighbour unless one robustly loves oneself is, both
psychologically and theologically, a deep truth. Meantime, by starting
from our self-love as it is, with all its inordinate elements, the 'golden
rule' vastly expands our sense of what love we owe to our neighbour. If,
for instance, I find myself longing to be listened to more and understood
better, there may well be sinful self-pity in my attitude, but that is not
relevant here; what matters is that the 'rule' makes me realize, from my
own feelings, how much more in the way of attentive patience and
imaginative identification love to my neighbour requires of me than I had
first thought – and so across the board.

*Second*, there is the scriptural teaching on our nature and destiny. This
is clear and emphatic. We are told that, being the creatures we are, we
can only find full happiness in making appropriate response to the love
of God; that each one's highest good lies in conscious fellowship with
God beyond this world, for which our present life is a kind of preparatory
school and training ground; and that the path to this prize is discipleship
to Christ, whereby through faith we die and rise with him, and live as
those for whom the world is not home, but a vale of soul-making where
our own decisions sow all the seeds of future joy or sorrow. This teaching
instructs us not only to see and live our personal lives as a homeward
journey, and to look straight ahead as we travel, but also to relate to others
in a way that will help them to know their dignity and potential as God's

creatures, and encourage them to embrace eternal life as their destiny too, and puts no stumbling block in their way at either point: which gives us a strong lead on very many issues, from human rights and business management to family ideals and the priority of evangelism.

*Third*, there is the summons to imitate God, who says, 'You shall be holy, for I am holy' (1 Pet. 1:16, referring to Lev. 11:44f.; cf. 19:2; 20:7,26), and Jesus Christ, who washed his disciples' feet as 'an example, that you also should do as I have done to you' (John 13:15), and spelt out the message of his action by saying, 'Love one another as I have loved you. Greater love has no man than this, that a man lay down his life for his friends' (15:12f.). The feet-washing symbolized the shedding of Christ's atoning and cleansing blood, and so John elsewhere writes: 'He laid down his life for us; and we ought to lay down our lives for the brethren' (1 John 3:16).

God's call to be holy, as he is holy, is a general summons to live by his revealed precepts and prohibitions, as embodying the loves and hates which make up his character and which his ways with us will always express; Christ's call to follow his example is a specific summons to unlimited self-humbling, and giving of ourselves without restraint, in order to relieve others' needs and make them great, which is what true love is all about. Paul, too, charges Christians to imitate Christ's costly and self-forgetful love (Phil. 2:1–8; 2 Cor. 8:9; Eph. 5:25–33, a word to husbands); and Christ's submissive but resilient patience in enduring human hostility is elsewhere held up for imitation as well (1 Pet. 2:21; Heb. 12:1–4). It is striking that all these references focus on Christ's cross, where the glories of his moral perfections are seen most clearly. It is striking too that the concern of each passage centres not on particular routines to be gone through, but on the spirit and attitude which our whole lives must express. Once again, the divine method of instruction is to 'tune us in' on the right wavelength and then leave the details of the application largely to us.

*Fourth*, there is the principle expressed in Paul's prayer for the Philippians, 'that your love will keep on growing more and more, together with true knowledge and perfect judgement, so that you will be able to *choose what is best*' (Phil. 1:9f., GNB). The principle is, of two goods choose the greater; don't let the good be the enemy of the best. It is the positive counterpart of the principle that, where one faces a choice of evils, the least evil should always be preferred. Here calculations of consequences must be attempted: for the best course, other things being equal, will always be that which promises most good and least harm. But since our capacity to foresee results is limited, differences of opinion here are in escapable, and so on policy decisions the most devoted Christians will not always be able to see eye to eye.

We find this in the New Testament itself. Acts 15:37ff. tells how Paul and Barnabas differed as to whether to take with them John Mark,

Barnabas' nephew, on missionary service. Barnabas knew his record but clearly expected him to make good; Paul 'thought best not to take with them one who had withdrawn from them in Pamphylia, and had not gone with them to the work.' Each of them insisted on making the best decision, and was not prepared to settle for anything less, but they differed as to what the best decision was. Being disagreed as to whether Mark was likely to prove an adequate colleague, they concluded that the best decision open to them was to split up, and each take the associate he judged best for the task; so Barnabas took Mark to Cyprus, and Paul went with Silas on a trip that ended in Europe. Some are embarrassed that Paul and Barnabas should ever have been involved in passionate disagreement, but there is no reason to regard this as a moral failure, any more than there is to see their parting as a strategic disaster. We can be sure that, God being who he is, no Christian forfeits blessing for parting company with his brother when both want the best, and only calculation of consequences divides them.

Should it be asked where the Holy Spirit's ministry in the conscience comes in, particularly in cases like this where Christian friends conscien - tiously differ as to what is wise and right, the answer is that as we pray and lay ourselves open to God, the Spirit quickens our minds and imaginations so that we are able to make the fullest use of the four aids listed, without either confusion of thought or perversion of purpose. But no man, no matter how saintly and devoted, is blessed with infallible perfection of judgment in this world, and (*pace* some charismatics) the idea that God will ordinarily give us experiences of being told, as by a human voice, exactly what to do is an unbiblical will-o'-the-wisp.

It is apparent that all these four aids to right conduct have the effect of maximizing the imaginative and creative element in morality, and of encouraging a spirit of enterprise and even opportunism in serving God – the spirit which so marked Paul (cf. Acts 16:35–39; 17:22ff.; 23:6–10). Within the boundaries set by God's specific commands, applications can vary and be better or worse, just as chess openings vary within the limits set by the pieces' permitted moves. And the best course will always be that which promises most in the total situation, just as the best first moves in a chess game will be those which promise most in the total situation, bearing in mind the game's importance, whether one is playing black or white, whether one should go for a win or a draw, the known strengths and weaknesses of one's opponent, one's own skill with this or that opening or line of defence, and so on.

Proper Christian obedience is thus as far away as possible from the treadmill negativism of the conscientious conformist, whose main con - cern is never to put a foot wrong and who conceives the whole Christian life in terms of shunning doubtful things. To be sure, a tender conscience which trembles at God's word (cf. Isa. 66:2; Ezra 10:3) and fears to offend him, 'hating even the garment spotted by the flesh' (Jude 23) is a Christian grace, and should never be frowned on as an introspective morbidity; but, just as one cannot maintain health on a diet of disinfectants only, so one cannot fully or healthily obey God just by trying to avoid defilements, evading risks, and omitting to ask what is the *most* one can do to glorify God. For that is the question which the Bible forces us to face all the time.

## Motives

The second criterion that Scripture yields for assessing choices is *the motive of the agent*. In Christian obedience the motive must be right as well as the action itself. The object of the action and the motive of the agent are distinct; the former we defined as the effect of successfully completing the action (healing, for instance, being the object of binding up a person's wounds), the latter is that in someone which moves them to attempt the action in the first place. Most motives are either reactions to situations or people, determined from without (e.g. fear, or gratitude), or they are personal goals determined from within (e.g. achieving wealth, or reputa - tion). Love, however, is a complex motive involving both these elements; it can be both a reaction of good will, occasioned and energized by appreciation of the beloved, and also a purpose of conferring benefit and happiness, irrespective of whether the recipients deserve it and of what it costs one to carry the purpose out.

That the Christian's supreme motive must always be the glory of God (cf. 1 Cor. 10:31), and that seeking his glory is the truest expression of love to him, will not be disputed. But love to men for the Lord's sake should motivate us also, and this has been an area of keen debate in recent years. How should love determine my behaviour towards my neighbour? It is necessary to reject the situationist idea that biblical rules of conduct are only rules of thumb, and that sound calculation of consequences can in principle make transgression of any of them right and good; [7] but at the same time it is important to realize that the more strongly neighbour-love operates as a motive, other things being equal, the more enterprising and skilful we are likely to be in devising, within the limits that the law sets, the most fruitful ways and means of doing others good. And when one finds oneself shut up to 'lesser evil' choices, love to God and neighbour will enable us to see the best that can be made of the bad job, and to choose in the least destructive way.

The role of love in our ethical decision-making is comparable to that of the referee in football. The referee's purpose is to apply the rules in a way which secures the best possible game, which is of course what the rules themselves are for. So he does four things.

---

[7] See Part 2, chapter 2.

First, he takes pains to familiarize himself with the rules and the proper way of interpreting them. Second, throughout the game he takes care always to be in the best position to make a decision. This requires close observation of all that is happening on the field, and anticipation, born of experience, as to how each situation may develop. Third, in order to get his facts straight, he will where necessary consult his linesmen, who are better placed to observe some things than he is himself; though he will pay no attention to the crowd, which is partisan and not well placed. Fourth, he will when appropriate invoke the difficult 'advantage rule,' which allows him to keep the game going though an infringement has occurred, if continuance is to the advantage of the wronged side.

Now, love to God and neighbour requires us to behave like the referee. Our purpose is to live in a manner that is as pleasing to God and as beneficial to our neighbour as possible, within the limits that God has laid down; and to this end love prompts a parallel fourfold proce-dure. First, it directs us to gain thorough knowledge of the whole range of obligations that Scripture requires us to meet. Without this basic knowledge, good decisions will be impossible.

Second, love directs us in each situation to get into the best position for decision-making, by securing as much relevant information about actual causes and possible consequences as we can. The legalistic mental-ity, from which so many of us suffer, is always in danger of pronouncing (negatively!) too soon, before the necessary minimum of information is to hand; we have to guard against that.

Third, love directs us when we are not well placed for decision, either from lack of specialist knowledge or through a personal involve-ment biasing our judgment, to turn to others who are better qualified to suggest what should be done, while at the same time declining to be swayed by loud noises from persons who are passionate but not well informed.

Fourth, love directs us on occasion to apply the Christian equivalent of the advantage rule, by not jeopardizing a greater good through needless enquiry into doubtful details. Thus, on the question of meat offered to idols, Paul writes:

> Eat whatever is sold in the meat market without raising any question on the ground of conscience . . . If one of the unbelievers invites you to dinner and you are disposed to go, eat whatever is set before you without raising any question on the ground of conscience. (But if someone says to you, 'This has been offered in sacrifice,' then out of consideration for the man who informed you, and for conscience' sake – I mean his conscience, not yours – do not eat it) (1 Cor. 10:25–29).

Paul's point is that though Christians should eschew any social activity of which sacrifices to pagan gods form part (verses 14–22), they need not ask, or bother their heads, whether food offered them in pagan homes was offered to idols first.

If a 'weak' person raises the issue, responsible Christians will then practise abstinence for their sake, but otherwise the question should be allowed to lie dormant, while Christians eat freely. As it is neither God-honouring, nor edifying, nor safe (says Paul) to join in sacrifices to pagan deities (for, after all, they really are demons), so it is not necessary in principle nor best in practice to spurn a pagan's hospitality in the interests of a thoroughgoing dietary witness against pagan beliefs (for, after all, 'the earth is the Lord's, and everything in it' (verse 26), and what is on the table, whatever has been done with it, remains God's gift). Knowing the overall value and potential importance of friendly social links with unbelievers, Paul counsels Christians to use their God-given liberty by waiving the idolatry issue, and thus in effect to play their own advantage rule in the situation.

But as referees, however experienced and well-intentioned, can still on occasion make bad decisions, so Christians from time to time have to acknowledge, looking back, that they missed the best course of action, either because an unnoticed cooling of their love left them in a particular situation or relationship thoughtless and apathetic, or else because love made them too eager and sympathetic to be truly prudent, so that they invoked the advantage rule inappropriately. Such acknowledgment is deeply humbling. But Christians live by the forgiveness of their sins; so they can afford to fail, and in humility they will learn from their mistakes.

## Choosing

So what is involved in making a moral choice? and how should it be done? The matter may be summed up thus. A moral choice is one involving standards (right and wrong) and values (good and bad). It presupposes a rational agent, that is, one who is free in the relevant respects to act rationally (not a demoniac, then, or a madman, or a baby, or a sufferer from an irrational behaviour pattern like kleptomania or agora - phobia). It presupposes too a field of freedom within which the agent sees that more than one course is open to them. The making of the choice involves, first, thinking out possible lines of action; second, envisaging their consequences; and third, measuring both action and consequences thus envisaged by the moral standards and scale of values that one recognizes as binding.

The Christian accepts the moral standards which are set forth in the Bible, acknowledging them as standing in a 'maker's handbook' relation to their own nature and as circumscribing the only way of life that can lead them to ultimate fulfilment and felicity. Their moral values, too, are determined by theology. They are, on the one hand, the characteristic qualities of those types of actions which God loves and delights in, and, on the other hand, that longed-for state of affairs in which God is being praised for his great glory and men whom he made and loves are being benefited according to their need. He knows that the best choice will always be choice of the best option, and that the way to choose between options is not by reference to rules apart from consequences, as if consequences were morally irrelevant, nor by reference to consequences apart from rules, as if rules had no intrinsic moral value, but by reference to both together. In his choosing he is constantly exercised with the question: 'Is this the *best* I can do?'

It is a law of life that our values become our motives, so that motive, where known (for we do not always admit our motives, even to ourselves), is the clearest indication of character that exists. It is possible, as we all know, to make a right choice from a wrong motive, and equally a bad choice from a good motive. The Christian's aim, however, in their game-plan for living, will always be to do the right thing for the right reason – that is, always to be found applying biblical standards for his guidance from the twofold motive of the glory of God and the good of people, understanding 'good' in terms not simply of currently felt need, but of godliness and glory (cf. the meaning of 'good' in Rom. 8:28). The Christian knows that only when their motives are right will his choices, however good in themselves, be the choices of a morally good man, who truly pleases God.

Is God's promise of a reward a motive, in the sense of a spur to right choice? Strictly speaking, no. The Christian's reward is not directly earned; it is not a payment proportionate to services rendered; it is a Father's gift of generous grace to his children, far exceeding anything they deserved (see Matt. 20:1–16). Also, we must understand that the promised reward is not something of a different nature tacked on to the activity being rewarded; it is, rather, that activity itself – that is to say, communion with God in worship and service – in consummation. [8] God's promise of reward, thus understood, may well be an encouragement to action and a source of strength and joy in it, but the motive must be love to God and

---

[8] 'There are different kinds of reward. There is the reward which has no natural connection with the things you do to earn it, and is quite foreign to the desires that ought to accompany these things. Money is not the natural reward of love; that is why we call a man mercenary if he marries a woman for the sake of her money. But marriage is the proper reward for a real lover, and he is not mercenary for desiring it. A general who fights well in order to get a peerage is mercenary; a general who fights for victory is not, victory being the proper reward of battle as marriage is the proper reward of love. The proper rewards are not simply tacked on to the activity for which they are given, but are the activity itself in consummation' (C. S. Lewis, 'The Weight of Glory,' in *Screwtape Proposes a Toast*, [Fontana, 1965], p. 95).

neighbour, as we said. We serve our God, not for reward, but because he is our God, and we love him. Francis Xavier's well-known hymn focuses this.

> My God, I love thee – not because
>     I hope for heaven thereby,
> Nor yet because who love thee not
>     Are lost eternally.
>
> Thou, O my Jesus, thou didst me
>     Upon the cross embrace;
> For me didst bear the nails and spear,
>     And manifold disgrace.
>
> And griefs and torments numberless,
>     And sweat and agony,
> And death itself – and all for me,
>     Who was thine enemy.
>
> Then why, O blessed Jesus Christ,
>     Should I not love thee well?
> Not for the sake of winning heaven
>     Or of escaping hell;
>
> Not with the hope of gaining aught;
>     Not seeking a reward;
> But as thyself hast loved me,
>     O ever-loving Lord.
>
> E'en so I love thee, and will love,
>     And in thy praise will sing;
> Because thou art my loving God
>     And my eternal King.

C. S. Lewis compares our position, as we move on in the Christian life, to that of a schoolboy learning Greek.[9] The enjoyment of Aeschylus and Sophocles to which he will one day come is the proper consummation of all his slogging at the grammar, just as the enjoyment of God in that glory compared to which, as Lewis elsewhere says, the raptures of earthly lovers are mere milk and water is the proper consummation of discipleship here. But at first the boy cannot imagine this enjoyment at all. As his Greek improves, however, enjoyment of Greek literature begins to come, and he begins to be able to desire the reward that awaits him (more of

---

[9] Ibid.

the same, at an intenser level), which capacity for desire, says Lewis, is itself a preliminary reward. Meantime, however (here I make a point complementary to Lewis'), it is the increased enjoyment in the present which sends him back to work at his Greek with increased energy and excitement; and so it goes on. I like this illustration, both because it is true to life (for when I learned Greek it happened to me) and because it shows the truth about Christian motivation so clearly.

The last and most important thing to be said about moral choice is that our choosing is a function of our character, just as our present character is largely the product of our past choices. Sin, that irrational, self-centred, anti-God surd in the soul, distorts character most fundamen - tally at motivational level; grace restores character there, but in a way that brings tension and struggle.

> 'I do not understand my own actions', writes Paul. 'For I do not do what I want, but I do the very thing I hate. Now if I do what I do not want, I agree that the law is good. . . . I can will what is right, but I cannot do it. For I do not do the good I want, but the evil I do not wand is what I do. Now if I do what I do not want, it is no longer I that do it, but sin which dwells within me.' (Rom. 7:15ff.).

What is going on here? New motivation, supernaturally restored by the coming of the Holy Spirit into a person's heart, is manifesting itself. This is Paul the Christian (the present tense, and the flow of the argument, prove this) testifying to the fact that now by grace he loves God's law and wants to keep it perfectly to God's glory. His reach, however, exceeds his grasp, and his qualified success feels like failure. Sin within him, dethroned but not yet destroyed, is fighting back. The intensity of Paul's distress at being less than perfect by the law's standard is, however, the index of the strength of his new motivation, and it is from this source that character grows and moral energy derives through the inward working of the Holy Spirit.

When elsewhere Paul says to Christians, 'Work out your own salva - tion with fear and trembling [awe and reverence]; for God is at work in you, both to will and to work for his good pleasure' (Phil. 2:12f.), what he means them to do is precisely to keep their motivational channels clear and work against whatever opposition indwelling sin may raise to make and follow out right choices, trusting in the Spirit's power. And as we do so, our capacity for so doing will increase; and thus God's work of grace within us will go on.

# Chapter 30

# Situations and Principles

The most obvious challenge to Christian morality today comes from a view of Christian morality itself which, if accepted, would sweep away most of the approach and conclusions for which this book contends. It is time for us to take a long hard look at it. 'Situation ethics' is its name.

'Situation ethics,' 'situationism' as we shall call it, burst with a shower of sparks on the English-speaking Christian world in the 1960s and is clearly here to stay for some time yet. Its best-known expositor has been J. A. T. Robinson; its most incisive spokesman the American, Joseph Fletcher.[1] It has a good deal going for it. It offers itself as a seemingly simple method of solving complex problems about what to do. It claims to correct the legalism and remove the artificiality which have in the past disfigured much Christian thinking about conduct. It endorses the modern (and, we might add, ancient and Edenic) disinclination to treat any external rules as unbreakable. Its exponents have a lot to say about sex, which to most people is a very interesting subject, particularly when handled in a way that sounds permissive.[2] In its rhetoric, situationism

SITUATIONS AND PRINCIPLES was originally published in *Law, Morality and the Bible*, G. J. Wenham and B. Kaye, eds. (Downers Grove: InterVarsity Press, 1978), pp. 151–167. Reprinted by permission.

This paper is indebted to three unpublished papers by Gordon Stobart.

[1] J. A. T. Robinson, *Honest to God* (SCM, 1963), Chapter 6; *Christian Morals Today* (SCM, 1964); *Christian Freedom in a Permissive Society* (SCM, 1970); J. Fletcher, *Situation Ethics* (SCM, 1966); *Moral Responsibility: Situation Ethics at Work* (SCM, 1967); 'Reflection and Reply', in Harvey Cox (ed.), *The Situation Ethics Debate* (Westminster Press, Philadelphia, 1968), pp. 249–264; 'What's in a Rule: A Situationist's View', Gene H. Outka and Paul Ramsey (eds.), *Norm and Context in Christian Ethics* (SCM, 1969), pp. 325–349.

[2] Unfortunately, Fletcher really did write 'Sex is not always wrong outside marriage, even for Christians' (*Moral Responsibility*, p. 138). No less unfortunately, H. A. Williams, on this showing a situationalist fellow-traveller, dabbled in his essay in A. R. Vidler (ed.), *Soundings* (Cambridge University Press, 1962) with the Freudian fancy of therapeutic and therefore valuable fornication. Of an episode in the film *Never on Sunday* he wrote: 'The prostitute gives herself to him

seems to endorse the hunch which popular music and pulp writing so often express, that love will justify anything and that in seeing this we are both wiser and more humane than our fathers were.

Not surprisingly, therefore, situationism allures as common ways of stating Christian morality do not. Frequently today the old formulations are dismissed as a bad brew of Victorianism and Puritanism, two outlooks which we are urged to abhor as unholy and oppressive blends of narrow-mindedness, pomposity, prejudice and hypocrisy – all law and no love, and dull as ditchwater into the bargain. The moral pendulum has swung with a vengeance, so that creative freedom in structuring caring relationships is now 'in' while the conscientious rigour of law-keeping is 'out.'

It could at once be objected that since loving action is what the Decalogue and the law of Christ are all about, the antithesis is false, just as are the proffered descriptions of Victorianism and Puritanism. Granted; but since situationism sees loving as the only prescribed duty and denies that there are any other, more specific, divine laws to keep, we cannot leave the matter there. Situationist claims must be examined on their merits. As we saw, this viewpoint owes much of its attractiveness to its identifying with what Fletcher called 'the whole mind-set of the modern man, *our* mind-set';[3] an outlook which Paul Ramsey correctly if turgidly summed up as 'prejudice in favour of individualistic freedom, normless-ness, traditionless contemporaneity, and modern technical reason.'[4] So, too, when J. A. T. Robinson calls for a recasting of Christian ethics, with Christian faith, on the ground that humanity today has 'come of age,' he is appealing to our un-selfcritical conceit in the same way that Fletcher does. No doubt, favour is gained this way. But the rights and wrongs of situationism cannot be settled at the murky level of popular prejudice, whether for or against. There are arguments to be weighed – complex and sophisticated arguments, as it turns out.

## What is Situationism?

First, let us note that though 'situationism' is usually thought of as a term referring specifically to one view of Christian morality, it is actually an

---

[2] *(continued)* in such a way that he acquires confidence and self-respect. He goes away a deeper fuller person than he came in.' And of something similar in *The Mark*: 'Will he be able to summon up the necessary courage or not? When he does, and they sleep together, he has been made whole. And where there is healing, there is Christ, whatever the Church may say about fornication' (pp. 81f.). All else apart, however, is it safe to assume that real life will be like what you see at the movies?

[3] *Situation Ethics*, p. 58.

[4] *The Situation Ethics Debate*, p. 202.

umbrella-word for all views which reject the idea that the way to decide what to do is always to apply rules, positive and negative, concerning types of actions (e.g. keep your promises, do not steal, do not rape, do not torture). The situationist does not regard such rules as *prescriptive*, i.e. as having absolute and universal authority, but as at best *illuminative*, in the sense of being relative, provisional and violable indicators of what behaviour may (though it may not) be right here and now. Thus, 'situationism' is a term of negative classification, clear only in what it excludes and covering many positive conceptions that are intrinsically different.

The word 'existentialism' is similar; it, too, is an umbrella-word for all views, Christian and non-Christian, which reject the idea that one can achieve authentic personal existence without total commitment, and it, too, in practice covers a wide range of outlooks. Now as a view about the way to determine what one should do, situationism can be part of an atheistic existentialist or humanist position no less than of a Christian one. The mark of existentialist situationism is its requirement that one should always act whole-heartedly, in conscious personal freedom (meaning by this, openness to variation from all one's actions hitherto). The mark of humanist situationism is its quest in all circumstances for the realization of personal values as it sees them. The mark of Christian situationism is its conviction that general moral rules applied to the matter in hand will not always lead you to what the command of God and the calculations of neighbourly love (which two things some identify and others distinguish) actually require.

The claim traditionally made for Christian morality is that love can be, and indeed has been, embodied in rules, so that in using the moral principles of Scripture prescriptively a Christian will always be expressing love, never frustrating it, and so will always be doing the will of God. Situationism diagnoses this claim as legalistic and declines to accept it, insisting that love itself requires one to go further and do more: namely, to pay fullest attention to the situation itself, which may be an exceptional set of circumstances requiring, for the fullest expression of love, an exceptional way of acting. Action which the rules would call wrong will yet be right if analysis shows it to be the most loving thing to do. For no types of action, as such, can be said to be immoral; only failures of love in particular situations can be called immoral or thought of as forbidden, inasmuch as the fullness of loving action is the whole of what God commands.[5]

---

[5] Fletcher writes: 'As a "Scripture" for the open-endedness of situation ethics turn to Romans 14:14. When Paul said, "I know . . . that nothing is unclean of itself," what he meant by "unclean" (once we step out of the situation in and to which he spoke), and what he could well have said, is "immoral". Nothing is immoral in itself, intrinsically. What love is, what morality is, always depends on

How, then, should we decide what to do in a given situation? Here the ways part. The *rational* situationism of the Anglo-Saxon Anglicans Fletcher and Robinson offers us a method of calculation; the *existentialist* situationism of the big B's of continental neo-orthodoxy – Barth, Bonhoeffer, Brunner, Bultmann – takes the line of attuning us for particular self-authenticating commands from God which will reach us via Scripture, though they will not be identical with, nor will they be simply applications of, moral principles stated in Scripture. Neither position (be it said) is intentionally lax or antinomian (that is, opposed to law); both think they achieve what the law in Scripture is really after; the differences between them, and between them both and Christian ethical stances which would not call themselves situationist, are theo - logical. This chapter is most concerned with the former type of situationism, but we shall grasp it better by comparing it with the latter, and this will be our next step.

## Pure Situationism

Neo-orthodox situationism may be called 'pure' as distinct from 'princi - pled.' Its main thesis is that as I face each situation, taking its measure and noting its complexities, God will speak, in some sense of that word, directly. The determining factor here is the dynamism or 'actualism' of the neo-orthodox conception of God: that is, the insistence that the Creator-God, who is transcendent, sovereign and free, is known to us and reveals his command to us only in the particularity of the present moment. So the

---

[5] *(continued)* the situation' (*Norm and Context in Christian Ethics*, p. 349). The text does not prove Fletcher's point, for Paul's 'nothing' denotes foodstuffs, not types of action, whereas Fletcher's 'nothing' signifies, apparently, types of action viewed formally and externally without reference to their motive and purpose (e.g. shaking hands, or signing one's name, or speaking, or keeping silent, or copulating). Nor in any case is Fletcher's external concept of an action always adequate; some types of action, e.g. rape and torture, are only definable in terms of an unloving and therefore (for Fletcher, as for everyone else) immoral motive and volition, so that to say that rape and torture are not 'immoral . . . intrinsically' would be self-contradictory. Robinson, trying to have it both ways, achieves this self-contradiction explicitly, affirming *both* that 'nothing can of itself always be labelled as "wrong" ' *and* that there are actions of which 'it is so inconceivable that they could ever be an expression of love – like cruelty to children or rape – that . . . they are . . . always wrong' (*Honest to God*, p. 118; *Christian Morals Today*, p. 16 and also *Christian Freedom in a Permissive Society*, p. 16): which, as Paul Ramsey notes, 'is simply saying that they are *inherently* wrong, wrong in themselves, . . . because of the lovelessness that is always in them' (*Deeds and Rules in Christian Ethics*, Oliver and Boyd, 1965, p. 28). For clear discussion with a situationist, the first question one should ask is how they define an action.

generalized ethical injunctions of Scripture are understood not as formulae embodying the fullness of God's will for all time, but as so many indications of the lines along which, or within which, particular commands of God may be expected to come. God's revealed will never takes the form of a universally valid rule for us to apply to all relevant cases, but only of particular summonses. 'God's commanding can only be this individual, concrete and specific commanding,' says Karl Barth.[6] Formally, then, the Christian ethic is obeying God in a most direct way; and materially it is neighbour love, in whatever mode God's self-authenticating command specifies here and now. Thus Brunner writes: 'Nothing is good save obedience to the command of God, just because it is obedience. No reasons of determination from content here come under consideration. The "form" of the will, obedience, is all. But to be obedient means: "love your neighbour!" '[7]

Bonhoeffer says this most starkly, forbidding us to ask 'What is the will of God for this particular case?' because the question embodies 'the casuistic misinterpretation of the concrete. The concrete is not achieved in this way . . . The will of God is always concrete, or else it is not the will of God . . . the will of God is not a principle . . . which has to be applied to "reality." '[8] These negations sound startling; but the guidance that Bonhoeffer takes away with the one hand, by denying that God reveals principles, he effectively restores with the other, by his teaching on the 'mandates' – church, government, labour and culture, and mar - riage and the family, spheres of delegated divine authority which the Reformers also recognized. 'Mandate' (which term Bonhoeffer preferred to the more usual 'orders,' because it denoted a God-given task) meant for him 'the conferment of divine authority (i.e. the right to command obedience as God's representative) on an earthly agent', and 'the forma - tion of a definite earthly domain by the divine commandment';[9] and the mandates themselves, conservatively conceived, define closely the limits within which God's concrete will is expressed and encountered. Barth and Brunner speak similarly. Barth also affirms that, while God's demand cannot be anticipated in abstraction, his constancy of character revealed in Christ means that like demands will be made in like situations: for Jesus Christ, who is the same yesterday, today and for ever, is 'the ground, content and form of God's command.'[10]

---

[6] K. Barth, *Church Dogmatics*, II.2 (T. & T. Clark, 1957), p. 673. Barth continues: 'We must divest ourselves of the fixed idea that only a universally valid rule can be a command.' See the whole section, pp. 661–708; op. cit., III.4, pp. 1–23; and D. Bonhoeffer, *Ethics* (Fontana, 1964), pp. 278, 285.

[7] E. Brunner, *The Divine Imperative* (Lutterworth, 1937), p. 59.

[8] Op. cit., p. 285.

[9] Op. cit., p. 287.

[10] H. Hartwell, *The Theology of Karl Barth: An Introduction* (Duckworth, 1964), p. 162.

In all this neo-orthodoxy is polemicizing against what Barth calls a 'theoretical casuistry' which assumes that the whole of God's command consists of a legacy of general principles left us in the Bible, to be applied by our own best wisdom. Their motive – a proper one – is a desire to display Christian obedience as direct response to God's present, personal address. But as anyone with a ripe doctrine of the Holy Spirit can and will make that point without denying that in what God says today he applies what he has said in Scripture once for all, so the 'pure' situationism to which these men resort seems to turn God's command, at least in its details, into an uncheckable private revelation every time.[11] Nor (to their credit!) do they sustain in practice the daunting notion which they profess. Thus, Bonhoeffer's concept of the command of God, which if it is not 'clear, definite and concrete to the last detail . . . is not God's command,' receives a crippling qualification when he admits that God's will 'may lie deeply concealed beneath a great number of available possibilities,' so that 'the whole apparatus of human powers must be set in motion when it is a matter of proving (i.e. discerning, as in Romans 12:2) the will of God.'[12] These admissions, and the whole excellent section on 'proving' from which they come, recognize realistically the perplexities which ethical choices involve, but hardly square with 'clear, definite and concrete to the last detail.' And Barth's treatment of areas of ethical decision in terms of God's work in Christ (which, he holds, is the basic subject-matter of ethics) differs little from the kind of casuistical reasoning which he professes to abhor.

The most problematical version of neo-orthodox situationism is Rudolf Bultmann's. Here the existentialist motif is strongest (for human-kind's existence consists wholly in our possibility of existence, and we are always seeking authentic selfhood by choosing who we are); here, too, God and his will are most elusive, for God is silent, and 'Jesus teaches no ethics at all in the sense of an intelligible theory valid for all men concerning what should be done and left undone,'[13] and obedience itself must be understood in a 'non- objectifying' way, not literally, that is, as response to God's command, but in a Pickwickian, that is, private and

---

[11] This brings 'pure' situationism into line with the position of sixteenth-century Anabaptists and seventeenth-century Quakers who relied on what they took to be immediate promptings of the Holy Spirit, not related to the Word in any direct or testable way. A similar tendency appears on occasion in charismatic circles, and in *Knowing God* (Hodder, 1975, pp. 263f.) I cite three horror stories along the same line from the 'fanaticism papers' which Hannah Whitall Smith compiled from her experience among American evangelicals a century ago. The doctrine of the Holy Spirit which underlies expectations of immediate guidance by private revelation is not so much ripe as overripe, and can be expected to produce ethical instability.

[12] Bonhoeffer, op. cit., pp. 278, 38, 40.

[13] R. Bultmann, *Jesus and the Word* (Nicholson & Watson, 1935), p. 84.

unnatural sense as decision in the situation, whereby authentic existence is achieved. The whole ethical process in humanity is reduced to successive crises of new decision each present moment. 'A man,' Bult-mann insists, 'cannot in the moment of decision fall back upon principles, upon a general ethical theory which can relieve him of the responsibility for the decision . . . man does not meet the crisis of decision armed with a definite standard; he stands on no firm base, but rather alone in empty space.'[14] Newness of decision is called for each new moment, for each new moment the situation itself is new.

So how should we act? First, we must realize the necessity of meeting the demands of the moment, for it always carries eschatological, that is, ultimate, significance for our existence; second, we must realize that each moment calls on us not just to do something but to be something – namely, persons who love their neighbours as themselves. We know how we love ourselves and how we want others to love us, so we already know how to love others. Jesus and Scripture do not therefore tell us what things love should make us do (that, if attempted, would be legalism); all we are told is that we should love, and that is all we need to be told, for 'if a man really loves, he knows already what he has to do'; [15] and he knows it, 'not on the basis of any past experience or rational deductions, but directly from the immediate situation.'[16]

General strictures on situationism will come later, and general criticisms of Bultmann on God, Christ and Scripture would not be in place here, but some particular shortcomings of his ethic may be noted at once. First, he takes an over-optimistic view of *humanity*. Does one who 'really loves' thereby always know what to do? Does real love keep us who are naturally daft from speaking and acting in character? Second, Bultmann takes an over-simplified view of *situations*. Do not most perplexities in moral decision stem, not from lack of loving intention or will to obey God, but from ignorance of past and future facts, so that one cannot with confidence calculate consequences? Is it not daunting to note, with Thomas Oden, that Bultmann lacks 'realistic understanding of the intense and endless *conflict of values* and interests and obligations that characterize human existence'? [17] Is it not disastrous that Bultmann neither will nor can develop a social ethic? Third, Bultmann gives an over-simplified account of the moral life, reducing it to a series of isolated decisions and allowing no significance to

---

[14] Ibid., p. 85.

[15] Ibid., p. 94 'The demand for love needs no formulated stipulations; the example of the merciful Samaritan shows that a man can know . . . what he has to do when he sees his neighbour in need of his help. The little words "as yourself" in the love commandment pre-indicate both the boundlessness and the direction of loving conduct' (*Theology of the New Testament*. I, SCM, 1952, p. 19).

[16] *Jesus and the Word*, p. 88.

[17] T. Oden, *Radical Obedience* (Epworth, 1965), p. 123.

factors like character, habit, aspiration and growth (all of which find a place in the New Testament!). Fourth, Bultmann gives an unrealistic account of moral decision itself, speaking as if there never need be – indeed, never should be – any doubt in a Christian's mind as to what they should do this moment, for if their heart is right God will have made the right course clear to them. I do not always find that, nor do you; who does?

## Principled Situationism

Set beside this, now, the 'principled' situationism of Fletcher and Robinson – 'principled' because it offers a constant method of deciding in each case what love demands. We may state it thus:

(a) Neighbour-love is God's absolute and only demand in each situation. God does not require invariable performance of particular types of action, as such, whatever the simple reader of the Decalogue and the ethical parts of the New Testament might think; he calls simply for love, first as a motive (good will) and then as beneficent behaviour, of whatever form the situation requires. 'Love is both absolute and relative by its very nature. An unchanging principle, it nevertheless always changes in its concrete application.'[18]

(b) 'Old' Christian morality lapses into Pharisaic legalism and so sins against love, because in determining how to act it 'begins from the deductive, the transcendent and the authoritative. It stresses the revealed character of the Christian moral standard . . . (and) starts from Christian principles which are valid "without respect of persons." '[19] The 'new' morality, by contrast, starts from persons rather than principles and from experienced relationships rather than revealed commandments, and in and from the situation itself works out, by reference to personal claims and probable consequences, what is the most loving thing to do. Fletcher, stressing that love maximizes good for all, assimilates love and justice and affirms a Christianized utilitarianism[20] so

---

[18] P. Tillich, *Morality and Beyond* (Fontana, 1969), p. 37. Tillich was a situationist of a kind, but he anchors morality in a private doctrine of 'Being' which sets him apart from Trinitarian Christianity.

[19] J. A. T. Robinson, *Christian Morals Today*, p. 34, and also *Christian Freedom in a Permissive Society*, pp. 31f.

[20] 'Justice is Christian love using its head . . . coping with situations where distribution is called for. On this basis it becomes plain that as the love ethic searches seriously for a social policy it must form a coalition with utilitarianism,' taking over 'the strategic principle of "the greatest good of the greatest number." ' (*Situation Ethics*, p. 95).

calculating that one reviewer called his book 'blood-chilling' and asked: 'Does this "calculus" of love not, in effect, dehumanize love?'[21] Robinson, by contrast, seems to think that the discerning of love's demands will occur spontaneously, through intuition rather than calculation. 'Love alone,' he writes, 'because, as it were, it has a built-in moral compass, enabling it to "home" intuitively upon the deepest need of the other, can allow itself to be directed completely by the situation . . . . It is able to embrace an ethic of radical responsiveness, meeting every situation on its own merits, with no prescriptive laws.'[22] At all events, it is part of the optimism of situationist faith that, by one means or another, love will be able to see what the personal claims in each situation require, without needing to run to God's law for guidance.

(c) Love may dictate the breaking of accepted moral rules of the 'do this,' 'don't do that' type. These rules, both in Scripture and in life, are no more than rules of thumb ('maxims,' Fletcher calls them; 'working rules' is Robinson's phrase); they give prelimi - nary guidance as to how love will normally be expressed, but sometimes for the sake of persons different action will be called for. This, however, presents no problem theoretically, for what the rules forbid is forbidden only because it is ordinarily unloving, and nothing that actually expresses love in a particular situation is actually wrong. 'Apart from (love) there are no unbreakable rules.'[23] Love as the end justifies its means; nothing is intrinsically evil, since what makes for good in a situation thereby becomes good in that situation. Fletcher notes that Paul rejects all thought of doing evil that good may come (Rom. 3:8), but sees Paul as here 'victimized' by 'the intrinsic theory,' that is, the false notion that things are good or evil in themselves.[24]

(d) No situation ever faces us with a choice of evils; the traditional view to the contrary is one more product of the mistaken 'intrinsic theory.' '*The situationalist holds that whatever is the most loving thing in the situation is the right and good thing*. It is not excusably evil, it is positively good.'[25] To illustrate, Fletcher is

---

[21] Norman P. Langford, in *The Situation Ethics Debate*, p. 63. Amazingly, Fletcher's reply is: 'All right, we accept that. Cold calculation for love's sake is indeed the ideal model' . . . the "warmer" love's calculations are, the more apt they are to be only interpersonal or even individualistic' (p. 261). Comment seems superfluous!

[22] Honest to God, p. 115.

[23] *Christian Morals Today*, p. 16, and also *Christian Freedom in a Permissive Society*, p. 16.

[24] *Situation Ethics*, p. 123.

[25] Ibid. p. 65; Fletcher's italics.

ready with blandest aplomb to justify – not as lesser evils, but as positively good – such acts as killing one's baby (p. 125), abortion (pp. 37ff.), therapeutic fornication (pp. 126f.), patriotic prostitu - tion (pp. 163f.), adultery to induce pregnancy (pp. 164f.), pre- marital sexual intercourse (p. 104), sacrificing lives on your own side in time of war (p. 98), suicide and euthanasia (pp. 66, 74, 165f.), and distribution of contraceptives to unmarried women (p. 127; *Moral Responsibility*, pp. 139f.). He also insists on saying that 'in principle, even killing "innocent" people might be right', and 'in some situations lying and bribery and force and violence, even taking life itself, is the only righteous and good thing to do in the situation'.[26] It is Fletcher's use of 'good', 'right' and 'righteous' that secures to situationism its well-known reputation of being desperately lax; here the 'new morality' and the old immorality do seem to speak in identical terms.

## Situationism Evaluated

Christian situationism claims to distill essential biblical teaching about decision-making. This claim must now be tested.

Let it first be said that fair dealing with situationism is not easy, for it is a very mixed bag. Viewed as a reaction of protest against the all-too- common legalism which puts general principles before individual persons and whose zeal for God ousts neighbour-love from the heart, it com - mends itself as making a healthy biblical point, namely that only by love and care for others can we acceptably serve God (Rom. 13:8–10; 1 Cor. 13:1–3; Gal. 5:14). But viewed as a method to guide us in choosing our behaviour, it appalls, particularly when Fletcher cracks it up as the panacea for all moral perplexity, delivering us from centuries of Christian ethical error.[27] When situationists detect provincialism, shallowness, negativism, thoughtlessness and lovelessness in our ethical thought and practice, we must humbly take the criticism, and be grateful for it. But when they treat God's revealed directives as working rules only, and invite us to hail as good what God calls evil, a different response is called for.

---

[26] *Situation Ethics*, p. 75; *Moral Responsibility*, p. 181.

[27] Fletcher the situationist is a convert turned evangelist. 'After forty years', he wrote in 1963, 'I have learned the vital importance of the contextual or situational – i.e. the *circumstantial* – approach to the search for what is right and good. I have seen the light, I know now that abstract and conceptual morality is a mare's nest' (quoted in *The Situation Ethics Debate*, p. 113; cf. *Situation Ethics*, p. 41). Robinson, by contrast, is concerned to claim that 'this "new morality" is, of course, none other than the old morality, just as the new commandment is the old, yet ever fresh, commandment of love' (*Honest to God*, p. 119).

Situationists are right to stress that each situation is in some respects unique, and that only by concentrating intensely on it shall we ever see what is the best we can make of it. Rightly too do they stress that love always seeks the best for all parties, and is betrayed if we settle for mere formal correctness, or avoidance of wrongdoing, without asking whether we could not do something better. Insistence that real love is creative, enterprising and unwilling to settle for the second-best in relationships is a substantial grain of truth in situationism, as is its further insistence that the lovingness of loving action should be thought out and spelt out in terms of the relationship itself. Robinson's casuistry of pre-marital sex, for instance, runs thus: 'To the young man asking in his relations with a girl, "Why shouldn't I?", it is relatively easy to say "Because it's wrong" or "Because it's a sin" – and then to condemn him when he, or his whole generation, takes no notice. It makes much greater demands to ask, and to answer, the question "Do you love her?" or " *How much* do you love her?", and then to help him to accept *for himself* the decision that, if he doesn't, or doesn't very deeply, then his action is immoral, or, if he does, then he will respect her far too much to use her or take liberties with her. Chastity is the expression of charity – of caring, enough.' [28] Though weakened by Robinson's unwillingness to declare sex relations apart from the full bed-and-board commitment of marriage wrong as such, this is surely right-minded. No; it is only in its denial that any particular action is intrinsically immoral, evil and forbidden that situationism goes astray. Unfortunately, this one mistake is ruinous.

Whence does it spring? Partly, from an unbiblical habit of defining actions externally, in merely physical terms, abstracted from their motive and purpose;[29] partly, from misconceptions about the place of the law of God as such. The New Testament says that while our relationship to God is no longer determined by law (Rom. 6:14), Christ having freed us from law as a system of salvation (Rom. 7:1–6; 10:4; Gal. 3:23–26), we are 'under the law of Christ' (1 Cor. 9:21; cf. Gal. 6:2) as a standard of sanctification; Robinson, however, seems to infer from the end of the law for salvation that it has no place in sanctification. The continentals, conceiving God's command as essentially specific and concrete, deny that the Bible's moral teaching, which was specific and concrete for its own situation, can be directly applied to ours.

The effect of denying that there are universal God-taught prohibitions is to enmesh love (good will, the commanded motive) in perplexities. How am I to love my neighbour now? By attending to the situation, I am told. But how should I define 'the situation'? Any circumscription of it will be arbitrary and open to challenge; I could always have included more, or less. And however I define it, how can I be sure what is really

---

[28] *Honest to God*, p. 119.
[29] See note 5 above.

the most loving thing to do in it? By trusting my 'built-in moral compass'? I do not know whether Robinson risks trusting his, but I dare not rely on mine. My love is often blind, or at least goofy, partly through sin, partly through natural stupidity (two factors with which situationism fails to reckon). Also, I know by experience that in moments when I have to make decisions the factors that ought to count most, and the long-term implications of this or that way of handling the situation, are often far from clear to me. So am I to calculate my way through all possible alternatives, both those which stick to the rules and those which break them? But time, brains and factual knowledge fail me; and in any case it is plain that, whatever I do, whether I keep the rules or break them, uncertainty about the consequences I calculated will leave me still unsure whether I did the most loving thing. James Gustafson observes that ' "love," like "situation," is a word that runs through Fletcher's book like a greased pig'[30] – how does one catch and tie down such slippery items? Fletcher's method, which in intention makes things easy and, as Gustafson notes, 'omits any possibility of a bad conscience,'[31] actually makes it impossible for me to know whether I have ever done what I should, and so leaves me with an anxious conscience every day. The way of relating love to law which requires the former to do duty for the latter does not make the life of Christian obedience easier for anyone.

But how are love and law related in the Bible itself? As follows:

*First*, no doubt ever appears about the universal applicability and authority of laws commanding and forbidding particular things – promise-keeping, payment of debts and care of one's children, for instance, in the one case; murder, adultery and theft, for instance, in the other – and John tells us 'this is the love of God, that we keep his commandments' (1 John. 5:3; cf. 2:3–5; 3:21–24, and Jesus' words, John. 14:15, 21; 15:10). In 1957, before the situationist storm broke, John Murray wrote: 'It is symptomatic of a pattern of thought current in many evangelical circles that the idea of keeping the commandments of God is not consonant with the liberty and spontaneity of the Christian man, that *keeping* the law has affinities with legalism.' He then quotes the passages referred to above, beginning with John 14:15, 'If you love me, you will keep my commandments,' and ending with 14:21, 'He who has my commandments and keeps them, he it is who loves me', and concludes: 'When there is a persistent animosity to the notion of keeping commandments the only conclusion is that there is either gross ignorance or malignant opposition to the testimony of Jesus.'[32] It is hard to see how this can be gainsaid.

*Second*, love of God has priority over neighbour-love. Jesus categorizes love of God as the great commandment, which comes first (Matt. 22:37f.).

---

[30] *The Situation Ethics Debate*, p. 81.
[31] Ibid. p. 80.
[32] J. Murray, *Principles of Conduct* (Inter-Varsity Press, 1957), pp. 182f.

Scripture is full of instruction on how to trust, fear, praise and serve the Lord, and for this we may be grateful – no utilitarian calculus could possibly take its place! It is odd that situationists regularly write as if love of God is wholly a matter of loving one's neighbour, but in Scripture it is certainly not so.

*Third*, neighbour-love is to be directed by law. So far from seeing an antithesis and possible clash between the claims of persons and of principles, Scripture assumes that we can only meet the claims of persons as we hold to the God-taught principles in dealing with them, and the principles take the form of directives as to what should and should not be done to them. The theology, in a nutshell, is that God our Maker and Redeemer has revealed the unchanging pattern of response that he requires, and that humanity needs if it is to be truly itself. The pattern is both an expression of God's own moral character, an indication of what he approves and disapproves, and also a clue to us about our own nature and that of our neighbour. By adhering to the pattern we express and further our own true humanness on the one hand, and true love for our neighbour on the other.

Our fellow human is always something of an enigma to us, just as we are something of an enigma to ourselves, but our Maker who knows our true nature and needs has told us how we are to do ourselves and each other real good. So love and law-keeping are mutually entailed, as Paul shows in Romans 13:8–10. The sixth, seventh, eighth and tenth commandments prohibit particular actions and attitudes (murder, adul - tery, theft, covetous jealousy) and Paul quotes them to make the double point that when we keep these commandments we love our neighbour as ourselves, and when we love our neighbour as ourselves we keep these commandments. The point is confirmed by John's striking rea - soning in 1 John 5:2: 'By this we know that we love the children of God, when we love God *and obey his commandments*.' Neighbour love fulfills the law.

Biblically, then, there is no antithesis between the motive of love and the divine directives which tell us what kinds of action on humankind's part God approves and disapproves. Situationism is, after all, gratuitous.

## The Lesser Evil

But if God's laws, and the actions which they prescribe and prohibit, have fixed intrinsic values, as expressing God's unchanging will for humankind, what are we to think and do when we find ourselves in situations where we cannot move at all without transgressing a divine prohibition, so that the best we can do is evil from one standpoint? Briefly, love's task then is to find how to do the most good, and the least evil; doing nothing is rarely the answer!

Rightly, different principles come out on top in different situations: two Christians armed with 'honour your parents' and 'do not steal' might well act differently if one could only prevent his parents dying of hunger by stealing, while the other was being told to steal by his heavily gambling father. We may agree with the situationist that love for persons must arbitrate between the conflicting claims of moral principles, that doctrinaire decisions in such cases will not make the best of the bad job, and that unwillingness to face the situation's full complexities, and insensitivity to the variety of rules and claims that apply, will lead straight into ironclad Pharisaic legalism. But we shall reject Fletcher's grotesque idea that in such situations adultery, fornica - tion, abortion, suicide and the rest, if thought the *best* course (which arguably in Fletcher's cases they might be – we will not dispute that here), thereby become *good*: which valuation, as Fletcher himself em - phasizes, leaves no room for regret at having had to do them. Instead, we shall insist that evil remains evil, even when, being the lesser evil, it appears the right thing to do; we shall do it with heavy heart, and seek God's cleansing of our conscience for having done it.

In the film of Nicholas Monsarrat's novel *The Cruel Sea*, a destroyer commander had to decide whether to drop a depth-charge that would kill dozens of desperate seamen struggling in the icy North Atlantic, but might also (*might* – there was no certainty) destroy the U-boat waiting on the sea floor to ravage the rest of the convoy. The alternative was to stop and pick up the swimmers. He headed through the men in the water and dropped the depth charge. One of his men yelled, 'Bloody murderer!' He did not know if he hit the U-boat. The experience temporarily shattered him. He said: there are times when all we can do is guess our best, and then get down on our knees and ask God's mercy. This is the most painful form of the lesser evil situation, that in which knowledge is limited and one does the evil that seems best knowing that it may not turn out best at all.

The poignancy and justice of the commander's words need no underlining. The most distressing feature of Fletcher's often distressing book (in which, incidentally, there is a reference to this episode) is that, if he knows what Christians feel at such times, he keeps quiet about it, and writes as if a dose of situationist casuistry will make them proof against it. One can only say: God help them if it does. Yet this is where situationism logically leads; Fletcher is only being clear-headed in pointing it out.

Cried Mr. Hardy to Mr. Laurel, not once nor twice, 'Here's another fine mess you've gotten me into!' Might not one have to say the same to any teacher who won him over to situationist ethics?

# Chapter 31

# Christian Morality Adrift

My title is meant to suggest a picture. Think of 'Christian morality' as a compendium of truth and wisdom that contains all that is involved in defining the Christian's obedience to God – all the principles, precepts, rules, standards, prohibitions, counsels, and statements of ideal that make up God's law; all the values and virtues that God tells us to seek for ourselves and promote in the lives of others; all the subjective factors – a good conscience, a heart grateful to God, reverent love for Christ, knowledge, thoughtfulness, self-distrust, reliance on divine help – that must be there if one is going to please God. Think of this body of truth and wisdom as a ship crossing the waters of this world. The place for a ship is in the sea, but, said D. L. Moody, God help the ship if the sea gets into it! That, however, is what has started to happen.

So think, now, of the good ship 'Christian morality' as drifting off course. Up on the bridge a crowd of people has been squabbling as to which of them should steer, with the result that the ship is not being effectively steered at all. It has already grazed some rocks and started to leak, and unless remedial action is taken (which will involve sorting out the confusions on the bridge) its condition is bound to get worse. God will no doubt ensure that it does not sink altogether, for if it did his promise of perpetual preservation for his church and his truth till Christ comes again would have failed. But the battering that Christian morality has received in this century, among both Protestants and Roman Catholics, has already done much harm.

Recently I saw in a leading Anglican weekly a pathetic letter from a man who said that if the church had taken a clear line about the unlawfulness of homosexual connections, his clergyman friend who had just died of AIDS might have been alive still. Let that 'if' haunt your mind and sear your heart as you recall that a century ago, in a pre-Freudian era, all the churches of Christendom did take such a line, and buggery was an indictable offence in both Britain and America. But the world slipped

CHRISTIAN MORALITY ADRIFT was originally published in *A Society in Peril*, ed. K. Perrotta and J. Blattner, (Ann Arbor: Servant Press, 1989), pp. 57–76. Reprinted by permission.

from its earlier standards at this point, as it has at so many other points and Christian morality has slipped with it.

That is the situation we face today. My aim in this essay is to try to achieve some in-depth understanding of what has happened, with a view to seeing what needs to be said and done about it by those who think the old paths of faith and life were right and deviations from them are wrong.

Our first step must be to get clear, if we can, on the fundamental structure of Christian morality – a matter on which, as I think you will agree, clarity is often lacking. I shall therefore give some attention to presenting a scheme which seems to me to catch what is essential regarding both the material and the method of Christian moral thought.

## The Nature of Christian Morality

### 1. Christian morality is an expression, function, and corollary of Christian theology

Our ethics are to be drawn from our *dogmatics*, and our view of both our ethics and our dogmatics will be deficient if we fail to see this. Christian morality is not to be equated with secular morality, or the morality of a national cultural heritage; Christian duty is determined by Christian doctrine; orthopraxy, as we may call it, follows from, and is controlled and shaped by, orthodoxy. Nor should any statement of Christian orthodoxy be thought of as complete till it includes a declaration of God's will for human behaviour, which is what Christian morality is about. Christian morality is precisely the doctrine of God's commands to mankind, set within the frame of the doctrines of his works for humankind and his ways with humankind.

God the creator, the God of the Bible, wants his human creatures to serve, please, and glorify him by specific types and courses of action that he likes to see, and he directs us accordingly, with sanctions to encourage us to do right and to discourage us from doing wrong. Christian morality, according to Scripture, is a blueprint for living under the authority of this awesomely and intrusively personal Lord, by whose grace we have been saved to serve, and to whom we must one day give account.

So Christian morality is a morality of divine command, based on the reality of a divine gift, and both the gift and the command are elements in the doctrine of God as such. Ethics, therefore, must never be thought of as independent of dogmatics, and study in either of these fields should be understood as obligating study in the other one as well. Otherwise, ultimate inadequacy in our chosen field, whichever of the two it is, becomes a foregone conclusion.

## 2. Christian morality is an expression, function, and index of Christian spirituality

It is the believer's whole life of communion with God by grace. The practice of Christian morality, which is the outward aspect of living the Christian life, must never be separated in thought, let alone in reality, from the inward aspect of that life – by which I mean such things as the exercise of conscience, the prayers for help, the joy of obedience, the grateful love of God, the active hoping for heaven, the cherishing of a sense of Christ's presence with us, and the constant battling against temptation, depression, apathy, and hardness of heart, which you may call sloth or *accidie*, if you like old names.

If our thoughts about doing God's will get detached from our thoughts about the inner spiritual life, as if these were two areas of reality and not one, or if – even worse – we define the Christian life entirely in terms of external obedience and forget that there is more to it than mechanically correct performance, then we can hardly avoid ending up in some version of legalistic Pharisaism, in which all the emphasis is on what we do rather than what we are, and into which the reality of Christian freedom does not enter. Then, like the Jews of Paul's day, we shall be rightly accused of going around to establish our own works-righteousness, and of lacking proper acquaintance with the Christ whose saving grace is for sinners only.

In the deepest sense Christian morality – the morality of faith, hope, and love, pursued with discretion, self-control, fair-mindedness and courage – is not Christian at all save as it is set in this evangelical context and made to rest on the truth that Christ's servants live only by being daily forgiven for their daily failures. We forget this at our peril; but a resolve to observe the connection between our morality and our spirituality will help us to remember it.

## The Norms of Christian Morality

Under the heading of norms of Christian morality, I have three points to make. They are substantial and weighty, and basic to the view of things that I wish to offer, so please be patient as I plod my way through them.

### 1. All the norms of Christian morality are both revealed and rational

As revealed, they are matters of divine command; as rational, they are embodiments of human wisdom; and there is no conflict between the morality of authentic revelation and authentic reason at any point. Let me explain.

Christianity is a revealed religion, and the Bible, which from one point of view is an explanatory record of God's revelation in history, in the process that found its climax in Christ and his church, is from another point of view God's revelation in writing. Epistemologically (that is, for the purpose of gaining knowledge), revelation is the fundamental Christian fact, and recognition of the Bible as the ultimate source and criterion of truth is basic to Christian theological method.

None of us, I trust, will quarrel with that, even if Catholic, Protestant, and Orthodox have to beg leave of each other to spell out this position in slightly different ways. Nor, I trust, will anyone quarrel with me when I go on to say that the biblical writers themselves affirm the universality of a 'natural' or 'general' revelation that no rational being in God's world is able to evade, namely a revelation of God as the creator who ought to be worshipped and the judge who will one day call everyone to account, and of the standards that theology describes as God's *natural law* for human life.

Paul is most forthright about this in Romans 1:18–2:16, the main part of the first section of his argument in that letter, in which he diagnoses all mankind, Jew and Gentile alike, as being hopelessly guilty of sin against their maker and so as standing helplessly under his wrath. God's wrath, as Paul and indeed all Scripture conceives it, is his characteristic judicial hostility to sin. God, says Paul, is already showing his wrath by letting sin have its head and breed more sin, and one day he will show that same wrath by catastrophic retribution upon all of sinning humankind.

Through the agency of Jesus Christ as judge, pronouncing sentence, there will on that day be 'tribulation and distress for every soul of man who does evil, of the Jew first and also of the Greek' (2:9 NASB). All deserve such treatment, for all have sinned against moral knowledge that they actually have. None will be able to plead ignorance of the law for breaking which they are condemned. Paul thus founds Christianity's claim to be the universal religion for humanity on the fact that it alone – perhaps I had better say, Christ alone – offers rescue from the wrath-provoking guilt that is humanity's universal predicament.

How does Paul make his point about the universality of moral knowledge? By the following line of reasoning. God's wrath, he says, is 'revealed from heaven' (revealed, that is, first in humankind's spiritual and moral downhill slide, then in each person's bad conscience, and then in the gospel message, as the ongoing context makes plain) against all human failure to worship and obey him (1:18). These failures are guilty because they flow from wilful suppression and distortion of knowledge that everyone is given of God as creator and source of all good (1:19–23). God in reaction has removed restraints on the manifold immoralities that humans do in fact crave to practice (1:24–31). Consciences, however, remain alive, so that all human beings have inward inklings that 'those who practice such things are worthy of death,' even while they themselves do them and applaud others who do them (1:32).

Proof of the universality of these God-given inklings, even where no biblical instruction has ever been received, lies in the reality of pagan moral experience: 'When the Gentiles who do not have the law do instinctively the things of the law, these, not having the law, are a law to themselves, in that they show the work of the law written on their hearts, their conscience bearing witness, and their thoughts alternately accusing or else defending them' (2:14f.). In other words, all humanity, however pagan and uninstructed, knows what it is to do some things that God's word shows to be really right, and to do those things because they are known to be right, and to have a good conscience for doing them and a bad conscience for omitting them.

What is contained in this universally revealed divine law? Paul's argument specifies, first, grateful worship of the sovereign creator (1:21) and, second, the opposite of all those types of action that Paul says people know to be 'worthy of death' (1:32) even while they engage in them. The list of these types of action is grim, but we had better hear it so as to be sure we know what Paul is talking about.

It starts with what is nowadays called same-sex loving on the part of both women and men, and goes on to cover 'all unrighteousness, wickedness, greed, evil . . . envy, murder, strife, deceit, malice' whereby people become 'gossips, slanderers, haters of God, insolent, arrogant, boastful, inventors of evil, disobedient to parents, without understanding, untrustworthy, unloving, unmerciful' (1:26–31). It is the opposite of these categories of conduct and character that the natural law, the law of our creation, prescribes. From this it becomes apparent that God's supernatu - ral verbal revelation from heaven of the kinds of behaviour that he loves and hates to see, the revelation, I mean, of divine standards in the Decalogue and in the moral teaching of the prophets, the apostles, and the Lord himself, is fundamentally nothing more, just as it is nothing less, than re-publication, confirmation, and reinforcement of the natural law that the world in a fashion knows already, but is resolved to ignore.

Empirical evidence goes far to confirm this contention. As C. S. Lewis showed in a striking appendix to his book *The Abolition of Man*, the 'Tao' (as he called it) of social righteousness according to the biblically revealed law of God has in fact been articulated by authoritative moral teachers in all developed cultures. Lewis's evidence indicates that in one milieu after another this part of the natural law surfaces spontaneously, which is what you would expect, since it is actually impressed by God through general revelation on all human hearts, however little particular individuals and groups may be willing even to try to live by it. Thus we may claim for the natural law of Romans 1 and 2, at any rate on its social side, the rationality that it is always proper to ascribe to matters of universal acknowledgement.

And a compelling case can be made for the entire natural law being rational in the further sense that it fits human nature, inasmuch as it points to the path on which the goal for which each person was made, and the ultimate contentment that each human heart craves, are actually found. The law of spiritual and social righteousness that God makes known by both natural and supernatural revelation is in truth the maker's handbook for humanity, of which we may and must say what has sometimes to be said of other maker's handbooks also – 'if all else fails' – rather, *when* all else fails – '*read the instructions!*' God's law, understood teleologically as setting out values, virtues, and behaviour patterns to aim at, and limits within which to stay, suits and benefits us by delineating to us what constitutes our own true fulfilment.

Abraham Maslow was not wrong to celebrate self-fulfilment, or self-realization, as a happy condition; he was only wrong in his analysis of it, and his ideas about the way to it. The true path here is the path of keeping God's commandments in the world of relationship to God and others that is ours. This is the path from which sin diverts us, and to which grace restores us. It leads us into the happy worship and devotion on the one hand, and the practice of love and justice and joy in human relationships on the other, that between them constitute our glorifying of God. And as we thus glorify God, fulfilment, contentment, and realization of who and what we are in terms of God's wise plan for us become increasingly ours.

Today's unbelieving world, which has no conception of fellowship with God and no adequate idea of human nature anyway, may well deny all this out of hand as ridiculous, and I suspect that here on earth we Christians do not know enough about our own identity and nature before God to see the full reason why, for instance, the law of God should tie us to heterosexual relations within marriage, and socially to the preserva - tion of human life in all its forms even when this means sacrificing personal convenience. Yet I think that thoughtful Christians are able to see enough of the overall effect on character of staying within these limits on the one hand, and of refusing to stay within them on the other, to argue effectively in any company for the intrinsic rationality of God's revealed norms, just as they have been doing since Christianity began. And when the argument is made, thoughtful unbelievers, even those who fight against it, cannot but acknowledge that it has real substance.

So much, then, for the dual character of the norms of Christian morality as both revealed and rational. I move now to my second point.

## 2. All the norms of Christian morality are both **creational** *and* **covenantal**

My thesis is that God's commands in the natural law, which the Decalogue restates and the New Testament moral teaching embodies, always remain the same in essence, for they are rooted in the realities of creation; although within that basic frame there appear angles, applications, and additions that are determined by the stage that God's gracious covenant purpose for his own needy people has reached at any one time.

I affirm this core continuity of God's law against all versions of the idea that Old and New Testament moralities are in direct opposition, or that the latter grew out of the former by some form of evolutionary development, or that the so-called 'kingdom ethics' of the New Testament are meant to replace, rather than reinforce, the 'creation ethics' of the Old Testament era. The basic moral norms for humankind are not arbitrary enactments on God's part, but are determined by two unchanging facts.

The first fact is the goodness and holiness of the divine creator, which we are all called to acknowledge by gratefully seeking to please him. The second fact is the nature of the human creature, whose capacity for freedom and contentment is only ever fulfilled through actively loving and serving God and others. It is true that some of the deeper dimensions of these norms are only seen by the light of the full Christian revelation; for instance, only when God is known as a triune fellowship of holy love, into which we hell-bent humans are brought by sovereign grace alone, can the relational implications of loving God and others as God loves us be adequately grasped.

Nonetheless, the norms as such, in relatively firm outline, are already revealed to mankind in and through our very existence as God's creatures in his world. And the identity in all ages of these basic norms, whether known through general revelation apart from Scripture or through the special, supernatural, verbal, historically contextualized revelation given in the Mosaic law and in the law of Christ, must be maintained, it seems to me, as a vital step towards clear thinking about Christian morality in this or any day.

How then are we to account for the differences that the Bible itself specifies between the Old and New Testament morality? The answer is: by drawing two distinctions. The first is the distinction between on the one hand the kinds of actions, defined in terms of behaviour towards God, one's neighbour, and oneself, that God's law requires and forbids, and that should therefore be seen as matters of divine command to all human beings as such, and on the other hand the special motivations of faith that arise from the realities of God's gracious covenant relationship, and that are therefore required only of those whom God has actually taken into that relationship. This distinction is crucial in itself, and very clarifying to the mind; let me illustrate what it means.

The first table of the Decalogue, as set out in Deuteronomy 5:6–15 and summarized in the *Shema* of 6:4–5, which Jesus identified as the first and great commandment (Matt. 22:35–58), states a motive for worship - ping the creator that applied only to Israel, namely, that the creator is also Yahweh, their covenant God, who redeemed them from Egyptian bondage. Romans 1:21, however, indicates that since all humans should be aware that they owe to God all the good they have ever received, starting with their very existence, grateful worship is a duty. This is implied also by Peter's statement to Cornelius that in every nation those who revere God and do what is right gain his favour (Acts 10:35) – a statement that can hardly be limited to the category of first-century God-fearers (Gentile fellow-travellers with Jews) to which Cornelius belonged, nor be invalidated by our total uncertainty as to whether the class of human beings who truly worship the creator on the basis of general revelation alone has nowadays any members. The point I am illustrating is simply that a type of action that is universally commanded on the basis of creation may be linked in God's economy with a further motive that is drawn from God's redeeming work; which can, however, be required only of the particular human group that God's redemption and covenant commitment have actually embraced.

Thus covenantal considerations, founded on the realities of redemp - tion, do in fact yield additional motives – reason, we would say – for observing the common principles of creational morality. Particular motives drawn by God's command from saving grace are to be con - sciously superimposed on universal motives deriving from creation and providence by those to whom that saving grace has come.

All mankind should be worshipping and serving the creator out of gratitude for creation, and believers should be worshipping and serving out of gratitude for redemption as well. Right motivation is a matter of divine command, just as right action is, but right motivation for Christians today, as for Jews of the Old Testament time, involves more than is required of persons who are as yet ignorant of God's redemptive action. Recognition of this difference – recognition, that is, that the correct theological answers to the question 'why should I do such-and-such?' have differed for different groups at different times in world history – seems to me to be another vital step towards clear thinking about Christian morality, though it is not possible to draw out the full implications of it here.

So far I have been speaking of behavioural commands that belong to the law of creation, Lewis's 'Tao,' and that therefore remain identical throughout human history. But now comes a second distinction that we must draw. Just as new specific motives for obeying this natural law flow from the facts of redemption and covenant, so new specific divine commands to particular communities rest on these same facts.

To demonstrate this, I now list the main differences between God's commands under the Mosaic dispensation (the old covenant) and the Christian order of things (the new covenant). Under the former, much of the divinely instituted pattern of life and worship was typical, tempo - rary, and designed specifically to educate God's covenant people to understand Christ when he came. Under the latter, the kingdom of God and life in the Spirit, foretasting heaven, are realities, and God's education of his covenant people has the hope of heaven's full joy as its new focus. Out of the progression from the one dispensation to the other came the following changes in the specifics of God's command to human beings in the realm of what is commonly called his positive, as distinct from his natural, law:

The typical priesthood, sacrificial system, liturgical calendar, and purity regulations of Old Testament worship were fulfilled, transcended, re - placed, and abolished by the mediatorial action of Jesus Christ, which in one way or another they foreshadowed. Therefore God's old covenant commands concerning these things are no longer in force for anyone.

The national life of Israel, with its home and foreign policy and internal legal system determined in the first instance by Mosaic legislation, was superseded by the international life of the Christian church, which is not one of this world's nations at all. Thus Mosaic legislation relating to Israel's national life ceases to have any direct application as God's command to particular persons or groups, and God no longer instructs his people to act as executioners of his judgement on his enemies by holy war, as he did on occasion in Old Testament times (cf. Rom. 12:19).

The Old Testament promises of material blessing for faithfulness, which had typical significance and an educational role, have been replaced by promises of endless glory at Christ's parousia and warnings to expect recurring tribulation until then. The hope of heaven, of being 'for ever with the Lord,' has new prominence and new force as a motive to holiness (cf. 1 John 3:2f.), as compared with the hints dropped about it in the Old Testament writings.

Christ requires Christians to distinguish between the divorce proce - dure that God permitted and tolerated under Moses and the creation ideal of lifelong monogamous marriage, and to recognize wilful divorce, with subsequent remarriage, as action that he does not favour (cf. Matt. 19:1–9; 5:31f.; Luke 16:18).

Obedience under the Christian dispensation has been given a Chris - tocentric and Christological focus: God commands Christians to imitate the love, humility, and entire moral character of their master out of gratitude for his saving mercy and out of loyalty to him as their Lord, and correlates this command with the revelation that the indwelling Holy Spirit is actively transforming them even now into the likeness of the risen Lord to whom they are united (2 Cor. 3:18, etc.). The Christlikeness that is commanded, and that Christians must therefore labour to practice, is achieved, insofar as it is achieved, by the enabling power of the Holy Spirit.

Christians, though consciously free from the typical and dispensational restrictions of the Jewish law with regard to the use and enjoyment of created things, are to be guided in using this liberty by the following explicit principles, all reflecting the new reality of personal and corporate life in Christ: They are not to do what their own conscience is uncertain about (Rom. 14:23), nor to press others to do what their consciences are uncertain about (Rom. 14:13–20; 1 Cor. 8), nor to induce addictions that enslave them (1 Cor. 6:12). These apostolic injunctions have the status of divine commands, given for the new situation to ensure that Christian liberty is not abused.

Divine commands to use the Christian sacraments (Matt. 28:19; 1 Cor. 11:25), to respect and provide for Christian presbyters (1 Cor. 16:16; Gal. 6:6; 1 Thess. 5:12; Heb. 13:17; 1 Pet. 5:5), and to show special love to Christians as such, as fellow-siblings in God's family (1 Cor. 13:34f.; Gal. 6:2,10; etc.), have replaced comparable Old Testament commandments regarding circumcision and Passover, provisions for priests, and the special obligations of Israelites to help each other.

All these specific changes in God's commands to men follow directly from the way in which his plan of world redemption has advanced beyond the era of Old Testament anticipation to that of New Testament fulfil - ment. But this law of Christ for his redeemed people should still be seen as meshing with the natural law to supplement its contents, and as focusing the frame of reference within which Christians must pursue the purposes and policies of love and justice that the natural law requires of them. The natural law remains the basis on which all that is distinctive in Christian morality is superimposed.

Now to the third point, which completes the picture.

### 3. All the norms of Christian morality are both regulational and relational

What I mean by this is that these norms are not abstractions but are commands of God that bear directly on all aspects of our living, and that under God we learn what they contain and how they bear on us not simply by applying moral universals to particular cases, but also by discerning the values and claims that are built into relationships. God's regulations determine the substance of right action, viewed as obedience, but it is relational awareness that imparts to right actions its temper and quality as love. And because this is so, full perception of these norms requires not only our analytical reasoning powers but also an empathetic use of our creative imagination within our relationships. This use, however, will only ever be sparked effectively when the motive of love is operating in us already in some shape or form.

In saying this, I extend the use of the word 'norms' beyond what I think is usual nowadays, to include in its meaning the exercise and expression of Christian virtue, or the graces of Christian character, as the older Protestant theology would have put it, along with the divinely commanded classes of actions of which I have been speaking so far. I make this extension because reality so requires. I am saying that 'be a certain sort of person' is, formally speaking, as much a Christian, and indeed a human, moral norm as is 'do these certain things.' I am affirming (and surely this is no new teaching!) that both natural law and biblical revelation require specific attitudes and dispositions, as well as specific actions and habits.

In the abstract, ideal virtue, that is, virtue of character in fullest manifestation, is a moral norm in itself no less than observance of the commands and limits of God's law is a moral norm. And in Christianity according to the word of God, the personal perfection of Jesus Christ is the ultimate norm and model for all moral action, which norm is only properly described by saying that here in Jesus you have perfect conform - ity to God's law as the foundation, with fully manifested virtue as the superstructure. But it was the love-relation of the incarnate Son to the Father, and to humankind for the Father's sake, that brought his moral virtue into the empathetic, imaginative expression that really constituted the normative quality of his obedience, and it is to imitating this, over and above committing and restricting ourselves to divinely approved types of actions, that we who are Christians are called. Let me illustrate.

First illustration: Jesus told the story of the Good Samaritan to teach a lawyer the universal scope of the moral norm of neighbour-love. 'That every person you meet, no matter how uncongenial, is your needy neighbour whom you must help if you can' is the regulational norm that he enunciates. But the story itself is of ideal, empathetic, imaginative neighbour-love, that is, of unlimited good-will and readiness to sacrifice convenience, time, and resources in order to help a stranger, and we can only ever expect such gestures of creative kindness to be called forth in real life by a prior relational reality, namely love to a loving God (think of Mother Teresa). When, however, Jesus says, 'Go and do the same' (Luke 10:27), he makes the Samaritan's spirit and style of action part of the norm; and such a norm, as everyone can see, goes far beyond the merely regulational.

Second illustration: Jesus, who was himself, of course, the archetype of the Good Samaritan in his own story, was confronted by a group of hostile Jewish theologians who apparently had just surprised a couple in the act of adultery. They brought the woman (not the man, note), and they 'set her in the midst' in order then to ask Jesus whether he thought the Mosaic directive to stone adulterers should be applied in her case. (It was one of those catch questions to which it was expected that any answer would discredit Jesus with somebody, in this case either the Jewish community or the Roman authorities, who would not allow the Jews to inflict the death penalty.)

Jesus first stooped down, deliberately taking his eyes off the woman, and wrote on the ground, thus indicating that the theologians' question was fit only to be ignored. Then, as it was pressed, he said, 'He who is without sin among you, let him be the first to throw a stone at her' (John 8:7), and wrote on the ground again, as if to dismiss the matter. When the theologians, stunned and shamed, had quietly vanished, Jesus faced the adulteress for the first time and told her simply that he was not there at that moment as a judge to condemn her; she was to go, and not sin that way again.

What amazing behaviour! And what creative, compassionate utterance on the Saviour's part! Jesus' sensitivity to the woman's inescapable feelings of guilt, fear, humiliation, and being destroyed by men, linked with such ingenuity in stymieing the theologians' malice to them both, in avoiding any further contribution to the woman's hurt, and in communicating forgiveness to her in the way best calculated to renew self-respect and so make psychologically possible a new start, is in truth breathtaking.

It displays a degree of wise and creative benevolence, springing from desire for another person's human and spiritual well-being, that the world never saw, nor dreamed of, until Jesus showed it. And this imaginative ingenuity, triggered by love, goes far beyond formal regulational correct - ness. Jesus here expresses, and so models for us, his followers, a quality of spontaneous good-will to God's human image-bearers that we can only ever enter into at all as a by-product, overflowing from our own responsive love-relation to the Father and the Son, who have so greatly and amazingly loved us. It is in this sense that the normative attitude and outlook (as distinct from the motivation) of our Christian lives is to be derived, partly at least, from our relation to God – which is the point I am here concerned to give substance.

Such, then, as I see it, in simple though not, I hope, simplistic terms, is the essential structure (maybe I should say substructure) of biblical Christian morality, in which the law of nature is also a matter of divine command, and God's commands make human sense as the means of leading us in righteousness to glorify and enjoy our Saviour-God, which is the goal and fulfilment of human life. It would be very satisfying to round off this overview with a study of how the Holy Spirit enables Christians to obey God's law and through that obedience transforms them into some measure of moral likeness to Christ, but that cannot be done now; we have to move on.

## What Undermines Christian Moral Thought Today

In light of our analysis we can now get clear on what has happened in modern times to send Christian morality off course. Three things call for mention, and the first is:

### 1. The erosion of Christian supernaturalism

This has been a problem particularly within Protestantism. Christian morality, so we said, is a department of dogmatics; orthopraxy flows from orthodoxy, and damage to our dogmatics is bound to mean that our ethics suffer too. This being so, it is ominous to observe how for almost two centuries Protestant dogmatics have been undergoing major damage from the rationalistic anti-supernaturalism that was begotten and bred up in the Enlightenment, found its home among Lutheran scholars in German universities, and is now entrenched, under the question-begging label of Liberalism, in many theological teaching institutions both sides of the Atlantic. Risky and odious as generalizations are, I think I may fairly offer a generic profile of it as follows.

Enlightenment theology conceives God in a unitarian rather than a trinitarian way, and denies that he communicates with us in language, or that he judges mankind for sins, or that he acts to redeem us in any other sense than by presiding over, or perhaps directing from within, the religious and cultural evolution of our race. Some of this is deism negating theism, and some of it is immanentism rejecting deism, but there is full agreement that the theistic supernaturalism of the historic trinitarian and incarnational faith must be rejected, and so it is. Process theology, calling itself pantheism and affirming the finitude of God, is the latest form of this rejection.

Against its unitarian background, Enlightenment theology develops non-incarnational Christologies that see Jesus as an ideal religious and prophetic figure from whom we can learn, rather than a divine Lord by whom we must be saved. They combine confidence that he did not die as a sacrifice for our sins with doubt as to whether he rose from the dead and whether the world will ever see him again.

As for the Bible, it is not in any sense a record and embodiment of revealed truth, for on Enlightenment principles there is no such thing. The Bible is, rather, a library of Judæo-Christian classics, a treasury of religious thought and feeling over a period of something like a thousand years. It links insight with superstition, and false history with true in a bewildering way that, fortunately, clever scholars can now sort out.

What was the effect of all this on Christian morals? At first, less than you might have expected. The deist thinker Kant, architect of the Liberal denial of verbal revelation, who has often (God save us!) been called the philosopher of Protestantism, was a moralist who maintained the reality of ethical absolutes in the form of the categorical imperative and identified many of the absolutes correctly by biblical standards.

The idea that the church's job is to set up on earth the kingdom of God, viewed as a Kantian 'kingdom of ends' (that is, a state of society in which each person is valued as an end rather than a means), soon gripped Liberal hearts, as indeed with some rephrasing it grips them still. To typical Liberals, Christianity was in essence, as they liked to put it, the ethic of the Sermon on the Mount, and they served their vision of moral people in a moral society with great zeal.

However, toward the end of the nineteenth century evolutionism came to dominate many Western minds, encouraging the belief that in culture and morals generally whatever is, is right, because it is the latest product of the evolutionary process. This inclined the practitioners of Enlightenment theology, which by then had exchanged Kantian deism for Hegelian immanentism as its characteristic philosophical outlook, to give up any notion of unchanging natural law and instead treat any latter-day community consensus as a revelation of the present will of God. That tendency led most German Liberals to support the militarism of two world wars, as it now leads most North American Liberals to support violence in the service of social change and to condone abortion, on the grounds, it seems, that you can meaningfully affirm the value of your neighbour, the pregnant woman, by killing at her request your other neighbour who is currently housed inside her.

Also, Liberal denials of verbal revelation make an ethic of divine command impossible. They oblige you to re-categorize biblical ethics as the fruit of human religious insight long ago, insight that is in principle relative to and open to question by the alleged insight of later generations. Thus the entire structure of Christian morality, as I have analysed it, is undermined. So I conclude that the long-term effect of Protestant Liberalism on Christian morals will continue to be, as it already has been, unhappy.

## 2. The assimilation of secular moral perspectives

This has become a vice of method in both Protestantism and Roman Catholicism in recent years. The reason is not far to seek. The post-Christian drift of the twentieth century has put Christian morality under great and sustained pressure. The cultural optimism with which the century opened was deflated by the First World War, and since then the prevalent mood of the West has been one of practical materialism and egoistic hedonism, fed by what Freud is supposed to have taught about the unhealthiness of sexual restraint. American pragmatism and European positivism have joined hands to create an atmosphere unfa - vourable to any moral absolutes, and in relation to our educational and cultural establishments historic Christianity has been comprehensively marginalized.

If, under these circumstances, persons who want to make Christianity sound relevant borrow the world's own thoughts in order then to present them to the world as Christian truth, it may make us sad, but it should come as no surprise. In fact, it has happened already, and will no doubt go on happening, over and over again.

At first the Roman Catholic Church stood resolutely aloof from Protestant Liberalism, and gave the parallel Modernist movement in its own ranks short shrift. But Vatican II was thought to sanction revisionist experiments, and one such, in the moral realm, has been the embracing of the view called consequentialism. Its central thesis corresponds to that proposed to Protestants by Joseph Fletcher in his well known book *Situation Ethics* (1966), namely, that there is only ever one criterion to apply for determining what it is right to do, and that criterion is the comparing of the likely consequences of the possible lines of action.

When I took moral philosophy in the 1940s, this procedure was called using the utilitarian calculus, which secular moralists have been debating for more than a hundred years. The thought behind it was, and for consequentialists still is, that no act is intrinsically evil, nor yet intrinsically good: only its consequences give it either quality. An obvious corollary is that, if the calculation of consequences so directs, it will become right to do what others, thinking in different terms, will regard as evil in order that good may come.

An obvious objection is that no publicly agreed version of the calculus can ever be established, because it is a fundamental fact about humankind that different people estimate the relative worth of particular good things – values, as we would say – differently; so any assessment of the quantity of good involved in each particular set of consequences is inescapably subjective or disputable.

But the overwhelming objection, in light of my argument so far, is that consequentialism, from the word go, ignores God's revealed com - mands in Scripture, and in the natural law as Scripture enables us to recognize that law. What God commands, in the first instance, is not that we calculate consequences across the board in order to determine what is good and bad – in fact, consequences only become relevant when we are choosing between equally legitimate options.

What he commands, rather, is that we observe and honour his own prior determinations of what is good and bad, that is, his teaching about the kinds of actions that he loves or hates to see, and that make for or against the fulfilment of our created human nature. Consequentialism has found eloquent advocates in Roman Catholicism in recent years, but, because it cuts loose from God's law, natural and revealed, it must be judged an egregious mistake.

One more unsettling factor for Christian morality remains to be mentioned, albeit briefly.

### 3. The prevalence of Romantic anthropology

The Romantic movement in European culture at the end of the eighteenth century threw up the dazzling ideal of the human individual as a pioneering hero, breaking all bonds of conventionality as he rises to unprecedented heights of achievement. Whereas the Enlightenment begot cool, destruc - tive skeptics, Romanticism produced passionate, creative rebels. Byron, Beethoven, Goethe, Wagner, and Nietzsche may be cited as archetypal exponents and embodiments of this ideal, and it is apparent that in a rather more trivial, lowbrow, and petulant form it has entrenched itself in the modern Western mentality. Human freedom and creativity are constantly celebrated, and voices from the existentialist camp are raised again and again to assure us that we shall never become real persons till we start to express these qualities in patterns of living that are entirely ours, learned from no one, devised entirely by following our own inner impulses. You must do your own thing, we are told: that's the only way to go.

One by-product of this mentality is that all thought of having to live under the rule of a law that has transcendent sanctions – a law, therefore, that it is beyond man's power to change – carries strongly negative vibrations. Boundaries, we feel, are for crossing, rules for breaking, locked doors for knocking down. This is the romantic hero syndrome, in its modern mutation – an anthropological Titanism, if ever there was one. Jean-Paul Sartre, himself an existentialist, complicated the scene by arguing that there is no such thing as human nature, but that our personal humanity is entirely what we make it out of the unformed raw material of potentialities that we find within ourselves. Small wonder, then, that utterance, from whatever quarter, declaring that, for instance, male and female homosexuality are contrary to nature, so that these alternative life-styles are actually pathological freaks, falls on deaf ears. Our culture conditions us to want to be bounds-breaking heroes, and life within limits is dismissed as a servile and unworthy goal.

What we really have here is the I-play-God mentality of the first sin in Eden, now reappearing in fashionable modern dress. Romantic anthropol - ogy, as such, is one of the many forms that original sin takes. By diagnosing it, however, we do not cure it, and as long as our culture, in both pop and sophisticated forms, lends it such thoroughgoing support as it does at present, it will continue to be an enormous obstacle to restoring any sense of the naturalness of the natural law, and the authority of the biblical ethic (the two, as I said earlier, are really one) to our benighted society. Many in our churches, quite apart from those outside them, are so intoxicated with this current cultural moonshine that they would deprecate any attempt to return to the time-honoured moral standards. Nothing less, however, can help our churches or our society back to the strengths of sanity. I say sanity because in its revolt against the law of God the Western world is more or less mad, and to the extent that the churches follow the world in this, they are mad too. And the prognosis for such madness is grim.

Declared Jeremiah:

> Thus says the Lord. 'Stand by the ways and see and ask for the ancient paths, where the good way is, and walk in it; and you shall find rest for your souls.' But they said, 'We will not walk in it.' And I set watchmen over you, saying, 'Listen to the sound of the trumpet.' But they said, 'We will not listen.' Therefore hear, O nations . . . hear, O earth; behold, I am bringing disaster on this people, the fruit of their plans, because they have not listened to my words, and as for my law, they have rejected it also (Jer. 6:16–19).

May it not be irrevocably so in modern North America. Lord, have mercy! Amen.

Now let me sum up in question and answer form some of the lessons that have begun to appear through our argument.

*Why, we ask, as we face today's moral landslide in Western society, do our churches fail so spectacularly to be clear, strong, and united in affirming biblical moral absolutes? In terms of our opening illustration, why is there so much disagreement about how to steer the Christian moral ship?*
The reason is that many of the steersmen, official and otherwise, have been infected with the cancerous moral relativism that post-Christian secularity has spawned. Those whose handling of the Bible is determined by secular frames of reference do not find moral absolutes in it.

*How then shall we draw from the Bible the moral absolutes that pre-twentieth century Christians found there?*
First, by categorizing its explicit teaching as didactic revelation from God; second by linking it with the equally explicit teaching of universally intuited natural law.

*But how, in today's skeptical world, can we give credibility to the claim that these standards of holiness make for man's highest good?*
By exhibiting them as the divinely revealed and empirically verified truth about the way of living that fulfils human nature, and by celebrating the power that the risen Christ through the Holy Spirit gives to practice the total self-denial and self-giving that this way of life demands. (The reality of that power has also been empirically verified; think again of Mother Teresa.)

*Finally, is it realistic to expect our culture to swing back to the Christian morality that it so badly needs?*
This can only happen as the historic gospel of Jesus Christ, the message of ruin, redemption, and regeneration, bears fruit in new lives and changed purposes. Commitment to Christian morals is a path of wisdom and duty that only Christians can be expected to understand, and ordinarily it comes as the fruit not of apologetic argument but of saving faith. So, while getting standards of conduct in the churches straight again and witnessing to our contemporaries about the way of righteousness are important, prayer for, and work in, Christian evangelism remains our prime task. It is thus that we most truly serve the world.

# Chapter 32

# Leisure and Life-style:
# Leisure, Pleasure, and Treasure

Carl Henry has won his spurs many times over as dogmatician, apologist, and ethicist, but I am not aware that he has ever dealt in print with my present theme. If he has, I have missed it and must apologize to him, for in a book such as this my oversight must appear both incompetent and discourteous. If, however, I am right in thinking he has not, I can appeal to that fact as symptomatic of the situation that I now attempt to address. Since the Second World War the West has grown affluent. Society practices and promotes spending rather than saving, self-indulgence rather than self-improvement, and amusement at all costs. (*Amusing Ourselves to Death* is the telling title of Neil Postman's assessment of television;[1] the same phrase might be used to describe the behaviour that has led to the AIDS epidemic.) Evangelical Christians have responded by emphasizing work rather than leisure,[2] activity rather than rest, and life commitments rather than life-style choices. Thus they have sought to tool themselves up to be salt and light in our dying culture. But on leisure and life-style they have had little to say.

To note this comparative silence is to state a fact, not to offer a criticism. Indeed, criticism would be out of place here. For Christians to be preoccupied with living and working for God is healthy, just as a preoccupation with leisure and luxury is unhealthy. If, as it appears, leisure and luxury are becoming the main interests of the Western world, a deadly decadence has already set in, against which Christians ought to be standing

---

LEISURE & LIFESTYLE: LEISURE, PLEASURE & TREASURE was originally published in *God and Culture: Essays in Honour of Carl F. H. Henry* , ed. D. A. Carson and John D. Woodbridge, (Grand Rapids: Eerdmans and Carlisle: Paternoster Press, 1993), pp. 356–368. Reprinted by permission.

[1] Postman, *Amusing Ourselves to Death: Public Discourse in the Age of Show Business* (New York: Viking Press, 1985).

[2] On the Christian view of work, see Carl F. H. Henry. *Aspects of Christian Social Ethics* (Grand Rapids: Eerdmans, 1964), pp. 37–71; and Leland Ryken, *Work and Leisure in Christian Perspective* (Portland: Multnomah, 1987).

with all their might, advocating and modelling something entirely differ -
ent. Christians must see this kind of decadence as a form of worldliness
and invoke against it such Scripture passages as 1 John 2:15–16: 'Do not
love the world or the things in the world. The love of the Father is not
in those who love the world; for all that is in the world – the desire of
the flesh, the desire of the eyes, the pride in riches – comes not from the
Father but from the world' (NRSV).[3] God forbid that paying any attention
to questions about leisure and life-style should have the effect of promot -
ing in the church a worldliness like that of the modern West.

Yet if these questions are not discussed, evangelicals will be in trouble
another way. All around the world, as capitalist consumerism and the
market economy grind on, carrying all before them, leisure and life-style
are becoming areas of entrapment for Christian people. Failure to see this
as a fact, to perceive it as a problem, to think about it in biblical antithesis
to the ruling secular notions, and to plan to operate as God's counter-
culture in these areas would indicate that we were already falling into the
traps, or (to change the metaphor) being blown up in the minefield. My
best hope for this essay is that it might offer the makings of a mine-
detecting survival kit. Carl Henry himself has worked prodigiously for
half a century as one of the leading mine detectors of our time, and these
pages will not be much of a tribute to him if they fall down at this point.

We begin with definitions, to make sure that we know what we are
talking about. My copy of Webster's defines *leisure* thus: 'freedom from
occupation or business; vacant time; time free from employment; time
which may be appropriated to any specific object.' *Life-style* is too recent
a coinage for my Webster's to take note of, but the contents of a junk
mail envelope that arrived recently, with the words 'Valuable Coupons
Inside – Save on All Your Life-style Needs' printed on its front, gives the
idea. Inside were coupons offering great deals on ornamental painted
plates; the world's greatest perfumes (that is what was claimed, anyway);
scenic address labels; items of personal hygiene; carpet shampooing; a
course in piano playing that focuses on leading singing at parties; wigs;
baseball cards; a doll built for lifetime companionship; family photos;
furnace cleaning; a machine for streamlining the female figure; videos
featuring Victor Borge; the *Encyclopedia Britannica*; skin cream; book club
membership; and deodorant. All one's life-style needs? Hardly, but the
selection points to the definition. *Life-style* is evidently an umbrella-word
used to describe the way of living that we achieve by our choices among
the various options that our affluent consumerist society makes available
to us – choices of clothes, food, hobbies, vacations, places of residence,
cars, clubs, careers, associates, amusements, and (of course) a church of
our choice, as well as choices of luxury items such as those listed above.

---

[3] See 'Hot Tub Religion: Towards a Theology of Pleasure,' chapter 4 in my
book *Hot Tub Religion* (Wheaton, Il.: Tyndale House, 1987).

'Life-style' is the label for both the ideal existence that our choices aim at and the actual existence that our choices produce. Our concept of our life-style hovers between being directional, stating how we want to live, and being descriptive, showing how we do live. In a day of multiple choices with regard to almost everything, we may well say: By their life-style you will know them; by my life-style you will know me. Where society sets us free to choose, our choices will show who and what we are, where we want to be, and where we are actually going.

Not all life-style choices are leisure choices, as we can see; but, as we can also see, all leisure choices are life-style choices, and they will say something about our view of life as a whole.

What sort of problems do we face in connection with leisure and lifestyle? There are three obvious ones, all with far-reaching theological, moral, and devotional implications.

The first problem is *idolatry*, the worship of false gods. The basic biblical insights here are that whatever controls and shapes one's life is in effect the god one worships, and that human nature is so constituted that no one can avoid a personal subservience to some god or other. As Bob Dylan sang some years ago, 'You've got to serve somebody,' and those who do not live to exalt the God of the Bible will inevitably be enslaved to some modern counterpart of the Baals and Molechs of the nature- and nation-worshipping cults that Scripture denounces. Then one's god may be some human individual or group – one's employer, perhaps, whose interests one devotes oneself to advancing; or one will worship and serve oneself directly, treating the gratifying of one's desires as all that matters and seeing everything as a means to that end – a life-style in which one constantly falls victim to 'greed, which is idolatry' (Col. 3:5). Greed, the mind-set that reaches out to grab things for oneself, becomes the liturgy of self-worship. In idolizing objects of desire, we idolize ourselves, the desirers; and so idolatry in this twofold sense becomes our life.

Regarding the matter in hand, we see that some people idolize work while others idolize play; some make a god of leisure activities (vacations, sports, hobbies, music, books, gardening, and so on) while others make a god of their bank balance and social position or of power; and others again make a god of their addictions (drink, drugs, sex, or whatever). Motivations and self-perceptions get very tangled here and need a lot of sorting out in particular cases, yet the bottom line is always the same. To the extent that we are not actively living to God, for God, and in the presence of God, seeking to glorify and enjoy him in and through all we do, we have lapsed into some form of idolatry whereby we worship and serve created things rather than the Creator (cf. Rom. 1:25). But idolatry must be avoided.

The second problem is *hedonism*, with which we may join, as its opposite, *anti-hedonism*. What is in question here is the place of pleasure in Christian living. Hedonism means the enthroning of pleasure as life's supreme value and therefore as a goal that everyone should pursue directly. Hedonism says, in effect, that pleasure-seeking is the height of wisdom and virtue and that maximizing pleasure is the highest service we can render them. Popular Western culture is largely hedonist, and modern Christians are constantly exposed to its brainwashing influences through the media and the relationships of life that draw them along the hedonist path. That God wants us all to be happy, right now; that total satisfaction is what Jesus offers, right now; that it is a good and godly thing to dismiss a spouse with whom one is not perfectly happy and marry someone else; that it is a good and godly thing to engage in genital homosexual behaviour, if that gives you positive pleasure – all of these notions have become very familiar in the church in recent years. That leisure is entirely for pleasure and that improving one's life-style means simply increasing one's pleasures are unchallenged axioms in today's advertising industry and unquestioned assumptions among many professed Christians. There is clearly a major problem here.

Recently, the phrase 'Christian hedonism' has gained prominence as a tag for the truth that the God who promises his people joy and delight in their relationship with him, both here and hereafter, does in fact fulfil his promise here and now.[4] As a corrective of what we may call 'Christian anti-hedonism' (the view that pleasure has no place in godly living, that God will always want us to do what we least want to do, and that the real Christian life on earth will always be, in Churchillian phrase, blood, toil, tears, and sweat – in short, sustained heroic misery), Christian hedonism speaks a word in season. In itself, however, 'Christian hedonism' is not a good phrase for its purpose; for it seems to say that rating pleasure as life's supreme value is something that Christianity itself teaches us to do, and that is not so. Biblical Christianity does not teach that any pleasure or good feelings, or any form of present ease and contentment, should be sought as life's highest good. What it teaches, rather, is that glorifying God by our worship and service is the true human goal, that rejoicing and delighting in God is central to worship, and that the firstfruits of our heritage of pleasures forevermore will be given us as we set ourselves to do this, but should we start to seek pleasure rather than God, we would be in danger of losing both. It is apparent that this is what the exponents of Christian hedonism do themselves think, so my difficulty is limited to their choice of words. But hedonism – real hedonism – must be avoided.

The third problem is *utilitarianism*, the view that the value of anything is to be found in the extent to which it is useful and productive as a means to an end beyond itself. Utilitarian thinking is very widely applied today in the realm of technology and business, but it has a radical built-in shortcoming: it overlooks the fact that what it values as a means to an end

---

[4] See John Piper, *Desiring God: Meditations of a Christian Hedonist* (Portland: Multnomah, 1986); Ryken, *Work and Leisure*, pp. 191ff.

may have an intrinsic value too, for the sake of which it should be promoted and preserved irrespective of how it rates in the means-to-end calculus. Leisure is a case in point. Utilitarianism says that the whole rationale of leisure and recreation is to 're-create' people for more productive work. Christianly speaking, this is part of the rationale of leisure, no doubt; after the sabbath rest one goes back to work. But where utilitarianism urges that leisure and rest be kept to a minimum so that productive work may be maximized (hence the fearfully long working hours of the early days of industrialization), Christian thinkers find intrinsic value in leisure activity that is, as Leland Ryken puts it,

> non-productive in the sense in which we ordinarily use that term. Leisure does not meet our needs of physical or economic survival. It does not put bread on the table or clothes in the closet. Leisure is a self-enclosed world that carries its own reward . . . [As Lee W. Gibbs puts it,] 'the purpose of play is in the play itself.'[5]

The Christian work ethic has sometimes been misrepresented as a sanctified workaholism, but this ignores the biblical celebration of God as the one who 'richly provides us with everything for our enjoyment' (1 Tim. 6:17) – a divine generosity that requires leisure for its appreciation, as the exponents of the authentic Christian work ethic well knew. So Christians should value leisure as more than a periodic pit stop before further work, and they should resist the narrowing impact of the money- and manufacture-mesmerized mind-set that marks utilitarian social think - ing. High though it rides as a public philosophy today, utilitarianism too must be avoided.

This identification of the three main problem areas in relation to leisure and lifestyle gives parameters for the rest of our study. We should not lapse into idolizing either work or leisure; it is not Christian to be either a workaholic or a drone. Nor should we lapse into hedonism, letting the pursuit of pleasure shape our lives, any more than we should lapse into anti-hedonism, censuring pleasure in Manichean style as a worthless and unhelpful distraction and treating pleasurelessness as an index of virtue. Nor should we lapse into utilitarianism, valuing work or leisure or any aspect of life-style purely as a means to an end beyond itself and not at all

---

[5] Ryken, *Work and Leisure*, p. 187, citing Gibbs, 'Ritual, Play and Transcendent Mystery,' paper presented to the American Academy of Religion, Midwestern Sectional Meeting, Chicago, Illinois, 17 February 1973, p. 4. Ryken's book, along with R. K. Johnston's *The Christian at Play* (Grand Rapids: Eerdmans, 1983), Johan Huizinga's *Homo Ludens: A Study of the Play-element in Culture* (1950; repr. Boston: Beacon Press, 1955) and Josef Pieper's *Leisure the Basis of Culture*, trans. Alexander Dru (New York: Pantheon Books, 1952), are basic for the Christian study of leisure.

as a field of creativity, a means of expression, or a form of enjoyment. So far, however, all of this has been negative; we have merely noted what we should not do. Now we have to ask, 'What positive principles of action should be guiding us in the area of life we are studying?' To answer this question is our next task.

Let us then stand back for a moment and look at the overall ideal of a redeemed sinner's life in Christ, which is the frame into which biblical teaching on leisure and life-style fits. The redeemed life is commonly spoken of these days in terms of *wholeness*; fifty years ago, it was thought of in terms of *balanced*; Thomas Aquinas saw it as life in *proportion*; and John Calvin spoke of it as a life of *moderation* – and indeed, it has all of these qualities. It is the life for which Jesus, himself the perfect man, is the model. Thomas's four cardinal virtues – prudence (wisdom), temper-ance (self-possession), justice (fairness), and fortitude (stick-to-itiveness, or guts) – are basic to it. His three theological virtues – faith, hope, and love – are central to it. And the ninefold fruit of the Spirit that Paul lists – love, joy, peace, patience, kindness, goodness, faithfulness, gentleness, and self-control (Gal. 5:22–23) – constitute a character profile of it, just as they do of the Lord Jesus himself. It is a superhuman version of human life, it is our natural life supernaturalized by grace.

On what principles is this redeemed life lived? Four may be briefly mentioned.

First, it is lived as a life of *duty to God*, glorifying him by our obedience out of gratitude for his grace. The phrase derives from the Catechism in Cranmer's Prayer Book (1549):

> My duty towards God, is to believe in him, to fear him, and to love him . . . to worship him, to give him thanks, to put my whole trust in him, to call upon him, to honour his holy Name and his Word, and to serve him truly all the days of my life.

Second, this redeemed life is lived as a life of *neighbour-love*. 'My duty towards my Neighbour,' Cranmer's Catechism continues, 'is to love him as myself, and to do to all men, as I would they should do unto me.' [6] Love seeks the well-being and advancement of the loved one in every way that it can; it is a matter of the mind and will more than of the feelings, and of sustained commitment rather than momentary intensities. The duty of love, to one's neighbour as to one's God, calls for discipline of life.

Third, the redeemed life is lived as a life of *freedom* (cf. Gal. 5:1) in four senses: freedom from the need to work for salvation; freedom from

---

[6] Cranmer's wording is retained in the catechism in the statutory *Book of Common Prayer* of the Church of England; I am quoting here from the 1962 Canadian revision, *Book of Common Prayer* (Toronto: Anglican Book Centre, 1962), p. 548.

the restrictions imposed by the typical enactments of God's Old Testa -
ment law; freedom for the use and enjoyment of all created things (1 Tim.
4:4–5; 6:17); and freedom in the sense of fulfilment and contentment in
working for God ('in whose service is perfect freedom,' as Cranmer's
Prayer Book declares).[7]

Finally, the redeemed life is lived as a life of *openness to God*, to receive
both his word and his gifts – including the providential gifts of leisure and
pleasure, which are our special concern at present.

Within this framework I now offer brief ethical reflections on our
theme to indicate the specific positives that should guide us through
leisure and life-style perplexities. Giving myself the pleasure of tidy titling,
I shall arrange my matter under three headings: the role of leisure, the
place of pleasure. and the use of treasure.

## The Role of Leisure

What is leisure? We have already cited a dictionary definition, but more
needs to be said.

*Leisure* is one of a pair of words, the other of which is *work*. Work
means not just one's wage-earning employment but everything that one
sees oneself as having to do as a matter of obligation, whether one enjoys
it or not. Jobs and commitments out of the house, jobs that need to be
done in the house, necessary studying, fulfilling promises one has made
– all of these count as work because of the sense of 'having to' that attaches
to them. By contrast, leisure means time that is ours to use for our own
pleasure on a discretionary basis. Some leisure time we fill with things we
choose to do for their own sake, just because we want to do them; these
are the activities of absolute leisure. Some leisure time we spend doing
things we both want and ought to do, from joining in public worship and
fulfilling volunteer roles at church or in a club to looking after pets and
reading to keep informed; these are better called activities of 'semi-
leisure.' All leisure, including semi-leisure, is a gift from God that, when
used wisely, 'provides rest, relaxation, enjoyment, and physical and
psychic health. It allows people to recover the distinctly human values,
to build relationships, to strengthen family ties, and to put themselves in
touch with the world and nature. Leisure can lead to wholeness, gratitude,
self-expression, self-fulfilment, creativity, personal growth, and a sense of
achievement.'[8] So leisure should be valued and not despised.

What Bible truths bear on our use of our leisure? At least the following:

*(1) The duty of rest.* In the quasi-liturgical, quasi-poetical, highly
stylized narrative of Gen. 1:1–2:3, God the Creator presents himself as

---

[7] 'Morning Prayer,' in the *Book of Common Prayer*, p. 11.

[8] Ryken, *Work and Leisure*, p. 38.

setting the world in order in six days, after which he rested on the seventh. Whether the six days should be understood as 144 of our hours, or as six vast geological epochs, or as a pictorial projection of the fact (the *what*) of creation that gives no information about the time (the *when*) or the method (the *how*) of creation is an interpretive question that need not concern us now.[9] What matters for us here is that on the basis of this presentation God directs that each seventh day be kept as a day of rest from the labours of the previous six (Exod. 20:8–11; 31:12–17). The day is to be kept 'holy' – that is, it is to be used for honouring God the Creator by worship, as well as for refreshing human creatures by the break from their otherwise unending toil.

This prescribed rhythm of work and rest is part of the order of creation. Human beings are so made that they need this six-plus-one rhythm, and we suffer in one way or another if we do not get it. The leisure or at least semi-leisure, of a weekly day for worship and rest is a divine ordinance that our work-oriented world ignores to the peril of its health. In today's community as Christian faith fades, society's standards fall, and economic competition becomes more cut-throat, the historic function of the Christian day of rest as a bulwark against employers' demands for a seven-day week is being increasingly circumvented, and the outlook is somewhat bleak.

*(2) The goodness of pleasure*. This has already been confirmed and will be fully discussed in the next section, so here I merely quote the pregnant words of Ecc. 8:15, 'I commend the enjoyment of life,' and move on.

*(3) The rightness of festivity*. The Bible is full of feasts. In Leviticus 23, six 'holy convocations,' at which work was prohibited, were prescribed for Israel each year; they are all called 'appointed feasts.' In John 2, Jesus is found at a wedding feast, miraculously creating extra wine; the fact that his critics were able to dismiss him as 'a glutton and a drunkard' (Matt. 11:19) shows that such festal celebrations were a recurring part of his life. All through the Bible the feast table is the place and the emblem of refreshing, celebratory fellowship – a very proper leisure activity, and certainly one to encourage.

*(4) The reality of stewardship* We are stewards of the time God gives us, of the abilities and skills that are ours, and of the opportunities that we find ourselves offered. We are also stewards of our own bodies and of this earth. Stewardship means responsibility for managing, caring for, and making the most of the resources God commits to our trust, and doing it in a way that squares with his known wishes. That does not in any way diminish our freedom to make use of created things for our enjoyment, but it does mean that in doing so we shall take care not to seem to approve what is immoral and demoralizing, nor to expose others to unhelpful influences, nor to play with fire ourselves. The Puritans closed theaters

---

[9]  See Henri Blocher, *In the Beginning*, trans. David G. Preston (Downers Grove, IL: Inter-Varsity, 1984), for an orientation to this question.

not because they did not enjoy drama but because the theaters of their day were immoral and demoralizing places. In a positive sense, recogni - tion of our stewardship – both its privileges and its responsibilities – should incline us to choose among the leisure activities that we enjoy those that bring us closest to God, to people, to beauty, and to all that ennobles. 'Whatever is true, whatever is noble, whatever is right, whatever is pure, whatever is lovely, whatever is admirable – if anything is excellent or praiseworthy – think about such things' (Phil. 4:8). We should not let the mediocre become the enemy of the good in leisure activity, nor should we let the good become the enemy of the best.

## The Place of Pleasure

What is pleasure? Webster's defines it as 'the gratification of the senses or of the mind; agreeable sensations or emotions; the feeling produced by enjoyment or the expectation of good.' Like joy, it is a gift of God, but whereas joy is basically active (one rejoices), pleasure is basically passive (one is pleased). Pleasures are feelings – feelings of stimulation or of tensions relaxed in the body, or realizations of something good in the mind, or conscious mastery in some performance or exercise of skill.

'Pleasure belongs to God's plan for humankind. As God himself takes pleasure in being God and in doing what he does,'[10] so he means human beings to find pleasure in being his. Adam and Eve's state was all pleasure before they sinned (Eden, God's pleasure-garden, pictures that), and when the redemption of Christians is complete, pleasure – total, constant, and entire – will have become their permanent condition.

> Never again will they hunger;
>     never again will they thirst.
> The sun will not beat upon them,
>     nor any scorching heat.
> For the Lamb . . . will be their shepherd;
>     he will lead them to springs of living water.
> And God will wipe away every tear from their eyes.
>
> (Rev. 7:16–17)

Thus the words of Ps. 16:11, 'You will fill me with joy in your presence, with eternal pleasures at your right hand,' and Ps. 36:8, 'You give them drink from your river of delights,' will find fulfilment. God values pleasure, both his and ours, and it is his pleasure to give us pleasure as a fruit of his saving love.

---

[10] See John Piper, *The Pleasures of God: Meditations on Gods Delight in Being God* (Portland: Multnomah, 1991).

Pleasure is Janus-faced: as a human reality it may be good and holy, or it may be sinful and vile. This is not because of the nature of the pleased feeling itself, for that in itself is morally neutral; it is because of what goes with it. If pleasure comes unsought, and if we receive it gratefully as a providential gift, and if it does no damage to ourselves or to others, and if the delight of it prompts fresh thanksgiving to God, then it is holy. But if the pursuit of one's pleasure is a gesture of egoism and self-indulgence whereby one pleases oneself without a thought as to whether one pleases God, then, however harmless in itself the pleasure pursued may be, one has been entrapped by what the Bible sees as the pleasures of the world and of sin (see Luke 8:14; 1 Tim. 5:6; 2 Tim. 3:4; Titus 3:3; Heb. 11:25; James 4:3; 5:5; 2t. 2:13; cf. Is. 58:13). The same pleasant experience – eating, drinking, making love, listening to music, painting, playing games, or whatever – will be good or bad, holy or unholy, depending on how it is handled.

In the order of creation, pleasures as such are meant to serve as pointers to God. Pleasure-seeking in itself sooner or later brings boredom and disgust, as the wise man testifies (Ecc. 2:1–11). Appreciating pleasures as they come our way, however, is one mark of a reverent, God-centred heart. A Jewish rabbi is credited with affirming that on the day of judgement God will hold us accountable for any neglect we have shown of pleasures he provided. Christian teachers have insisted that contempt for pleasure, far from demonstrating superior spirituality, is actually an expression of the Manichean heresy (the view that the material world and everything that it yields have no value and are indeed evil) and a manifestation of spiritual pride. Pleasure is divinely designed to raise our sense of God's goodness, deepen our gratitude to him, and strengthen our hope as Christians looking forward to richer pleasures in the world to come.

This truth about pleasure was not fully grasped in the first Christian centuries. The Greco-Roman world that the early church confronted was in the grip of a frenzied pleasure-seeking mentality, so it is no wonder that patristic writers spent more time attacking sinful pleasures than celebrating godly ones, nor that this perspective was carried into the Middle Ages, in which the world-renouncing asceticism of the monastery was thought of as the highest form of Christianity. But through the Reformers' and the Puritans' appreciation of God's grace and insistence on the sanctity of secular life, the biblical theology of pleasure finally broke surface. John Calvin states it best, in a chapter of his *Institutes* entitled 'How We Should Use This Present Life and Its Helps,' where he warns against the extremes of both overdone austerity and overdone indulgence. He affirms that not to use for pleasure those created realities that afford pleasure is ingratitude to their Creator. At the same time, however, he enforces Paul's admonition not to cling to sources of pleasure since we may one day lose them (1 Cor. 7:29–31); and he recommends moderation

– that is, deliberate restraint – in availing ourselves of pleasures, lest our hearts be enslaved to them and we become unable cheerfully to do without them.[11] Here as elsewhere, Calvin's Christian wisdom is of classic quality.

It is ironic that Calvin, who is so often considered the embodiment of gloomy austerity, should actually be a masterful theologian of pleasure. It is no less ironic that the Puritans, whose public image is of professional killjoys (H. L. Mencken defined Puritanism as the haunting fear that somewhere, somehow, somebody may be happy), should have been the ones who have insisted again and again that, in the words of Isaac Watts, their leading songster, 'Religion never was designed / To make our pleasures less.' And it is supremely ironic that, after two millennia of Christian culture, the West should now be plunging back into a self-defeating hedonism that is horribly similar to the barbaric pagan life-style of the first century, and that it should be doing so in the belief that the Christian religion is basically anti-human because it does not set up pleasing oneself as life's highest value. But Calvin's wisdom about pleasure remains basic to authentic Christian living, in this or any age.

## The Use of Treasure

Should I apologize for dignifying our money with the label 'treasure,' when the word suggests something of enormous value, even though I know firsthand that I – and I suspect most of my readers – do not rate among the world's wealthy? Not necessarily. One does not have to have a lot of money for it to become 'my precious,' as Gollum constantly calls the fateful ring in J. R. R. Tolkien's epic, and for it to affect one as Jelly-Roll Morton sang that jazz affected him – 'The more I have, the more I want, it seems; I page old Doctor Jazz in my dreams.'[12] Small sums of money are almost more effective than large ones in grabbing the heart and setting one dreaming and scheming about ways of getting more.

In his wise and searching book *Money, Possessions anal Eternity*, Randy Alcorn quotes Cyprian's description of the affluent of his day:

> Their property held them in chains . . . chains which shackled their courage and choked their faith and hampered . . . their judgement and throttled their souls . . . They think of themselves as owners, whereas it is they rather who are owned; enslaved as they are to their own property, they are not the masters of their money but its slaves.

---

[11] Calvin, *Institutes of the Christian Religion*, 3.10.

[12] 'Doctor Jazz,' by Jelly-Roll Morton and his Red Hot Peppers (Victor Records, 1926; various reissues).

Alongside this Alcorn sets the testimony of John Wesley, whose word to his preachers and society members was: 'Gain all you can, save all you can, give all you can . . . Money never stays with me. It would burn me if it did. I throw it out of my hands as soon as possible, lest it find its way into my heart.'[13] From these quotations the impossibility that Jesus announced – that of serving both God and mammon (money) – becomes plain (Matt. 6:24). A conscious refusal to serve money is therefore a necessary part of the Christian life-style, as the following quotations show:

> Do not store up for yourselves treasures on earth, where moth and rust destroy, and where thieves break in and steal. But store up for yourselves treasures in heaven, where moth and rust do not destroy, and where thieves do not break in and steal. For where your treasure is, there your heart will be also. (Matt. 6:19–21)

> Command those who are rich in this present world not to be arrogant nor to put their hope in wealth, which is so uncertain, but to put their hope in God, who richly provides us with everything for our enjoyment. Command them to do good, to be rich in good deeds, and to be generous and willing to share. In this way they will lay up treasure for themselves as a firm foundation for the coming age, so that they may take hold of the life that is truly life. (1 Tim. 6:17–19)

The point is plain. Money is for giving, and it is to be used to do good. It is not to be loved and hoarded; rather, it is to be stewarded for the service of God and one's neighbour. Frugality, rather than conspicuous consumption, must mark the Christian, and if that means that he or she cannot keep up with the world's wealthiest Joneses, well, so be it. There are in any case more important things to do.

In a post-Christian era such as ours in the West, an authentic Christian lifestyle – with its built-in balance of work and leisure, worship and witness, self-denial and self-giving for the glory of God and the good of others – is bound to seem countercultural and implicitly censorious, just as it did in the pre-Christian world of first-century Greco-Roman paganism and in the pre-evangelical world of Elizabethan and Jacobean England, where the Puritans sought the conversion of their country and became highly un - popular for doing so. Some unpopularity is inseparable from the practice of consistent Christianity, and we had better brace ourselves to meet it; for as things stand now in the West, it can only increase. But as Jesus has told us, 'wisdom is proved right by her actions' (Matt. 11:19). The motto of the first institution at which I taught was 'Be right and persist'; that is a word in season for all who would honour their Lord by their lives today.

---

[13] Alcorn, *Money, Possessions and Eternity* (Wheaton, Il: Tyndale House, 1989), pp. 402–3.